Adventuring in Alaska

The Sierra Club Adventure Travel Guides

Adventuring
in Alaska

COMPLETELY
REVISED
AND UPDATED

PEGGY WAYBURN

ILLUSTRATIONS BY JODY HORST

SIERRA CLUB BOOKS • SAN FRANCISCO

The Sierra Club, founded in 1892 by John Muir, has devoted itself to the study and protection of the Earth's scenic and ecological resources—mountains, wetlands, woodlands, wild shores and rivers, deserts and plains. The publishing program of the Sierra Club offers books to the public as a nonprofit educational service in the hope that they may enlarge the public's understanding of the Club's basic concerns. The point of view expressed in each book, however, does not necessarily represent that of the Club. The Sierra Club has some sixty chapters coast to coast, in Canada, Hawaii, and Alaska. For information about how you may participate in its programs to preserve wilderness and the quality of life, please address inquiries to Sierra Club, 85 Second Street, San Francisco, CA 94105. www.sierraclub.org/books.

LIBRARY OF CONGRESS CATALOGING-IN-PUBLICATION DATA
Wayburn, Peggy.
　　Adventuring in Alaska.
　　Rev. ed.
　　Bibliography: p.
　　Includes index.
　　1. Alaska–Description and travel–1981–　Guide-books.　2. Outdoor
recreation–Alaska–Guide-books.　I. Sierra Club.　II. Title.　III. Title:
Ultimate travel guide to the Great Land.
F902.3.W33　1988,1998
917.98'045　　　　　　　　　　　　　　　　　　　　87-23578
ISBN 0-87156-950-7

Production by David Peattie · Cover and book design by Amy Evans McClure · Illustrations by Jody Horst · Maps by Joan Rhine and Hilda Chen · Front cover photo by Michio Hoshino /Minden Pictures.

First edition: 1982 · Second edition: 1988 · Third edition: 1994 · Fourth edition: 1998

To my husband, Edgar Wayburn, for his vision, dedication, and effective leadership: he continues to inspire and inform the great national effort to preserve Alaska's unspoiled wilderness. And to our grandchildren and the countless other people whose lives will be the richer because that effort, in large part, has succeeded.

There is one word of advice and caution to be given those intending to visit Alaska for pleasure, or for sight-seeing. If you are old, go by all means, but if you are young, wait. The scenery of Alaska is much grander than anything else of its kind in the world, and it is not well to dull one's capacity for enjoyment by seeing the finest first.

Henry Gannett, Harriman Alaska Expedition, 1899

Contents

IV• Interior and Arctic

Appendices

Index   406

Acknowledgments

It has been my great good fortune over the years to come to know many Alaskans. Their hospitality has nurtured me, their knowledge informed me, and their friendship warms my heart. A number of them have, directly or indirectly, had to do with this book. Among them are Jack and Mary Kaye Hession; Nancy Tileston; Sharron and Cliff Lobaugh; Peg, Anna and Jules Tileston; Bob and Judy Weeden; Mike and Marilyn Miller; Jan Wrentmore; Joel Bennett; Jack Calvin; Jay and Bella Hammond; Bruce and Gail Gilbert; Bob Howe; Skip Wallen; Carmen and Orvel Holum; Lisa Shon; Will Troyer; Larry Edwards; Sally Gibert; Clem and Diana Tillion; Jim Barnett; Claire Fejes; Darlene Billings; Jim King; Cal Lensink; Sterling Bolima; Nancy Michaelson; Jerry and Jan Brookman; K. J. Metcalf; Carol Bodenhamer; Richard Nelson; Mark and David Hickok; Charles Evans; Dave Spencer; Sandy and Monda Sagalkin; Lin Sonnenberg; Averill Thayer; Evelyn Reynolds; Doris Hugo; Ed LaChapelle; John Adams; Keith Schreiner; Ginny Wood; Celia Hunter; Lucy and Harold Sparck; Ed Gamble; Dave Hardy; David Finkelstein; Neil Davis; Dick Hensel; John Sackett; Stan Williams; Riley Morrey; Ken Middlemist; and Douglas Anderson, who is Alaskan by virtue of his anthropological studies in the state. To them all goes my appreciation. In particular, I am grateful to Rich Gordon of Juneau, whose knowledge of Alaska is encyclopedic: he read my entire manuscript and contributed invaluable corrections and suggestions.

I am also grateful for the cooperation of the staffs of the National Park Service, the U.S. Fish & Wildlife Service, the USDA Forest Service, the University of Alaska, the Bureau of Land Management, Knik Kanoer and Kayakers Association, and the Arctic Environmental Information and Data Center.

Closer to home, my friend Connie Parrish has been of invaluable help in updating this book. My copy editor, Mary Anne Stewart, has, as always, done a superb job on the style and consistency of my text: I'm greatly indebted to her. My husband, Edgar Wayburn, has borne with me lovingly throughout the trials and tribulations of creating, editing, and revising this book. Without the support of Mary Watson, my friend of over thirty years, the work that went into the book would not have been possible. And without the interest, generosity, and flying expertise of Jim Roush, I could never have learned to know and love Alaska as I do.

With the assistance I have had in preparing this book, there should be few errors. I am, however, responsible for any that might occur in my text.

PART I

The Great Land

1. Introduction

Alaska is many things. It is nearly a continent in size—a land so vast that to see it all would take more than a year of viewing 1 million acres every day. It is a land of few people; were Manhattan Island populated to the same density, it would have only seventeen residents. And it is a place of fascinating extremes: its topography includes the lowest ocean trough as well as the highest mountain on North America; between these two points there are 45,000 vertical feet. Its Arctic winter is one long night and its summer one long day; temperatures can zoom to 100 degrees and skid to minus 80; frozen tundras can receive as little as 2 inches of rain a year, while lush Southeast forests may get over 300. Alaska is also a place of superlatives: its mountains dwarf the Alps; its fjords surpass Norway's; its large, free-roaming animals rival Africa's; its glaciers are outnumbered only by Greenland's and Antarctica's; its avian and marine life are unmatched anywhere; its oil pipeline was the most costly private construction project ever, when built—the list goes on. And while Alaska is a treasure house of natural resources as well, it is still a land of wilderness, with untracked terrain, unclimbed mountains, and lakes and rivers as bright and pure as liquid jewels. Varied, unique, challenging, still relatively unspoiled—Alaska is, in sum, one of the great places on earth to adventure.

Alaska is also in the throes of major change. Virtually unknown and little touched until after World War II (which itself initiated great changes in the state), and having achieved statehood only in 1959, Alaska became front-page news all over the world when oil was brought in in quantities at Prudhoe Bay in 1968. Since then, Alaska's economy (never stable) has been tied to the global oil situation and has skyrocketed and plummeted accordingly—and the state's population has more than doubled. Perhaps more importantly, during recent years Alaska has been the scene of major environmental changes. With statehood came the opportunity—and the responsibility—for Alaska to select 104 million acres of land for state property out of the 375 million acres within its boundaries. (Until that time, almost all of Alaska had been classified as "vacant, unappropriated public land" by the United States government.) Under the Alaska Native Claims Settlement Act (ANCSA, signed into law by President Richard Nixon in 1971), Alaska's Natives were allotted another 44 million acres of Alaska's land (and incidentally were plunged into the corporate mainstream). And under the Alaska National Interest Lands Conservation Act (ANILCA, signed into law by President Jimmy Carter in 1980), 105 million acres of Alaska's land were designated for lasting protection as national parklands, national forests, and national wildlife refuges. This vast subdivision of Alaska has understandably caused major upheavals, and it is still in process; boundaries are still being drawn, and there is still contention over various metes and bounds. At the same time, Alaska's vast "bush" has been opened up increasingly with better transportation and communications. And Alaska's tourist industry has blossomed into one of the state's major economic assets: many more people now visit Alaska every year than live in the state. With all of this, the Great Land still offers magnificent opportunities for those who enjoy the unspoiled out-of-doors.

It is manifestly impossible for a single small volume to deal fully with the scope and diversity of Alaska, and *Adventuring in Alaska* does not attempt to do so. (Every section of this book could probably be expanded into a volume of its own, and many have been, as the Suggested Reading list in the Appendices shows.) Instead, this book provides pertinent information and know-how for you who want to adventure in Alaska with both understanding and enjoyment. Be you traditional tourist, footloose traveler, rugged outdoors-person, hiker, biker, river runner, student, senior—or even an armchair adventurer—you will find facts, details, and background material that will add to your knowledge and appreciation of one of this world's most beautiful areas.

What is the climate really like in Alaska? How can you best take a bicycle to Alaska? On which wild river could you spend an entire summer and still come back for more? What places should you *not* visit, and why? What is "the bush"? What is a Cheechako? How can you minimize your impact on Alaska's fragile wilderness? What should you wear? When is the best time to visit the Arctic or Southeast? Why did Congress pass an Alaska Lands Act—at such a late date, 113 years after the United States acquired Alaska—declaring who should administer what land, and how does this affect your travels in Alaska? What is the proper way to visit a Native village? Are the mosquitoes in Alaska really as bad as everyone says? You will find the answer to these and many, many more questions in the following pages.

These pages reflect my personal experiences in Alaska during more than three dozen visits there, which add up to more than three years out of the last thirty. *Adventuring in Alaska* also represents a great deal of research conducted both inside and outside Alaska. To organize and present the material I have gathered on this large and complex subject, I have necessarily had to make a number of choices, many of them arbitrary. In making these choices, I have generally followed three guidelines. First, I have heeded my curiosity and attempted to answer many of the questions for the reader that arose in my own mind as I traveled in Alaska. Second, I have looked for and described opportunities for travelers in the parts of Alaska that are the most accessible, and the least expensive, to visit. Third, I have discussed only those more inaccessible areas that have been identified by the Congress or the state of Alaska as having exceptional scenic, wildlife, historical, or recreational values; thus the off-the-beaten-track traveler in Alaska can turn to the federal and state agencies that administer these areas for additional information and help.

The book is organized to provide ready reference to the information it contains. The first part gives general, overall, and background facts and figures about Alaska; this will be useful to anyone interested in Alaska as well as to those who contemplate traveling there. The next three parts of the book—II, III, IV—present more in-depth and detailed information about the three major regions of Alaska: the Southeast, the Southcentral and Southwest, and the Interior and Arctic. My division of Alaska into these three general areas is one of my arbitrary choices; it was influenced not only by major physiographic features of Alaska but also by the fact that journeys into Alaska routinely start in one of the state's three principal cities—Juneau, Anchorage, or Fairbanks. Each city serves, then, as a natural gateway to one of the regions I have described as well as a destination of its own. A fifth part of the book provides Appendices, including information on ordering Alaska topographic maps; checklists of Alaska birds and mammals; a key to Alaskan colonial seabird habitats; lists of International Youth Hostels in Alaska, Alaska Native Regional Corporations, and Alaska zip codes; a Suggested Reading list; and an Index.

The material in *Adventuring in Alaska* is presented in more or less short essays that discuss both subjects and places. Although these essays deal with specifics—and can be referred to separately—virtually all of them also contain general information about Alaska. It is therefore my suggestion that the book be read as a whole before it is used more specifically for its parts. That way you will have a better overall picture of Alaska before you decide how you will adventure there.

Throughout the text of the book, I have had to emphasize the fact that the topical information presented is "as of this writing." This is because Alaska, as noted, has been and continues to be changing so rapidly. While major and far-reaching changes occur almost daily in such important arenas as land use, little, mundane things like telephone numbers and addresses seem to be in a state of perpetual flux. For one example, all the telephone numbers in Anchorage were recently changed; for another, friends of mine in Juneau have had their address changed five times during a period of twenty years—while living in the same house! Thus, my apologies and disclaimer in advance if the book gives an obsolete phone number or address. (I note in passing that in updating this book for new printings, I make several changes a year; in revising the book, I have made literally hundreds of changes.)

One thing, however, has stayed the same in Alaska: the area code for the state has been, and continues to be, 907. Because this is a universal area code, I have omitted repeating it in many of the phone numbers, while occasionally reminding the reader that 907 is always to be used. (Note also: Some Alaskans claim that mail addressed to "AK" may end up in Arkansas! Just be sure to use the right zip code! Zip codes are provided throughout this book.)

It is manifestly impossible to list all of the services available to tourists in Alaska. (Other publications are devoted to this; see Suggested Reading.) I have, however, included as many references as possible to various facilities, using my own experience and the recommendations of knowledgeable Alaskans as a basis for selection. This does not imply an endorsement by either myself or the publisher of the book, but it will give the reader some options. My apologies to the many excellent operations that have been inadvertently omitted. I welcome suggestions and corrections; write me in care of the publisher.

When I first began writing this book, I wondered if, by introducing prospective travelers to the beauties and wonders of many of Alaska's wild and vulnerable places, the book would contribute to the overvisiting of these spots and so impair their special values. I decided that the opposite should be the case. Along with the rest of Alaska, these wild places have been identified and officially classified for particular uses that include and, indeed, emphasize wilderness recreation. They will inevitably be visited by an increasing number of people—and, unquestionably, many more books will be written about them. How these wilderness travelers—and Alaska's land administrators—treat these precious wild places will determine their ultimate fate. I wanted my book to be not only a guide to adventuring in Alaska but a guide to understanding, appreciating, and ultimately protecting Alaska's superb wilderness and the life and lifestyle it has traditionally supported.

In the years since then, the world has become ever more crowded and pressured, and visitation of Alaska's wild places has indeed increased. (The increase has been so dramatic in places that land managers want to slow down visitation.) Alaska's wilderness has become more and more precious—and vulnerable. And several other books for travelers to Alaska have indeed been written, as well. The intent of this book remains as it was: to heighten the appreciation and protection, along with the enjoyment, of Alaska's superb public lands. These wildlands and parklands are the heritage of us all, and their fate remains in our hands. Whether or not they and the life they support will survive—whether or not future generations will have these to enjoy—is for us to decide.

2. Size

Think of immensity: of lakes that stretch like inland seas, of mountains that fill up half the sky. Consider distance: the faint shimmer of mountains 100 miles away across the tundra or a wild river so long it takes a month to run. Then let your mind dwell on space—uncluttered, infinite, pristine. This small exercise gives just the barest hint of Alaska's scale. The size of Alaska, in fact, has been a challenge to convey since the first explorer found the place. Explorer-geologist Alfred Hulse Brooks could only come up with a continent as an adequate measure of comparison. John Muir, rarely at a loss for words, found the magnitude of Alaska's scenery "hopeless beyond description." Perhaps the Aleuts did best when they simply chose the name *Alaska,* "the Great Country."

Consider the figures: Alaska's land area is 586,000 square miles, or a little over 375 million acres. Its tidal shoreline is around 47,000 miles. Its span from north to south is about 1,400 miles, and from east to west it is nearly 2,400 miles.

These dimensions make Alaska a record holder on several counts. Worldwide, it is one of the biggest peninsulas on the planet. Nationwide, it is the largest by far of the fifty United States, or—as Alaskans like to put it—their state is not only first in size, but, if Alaska were divided in half, Texas would still rank third. Alaska has more coastline than all the other states put together. Its landmass equals one-fifth that of the forty-eight conterminous states—actually totaling more land than the twenty-one smaller states (measured in ascending order of size).

For one last mental yardstick, try this: to cover the entire terrain of Alaska, a surveyor would have to measure 6 square miles every day for more than 267 years. (This helps account for the fact that Alaska was largely unsurveyed and unmapped until the advent of aerial and satellite photography.)

Alaska's size offers any adventurer both challenges and hard choices. If you are a mountaineer, for instance, you'll find some of the world's greatest mountains in Alaska, and many of them are unclimbed. But you will also have to accept the fact that you'll never live long enough to climb them all. The same thing goes for Alaska's beautiful wild rivers, if you're a river runner. And if you like backpacking, unless you're a Paul Bunyan, don't count on covering all the wilderness of this state.

If you want to travel just to see and enjoy Alaska, you might find it useful—because of the size of the place—to consider it as you would Europe. If you have only a couple of weeks to visit, you may elect to take a general overview, traveling perhaps on an organized tour and foregoing

The Nabesna Glacier, one of the Wrangell Mountains' largest. Source: National Park Service.

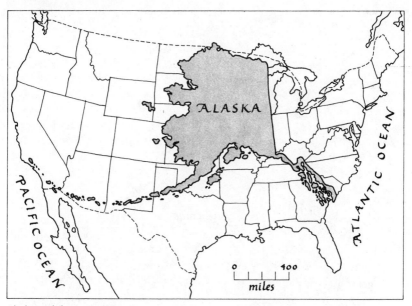

Alaska and the Lower 48

the more intimate experiences. Or you may decide, instead, to spend your time exploring a particular part of the state more in depth, getting to know the country and the people there a little better.

Whichever way you choose to travel in Alaska, expect to be awed by the scope, the space, and the sense of limitless horizons.

3. Location
and Neighbors

Close to one-third of Alaska's land area falls inside the Arctic Circle, and its northernmost tip, Point Barrow, is very near 72 degrees north latitude—less than 1,300 miles from the North Pole. Thus Alaska gives the United States a firm, important presence in the Arctic.

Distances in Alaska

From north to south, Alaska spans over 20 degrees of latitude; its southernmost tip, Amtignak Island in the Aleutians, juts south of 52 degrees north latitude—lining it up closely with Portsmouth, England. Eastward, Alaska stretches to Camp Point on the Canadian border at 130 degrees west longitude. To the west, it sweeps across the planet so far into the Aleutian chain that it crosses the 180th meridian, the boundary between the east and west longitudes. This means that Cape Wrangell on Attu Island, near 172 degrees east longitude, is more than halfway around the world from the prime meridian in Greenwich, England. It is therefore the easternmost point of the United States and, indeed, of the North American continent.

Anchorage, the population center of Alaska, is situated approximately on 61 degrees north latitude and 150 degrees west longitude—a strategic location on the great circle route. This puts it about midway between New York and Tokyo by direct air flight.

On its eastern side, Alaska borders Canada for 1,538 miles. This boundary was set by agreement between Russia and Great Britain in 1825, forty-two years before the United States acquired Alaska by purchase from the Russians. Alaska's other near neighbor is Russia, which is separated from the Seward Peninsula by the shallow waters of the Bering Strait. The distance between the two countries—and two continents—is less than 55 miles. (Road builders and road-building engineers dream of linking Russia to the United States by highway.)

The approximately 1,000-mile water boundary between Russia and the United States was established by the United States–Russia Convention of 1867, and it runs along the 169 degrees west longitude between the Seward Peninsula and Siberia. This border falls between the two Diomede Islands, so that Big Diomede belongs to Russia and Little Diomede to the United States. During the Cold War, all commerce between these two islands was forbidden. The Eskimos of the two Diomedes spring from common roots and are closely related; now they can and do freely visit one another.

To accommodate the boundary drawn between Alaska and Russia, the International Date Line had to be manipulated considerably. It was first bent to the east to pass through the Bering Strait, then to the west to give most of the Aleutian chain to the United States. On a clear day, you can see Siberia while flying from Kotzebue to Nome—looking west, of course, into tomorrow. And the people on the two Diomede Islands live one day but less than 5 miles apart.

4. Geology

Geology is something like science fiction. It deals only in part with proven facts; it sets forth scenarios that may or may not turn out to be true; and it benefits greatly from innovative thinking.

Of course, a major difference between the two fields is that geology is largely concerned with the past, while science fiction projects into the future. It might seem that looking backward would be easier than looking forward, but this is not the case for geologists; the time frame they deal with is mind-boggling—4.5 billion years, the estimated age of our planet. Furthermore, expanding the catalog of geological facts is difficult; the evidence is diverse, fragmented, widespread (indeed, global), and often hard to decipher and interpret. Geology is, in fact, full of fascinating mysteries and challenges, and perhaps nowhere on earth are they presented in a more vivid way than in Alaska.

Consider the geological scene in our forty-ninth state. To begin with, the terrain is incredibly varied. It ranges vertically from the offshore Aleutian Trench, where the ocean bottom plunges 25,000 feet below the sea, to the highest mountain on the North American continent, 20,320-foot Mount McKinley; this is a distance of close to 9 miles. Horizontally, there are 586,000 square miles to take into account. Three impressive mountain systems demarcate this landmass. The Coast Range outlines the southern arcuate sweep of Alaska and includes the Saint Elias and Chugach-Kenai-Kodiak Mountains; it dips below the sea southwest of Kodiak. The Alaska-Aleutian Range is separated from the Coast Range—which it roughly follows in its curving sweep—by a discontinuous trough that is partially filled by the Wrangell and Talkeetna Mountains. To the east, the Alaska Range peters out in the immense plateaus

Aniakchak Crater, now quiescent; one of the forty-seven active volcanoes in the Aleutian Range. Source: National Park Service.

of Yukon Territory and British Columbia; to the southwest, the active volcanoes of the Aleutian Range comprise part of the Pacific's "ring of fire." The Brooks Range more or less delineates the Arctic Circle and lies to the north of it. In between the Alaska-Aleutian and the Brooks Ranges is the Interior of Alaska, an immense plateau that undulates into lower mountains in places and contains great river valleys. To the north of the Brooks Range is the Arctic Slope, a wide apron of land that tilts very gently to slip beneath the Arctic Ocean.

To put Alaska's vast terrain into perspective, it helps to look at its relationship to the rest of the North American continent. The Coast Range is analogous to the Olympic and Klamath Ranges, the Alaska-Aleutian Range to the Cascades and the Sierra Nevada. The trough between these two ranges corresponds roughly to the Puget-Willamette lowlands and California's Central Valley. Alaska's immense Interior corresponds geographically to the Great Basin. The Brooks Range is the geographical northern arm of the Rockies, although it was upthrust at another time, and the Arctic Slope is analogous to the Great Plains.

The extraordinary landmass that makes up Alaska is relatively new when looked at in terms of geologic time. (The Arctic, in fact, is the youngest ecosystem on earth, and approximately one-third of Alaska lies within the Arctic Circle.) Alaska's most ancient rocks are mica-schists that date back only 600 million years, plus or minus a few million years, and its youngest rocks are mere decades old. Forming part of the edge of a continent, this is a very uneasy piece of the earth's crust; more than half of the state is seismically active, with some regions being wracked by earthquakes frequently and others often showered with volcanic debris. Bush pilots remember their small planes being covered with grit spewed out by Mount Wrangell, one of the world's highest active volcanoes, not all that long ago; the city of Anchorage lies in the "ash shadows" of both Mount Spurr and Mount Augustine, and is used to having clouds of ash (which, incidentally, may activate the fire alarms in airplanes flying over an eruption of these active volcanoes in Cook Inlet) rain onto streets and lawns and roofs; skiers hate this when it gravels the runs! Ten percent of the world's earthquakes occur in Alaska, demonstrating the current activity level of tectonic plate collisions. The town of Valdez on Prince William Sound averages something like a major earthquake (one that measures 5.0 or more points on the Richter scale) a year. The devastating 1964 Good Friday shake (over 8.0 on the Richter scale) not only destroyed large parts of Anchorage, but virtually leveled Valdez.

This is a great time in the history of geology. The theory of plate tectonics—which has been characterized as being as significant to the earth sciences as the atomic theory is to chemistry or as evolution is to biology—has revolutionized geologists' thinking. Many fresh ideas are presently being examined and tested, and many interesting new aspects of the plate tectonic theory are being explored as well.

According to this theory, the earth can be thought of as something like a lightly boiled egg with a cracked shell. The yolk corresponds to the earth's dense, partly molten core, the white to its somewhat gelatinous mantle, and the shell to the earth's crust. The earth's crust, as it happens, is fractured into a dozen or so large fragments that are called tectonic plates; these plates rest on and are being moved over the mantle continuously. How does this happen? To perhaps oversimplify it, the extrusion of molten magma through large seams or cracks that run the length of the two great ocean floors constantly produces new crust: the older crust is thrust away from the seams by the new and pushed onward until it encounters another chunk of crust, such as a continent.

Continental crust is older than ocean-floor crust and is made of less weighty rocks: thus continents float on the molten magma beneath them. When the heavier ocean floor meets the lighter continent, it is "subducted," or pulled beneath it, and then recycled in the depths of the earth. (The action is sometimes compared to that of a giant conveyor belt carrying newly formed and forming rock up to, across, and then below the surface of the earth.) Or, if it is not readily subducted, the plate may shear or buckle. This fundamental process is believed to have been going on for eons, and as a result of many inevitable collisions of moving rock, the continents themselves have been formed; new portions of the ocean's floor have been pasted onto them; moving plates have scraped off bits and pieces of distant continents, rafted them around the world, and pressed them into alien continents (for example, rocks around Homer started out in Mexico!); and the moving plates, jamming into one another, have formed mountain ranges, ground one another's edges, and, in places, overridden one another like huge slabs of pack ice. This often-violent tectonic action continues, and accompanying it there may be massive earthquakes, more mountain building, volcanism, and referred movements along faults in related landmasses.

All of this explains very well what has "built" Alaska and what continues to shape Alaska's landscape today. Indeed, a description of Alaska's present topography and tectonic activity can read like a textbook illustrating the theory of plate tectonics. Along southern margins of Alaska, for instance, a collision of tectonic plates is occurring: the ocean floor (part of the Pacific plate) is pushing generally northwest and is being subducted beneath the resistant landmass (the North American plate) that it is encountering. Hence the Aleutian Trench, which marks one junction of the two plates where the ocean floor is plunging beneath

MAGNITUDE
- · 5.3–5.9
- • 6.0–6.9
- ● 7.0–7.7
- ⬤ 7.75–8.5

Epicenter 1964 Earthquake

ALASKA RANGE

ALEUTIAN TRENCH

Earthquakes in Alaska

Glaciation in Alaska

the land. Alaska's numerous (forty-seven) active volcanoes provide another index of the massive collision now in process.

The frequency and magnitude of earthquakes offer further evidence of how Alaska has been formed. Past encounters between the plates have produced—and continue to produce—the great mountain systems that curve through Alaska. The numerous pieces of "nonconforming" landmasses, believed to have originated in distant parts of the planet (some match the continents of the South Pacific), that are being identified in many parts of the state can be explained by the "rafting" action of tectonic plates, which move pieces of the planet around and reassemble them like gigantic jigsaw puzzles. As a final, more specific example, a major fault is well defined in Alaska's Southeast; with the help of earlier glacial action, this fault has gashed open the earth and allowed the ocean to intrude to form the Lynn Canal and Chatham Strait. Known as the Farewell fault at its eastern end and as the Denali fault at its western end, this fault extends north and westward and can be observed in several

Takahula Lake, Gates of the Arctic National Park and Preserve. Source: National Park Service.

places from the air. According to at least one school of geologists, it does not stop until it reaches Bristol Bay, and thus it generally marks the arcuate curve of upthrust land that has resulted from past plate collisions. Perhaps as significantly, earthquakes continue to occur along this immense fault. It is worth noting that the Southeastern mountains more or less outlined by this fault not only rise abruptly from the sea but tower higher than any other coastal range on earth.

The tectonic plate theory continues to be explored and defined, and new ways of looking at the planet's geological structure are still opening up. Along the way, many older ideas are being discarded, such as the beliefs that continents are more or less stable and that the ages and composition of their rocks are indices of their chronology in situ. However, certain long-held theories continue to be subscribed to. Among these are that most of Alaska has at one time or another been underwater (as has most of the earth); that the climate of what is now Alaska once supported broadleaf trees and conifers (at least one species, *Pinus monticula,* grew simultaneously in what is now Siberia); and that from the beginning of the Quaternary period to the present—a very brief period in geologic time—Alaska's landmass has remained generally in place. Thus, for all its upheaval, Alaska's recent geological record appears to be relatively clear.

Sometime between 1.5 and 2 million years ago, the earth's climate began to undergo a series of extreme changes, swinging from warm to cold and back again. During the ensuing millennia, there were four periods of heavy glaciation interspersed with periods of warming. This glaciation did much to shape the Alaskan landscape that you can see today, for about 50 percent of the state's area, it is believed, was buried under ice at one time or another. The glaciation that persists today—largely in the Southeast—may give a clue to what other periods of snow and ice were like, but the present ice sheets are positively meager compared with the grand, 4,000-foot-thick slabs of ice and snow that once weighed down large areas of Alaska.

Glaciers soften the harsh edges of new rocks. They round off low hills as they move over them. When glaciers melt, they leave behind potholes and lakes and great deposits of glacial debris that form ridges, eskers, and hill-like moraines. Glaciers also spawn great rivers. They carry rocks great distances before they drop them. They quarry valleys into rounded U shapes, and the dust from their till is swept up by the wind and deposited as fine soil or loess over vast regions of the landscape. All these phenomena can be observed in different parts of Alaska.

The monumental sheets of ice that built up at times in Alaska had other interesting side effects. They formed immense and nearly impenetrable walls that cut Alaska off from the rest of the continent in places. They also stopped short of Alaska's Interior; being more or less ice-free, the Interior became a refugium—or place of refuge—for many different plants and animals that were unable to disperse or travel freely during those frigid times. (The Interior may also have been a refugium for people during the past 25,000 years. See History, below.) Migratory birds, however, were able to fly above the vast frozen land and to use the Interior as they had through the millennia; they continue to do so today. Earth scientists and biologists sometimes refer to this refugium as being part of an area they have named "Beringia."

When the earth's waters were locked into ice, the sea level dropped everywhere. At times of maximum cold, it was around 400 feet lower than it is today—and possibly more. During these bleak glacial periods, what is now the northern part of the Bering Sea did not exist; instead, the Bering Land Bridge linked Alaska to Siberia. This was no mere narrow strip of land, however, as the word *bridge* suggests. It was a stretch of land from 900 to 1,000 miles wide that actually joined the two continents. (Although now submerged again, this land still joins North America to Eurasia.) The bridge was ice-free and provided access for wandering animals and, later, it is believed, for the first people to enter the New World. This region made up the rest of the area now referred to as Beringia, and it, too, acted as a vast refugium for many kinds of living things. It is worth noting that during warmer periods, when part of Beringia is inundated (as it is today), exchange of plant and animal life between the Pacific and Atlantic Oceans can take place through the waters of the Bering Sea.

The permafrost that presently and persistently grips so much of Alaska is believed by some geologists to be a relict of those earlier, cold Pleistocene times. Its effects are many (see Permafrost, below), and it has resulted not only in fascinating land patterns but in thousands of thaw lakes and puddles. (Alaska has a total of more than 3 million lakes.) The more straightforward processes of freezing and thawing affect the earth's surface as well.

As you travel through Alaska, you will have the chance to observe— just as the geologists do—how the marvelous forces of the earth have shaped this landscape in the past and are actively continuing to shape it today. Alaskans in many parts of the state have learned to live with these irresistible earth forces, but the potential for radical change and even for disastrous geological events is always with them. This is, of course, one of the things that makes Alaska not only a paradise for curious geologists but also a very exciting place to live and to visit.

5. Climate

That Alaska is a land of extraordinary contrasts is nowhere better illustrated than in the wide—and even wild—extremes of its weather. Alaska has places with the highest precipitation of any of the forty-nine conti-

nental states and places with nearly the lowest. The difference between
the precipitation in two such places can amount to over 300 inches. For
example, at McCleod Bay on Montague Island in Prince William Sound,
the precipitation has been as high as 332 inches in one year. Less than
1,000 miles away at Point Barrow, it has added up to as little as 1.61
inches in a similar time span. Snowfall in Alaska is also record setting
and extraordinarily variable. In the Southeastern mountains, the overall
snowfall ranks among the highest in the world. An average of 10 feet of
snow per month in the higher elevations is common enough, and 225
inches of snow—almost 20 feet—was once measured as falling in a single month at Thompson's Pass near Valdez. North America's greatest
recorded snowfall in one season was chalked up on the Wolverine Glacier in the Kenai Mountains in the winter of 1976–77, when 356 inches of
snow piled up and stayed. Yet on the North Slope only 3 or 4 inches of
snow may fall in an entire winter. (This snow may confound a visitor by
appearing to be totally airborne, kept aloft by 60-mile-per-hour winds.)

Alaskan temperatures can gyrate as wildly between record highs and
record lows, and they do—often in the same spot. In the Interior, a winter reading of minus 50 to 60 degrees Fahrenheit hardly raises eyebrows
(although it may frost eyelashes), and in Fairbanks, the smog routinely
freezes. Summer readings of 80 to 85 degrees in the same location are
common. At Fort Yukon, not far from the Canadian border, a minus-78-
degree reading was racked up (or down) one midwinter, and a plus-100-
degree temperature was recorded late one June—giving the place a
temperature range of 178 degrees. Interesting to try dressing for life in a
climate like that!

All of this emphasizes the fact that while it can be very cold in winter,
Alaska is not a land of perpetual ice and snow, as the ancient myth goes.
It can and obviously does get very hot in many areas in summer. After all,
in about one-third of the state, the sun remains above the horizon for
twenty-four hours a day for more than two straight months. Actually,
over 97 percent of the Alaskan land thaws under the summer sun and
stays snow-free.

Alaska's overall climate can be broadly classified into zones. These can
cue you in to what to expect generally in different parts of the state. One
zoning system uses the presence or absence of a marine influence as the
principal index. By employing this measure, Alaska's Southeast, Southcentral coasts, and most of the Aleutian chain are in a maritime zone,
with heavy rainfall, frequent fog and clouds, strong winds, and moderate
temperatures. The Alaska Peninsula and the lowlands along Alaska's
western coasts are in a transitional zone, with less cloudiness and rainfall,
strong winds, and a mean annual temperature of about 25 to 35 degrees

Climatic zones of Alaska

Fahrenheit. The area north of the crest of the Brooks Range is in the arctic zone, with light but persistent foggy clouds and precipitation, strong winds, and a mean annual temperature of 10 to 20 degrees Fahrenheit. (Note the presence of strong winds in all three of these zones—making for a potentially severe chill factor.) The rest of Alaska—the vast reaches of the Interior—are in a continental zone, with enormous daily and yearly temperature variations, little rainfall, generally light winds, and a mean annual temperature of 15 to 25 degrees Fahrenheit.

Using another, more traditional, weather zoning system, the great body of Alaska can simply be considered subarctic; that is, it has at least one month with a mean temperature of 32 degrees or colder and no more than four months with a mean temperature greater than 50 degrees. According to this measure, only a fairly narrow strip of the Arctic Slope is then classified as being within the arctic zone, or having at least one month with a mean temperature of 32 degrees or colder and no months with mean monthly temperatures greater than 50 degrees. The Southeast then falls into the temperate zone, along with other areas of the forty-eight contiguous states.

I find the best indications of Alaska's climate—and the most interesting to use—the presence or absence of forests, and, where present, the kind of forests that grow. For example, the lush Southeastern forests of spruce and hemlock are clear indications of a moderate climate, relatively warm winters, pleasantly cool summers, and lots of rain. The boreal forests of the Interior—or the taiga community (*taiga* is a Russian word that came from a Turkish word meaning "rocky high places")—on the other hand, are sparse in places and comprised of hardy trees and plants, white spruce and stunted black spruce, willows, birch, balsam poplar (cottonwoods), and aspen. These more marginal forests bespeak much harsher climatic conditions, long periods of cold, and a mean annual temperature below freezing. The tundra communities (*tundra* is a Finnish word that means "barren land") of the west and the north of Alaska are virtually without trees except for dwarf spruce and birch. These tundras tell of consistently cool to cold weather, of frequent cloudiness, and of harsh, compelling winds that sweep across the low-growing grass and lichens and forbid the growth of tall forests.

Wherever you travel in Alaska, you will find miniclimates. These can vary enormously within a fairly circumscribed area, too. For instance, you can expect to bake in the heat of Interior Alaska for at least a few days during July, but if you fly only a hundred or so miles from Fairbanks into the Brooks Range, you may find snow powdering the lower foothills.

The most important thing about Alaska's climate to keep in mind is how rapidly it can change. In every part of the state, from the temperate regions of the Southeast to the frigid reaches of the North Slope, you can expect the weather to deteriorate or to improve dramatically in just a matter of minutes. Clouds can clot a flawless blue sky as you watch, and rain can pour down almost before you can rig a shelter. The thermometer can drop 10 or 20 degrees in an hour, and fog can well up to blot out the daylight or white out a mountaintop. Fierce winds can suddenly roar in—winds strong enough to whip up high waves on inland lakes, set the spindrift scudding off ocean coasts, blow a raft upstream, or skid a small aircraft across the ground.

Camping on a lake in Southwest Alaska, I once had a free-standing tent wrenched from my hands by the wind one cloudy July morning. The gale bore down with the speed, force, and sound of a racing locomotive, and the tent took off. Tumbling and touching the ground now and then like a big blue balloon, it finally soared skyward in an updraft, skimmed over some treetops, and disappeared completely from sight. Fortunately, our party retrieved it, unscathed, a good quarter of a mile away.

Remember, however, that bad weather can change just as rapidly into good. Winds can silence, rains can let up, fog can vanish before delighted eyes, and the sun can return while a glorious blue day embraces you, all in a matter of minutes.

When you visit Alaska, rely less on official weather predictions than you would elsewhere. Meteorologists work under handicaps that are compounded by the normal capriciousness of the local climates. Be ready to seize the blue days—or portions of them—that come your way and enjoy them thoroughly. Alaskans all over have learned to do just this. At the same time, be prepared to sit out foul weather and have adequate shelter in which to do so. This book will help you select the right equipment. With proper gear, rain or cold alone should not ground you; but winds, fog, or a heavy storm can. Should you encounter such bad weather, a paperback will help, but good company is immeasurably better—another good reason to plan an Alaskan trip with someone whose company you enjoy.

6. Permafrost

A unique feature of Alaska's terrain is the phenomenon known as permafrost. Permafrost is defined as any part of the ground—rock, soil, or sand—that has remained frozen for more than two years. Permafrost requires a "frost climate," an average annual temperature generally below freezing, to form and persist. The weather over most of Alaska is ideal for it, and permafrost underlies more than 80 percent of the state. North of the Arctic Circle and in extensive regions of the Interior, permafrost is continuous. Farther south and in the west, it occurs sporadically—on the northern slopes of hills, for example, but not on the southern. Only in the warmer parts of Alaska, particularly along the Pacific coast, is there no permafrost. Much of Alaska's extensive permafrost has probably been around not just for two years or even for two hundred but for many millennia; it is a relict of the great ice ages.

Permafrost has some interesting characteristics and side effects. The lens of frozen ground may lie one or two inches or a few feet below the surface, and it can vary in thickness from a few inches to hundreds of feet. Around Tok, in the Interior, the permafrost is 100 feet thick; around Bethel, in the Southwest, it is 600. On the Arctic Slope it is up to 2,000 feet thick, a condition that posed problems for the oil drillers near Prudhoe Bay and even more problems for the builders of the oil pipeline.

An essential part of permafrost is the integral "active layer" that forms its upper, insulating skin. This active layer thaws in the summer, while the ground beneath it, being protected, remains frozen, a condition required for its perpetuation. The skin of permafrost can be composed of debris—for example, rocks that have been shattered by the freezing process—or it can be a tundra or forest community of one kind or another. On the Arctic Slope, for instance, the permafrost wears a velvety green cloak of tundra that is embroidered with wildflowers in the summer. In the Interior, a thick layer of living and dead mosses often carpets the frozen ground. In areas of greater rainfall, on the other hand, permafrost can be covered by peat or other moss communities, or its active layer can be a soggy meadow with big clumps of coarse grasses, or tussocks—bad news for hikers. (*Note:* in some areas it is warming.)

Without the active layer of ground protecting it, the upper stratum of permafrost is exposed to the summer sun. It then melts and collapses upon itself, forming a declivity that becomes an icy puddle—or thermokarst. As Arctic erosion proceeds, the puddle—being alternately frozen and thawed—may grow into a pond or lake. In regions of extreme cold, where the active layer can be cracked and torn by weathering, this process occurs as part of the natural evolution of the frozen landscape. Thus you will find hundreds of thousands of ponds and lakes dotting the North Slope tundra. Erosion is often initiated by other means today, however: when you see twin canals cutting across the same Arctic tundra, you can be sure that heavy equipment has passed this way—it might have been many decades ago, since it takes this fragile land so long to heal itself—or it might be a recent occurrence.

In many parts of Alaska, spectacular ground patterns are associated with permafrost. Frost circles and immense networks of polygons (like slices of honeycomb) are fractured into the Arctic tundras. On slopes where the frozen land thaws in summer and creeps downhill, solifluction lobes scallop the hillsides. Pingos, or large ice blisters, like 100-foot-high frozen volcanoes, relieve the flatness of the Arctic landscape.

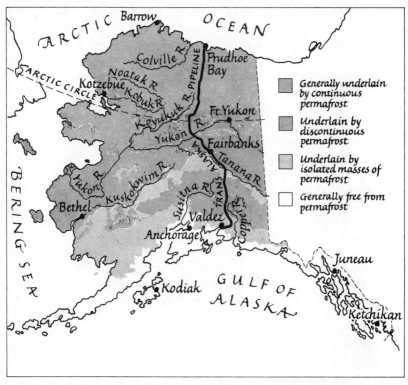

Permafrost in Alaska

Because it is frozen solid, permafrost functions as bedrock in the Arctic. This causes heavy runoff of surface water and makes the construction of standard reservoirs or the use of conventional water and sewage systems impossible. Not only do water pipes and septic tanks freeze in permafrost, but the act of installing them opens up the active layer, and the permafrost starts to erode. To locate any kind of structure, in fact—whether railroad ties, roads, piers or bridges, an office building, or even a small house—in or on permafrost is a major challenge to a builder or engineer. Digging a cellar for a house and putting in a furnace, for instance, can cause the house to collapse. Putting a house on blocks on the frozen ground can still cause the permafrost to sink and heave, which means buckled floors, leaning walls, and doors that won't close. Standard road building also invites disasters—such as huge thermokarsts that swallow up sections of pavement. Unwary farmers clearing frozen ground have been known to have their tractors swallowed up, too.

As construction (of all kinds) has increased in Alaska, engineers have been offered unique challenges. The oil pipeline builders, for example, would have liked to bury most of the 48-inch-diameter pipe from Prudhoe Bay to Valdez. But the oil they were arranging to move leaves the deeply permafrosted ground at 150 to 180 degrees Fahrenheit and may lose only a few degrees as it enters the pipe. How to keep the ground frozen and avoid the damage of disrupted permafrost under these circumstances? Elevation of the pipeline on deep-sunk vertical members (VMs), or steel pipes, for 420 miles—over half the length of the pipeline—was one answer. For another, they buried the pipe in various optimum lengths and at various optimum depths where they could, and then refrigerated portions of it. They refrigerated the ground under most of the dozen pump stations as well, using a complicated system of circulating brine through coiled pipes underneath an insulating layer of plastic foam. Then they equipped the VMs with finned radiators to carry off extra heat where necessary.

When you travel through the Arctic, look for other freezer systems incorporated into the foundations of structures—and if you see slabs of plastic foam, you'll know what they're being used for. (Several buildings in Kotzebue are underlain with this kind of insulation.) Time will tell how these systems hold up. Meantime, more and more of Alaska's picturesque old buildings, once skewed by permafrost, are being straightened out. You still find, here and there, however, a slightly tipsy-looking cabin—a reminder of the way things were not all that long ago.

When you run an Arctic river, you may have a chance to see permafrost at work firsthand. Along the cut-back banks where the frozen ground is exposed, the earth erodes easily, leaving the topsoil layer draped over like a torn curtain and the trees and plants rooted in it canted at crazy angles. On Interior rivers like the Charley, you can see the icy lenses of permafrost exposed in the open banks.

7. Light

In Alaska, the sun is never directly overhead. Furthermore, there are long months of complete darkness or dim twilight during the winter in many parts of the state. Despite these phenomena, Alaska receives more light overall (sunlight and twilight together) during a year than do territories in the lower latitudes. Fairbanks, for example, located at 65 degrees north latitude, receives light of one sort or another for more than 62 percent of the year. In the tropics, the light is stronger, but the periods of sunlight and twilight add up to only a little more than 53 percent of the year. There are two reasons for this seemingly odd discrepancy. First, in the northern latitudes the sun moves across the sky at an angle low to the horizon, which means it takes longer to rise and to set, and consequently there are longer periods of twilight. Second, refraction—the atmospheric bending of the sun's rays—which occurs only slightly at the equator, becomes more pronounced the farther north you travel, and this causes the sun's rays to remain visible even after the sun itself has dipped below the horizon. The energy delivered to the ground by the sun's rays is less in Alaska than in the tropics, but because of the total sunlight and twilight received during the summer in these northern latitudes, the radiation effect is fairly close to that received in lower latitudes.

It is noteworthy that light is bent in the direction of increasing air density—that is, toward cold dense air—and this phenomenon pulls the image of distant landscapes above the horizon. Thus, mountains that are invisible in warm weather may be clearly seen when it is cold. This is called the "looming" effect.

The pattern of the seasons in the north is dramatically different than elsewhere. In the Arctic, the summer is one long day, while the winter is one long night. At Alaska's northernmost point, the sun remains above the horizon for over two and one-half months—from the second week of May until early August. But for the two-plus months from mid-November to late January, the sun never shows its face; twilight takes its place. Once the sun returns, the hours of sunlight lengthen dramatically from day to day. The seasons—a function of the sunlight, of course—must race to change: with sunlight going from zero minutes to twenty-four hours per day in a matter of less than four months, the passage of spring and early summer is a particularly exciting time.

Even in Alaska's more southern areas, this same pattern of light is felt. Although the sun slips below the horizon in summer, the twilight lingers all night long, and in many places the skies are starless and the only heavenly body to be seen is the moon. In deep winter, the sun barely clears the mountains to slant its light against the snowy ground.

Displays of the aurora borealis frequently light up Alaska's skies. (Near the South Pole, an equivalent effect is called the aurora australis.) These stunning light shows are caused by the solar wind—a burst of the sun's particles released when its surface flares up in sunspots—encountering the earth's polar magnetic fields, where charged particles appear to

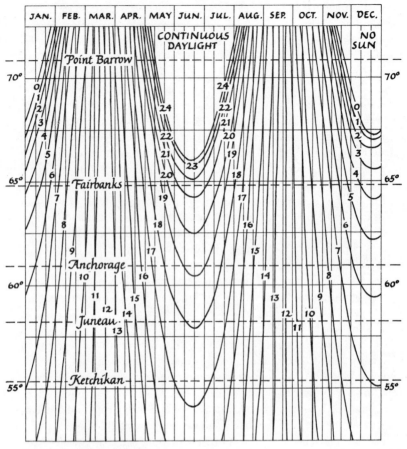

| JAN. | FEB. | MAR. | APR. | MAY | JUN. | JUL. | AUG. | SEP. | OCT. | NOV. | DEC. |

Sunlight in northern latitudes

erupt in "fountains." The energy released in these collisions strikes the molecules of earth's common atmospheric gases, oxygen and nitrogen. When such encounters occur in the upper atmosphere, oxygen reacts by giving off a red glow, while nitrogen glows yellow. Closer to the earth, oxygen ionizes violet, and nitrogen ionizes green. In Alaska, look for the aurora borealis in clear night skies from August through May. The aurora, the subject of many Eskimo legends, can also be seen from a distance of 1,000 miles when you are flying 30,000 feet high; look for it on clear winter nights on the flight from Seattle to Anchorage or Fairbanks. If you have a good show, you may be able to view about a quarter of the entire aurora in the Northern Hemisphere. (Sit on the right side flying north.) If you're in a position to photograph the aurora from the ground, use ASA 400 film, a wide-angle lens, and a time exposure of from three to thirty seconds. An object, such as a tree or a lighted cabin in the foreground, will add scale to your picture.

The intense electrical currents generated by the aurora in the ionosphere (70 miles up) induce secondary currents on the earth's surface that have caused interesting effects in the Trans-Alaska Pipeline—a particularly good north-south conductor.

Because of the slanting light in Alaska, you will always have a shadow on sunny days. Trees do, too, of course, especially in the sparse forests of the Interior. Flying over these forests on a late summer afternoon, watch for traceries of parallel tree shadows on the ground; they look as though they had been penciled lightly onto the soft, green landscape. In the winter, the tree shadows make blue stripes on the snow.

Alaska's flora and fauna—including its people—have adapted to the rhythm of the Nordic sunlight. They cram much of the whole year's living into those months of daylight. The conifers nearly burst with cones, the alders hang out their tassels thickly, flowers bloom everywhere. (Because of the steady light, cabbages grow to be 4 feet in diameter; delphiniums shoot up as high as 12 feet.) Children play all night, and some adults do, too. You can find yourself making camp at 1 A.M. with no difficulty or taking off in daylight at 3 A.M. People also take advantage of the long hours of twilight in summer and in winter—thus you will have more hours in the day in which to enjoy the outdoors. Alaskans seem to need less sleep during the summer, and you may find yourself getting by on less than you do in lower latitudes. But remember, Alaskans can sleep it off in their long, dark winter.

The quality of Alaska's slanting light reminds some people of the glowing illumination that seems to flood many paintings of the Dutch school. Photographers are apt to go slightly crazy over it, especially when, around midnight, the sun backlights a field of dryas or the ice floes of the Arctic Ocean or a caribou standing on the riverbank and curiously watching the creatures bobbing by on their strange craft.

Alaskan light is soft: it gentles hard and vivid colors. When you return from Alaska to the Lower Forty-Eight, you will probably find yourself blinking at the glaring brightness of the colors around you and the newly seen harshness of the neon signs.

8. The Miracle of Migration

Each year, when the days grow longer and the sunlight works its magic more and more upon the land, pageants of migration begin to unfold all over the state of Alaska. Some of these extraordinary rites of passage occur across the land, as when tens of thousands of caribou leave their wintering grounds and commence their steady drift across the spacious tundras, through the mountain passes, and across the braids of rushing rivers to reach their chosen calving grounds. Other migratory travels occur in offshore waters: the Bering Strait, for example, funnels a prodigious population of marine mammals—whales and walruses and ringed, spotted, and bearded seals—through its frigid waters when April and May bring the first breakups of ice. Starting in late May, salmon fill the streams and lakes and rivers all up and down Alaska's coast, navigating the waters they move through unerringly. They arrive in rhythmic run after run of species, first the chinooks (or kings), then the chums (dogs), followed by the pinks (humpbacks), and finally, in July, the cohos (silvers) and the sockeyes (reds). Equally spectacular are the breathtaking numbers of birds that return each summer to the shores and the rich wetlands of Alaska, following the traditional pathways of their species: as many as 24 million shorebirds and waterfowl may occupy the Yukon-Kuskokwim delta, nesting or resting during the light-filled months of May through September.

Although the "whys" of migration are generally understood (animals pursue survival, following seasonal ancestral patterns in search of food and sites to bear their young), the "hows" are still full of mystery. We know that animals respond to their own innate biological clocks (even as do we). But how do the caribou know to move, in perfect tempo, at one particular moment in the spring? What guides their footsteps to their calving grounds through blinding late-spring sleets and snows? How does the Arctic tern chart its incredible course as it wings from pole to pole each year, forever following the sunlight? How do the snow geese know to crowd the sky, flying southward like skeins of pearls through the cool dark of one October evening? What knowledge lies within the salmon to bring it back, after years in the ocean, perhaps thousands of miles to the place where it was born, there to spawn and then to die? Do these creatures, indeed, navigate by the stars as have human travelers through the eons? Do they "follow their noses," using their sense of smell to steer their courses? Do birds follow landmarks, perhaps the silhouette of a certain mountain here or the curve of the seacoast there, to stay on their chosen pathways? Is it a deep magnetic force, acting upon the iron within their very blood, that pulls the migrating creatures northward or sends them southward at a given moment? Or is it, in fact, something preordained by an unknown cosmic force? Something so magical that we mere mortals can never comprehend it?

Whatever the answer, certain parts of Alaska's land and waters become the scenes of unequaled spectacles every spring and summer. Ask someone who has stood beside a stream in the Southeast—say, the Mendenhall River, right outside of Juneau—and seen its clear waters all but bursting with beautiful fish bent on achieving their destiny. Or talk to one who has listened to the gentle thunder of thousands of wingbeats in the night. Or inquire of one who has witnessed the tawny stream of caribou flowing effortlessly across the tundra. Barry Lopez, in his eloquent book *Arctic Dreams,* speaks of "those few weeks when life swirls in the water and on the tundra and in the balmy air. Standing there on the ground, you can feel . . . something physical in [the land] under the influence of light, an embrace or exaltation." It is indeed a particular affirmation of life and beauty that cannot be experienced anywhere but in the northern lands of the world.

As you enjoy this annual phenomenon, it is worth noting that the rhythm of all living things in the far north is tied in to the arrival and departure of the countless migratory creatures that visit this part of the earth. Not only are the plants ready to provide them food, but the cycle of insect life peaks when the birds and the fish arrive. Perhaps more subtly, there are global echoes, as well: both nutrients and life are being cycled and recycled by the millions of world travelers that, for part of their lives at least, spend their time in Alaska.

9. History

No one knows when people first found the land that would one day be called Alaska. Recent discoveries in Alaska's Yukon Territory—and in Canada's Old Crow Basin not far from the Alaska border—suggest the presence there of human hunters more than 27,000 years ago, and some anthropologists believe that people migrated from Asia to North America as long as 30,000 to 40,000 years ago or more. Others argue that the date of human arrival was closer, perhaps, to 15,000 years ago, when wanderers may have found the place in Alaska now known as Onion Portage. Whenever the actual event occurred, it certainly went unnoticed and unremarked, for the people reaching Alaska were not intent on exploring the world; they were simply pursuing their way of life and following the animals that provided them their food.

These first Alaskans may have arrived during a warm interglacial period when they could easily cross the narrow body of shallow water that separated Siberia from Alaska. It is likely, however, that nomadic hunters and fishermen first entered Alaska during an ice age when the sea level was low and the Bering Land Bridge, extending perhaps 900 to 1,000 miles from south to north, joined what are now Alaska and Siberia into one continuous landmass.

Never glaciated, the land bridge was probably similar in character to regions in western and Interior Alaska today. A grassy tundra community covered broad stretches of gentle plains, or steppes. Low hills delineated the horizon, with a mountain thrusting up only here and there. There were few trees, but streams and braided rivers meandered through the lowlands. The weather was frequently stormy and chilled by icy winds. Then, as now, great mountain walls barricaded the land to the southeast and the north, but then glaciers radiated in every direction from high cirques, and snowfields and ice choked many of the mountain passes.

It was not a particularly hospitable land, but the coastal areas, especially in the south, were exceptionally rich in shellfish, fish, and sea mammal populations. The streams were full of salmon, and there were many land animals. And so the hunters and fishermen came traveling in small bands or family groups, new families forming and budding off to make their way on their own. They came sporadically through many millennia, starting from different places, taking different pathways, and bringing different ways and ideas with them. As the ice ages drew to a close and the seas began to rise, these people moved to higher and drier places, the land that would become Alaska.

During times when the ice melted from the mountain passes, some of these first adventurers continued to migrate through Alaska to more distant places, perhaps as far as South America, so that the Bering Land Bridge may have served as a human gateway to both of the American continents.

It was during the colder times, some anthropologists believe, that people were confined to the Interior refugium, or the Arctic (which also escaped glaciation at times), and they settled in and stayed. Whatever the reason, members of four ethnic groups—the Eskimos, Athabascans, Tlingits and Haidas, and Aleuts—that came into North America remained in Alaska and made it their permanent home.

While all four groups shared certain basic similarities—they all hunted, fished, and gathered food; had no written language; and were skillful and ingenious people—there were distinct and sometimes subtle differences between them. Some of these were physical, but, more importantly, as they settled into their different environments, they developed distinctive cultures and sets of skills.

The Eskimos, perhaps the last to come to Alaska, were primarily a coastal people, although some of them lived inland as well. Groups of Eskimos moved both south and north along Alaska's shores, and some continued across the Arctic coast as far as Greenland. Many of them learned to live successfully under the demanding conditions of the Arctic. They developed an extraordinarily fine, almost uncanny, directional sense. Traveling in a straight line, noting which way the wind blew, knowing the features of the terrain as they knew the faces of their families, they could find their way through blinding snowstorms, whiteouts, and dense fogs. They also mastered the art of making their way through ice-choked waters, and they became adept at spearing seals and harpooning the white beluga and bowhead whales long before Europeans brought metal to their culture. Gifted carvers, they fashioned exceptional toggle harpoons and such things as snow masks to protect their eyes from wind-driven snow and the glaring eye-level sun. They traded extensively among themselves—seal oil, walrus, sealskins, ivory—and regularly with the Chukchi of Siberia and the Athabascans. They also fought frequently

with the latter, who were their immediate neighbors. Some were nomadic; they returned over and over again to favored fishing, sealing, and
caribou-hunting camps, to such places as Cape Krusenstern, Point Hope,
and Shishmaref—where they left their traces in arrowheads, chippings,
bones, and the faint outlines of their dwellings—and to Anaktuvuk Pass,
the "Place of Caribou Droppings." (It is noteworthy that the descendants
of these ancient people are directly involved in current archeological digs
in Alaska.) Needing the caribou, as well as sea mammals, for many purposes—food, clothing, to make bone implements or needles and thread—
they were skillful at intercepting the animals in their far-sweeping
migrations, knowing through which passes the great herds would funnel.

Their neighbors, the Athabascan Indians, may have been the first people to come into and, indeed, to continue through Alaska; some Athabascans went as far east as Hudson Bay, and others filtered southward to
become the ancestors of the Apache and Navajo Indians. Like the Eskimos, the Athabascans were skillful hunters, but they depended more on
large land mammals, such as caribou and moose, and on salmon and
other fish that traveled the Yukon and its tributaries for their major subsistence. The Athabascans became adept at corralling caribou, tracking
moose, and using snares, traps, and pits to catch smaller game, which
they used for food as well. They also devised ingenious hooks, lures,
traps, and nets to snare fish. Generally nomadic, the Athabascans looked
for forested land to pitch their camps, seeking the warmth and shelter afforded by the white spruce trees of the Interior.

In winter, bands of related people frequently joined together to spend
the long dark months in small settlements, and at these times songs, stories, and dances told the history of the tribes and so perpetuated the past.
But subsistence for the Athabascans was never certain: they had to cope
with a harsh and often cruel climate and with undependable food supplies. They lived precariously from season to season, needing an inner as
well as a physical strength to survive. Believing reincarnation of the spirit
was possible into both human and animal forms, they identified closely
with the animals they depended upon. They also developed a complex
system of beliefs that helped answer the worrisome philosophical questions that arise in the minds of all people.

The Tlingits and Haidas (known collectively as the Koluschan) and
the Aleuts lived under more benign environmental conditions. It is prob-
able that the Aleuts originally populated the rich southern shores of the
Bering Land Bridge as well as the Aleutian Islands. The Tlingits and
Haidas occupied the lush forested shores of the Southeast, where the
food supply was also dependable and easily harvested. The weather in
both Alaska's Southwest and its Southeast became what the Russians

Mount Saint Elias viewed from Icy Bay. Source: National Park Service.

later described as "surprisingly warm," although fog and rain were part of the daily lives of the people living in both regions; for the Aleuts, storms were commonplace and so were winds strong enough to blow rocks around.

The rich culture that flourished among the Tlingits and Haidas has been well studied and frequently described. These people developed a complex society, took slaves, gave lavish potlatches, and lived their lives in accordance with highly organized social structures while observing clan rituals and strictly regulated relationships. Their artwork—magnificent totem poles, beautiful blankets, fine cedar-bark and spruce-root baskets—and their architecture are well known and notable for bold and highly stylized designs.

Less well known is the culture of the Aleuts; it was almost totally changed by a handful of Russians in a matter of a few decades. However, it was evidently as complex and fascinating as that of the Aleuts' neighbors across the Gulf of Alaska. Since their food supply also was rich, varied, and readily available, all age groups in Aleut society could play a role in bringing it in; old people and children, for instance, gathered shellfish while the stronger, more skillful hunters brought in the sea mammals. It is known that the Aleuts practiced surgery and that their elaborate ritual burials included the practice of embalming the dead. They lived in villages, and, although not as aggressive or warlike as the Tlingits, like the Tlingits they took slaves.

Lacking a written language, they left no records themselves, but early European visitors wrote at some length of their charm and well-developed culture. Among those who traveled among the Aleuts (and the Russians) in the late eighteenth century was Martin Sauer, who was greatly impressed by the Aleut people and their artful handiwork. "Their instruments and utensils," he wrote, "are all made with amazing beauty and exact symmetry . . . their darts are adapted with the greatest judgment to the different objects of the chase." (The Aleuts, in fact, used thirty different kinds of harpoon heads for different species of game.) Sauer found their baidars, or skin boats, especially fine, and said of them: "If perfect symmetry, smoothness and proportion constitute beauty, they are beautiful: to me they appeared so beyond anything I ever beheld. I have seen some of them as transparent as oiled paper, through which you could trace every formation of the inside, and the manner of the Natives sitting in it; whose light dress, pointed and plumed bonnet, together with their perfect ease and activity, added infinitely to its elegance." The Aleuts, he went on to say, maneuvered their baidars with ability and skill, and "paddled in among the breakers which reached to their breasts, and carried the baidars quite under the water, sporting more like amphibious animals than human beings."

Sauer was incensed at the treatment the Aleuts received from the hands of the Russian *promyshleniki* (hunters and traders): the Aleuts' behavior, he noted succinctly, "is not rude and barbarous, but mild, polite and hospitable . . . they by no means deserve to be termed stupid, an epithet so liberally bestowed on those whom Europeans call savages."

Bishop Innokenti Veniaminof, writer, anthropologist, and priest, lived among the Aleuts for seven years during the first part of the nineteenth century. He learned their language, and he gained great respect for their intelligence and gifts of artistry. His notes are still among the most definitive made about these people.

By the time European explorers first came to Alaska, a relatively large Native population—perhaps larger than Alaska's Native population today—had become well established there. Some estimates put the number of Eskimos in the early eighteenth century at around forty thousand, the number of Aleuts at twenty-five thousand, and that of the Tlingits and Athabascans at around ten thousand each. Although relationships between the Native peoples were not always cordial, they had by then more or less defined their respective territories, and their unrecorded boundaries were generally honored. And while other cultures might have developed land use and exploitation and erected sophisticated buildings and monuments, the Alaska Natives had disturbed their land almost not at all, for they lived in profound harmony with it. (What a legacy!) Vigorous, resourceful, and adapted to their various environments, they lacked metal, guns, and gunpowder to defend themselves. Without these, they were helpless before the Europeans.

The first Europeans to claim Alaska successfully were the Russians, who were engaged in exploring to the east just as the English, French, and Spanish were then probing the mysteries of the world that lay to their west. Vitus Bering, a Dane sailing under the Russian flag (as did adventurous young men from many countries at that time), became a sort of Alaskan Christopher Columbus. Commissioned first by Peter the Great and then by Anna Ivanovna to take part in an ambitious attempt to find the New World and to chart its coast north of Mexico (and the entire coast of Siberia), Bering was allotted the finding and exploring of the American coast. The expedition he led in 1741 would change the course of Alaska's history.

Bering made his initial landfall in Alaska after fifteen heartbreaking years of preparation and then unsuccessful sorties from Kamchatka. (On one early trip, he did, however, discover and name Saint Lawrence Island and Big Diomede in what would come to be named the Bering Sea.) He set forth from Russia in the spring of 1741, captaining the *Saint Peter* while Lt. Alexei Chirikof captained a sister ship, the *Saint Paul,* and sailed with him. The two soon became separated, and Chirikof proceeded on a less eventful course. After poor weather and difficult sailing, on July 16, the birthday of Russia's Saint Elias, Bering found himself near the 60th parallel, with a longitude of 140 degrees east. The day was clear, and looming against the eastern horizon was a magnificently high white mountain that seemed to rise from the sea. Looking at a future major

landmark of Alaska, Bering—who was already in failing health and suf-
fering from exhaustion—is reported by one of his crew to have simply
"shrugged his shoulders in the presence of all on board the *Saint Peter.*"
He did, however, on July 20, give the name of Saint Elias to a prominent
cape of land nearby. And he did drop anchor and put to shore on an island the Russians later named Kayak Island because it was shaped like a
Native boat. (Mount Saint Elias was named later; the American explorer,
scientist, and writer William Healy Dall referred to this grand mountain
by that name in 1880.) Georg Wilhelm Steller, the headstrong and gifted
naturalist who accompanied Bering on this trip, verified the fact that they
had indeed found North America because he saw an American blue jay,
known to be native only to that continent: hence, Steller's jay.

Although Bering found the New World on this fateful voyage, it was
ultimately a disastrous expedition. (Chirikof actually found Alaska—
probably Prince of Wales Island—the day before Bering landed on Kayak
Island, but he lost at least thirteen men in landing attempts and returned
to Russia without having set foot on the North American continent.)
Along with many of his crew, Bering came down with scurvy and became
weak and ultimately disoriented. Bad luck dogged him, and fierce head
winds and storms battered the *Saint Peter* as it sailed for its home port in
Siberia. Steller wrote: "The wind seemed as if it issued from a flue, with
such a whistling, roaring and rumbling, that we expected every moment
to lose mast and rudder, or to see the ship crushed between the breakers." The crew became too feeble to man the ship or to stand watch, especially after their water supplies ran out. "Their courage," Steller noted,
"was as unsteady as their teeth." Finally the *Saint Peter,* unguided,
drifted ashore on what would one day be called Bering Island. There
Bering and several of the crew members died and were buried. After rebuilding the wrecked ship, the tattered survivors of the crew—Steller
among them—managed to limp back home.

The reports brought back by the *Saint Peter*'s crew of Alaska's fabulous sea otter and fur seal populations and Steller's excellent and detailed
descriptions of these and other animals excited the Russians and pro-
moted bands of adventurous and ambitious *promyshleniki*—the hunters
and traders—to set forth into the Bering Sea, seeking their fortunes.
Their onslaughts initiated the near extinction of the fur-bearing sea
mammals as well as the Aleut people, whom the Russians had subdued
and enslaved by 1766. Sauer wrote of them: ". . . The Russian *promyshleniki* . . . are infinitely more savage than any tribes I have hitherto met
with." A Russian naval officer later wrote sadly of the brutality: ". . .
Wives were taken from their husbands, and daughters from their moth-
ers . . . they [the *promyshleniki*] used not infrequently to place men close

together, and try through how many the ball of their rifle-barreled musket would pass." (It should be noted that not all the *promyshleniki* were so brutal.)

Along with the *promyshleniki*, several Russian explorers set out on new expeditions of discovery. They eventually managed to sail as far north as Cape Krusenstern and then up the Yukon River as far as Nulato, where they left their names and religion among many of the Athabascan Indians. (They also eventually traveled southeast as far as California.)

The English, French, and Spanish explorers were not far behind the Russians, however. In 1778, Capt. James Cook, with George Vancouver along, reached the Arctic Ocean. (Another Englishman, Capt. Frederick W. Beechey, pushed on farther north to Point Barrow in 1826, and the New England whalers soon followed him.) George Vancouver made a second trip to Alaska in 1793; he charted the complicated coastal area of Southeast Alaska so accurately that his maps were used for more than a hundred years afterward. The Frenchman Jean François de Galaup, comte de La Pérouse, explored as far north as Lituya Bay in 1786, searching for the Northwest Passage. He lost twenty-one of his crewmen to the treacherous waters of Lysianski Strait and died himself on his return voyage to France. Between 1774 and 1792, Spain sent several of its greatest navigators, including Juan Francisco de la Bodega y Quadra, into Alaska's southeastern waters.

By this time, Gregor Shelikof had established Russia's first permanent settlement at Three Saints Bay on Kodiak Island, and, in 1799, the Russian-American Company was formally established with the blessings of the emperor Paul I. This company, patterned after the British East India Company, was expected to promote further discovery, expand trading, develop architecture, and spread Russian Orthodox religion in the New World. According to William Healy Dall, the early Alaskan explorer, Alaska's Natives were easily converted to the Russian faith because they believed that a god who could save such cruel souls as the *promyshleniki* must be all-powerful indeed. The Russian establishment, however, was more benevolent, despite occasional warlike incidents.

Under a series of managers (sometimes called governors)—the first, Alexander Baranof, and later Adm. Baron Ferdinand von Wrangell—the Russian-American Company became in effect the governing body of Alaska for the next sixty years, the managers running things much like lords of a fiefdom.

Baranof started his company operations in Aleut territory, but when the sea otter and fur seal were nearly exhausted, in 1799, he moved from Kodiak and the Aleutian Islands southeast. There he established the first Russian capital, Mikhailovskii Redut (Fort Saint Michael), on Baranof

Island. Although the Tlingits succeeded in burning and sacking this fort in 1802, they were not so successful at getting rid of Novoarkhangelsk (later Sitka), especially since the Russians had reciprocated with a devastating reprisal in 1804. For the next several years, Baranof presided over a lively society in Sitka, which was called the Paris of the Pacific. During the years the Russians occupied Alaska, there were rarely more than five hundred or six hundred of them living in their immense colony. (An early census showed that there were more Hawaiians—brought in for work— in Alaska than Russians by nearly two to one.)

Despite such a low population, the Russian settlers could not produce enough food to live on. Russian holdings in California also failed to supply the needed agricultural base, and as time went on, the fur seal and sea otter became more and more scarce. Trade became more competitive as well, with both England and the United States pushing northward and vying for the available resources. In addition, Sitka was a long way from Saint Petersburg and a fatherland that was devoting its energies to wars with Napoleon's France. So it was that after little more than a century in the New World, Russia began to find itself overextended. In 1867, Russia sold Alaska to the United States for $7.2 million. (Russia's Baron Stoeckl, who handled negotiations with United States Secretary of State William H. Seward, is reported to have taken $200,000 to reimburse himself for the amount he had spent out of his own pocket enlisting the support of key congressmen for this purchase.) It is noteworthy that no treaties were made with the Native Alaskans at the time of this transaction. Seward changed the name of the territory then known as Russian America, rechristening it Alaska.

Although he considered the acquisition of Alaska the greatest achievement of his life, the Alaskan purchase was not entirely popular with the American people. Some called the new territory Seward's Folly, Walrussia, or Icebergia. The myth of a land locked perpetually in ice and snow, where only an Eskimo or a polar bear could survive, became all too quickly and firmly established. For the thirty years after it was acquired, Alaska—remote and inaccessible—was left virtually alone by the United States. It was first called Indian Country, then, in 1884, by virtue of the first Organic Act, it became the District of Alaska. Around that time, as the explorer-historian William Healy Dall wrote, it was a place where "no man could make a legal will, own a homestead and transfer it, or so much as cut wood for his fire without defying a Congressional prohibition: where polygamy and slavery and the lynching of witches prevailed, with no legal authority to stay or punish criminals." An early Juneau miner put it more colorfully: "We had an earthquake a while ago, so we know the Lord ain't forgotten us, even if the government has." It took

Abandoned miner's cabin near the Yukon-Charley Rivers National Preserve. Source: National Park Service.

the gold rushes—which brought Alaska its first recorded population boom—at the turn of the twentieth century to establish some semblance of authority and order; and even then the law was often decided by the miners themselves and on their own terms.

In 1900, Alaska's population was estimated to be about sixty thousand people, including almost thirty thousand non-Natives, most of whom would leave after failing to find gold. One of the census takers was an "outsider," who found life in Alaska to be rough and ready; in fact, he described the place as being "the worst country in the world for swearing." He told of meeting one relatively pious Alaskan who named every dog on his team with a four-letter word so he could swear as much as he wanted all winter long without disturbing his conscience. (It is worthwhile reading Robert Service, whose Yukon poems capture the spirit of this period in Alaska's history so well; see Suggested Reading.)

Alaska may have been far from civilization, but American industry was not entirely idle in the newly acquired district. When whaling declined in Alaska's waters, the whalers turned to taking walrus for their oil and tusks. (It is estimated that between commercial take by whalers and the subsistence take by Eskimos, two hundred thousand walrus were killed in Alaskan waters between 1860 and 1880.) There were also the rich salmon fisheries in the Southeast and Southwest, and these attracted increasing commercial exploitation too. Canneries went up—first small, then rambling wooden buildings—and stationary fish traps, or nets, were set across the mouths of the major migratory streams and rivers. Workers came from China, Japan, and the Philippines. (A machine that speeded up the processing of the fish was named the "Iron Chink.") In the meantime, the Americans continued to hunt the sea otter and fur seal. By the early twentieth century, people were beginning to worry about Alaska's fisheries and the vanishing populations of the sea mammals. Finally, the federal government stepped in to end pelagic seal fishing and to initiate strict controls on the hunting of sea mammals, with a measure of success: both sea otter and fur seal have since become reestablished.

Meantime, in the 1860s, Alaska (still Russian America) was considered for a launching point for the newly developing Western Union Company's telegraph system. This led to a period of major scientific exploration in Alaska, funded by the U.S. government. Eventually, however, a preferable route for the cable was found, from the East Coast to Europe. Copper mining became a more successful venture. Soon after the beginning of the twentieth century, capitalistic tycoons moved in to build a railroad into the heart of the Wrangell Mountains, and the Kennecott copper operation went into major production. (See Wrangell–Saint Elias Park and Preserve, in Part III.) The salmon fishery also came to be a major industry.

In 1912, Congress finally passed the second Organic Act for Alaska. This one at last gave Alaska its own territorial legislature. (In 1906, it had been allowed a voteless congressional delegate.) Near that time, the Bureau of Forestry (later the USDA Forest Service), led by Gifford Pinchot, was consolidating its Alaska holdings into 24 million acres of the choicest forested land in Alaska's Southeast and Southcentral regions. The federally built and operated Alaska Railroad was authorized in 1914 and completed in 1923. This played a major role in opening up and developing Southcentral and Interior Alaska. (The Alaska Railroad was acquired by the state of Alaska in 1984. It continues to serve a number of homesteads that are inaccessible by road or by air.)

In 1920, a pioneer flight from New York to Nome (by the army) ushered in a new era for "the bush." But it was not until World War II that major change hit Alaska. At that time, the military constructed numerous airfields and established several large installations there. Soldiers spent long lonesome and dangerous months on the foggy and windy Aleutian Islands; in 1942, Dutch Harbor was bombed, and Attu and Kiska were both invaded by the Japanese. It took the Americans more than a year to reoccupy these islands, and during the bloody battle on Attu Island, only 28 out of 2,600 Japanese were known to have survived. (This count was possible only because they were taken prisoner.) The island of Kiska had 1,255 tons of bombs dropped on it, and the Japanese managed to evacuate their force of 5,183 men in a record fifty-five minutes—to make for a somewhat hollow American victory.

Perhaps most significantly for the future, many new roads were built during the war, including the AlCan Highway (now called the Alaska Highway), which joined Alaska to the "Outside" once and for all. In total, the military spent over $1 billion for its various Alaskan efforts between 1941 and 1945, and Alaska's population grew from 74,000 to 112,000.

Alaska continued to grow after World War II. In the fifties, oil was brought in on the Kenai Peninsula, a major finding. The USDA Forest Service began to open its forests to "harvest," and the commercial fishing business continued to prosper. Still, the territory felt itself a stepchild. With a growing population, pressures for statehood increased. Congress finally responded with a statehood act. When President Eisenhower proclaimed Alaska a new state on January 3,1959, the story goes, every church bell in Alaska pealed in celebration. Because Alaska still had what was then considered a meager economic base, Congress was especially generous with the new state (see Who Takes Care of Alaska's Lands, below), but it failed to define and settle the Native land claims.

Of course, it turned out that Alaska's natural resources—particularly its oil—were richer than anyone had dreamed. When oil was brought in on the North Slope in 1969 (the presence of oil there had been known since before the turn of the century) and the oil pipeline was built from Prudhoe Bay to Valdez, Alaska gained an economic base that became the envy of many other states and even nations. With an overall population of about 500,000, Alaska had for a time the highest per capita income of any of the fifty states—a budget in the billions and in the black. Tied to the price of oil, however, Alaska's economy has since gyrated accord-

Day 19
April 11
250 Mi

Day 38
April 30
280 Miles

SHELIKOF STRAIT

ALASKA PENINSULA

Day 40
May 2
350 M

Day 56
May 18
Farthest
Southwest
Observation
470 Miles

Composite overview of the Exxon Valdez oil spill, tracking from March 24, 1989 (date of the spill) to May 18, 1989. In just fifty-six days, the oil slick traveled 470 miles southwest from Bligh Reef, and the cumulative area of slick spread out over 11,000 square miles. Years later, oil was still present in the substrate of extensive areas of the impacted coasts. Source: State of Alaska Department of Environmental Consevration.

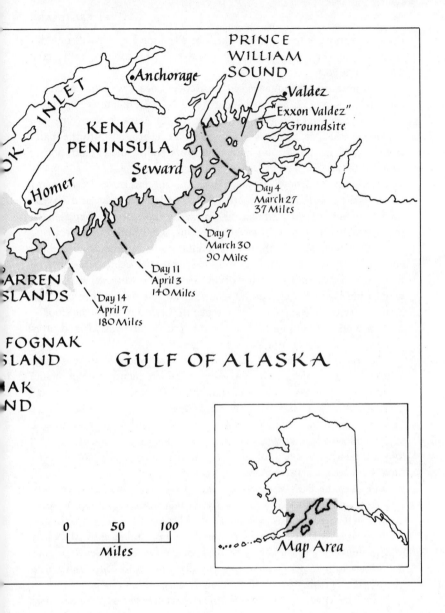

PRINCE
WILLIAM
SOUND

•Anchorage

•Valdez

"Exxon Valdez"
Groundsite

KENAI
PENINSULA

OK INLET

Seward
•

•Homer

Day 4
March 27
37 Miles

Day 7
March 30
90 Miles

Day 11
April 3
140 Miles

ARREN
SLANDS

Day 14
April 7
180 Miles

FOGNAK
SLAND

GULF OF ALASKA

AK
ND

0   50   100
        Miles

Map Area

ingly, and there is the certainty that the Prudhoe Bay oil will one day soon run out. (Pressures to open up new Arctic areas for exploration continue unabated.)

An important consequence of the discovery of oil was the passage of the Alaska Native Claims Settlement Act (ANCSA), in late 1971. This at long last gave legal recognition to the rights of Alaska's Native people. Because of this act, Alaska's Natives have been brought into the mainstream, both in Alaskan business endeavors and in the exploitation of Alaska's resources.

As you travel through Alaska today, you can find traces left by many of its earliest settlers. There are totems, lodges, umiaks and kayaks (many are built of different materials now, but they are still shaped in the traditional way), frames for stretching skins, whalebone enclosures, and subsistence tools such as the Tlingit halibut hook and the Eskimo ulu (a curved blade used as a knife in food preparations). Almost everywhere you go, you will find racks for drying fish. The traditional subsistence way of life is still practiced and cherished to one degree or another in many parts of Alaska, with Native people savoring succulent smoked salmon filet; muktuk, another delectable morsel of seafood; and often beluga whale. (See Visiting Native Villages, below.)

The artwork of Alaska's Native people can be exceptionally beautiful. You will find it—along with not-so-beautiful (frequently foreign-made) copies—in any Alaskan city and in many of the villages. Look for fine carvings: although Alaska's Natives are legally allowed to gather walrus tusks for ivory (non-Native Alaskans are not) and work with it, you might prefer to buy carvings of fossil ivory, soapstone, and bone. Also look for beadwork and baskets. If the articles seem costly, consider the time spent by the artists in creating them.

Wherever the Russians traveled, they, too, left their marks. You will find Russian churches and graveyards in many places. Later, the sourdoughs left their cabins, worn-out dredges, picks and shovels, and kitchenware. (It is said that more metal has been taken into Alaska by miners than has been taken out.) And, of course, the evidence of contemporary humans is proliferating rapidly and profusely, making new history in everything from plush hotels to gargantuan pipelines.

Note: On March 24, 1989—almost twenty-five years to the day after the great Good Friday earthquake—another catastrophe struck Alaska. The Exxon tanker *Valdez* ran aground in Prince William Sound and spilled more than 11 million gallons of oil into the sound's pristine waters. As a result, more than 1,500 miles of shoreline were befouled; hundreds of thousands—some estimates say over 1 million—of birds were known to have perished; around five thousand sea otters died; the subsistence harvest in affected communities declined by as much as 77 percent; and there were untold other losses. Despite "cleanup," the effects of the spill still reverberate. No one knows how many years—or decades—it will be before the oiled area recovers completely.

In 1991, Exxon agreed to pay $100 million in criminal fines and $925 million in civil fines to the state of Alaska and the United States. Over $200 million of this money went immediately for damages and initial cleanup activities. The remainder has been and is being used for replacement of lost resources, for acquiring new resources of equivalent value to those lost, for restoration where possible, and for research. The monies are managed by a six-person joint state-federal Trustee Council.

10. Place Names

One way to trace Alaska's history is to study the place names on a good map of the state. You will find Native names everywhere you look, of course: musical and fascinating names like Tazlina, Iguigik, Sagavanirktok, Hoonah, Unalaska, Eek. Each name has its meaning, although some have been lost to time. It is not always easy to tell whether the names are Eskimo, Aleut, Athabascan, or Tlingit, but their location on the map may give you a clue. Sagavanirktok, for example, is a river that flows north from the Brooks Range into the Beaufort Sea through Eskimo country: the name means "strong current." Although Tazlina is the Ahtna (Athabascan) word for "swift river," it was given to a lake, a glacier, and a river as well in Southcentral Alaska. Iguigik, in the Southwest, is in Aleut terrain: the word means, fittingly enough, "volcano." Hoonah, a village on Admiralty Island in the Southeast, is a Tlingit word meaning "cold lake." Unalaska, another Aleut word, means "dwelling together harmoniously": look for the village with this name among the Aleutian Islands, where the Russians found it early in their quest for sea otters. Eek, an Eskimo name, means "the two eyes": it is a small village near Bristol Bay.

To find Russian names—and there are a great many of them—start along the Aleutian Chain and the Alaska Peninsula, Kodiak, and Kenai. You will find that these names, given for many different reasons, are often apropos and instructive as well. Mount Veniaminof, for instance, in the Aleutian Chain, is a volcano of immense stature, and it commemorates a man who was likewise. Not far away from it is Chirikof Island, named for Lt. Alexei Ilich Chirikof, who sailed with Bering in 1741 commanding the *Saint Paul,* a sister ship of the *Saint Peter.* (According to some historians, Chirikof identified the New World before Bering did.) Another great volcano in the Aleutians is Mount Pavlov (which has recently been active): its naming was probably for the Russian emperor Paul I, but it also remembers all the other Russian "Pauls" who came this way. The Shumagin Islands were named by Vitus Bering for a crew member of the *Saint Peter* who died of scurvy and was buried on one of these islands on August 30, 1741. Many Russian place names celebrate Russian explorers. The Krenitzin Islands, for instance, were named for Lt. Peter Kuzmich Krenitzin, who traveled through these waters between 1758 and 1769. Other names mark features of the local geography; thus Seldovia on the Kenai Peninsula translates from the Russian as "Herring Bay."

As you look to the northwest, note Russian Mission on the Yukon River, the site of the first Russian Orthodox church on that waterway; it was built in 1851. Further north, find Shishmaref, named by Lt. Otto von Kotzebue, a German who sailed in Russia's name in search of the Northwest Passage and who, incidentally, did not find the Eskimos as docile as the Aleuts (the Eskimos gave the Russians short shrift near the place that would one day bear his name); Kotzebue's second-in-command on the brig *Rurik* was Gleb Shishmaref. Still further north, note Kotzebue Sound, the village of Kotzebue, and Cape Krusenstern, which marks the northernmost limit of Russian exploration. The cape was also named by Kotzebue, to honor Adm. Adam Johann von Krusenstern, the first Russian sailor to circumnavigate the world.

Turning to the south, look for Cape Saint Elias, Kayak Island, the Bering Glacier, and Mount Saint Elias, all reminders of July 16, 1741. Further south you will find many more Russian names: Baranof, Sitka, Wrangell, the Alexander Archipelago. The latter was named by the United States in honor of Alexander II, czar at the time Russia sold Alaska. Chichagof Island honors the Russian explorer Adm. Vasilii Yakov Chichagof. The Kupreanof Islands were named for Capt. Ivan Andreevich Kupreanof, governor of the Russian-American Company from 1836 to 1840.

In the Southeast, look also for place names that commemorate explorers from other countries. Note Mount La Pérouse, named for the French explorer, and the Malaspina Glacier (1,500 square miles and larger than the state of Rhode Island), named for an Italian, Capt.

Alessandro Malaspina, who sailed near here in 1791. There are many English names, most given by Capt. George Vancouver, who chose more than three hundred place names for various spots in Alaska. He named Prince of Wales Island for the man who later became England's George IV. In Chatham Strait, he honored John Pitt, second earl of Chatham, who was first lord of the admiralty while Vancouver was charting Alaska's waters. Note Revillagigedo Island: this name was Vancouver's confirmation of an earlier Spanish choice; it commemorates the Spanish viceroy of Mexico from 1789 to 1794. Look also for Muir Glacier, honoring John Muir, who was the glacier expert on the Harriman expedition in 1899. (John Burroughs, the noted naturalist, was also on that trip, and he wrote that Muir was such an expert that "no one else was allowed an opinion.") You will find Seward's name on both the Kenai Peninsula and the northwest peninsula that approaches Russia most closely.

Along the Yukon River and throughout the Interior country, there are many names left by the early sourdoughs: names like Fortymile, Chicken (so named, the story goes, because the miners couldn't spell Ptarmigan, their first choice), Eagle, Purgatory, Cache, Dome, Happy, Circle, Rampart, Fairplay, Crazy Mountains. And the names along the railroad between Fairbanks and Anchorage tell a whole series of stories: Berg, Clear, Lignite, Moody, Carlo, Windy, Summit, Broad Pass, Colorado, Honolulu, Hurricane, Gold Creek, Fish Lake, Sunshine, Montana, Nancy. Hope, on Turnagain Arm (named by Cook) near Anchorage, was named by miners, and, to the far west, Bethel was named by missionaries. Point Hope, in the northwest, however, was named by neither miners nor missionaries but by Capt. Frederick W. Beechey, who on his 1826 voyage wished to honor his friend Sir William Johnstone Hope.

There are, of course, the names of many American explorers (Stoney and Kennicott, for example), geologists, miners, and other settlers in Alaska. And there are names that are descriptive of the climate and certain features of the landscape: names like Cold Bay, Danger Island, Icy Strait, Dark Point, Swift Creek, and Slow Fork. North of Merrill Pass in the Alaska Range, Another River heads in an unnamed lake: its name memorializes not only the country around it, which is full of streams, but also the exasperation of the 1927 U.S. Geological Survey (USGS) team exploring the area, which must have run out of new names to give.

Robert Marshall, who explored the Brooks Range between 1929 and 1939, happily named many of the geographical features of this particular region, which he loved. In fact, he was responsible for adding 169 official place names to the map of Alaska.

The names of Alaska's various fauna keep cropping up as you look at your map. Porcupine, Bear, Whale, Walrus (which comes, incidentally, from an old Norse word *hrossvale*, which means "whale horse"), Fox, Seal, Salmon, Sheep, Wolverine, and more. See how many Beavers you can find, counting waterways, lakes, dams, bays, and settlements: the name appears on the map more than eighty times. There are also seventy Bear Creeks listed in the excellent USGS publication *Dictionary of Alaska Place Names*. And Moose Creek shows up forty-seven times; there is even a Moose Creek Number One and a Moose Creek Number Two near Fairbanks. At the other end of the spectrum, it is noteworthy that use of Native names is rarely duplicated; thus they have been traditionally used to identify flight routes.

Mount Fairweather, by the way, near Glacier Bay, was named by Vancouver one bright, beautiful day, the story goes: the clouds closed in the next day, and the mountain wasn't seen again for fifty years.

11. How to Get There

You can get to Alaska by air, by water, or by highway. Jet service to Alaska's three major cities—Juneau, Anchorage, and Fairbanks, the state's principal gateways—is good. (Anchorage has one of the busiest international airports in the country, being a way station on the great circle route.) The air tariff may seem high. As long as airlines are competing and expanding their services, you may find a good fare.

If you enjoy traveling by water, you'll find Alaska's state ferry-liner system a super way to go—with or without your car. (Without a car, the ferry is a real bargain; overnight options include comfortable staterooms, which you must reserve, and lounge chairs, or you can roll out your sleeping bag topside.) Known overall as the Marine Highway, Alaska's two ferry systems operate on two separate routes. One system travels the Inside Passage from Bellingham or Prince Rupert in Canada, to Haines or Skagway, and to Valdez and Seward, 1,130 miles with many stops along the way. The other serves Prince William Sound, Kodiak, and parts of the Kenai Peninsula. In 1998, a new ocean-going ferry liner was added to go from Bellingham to Seward, on the Kenai Peninsula. All three routes carry you through magnificent scenery. From Bellingham to Skagway takes about four days, but you can make it a longer trip if you

Moose (Alces alces gigas), *the largest member of the deer family. Range: throughout Alaska.*

wish; there's only a modest charge for stopping over along the way. You buy a stopover pass from the purser. (If you bring your bike, you'll find good bicycling opportunities in the accessible parts of Alaska.) When you reach the northern end of the Inside Passage, you can continue your journey, if you wish, by bus (in summer) or in your car. There are roads from both Haines and Skagway that lead into Alaska's Interior road system.

Driving the Alaska Highway, which you pick up at Dawson Creek, British Columbia, can be a real adventure, but it takes a lot of time (at least five days on the road) and is demanding of both driver and passengers. While there are adequate accommodations along the way, you'll enjoy this trip more if you really love the out-of-doors and have a feeling for roughing it.

(A possible alternative to driving the Alaska Highway is to take the Cassiar Highway—an even more adventurous road—through Canada to the little town of Hyder, Alaska, and there pick up the Alaska State Ferry. Contact the ferry people at 1-800-642-0066 for latest information on this service.)

Another real adventure is traveling the Alaska Highway by bus—a possibility when stateside bus lines ferry their vehicles north out of Seattle in May and south in October. For starters, call Gray Line at 1-800-544-2206.

The principal roads in Alaska, including the Alaska Highway and the access roads from Haines and Skagway (ferry) ports to the Alaska Highway, are paved. But it's a small highway system, totaling only a few thousand miles, and the roads are not all contiguous, either. Do not expect an Interstate 80 anywhere in Alaska; freeways are few and far between. The Glenn Highway, north of Anchorage, is the best there is, and it's also the most heavily traveled. (More moose are killed on sections of this highway, incidentally, than die by hunters' guns in the same area.)

12. Words About the Alaskan Wilderness

Being Prepared

Expect Alaskan wilderness to be unlike any wilderness you have encountered before. It is different because of its weather, its size and scale, and its wildness. Weather is emphasized throughout this book because it plays such an important part in any Alaskan adventure: you will meet unpredictable and cantankerous weather—and on its terms, not yours—on any travels you make in Alaska's wilderness. (Remember, though, that Vilhjalmur Stefansson wrote a book called *The Friendly Arctic;* it is possible to enjoy Alaska's weather.)

As to size and scale, they will color all your perceptions of Alaska. You will find intimate spots in this wilderness, perhaps in an alpine meadow or beside a glossy black lake studded with yellow water lilies, or along a clear chattering stream. But when you lift your eyes, the immensity of the landscape will always be around you. Outside of the Southeast and regions around Anchorage and Fairbanks, you will not often be able to drive or walk to a roadhead or trailhead; you will have to fly to your point of departure or to your camping spot in the wilderness. (A few notable exceptions are mentioned in the text.) If you go by air taxi, once the plane leaves you, you may be several days away from the nearest civilized place, whether you travel by land or by river.

As you travel through this wilderness, you will, for the most part, be in wild and relatively untouched country. Although it is being used more and more by people (and certain areas of it have passed into private Native ownership), your chances are still good of seeing only a few other travelers. Instead, for company you will have the wild animals whose territory you are crossing. Respect these fellow creatures, please; wild Alaska is their home. Respect, too, the rights of the Natives whose territory this has been through the millennia (see Visiting Native Villages, below).

Before you start on an adventure in Alaska's wilderness, it is wise to ask yourself if you are ready not only for the best but for the worst. (This is a worthwhile exercise even before starting on a day hike in Alaska.) Are you prepared to spend an unspecified length of time comfortably in heavy rain, wind, and cold? Are you prepared—mentally as well as physically—to wait for your bush pilot, especially if the sun is out and you cannot see any good reason for a delayed pickup? If this is your first trip, are you prepared to go with a friend or a group? Most important of all, if yours is a private party, have you prepared your trip plan and told someone about it and where you expect to be when?

Don't let all of this put you off; it is not much more than common sense in an uncommon wilderness. In Alaska, you will have the rare opportunity to be entirely on your own in one of the most magnificent parts of the earth. If you are prepared and know what you are doing, your adventure here should be one of the great experiences of your life.

Firewood

Firewood is inadequate in many parts of Alaska. It is unavailable above tree level and also in much tundra and coastal country. Where it is readily available—for example, in the Southeast—the wood is often damp and difficult to burn. (Under these circumstances, search out dead spruce fronds or red cedar bark, preferably from the protected part of a dead tree.) You may or may not find firewood on sand- or gravel-bars in the rivers, depending upon the location and time of year.

For all these reasons, it is a good idea to carry a small stove if you are taking any kind of an extended trip into Alaska's wilderness. Even on a short trip, a quick cup of hot tea or bouillon (made in a Sierra Club cup, if nothing else) can be highly restorative.

If you do build a campfire or cookfire in Alaska's wilderness, do so carefully and do not cause a scar. When you leave, be absolutely certain your fire is out; douse it thoroughly with water. Although the countryside can look wet and fireproof, it may not be. If a fire gets started in peat or tundra, it can travel underground almost indefinitely. Forests, even when damp, can burn easily once flames get going. Lightning-caused fires have burned hundreds of thousands of acres in Alaska; so have human-caused conflagrations. In fact, in peak years as much as 2 million to 5 million acres have been consumed. Firefighting is difficult under the circumstances and very costly (mostly to the federal taxpayer, since the Bureau of Land Management [BLM]—a federal agency—is Alaska's principal firefighter). While fire is important to the natural succession of plants and animals in many ecosystems, its role in Alaska is still being studied. Human intervention in this process—one way or another—can be disastrous.

Stream Crossings

If you plan to cover much Alaskan territory on foot, it is almost certain that you will be fording one or more streams or rivers. Your former wilderness experience elsewhere may not have prepared you for Alaska's waterways. The water here may be icy, the currents swift and strong. Streambeds may be lined with unstable or rolling rocks, and if the waterway is glacial in origin, the depth of its silty waters may be difficult to gauge. Here are a few tips that can help speed your crossings.

If it is not feasible to build a ford of logs or big rocks—and it rarely is—look for the widest place you can find to cross the stream or river. Usually, the farther downstream you go, the wider and more shallow the water is apt to become, and many rivers break into braids in their lower courses. When you have chosen a spot, see if you can find a long stick to help you gauge the depth of the water and keep your balance. If the water is swift and deep and you are wearing a large pack, uncinch your waistband so that you can shed your pack easily if necessary. With several people along, you have certain advantages crossing rivers; you can string a rope across the water, which will give you both physical and moral support. You can hold hands as you wade across, or you can pair off and travel in tandem, the stronger person behind, with his or her hands on the shoulder of the person in front. (Some people put the stronger one in front.) As much as possible, angle into the current and keep your feet as wide apart as is comfortable.

As to what to do about your feet when fording Alaskan waters, you have four choices. You can carry old sneakers or running shoes and wear them on bare feet, hauling your boots and socks across in your pack: since your feet will probably get very cold, dry shoes and socks will feel wonderful when you put them back on. Or, as many Alaskans do, you can remove your socks and wear your boots on your bare feet: this means you will have damp, if not wet, feet when you continue hiking. The other two obvious stream-crossing methods—neither of which I recommend—are to simply leave on your shoes and socks and walk across, or to wade across barefoot. The latter option can be disastrous if you encounter poor footing or big rocks, or if you have tender feet.

It is not smart to try stream crossings wearing a long rain poncho or cagoule. The water can catch in such a garment and act like strong wind against a sail, tipping you off your feet and into the water. I had this happen twice in a matter of minutes trying to cross the Toklat River, a swift glacial stream, in Denali National Park one July day. By being "rolled in a river," I passed through one of the initiation rites for becoming Alaskan but also ended up with a not-so-mild case of hypothermia.

I learned another lesson from that particular venture on the Toklat. Alaska's rivers, especially those that flow through areas with permafrost underneath, can rise several feet during the day in both fair and foul summer weather. When the weather is hot and sunny, snowmelt can add measurably to the stream flow. During rains, the volume of the rivers is likewise increased. On our Toklat outing, we had started about 4 A.M. and had easily crossed and recrossed the river. Then we hiked several miles downstream during a day of drizzly rain. When we returned in the late afternoon we found that the river had risen at least 2 feet in the area where we had made our crossings.

Hypothermia

The word *hypothermia* derives from two Greek words: *hypo,* meaning under or beneath, and *therme,* meaning heat. It accurately describes a condition brought about by the abnormal decrease of body temperature. And it can be more dangerous to wilderness travelers than are encounters with bears.

The human body can lose heat outdoors from at least three causes: cold, wind, and moisture. The combination of any two of these speeds the cooling process, and the combination of all three compounds it even more. Add fatigue to this, and you can be in real trouble.

The first symptoms of hypothermia are shivering, the presence of goose bumps, and an accelerated heart rate. (These are all automatic body reactions to compensate for heat loss.) Then comes clumsiness, loss of body functions, loss of judgment, and finally disorientation. Even when arrested, hypothermia can lead to serious complications; if not arrested, it can lead to death, but hypothermia can almost always be avoided.

The first way to avoid hypothermia is to be responsible for your own

Equivalent Chill Temperature

Wind Speed (mph)	Temperature (°F)																				
	40	35	30	25	20	15	10	5	0	-5	-10	-15	-20	-25	-30	-35	-40	-45	-50	-55	-60
	Equivalent Chill Temperature																				
Calm	40	35	30	25	20	15	10	5	0	-5	-10	-15	-20	-25	-30	-35	-40	-45	-50	-55	-60
5	35	30	25	20	15	10	5	0	-5	-10	-15	-20	-25	-30	-35	-40	-45	-50	-55	-65	-70
10	30	20	15	10	5	0	-10	-15	-20	-25	-35	-40	-45	-50	-60	-65	-70	-75	-80	-90	-95
15	25	15	10	0	-5	-10	-20	-25	-30	-40	-45	-50	-60	-65	-70	-80	-85	-90	-100	-105	-110
20	20	10	5	-5	-10	-15	-25	-30	-35	-45	-50	-60	-65	-75	-80	-85	-95	-100	-110	-115	-120
25	15	10	0	-5	-15	-20	-30	-35	-45	-50	-60	-65	-75	-80	-90	-95	-105	-110	-120	-125	-135
30	10	5	0	-10	-20	-25	-30	-40	-50	-55	-65	-70	-80	-85	-95	-100	-110	-115	-125	-130	-140
35	10	5	-5	-10	-20	-30	-35	-40	-50	-60	-65	-75	-80	-90	-100	-105	-110	-120	-130	-135	-145
40*	10	0	-5	-15	-20	-30	-35	-45	-55	-60	-70	-75	-85	-95	-100	-110	-115	-125	-130	-140	-150

Little Danger

Increasing Danger
(Flesh may freeze within 1 minute)

Great Danger
(Flesh may freeze within 30 seconds)

*Winds above 40 mph have little additional effect.

clothing needs. Travel with enough clothing to protect yourself under any possible adverse situations you could encounter. Enough clothing includes warm headgear, handgear, and footgear, since the body loses heat first from its extremities. The head, in particular, should be protected. Enough clothing also includes enough layers to protect you against rain and wind. (See Summer Clothing List, under Equipment, below.) Second, avoid getting overheated and sweaty; damp clothes can act as a refrigerating agent. Third, do not push yourself when you begin to feel exhausted.

If a member of your party shows symptoms of hypothermia—slurred speech, a slowing of pace, apathy, and unusual behavior or poor judgment—stop traveling immediately and build a fire if possible. Get the victim as warm as you can and give her or him a hot drink (not alcohol). If the hypothermia persists, get into a sleeping bag with the victim and warm her or his body directly with yours—without clothing. Send for help if you can, but if there are only two of you, stay together: a person in this condition should not be left alone.

Insects

I know that the native dogs are killed by the mosquitoes under certain circumstances, and I heard reports, which I believe to be well founded, both from Indians and trustworthy white persons, that the great brown bear—erroneously but commonly called the grizzly—of these regions is at times compelled to succumb to these insects. The statement seems almost preposterous, but the explanation is comparatively simple. Bruin having exhausted all the roots and berries on one mountain, or finding them scarce, thinks he will cross the valley to another range, or perhaps it is the odor of salmon washed up along the river's banks that attracts him. Covered with a heavy fur on his body, his eyes, nose and ears are the vulnerable points for mosquitoes, and here of course they congregate in the greatest numbers. At last when he reaches a swampy stretch they rise in myriads until his forepaws are kept so busy as he strives to keep his eyes clear of them that he can not walk, whereupon he becomes enraged, and bearlike, rises on his haunches to fight. It is now a mere question of time until the bear's eyes become so swollen from innumerable bites as to render him perfectly blind, when he wanders helplessly about until he gets mired in the marsh, and so starves to death.

Frederick Schwatka,
A Summer in Alaska

According to the Koyukon people, when Raven finished creating humans, a man came and stole Raven's wife. So Raven went out and found some rotten willow wood, ground it into a fine dust, and tossed it high into the air. The powdery specks all became mosquitoes, which from then on would torment humankind.

Chances are that you have heard horrific stories about Alaska's insects. Sadly, they are probably true. Alaska is something like a giant sponge: it freezes solid in winter, but in summer its top layer thaws and water gathers everywhere to make hundreds of thousands of ponds and puddles. Add to this lakes and overflowing rivers, once spring breakup occurs. All that shallow stagnant water is haven for breeding insects. These conditions do not persist, but while they are in effect, the bugs mass in the billions (or so it seems). This is one reason, of course, why birds come from all over the world to Alaska. The insect food supply is unsurpassed.

Like humans, Alaska's insects thrive in the best weather. May, June, and July are the months for mosquitoes. July and August are the months for the midges (no-see-ums) and blackflies (whitesox). Here's what you're up against with these pests.

Mosquitoes, midges, and blackflies are all flies, although each belongs to a different family. While each has its own characteristics, they also have similarities. Among all of them, the female requires blood (for protein), and the male gets by on either nectar or other vegetative material. All require still water for their larval stage, and all the females feed by inserting a tiny stylus into the skin of an animal and sucking blood. Compounding this outrage, they also inject an anesthetizing agent—which varies in degree of toxicity—that numbs you to the attack. It is this little squirt of poison that causes complications.

Mosquitoes belong to the family Culcidae, subfamily Culcinae (there are hundreds of species). They are, of course, familiar to people all over the world. In Alaska there are some twenty-five to forty species, the principal ones being *aedes, anopheles, culex,* and *psorophora*. None of them carry diseases, and—if it's any comfort—they feed on animals and birds as well as on people. (A young, weak caribou can be killed by mosquitoes.) Some large adult mosquitoes hibernate during the winter in places such as leaf litter. These are the ones that are ready to pounce at the first sign of warm weather.

Since Alaska mosquitoes tend to stay in the general region in which they originated (puddle, pond, lake, or overwash of stagnant water), you may be able to avoid major confrontations by moving out of a heavily infested area. But don't count on this; swarms will often simply follow you, even down the middle of a river. Higher ground with a breeze is usually less populated by these small creatures.

Biting midges (commonly called no-see-ums or punkies) belong to the

Alaska brown bear fighting mosquitoes. Source: Frederick Schwatka, A Summer in Alaska.

family Ceratopogonidae. These insects are so tiny that it is hard to see them, and they can usually get through a standard mosquito net with no trouble. They announce themselves by a high whine and a swift, light sting. Later, you may develop a fine case of welts or hives from their poison. Since these minute pests are even more home oriented than mosquitoes, they can sometimes be avoided by moving just a few yards away. Watch out for them along streambanks and around the edges of lakes.

The most poisonous of Alaska's winged and stinging insects are the blackflies, also called whitesox and buffalo gnats. (A Yupik story tells how two young orphan boys became so frightened by a higher-than-usual tide that, to save themselves, they turned into little flies, and that is why we have gnats today.) These tormentors belong to the family Simuliidae; they are small and dark, and have short legs (sometimes white), broad wings, and a humpbacked appearance. They breed in streams and tend to remain close to their home base, but don't always; some of them travel widely. The bite of one of these insects not only can be painful but can draw blood. Frequently it will cause major swelling, as many people are sensitive to the toxic agent injected. As with wasps and bees, certain people react violently to the toxin, and a bite can be, though very rarely is, fatal.

Covering up is your first line of defense against Alaska's stinging insects. Since they seem to prefer dark colors, you can wear outer garments that are light colored—but not light in thickness! The stinging apparatus of all these bugs, and the whole bugs of the tinier species, can go right through thin or loosely woven clothing. A cotton flannel shirt is good armor; you can get one that is light colored and thick enough to give you protection. Of course, you will also want long sleeves (and long pants) when you are in bug country.

A head net is helpful, and I would consider it a necessity if insect bites bother you and you are going into the Alaskan bush. You can find head nets at most sporting goods stores. You should also be sure that your tent has a good, tight mosquito screen; it can be a marvelous haven when you are under attack. You can get tent screens with a small enough mesh to keep out midges, but they will also cut down on the airiness of your tent.

Insect repellents are another line of defense. These usually contain diethyl-metatoluamide in varying amounts. You can look for lotion, liquid, stick, aerosol spray, or towelette. (Interestingly, the repelling agent does not send mosquitoes away because of its bad smell or taste; instead, its heavy and irregularly shaped molecules befuddle a mosquito's sensory functions and send her buzzing off in confusion.) If you don't want to cover yourself with chemicals, you can try taking large doses of vitamin B (or another "systemic repellent") or using an electronic device, but most researchers are skeptical about the effectiveness of these methods.

Just keep in mind that there are few wildernesses anywhere that do not have pests of one kind or another. Alaska makes up for a spectacular insect population by having few large stinging insects such as hornets or wasps, no plants that are poisonous to the touch (albeit devil's club is spiky), no scorpions, and no poisonous snakes (in fact, no indigenous snakes at all).

Giardia

Alaska's clear and sparkling streams are tempting indeed to thirsty travelers. But, alas, beware of drinking the water! Like the wilderness of too much of North America, Alaska's wilderness is home to a growing population of the nasty little parasite (a protozoan) *Giardia lambia*. Once inside your intestines, this unwelcome visitor digs in and can make you feel rotten indeed, causing, for example, nausea, abdominal cramps, diarrhea, and weakness. (The symptoms are often compared to those of mononucleosis.) All this can be avoided by: (a) boiling any water taken from wilderness sources for at least five minutes; or (b) availing yourself of a small portable filter (Recreational Equipment, Inc. — REI — and other outdoor equipment stores have them) and filtering water you're going to drink (or brush your teeth with). Unfortunately, beavers are a principal vector in the life cycle of *Giardia lambia,* and these delightful little mammals are widespread in Alaska's streams, lakes, and rivers. It is noteworthy that the incidence of giardiasis — a disease that has always been endemic in North America — has increased proportionately to the number of people who in ever growing number are traveling in the wilderness.

The Good News

Despite the inconveniences and possible dangers you might encounter in Alaska's wilderness, there are unexpected pluses that are quite apart from the magnificence of the scenery and the wonders of the wilderness and wildlife. Although it can be cold, wet, and muddy — or warm, sunny, and dry — Alaska's wilderness is relatively clean to travel through compared with, for example, the wilderness of the Sierra Nevada, where your socks turn grimy your first day in. You may sometimes slog through mud or sand, but you are not likely to encounter heavy dust on the wilderness trail (if you find a trail, that is). An exception to prove this rule is glacial country, where the wind whips up deposits of glacial silt. (Also note that if you fall into a glacial stream it will take you several washings to get all the silt out of your clothes and hair, and you'll have to have your watch cleaned if it isn't waterproof.) With certain exceptions, which have been well emphasized, you will find the temperature generally pleasant for summer hiking or backpacking, and you won't, as a rule, find yourself working up a great sweat. And last, but not least, while some tundra is rough going, a lot of it is such good walking that you'll feel as nimble as a ballet dancer or, perhaps more appropriately, a mountain goat or a Dall sheep.

13. Equipment

What to Wear

The kind of clothing you choose to take to Alaska will depend, of course, on which part of the state you plan to visit, the time of year that you visit, and what you want to do while you're there. Clothing needs and gear lists for wilderness travelers follow. For general travel, be guided by the fact that Alaskans for the most part are not only very informal but completely unpretentious. In Juneau, Anchorage, and Fairbanks, you will see people in business clothes, but you will also see businesspeople in the most casual kind of dress. You will look and feel more at home in these Alaskan cities if you dress primarily to be comfortable. Jeans or informal slacks or skirts, sweaters, open-neck shirts, parkas, and running shoes or boots are acceptable almost anywhere. (There are elegant and excellent restaurants in Alaska but almost none that require ties or jackets for gentlemen.) Try to stay away from traditional tourist garb if you want to fit in.

Some Thoughts About Clothing and Equipment

Get the Best You Can Afford

Whether you are buying boots, bandannas, or sleeping bags, get the best you can afford for your Alaska travels. You might be able to economize in the Sierra Nevada or Great Smokies with a cheap air mattress that you plan to discard after your trip, but that system—a wasteful one under any circumstances—will definitely not work for Alaska. If you are going into the Alaskan wilderness, you will need the sturdiest and most reliable equipment you can manage to obtain—not only for your comfort but, possibly, for your survival.

Be Sure Your Equipment Is in Good Shape

You won't find shoe repair shops outside the larger communities, and you might even have trouble finding new shoelaces. It is even harder to find sporting goods stores that will repair a tent or backpack once you leave Alaska's main cities. You can avoid a lot of headaches by getting all your equipment into top condition before you leave home.

On Tents and Such

A good tent is essential. There are some campers, notably those who have traveled frequently in the Sierra Nevada, who like to carry only a lightweight tarp that can be used as a ground cloth or rigged as a shelter. I strongly recommend against this practice in Alaska. You may get by with this arrangement for one or two trips, but almost certainly you will eventually wish you had brought along a snug tent. If you encounter severe winds and weather or have an accident, such a tent could mean the difference between life and death.

Your tent needs to be lightweight, waterproof, and as windproof as possible, and you will need a fly. I prefer a freestanding tent that can be rigged and then moved easily to the optimum level and sheltered spot. Be sure, however, that you have good strong stakes with which to nail it down and extra line to tie it down more securely, if necessary. I travel with a geodesic-dome-type tent, but many friends use standard tepee types or the caterpillar type.

You should be prepared to whisk wet dirt off the bottom of your tent in Alaska's backcountry and to sponge moisture off your tent fly; even after a clear night, there can be heavy condensation. A small, lightweight whisk broom, a good-sized sponge, and a piece of old lightweight canvas big enough to sit on always go inside my tent bag. This canvas porch is extremely useful. You can sit on it to remove your boots before entering your tent and so avoid tracking in mud or caked dirt; or you can clean your wet boots off on it before diving into your tent during rains.

Although certain tundra communities in Alaska are wondrously soft and springy and a delight to sleep on, you should always have some kind of mattress or pad to go under your sleeping bag, and a waterproof tent floor is a great comfort. In the Southeast, I prefer a good old-fashioned air mattress, since it keeps one well off the tent floor, which may become clammy. Many people prefer a foam or other composition pad because it is lighter and provides good insulation when the weather is cold. You can also get a combination type.

The question of down versus synthetic fibers for sleeping bags (as well as for vests, sweaters, and parkas) gets lots of going over among people who travel in the Alaska bush. I prefer down (and, generally speaking, other natural materials). There's nothing like a down sleeping bag (inside a snug tent, of course) to crawl into after a cold, hard day. Remember, though, that it can get very hot in Alaska during summer in some places,

Summer Clothing List for Alaskan Wilderness Adventurers

Item	Wilderness Foot Travel & Camping	River Running & Kayaking	In SE	In SC & SW	In Int. & Arctic	Comments
Warm underwear top and bottom	X	X	X	X	X	• Can double as pajamas.
Three pairs inner and outer wool socks	X	X	X	X	X	• Four pairs of each is better, if you can find the room. There is nothing like warm, dry feet.
Wool pants	X	X	X	X	X	• I would rather be too warm in wool pants than cold and wet in jeans, but lots of people wear jeans anyway.
Cotton flannel shirt	X	X	X	X	X	• A good all-purpose garment. Be sure it has plenty of pockets.
Wool shirt or long-sleeved warm sweater	X	X	X	X	X	• A wool shirt is easier to get into and out of, but suit yourself.
Down vest or down sweater	?	?	?	?	?	• I happen to like down (well protected), but for wet environments, you might prefer a synthetic.
Windproof hooded parka	X	X	X	X	X	• The Eskimos discovered the advantages of this design long before we arrived on the scene.
Hooded down parka	X	?	?	X	X	• You will not need a down vest or down sweater, of course, if you carry this warmer item.
Wool hat or wool stocking cap	X	X	X	X	X	• Wear it to bed if it is really cold.

Item				Notes
So'wester hat		X	?	• Introduced by early whalers and beloved of Southeasterners.
Pile or bunting jacket		X	X	• Some Southeasterners swear by these synthetics.
Rain parka	X	X	X	• Stay away from long ponchos and cagoules if you plan to cross any streams or rivers.
Rain pants or rain chaps	X	X	X	• Although you may not need these for rain in Interior or Arctic, they are good everywhere for wind and cold protection, and for traveling through wet vegetation.
Warm gloves	X	X	X	• If you can get tight-knit wool gloves, do so. Leather is good until it gets wet. Also consider fishermen's handgear or leather mitts with wool or silk liners.
Knee-high rubber boots	X	X	X	• Standard footgear for most of Alaska.
Shoepacks, or hunting boots		X	X	• Good for light use outdoors.
Hip boots	X	X	X	• Unless you plan to wear a wetsuit.
Sturdy hiking boots	X	X	X	• Hopefully, yours are tried and true friends. Be sure to wear good innersoles as well. Waterproof the seams and carry extra laces.
Sneakers or old running shoes	X	X	X	• My recommendation for stream crossings and for kayakers to use as a change of footgear, although you may want boots instead, particularly if you plan to hike on your river trip.

and a down bag that feels only mildly toasty in the Arctic can roast you alive in the Interior heat. Since you are probably going to carry only one sleeping bag, you will have to decide whether to go light or heavy. I would rather unzip my warm bag (a plus-thirty-year-old, 3-pound down bag) on a hot night or even sleep on top of it than be caught cold. You may belong to the school that keeps adding clothes inside a light bag when it gets chilly. Take your choice.

If you do decide to take down, remember that it is practically useless when it is wet. Carry your sleeping bag inside a good heavy plastic bag— I line my stuff sack with a heavy-gauge garbage bag (and I carry a spare garbage bag in case the first one tears). Synthetic fibers do provide greater insulation when wet, and you should give them your careful attention if you are thinking of acquiring a bag or protective clothing. (Some Southeasterners say you should definitely use a synthetic-fill sleeping bag in their wet climate.)

Backpacking Equipment

If you are into backpacking, you probably have a pack of your choice, and any good design that is sturdy and comfortable (and relatively waterproof) is fine for Alaska. However, if you are starting fresh, you should consider the pros and cons of the rucksack-type pack with internal frame versus the pack with an external frame. In the Southeast and in other areas of heavy brush, the pack with an inside frame has certain advantages because it will not hang you up. However, for open country, a pack with an external frame is my choice, and I recommend getting the kind that will stand up alone when you put it down. Of course, try to select material as waterproof as possible for the body of the pack.

Carrying different items in plastic bags inside your pack will add to your chances of keeping your stuff dry, and it is also a good way to see what you've got where. Be sure the plastic bags you carry are reasonably sturdy. I usually get two sizes of freezer bags that snap shut. (By all means, reuse them year after year.) Heavier-gauge plastic bags are available in outdoor equipment stores.

Heavy-gauge plastic garbage bags are also useful for protecting the outside of your pack, but be sure to take along one or two extras since even the best of them will not hold up well with heavy wear. You can also look for a pack that comes with its own separate raincoat. A brightly colored day pack is a good item to carry if you plan to do any day hiking on your trip.

Footgear

Rubber boots of one kind or another are standard equipment for most Alaskans who live in the Southeast or anywhere in the bush. They have

Backpacking near Nikolai Pass, Wrangell Mountains. Source: National Park Service.

a special, invaluable use in a country that is full of wet places. However, waterproof footgear is not ideal for most real hiking, and it can certainly add a lot of weight to a pack. But if you are gong to spend your time in Southeast Alaska, by all means consider getting a pair of knee-high rubber boots, sometimes known as "Southeast sneakers" or "dancing shoes." They are ideal for slogging around on birdwatching outings, traveling in the low country, exploring muskegs, and general wear on wet days. A good pair will be worth the money; look for them in Southeast communities like Ketchikan and Juneau if you cannot find them in your home town.

For kayaking or river running, you will probably want hip boots for at least a few members of your party, unless you decide to use wetsuits and sneakers. (Or you can just decide to get wet when you have to line your river craft, which you will probably have to do a time or two since even the finest of Alaska's rivers may require lining when the water is high.)

Assuming that you're going to hike a lot also assumes that you have a good pair of boots with which you're well acquainted and on, shall we say, a good footing. Just be sure your boots are sturdy and remember to waterproof the seams and oil the leather well. (Completely waterproofed boots, even if you can achieve them, have the same drawback as rubber boots, and you may end up with wet feet in them.)

If you plan to do only light hiking—you might, for example, be going to visit a wilderness lodge such as Camp Denali and plan to wander only locally—you may find shoepacks (that is, boots with rubber bottoms and leather tops) both adequate and comfortable. A great many Alaskans wear this kind of footgear, too. You can purchase shoepacks in Alaska or obtain them by mail from L.L. Bean, which sells them as "Maine hunting shoes." Whatever your footgear, good insulating innersoles will add to your comfort, as will, of course, two pairs of wool socks.

The Merits of Wool

Many Alaskans swear by wool clothing of all kinds for outdoor wear (or for any kind of wear). Wool is not only warm, but it also sheds water, and if it does get wet, it is still good insulation. Except for the already mentioned Interior summer heat, there are few places in Alaska where a pair of wool pants and a wool shirt will not feel good year-round. You may see some old-time Alaskans wearing dark-green wool whipcord pants and matching battle jacket, a light wool shirt, and a bolo tie with a gold or ivory Native artwork clasp: this was once known as the "Alaska tuxedo." Another popular piece of clothing, especially in the Southeast and other fishing areas, is referred to as a "halibut jacket"; this is simply a heavy wool shirt. If wool is hard to come by where you live, you'll find a good selection of wool clothing in places like Juneau. (If you can find a pair of tight-knit wool gloves, they will give you a lot of comfort in Alaska's summertime.) Remember not to wash or dry-clean wool any more than is absolutely necessary: lanolin is removed by cleaning processes of any kind, and the lanolin is what gives wool some of its marvelous qualities. Since good wool has the property of shedding dirt as well as water, quality wool clothing can be kept clean without washing or dry cleaning for a surprisingly long time. When you get it home from a trip, give your wool clothing a good brushing, spot-clean with a cloth wrung out in cold water, and hang it in the sun. Store it, of course, with mothproofing.

The Onion or the Artichoke

When you dress for the outdoors in Alaska, use layers of clothing. (Some people refer to this as the onion method, some as the artichoke; take your choice.) The air trapped between the layers provides excellent insulation; it also allows condensed body heat to dry, thus avoiding the dampness of perspiration. A further advantage is that it allows easy regulation of how much clothing you want or need for the current temperature. The best outer layer for summer is a light, windproof (and, if possible, breathable) waterproof parka with a hood and with a front zipper that makes it easy to get into and out of. A hood avoids drafts around your neck, and, if it is cold, you can add a snug wool cap. If you are carrying a sweater, a cardigan is convenient. In harsh weather, you can let the layering system help keep your hands warm: wear your wool gloves inside a pair of ski mitts, or, if the weather is wet, wear your gloves inside a large pair of fisherman's gloves (available in marine supply stores).

Other Tips

Try replacing the buttons on your shirt sleeves with Velcro tabs; this makes it easy to roll your sleeves up and down if you want to. Buy shirts with enough pockets; pockets can provide many needed places to keep "everything in its place." Be sure your shirt pockets have fold-over flaps and buttons (or Velcro tabs) to keep things from falling out when, for example, you lean over a swift-flowing stream. When you are wearing rubber boots, pull your socks over the bottoms of your pants—this is not only tidier, but it makes getting boots on easier. Use large rubber bands to cinch your pants around your ankles when hiking through brush. Avoid pants with cuffs; cuffs collect debris, which falls out inside your tent. Another handy item is a safety pin; fasten a couple in your hatband.

Waterproofing

Seam sealing is a real necessity for tents and rain gear if you are going into country where it rains, so don't stint on it. What rain gear you use in Alaska will depend upon the kind of outdoor activity you will be doing. For canoers or raft travelers who aren't going to be getting steady or heavy exercise, a good fisherman's waterproof outfit may be the answer. You'll find a selection at Alaska stores, especially in the Southeast. Hikers and backpackers who want a lighter garment have more of a choice. There are several companies making lightweight rain gear that is designed both to be waterproof and to breathe. I suggest that you try out any new rain gear ahead of time. For Alaska, you need to be certain that you have rain protection that you can depend upon in a steady downpour—especially if you're going to be traveling in an open raft for one or more days. (You might test new rain gear in your shower.)

Important Incidentals

Someone once said that to really see and appreciate Alaska, you need both a telescope and a microscope, and it is true that you will enjoy your travels more and certainly add further dimensions to your Alaska experience if you carry field glasses and a small magnifying lens. The magnifying lens is perfect for looking closely at the incredibly beautiful structure of flowers and examining other small flora of the tundra and forests. Both glasses and lens should be lightweight, inexpensive, and, if possible, waterproof. If you are going to do any kayaking or river running, field glasses that float are a good idea. If you cannot find bright orange binoculars—they are available—be sure to tie or stick bright orange tape on your binoculars and tie bright orange yarn on your small lens so that they will be easy to see if dropped on the ground. A brightly colored string or a leather thong makes a good necklace on which to wear your small viewer.

Tips for Photographers

Small, do-everything automatic cameras are tempting to anyone carrying a pack, being lightweight and both quick and easy to use. Be mindful of their limitations, however (even their zoom lenses, being necessarily short, are limited). They are great for record shots, but if you're interested in photographing wildlife or doing close-ups of flowers, you'll want to consider a more flexible camera system—keeping in mind the telescope and microscope idea. It is worth carrying a long lens (minimum 200mm with a 2x ring) and a macro or micro lens, or you can opt for a good zoom lens. A wide-angle lens is also desirable—indeed, a necessity for many a scenic vista. (Either a 24mm, 28mm, or 35mm is a good choice. Throw-away cameras—they are actually recycled—are good for landscapes.) Since it is all too easy in Alaska to get your photographic equipment wet, especially in the Southeast, a good waterproof camera bag is an excellent investment. If you can't afford one, then heavy plastic bags are a must.

Again, be sure to tie string or stick tape that's bright orange onto your camera, camera equipment, and camera bag. It can be virtually impossible to find a small dark object like a camera, field glasses, or even a camera bag in Alaska's wilderness. I learned this the hard way on a foothill of Mount McKinley when I put my camera down in the tundra during a lunch stop and inadvertently went off without it. A two-hour search, initiated almost immediately, proved unsuccessful, and my camera (a beloved Nikkormat with a macro lens) was gone forever.

If you like to work with high-speed film, you will find many opportunities in Alaska, where the light is often not very strong. I always take along a few rolls of ASA 100, 200, and 400. However, ASA 64 is a good all-around film and is preferable in glacier country and on bright winter days. Note that in extremely cold weather film and fingers can freeze. (Be sure to carry extra film, and, if you are using a new camera, be sure to shoot a couple of rolls of film before your Alaska visit so that you are completely familiar with it.)

Carry your unexposed film in a bag of one color and your exposed film in a bag of another color. This helps to keep things separate and readily identifiable.

Travel Light

A final word of advice: keep your gear to a reasonable minimum. You will want to spend your time and energy in Alaska doing other things besides packing, sorting, and hauling gear. Always keep your things organized. This will save you a remarkable amount of time and trouble.

Twenty Necessities for Alaskan Adventuring

Note: Except for the extra clothes, all of the following items are small, lightweight, and easily carried in a day pack. (You can separate them into plastic bags, if you wish.) The dozen **boldfaced** items are an absolute must whenever you leave civilization in Alaska; I recommend that you carry these items with you routinely.

Knife: Swiss Army knife with scissors (recommended) or hunting knife.

Space blanket: Use for wind, rain, and cold.

First aid kit: If nothing else, carry Band-Aids and a small piece of soap to clean any wound.

Bandanna or diaper: Wonderful multipurpose item. Use for bandage, sweatband, towel, hot pad, napkin, scarf, head net, and so on.

Safety pins: Pin a couple into your hatband or along an inner seam of your parka.

Sierra Club cup or one similar to hang on your belt: Another multipurpose item, useful for noisemaking to keep bears away and for washing small wounds, heating water for tea or bouillon, and, incidentally, for simply taking a drink.

Extra candy bars, nuts, or gorp; a tea bag or two bouillon cubes: Survival fare.

Extra clothes: Wear a T-shirt and shorts, if you must, but always have long pants, a warm shirt, parka (if possible, waterproof), and warm headgear and handgear in your pack—survival items.

Waterproof matches: Dip big kitchen matches in melted wax.

Old candle stub: Fire starter deluxe.

Flashlight: Check batteries before starting; or carry a flare or try a small solar- or lithium-powered flashlight.

Maps: So you'll know where you are.

Compass: Know how to use it in the higher latitudes.

Toilet paper: Please cover it with rocks, or bury it; think how you feel when you find someone else's.

Sunglasses: Requisites for snow or water travel. In fact, the sun's angle in winter makes these a year-round necessity.

Bug juice or other insect repellent: A stick has the advantage of not leaking.

Head net: A small, priceless item.

Duct tape: Roll up a foot or two to carry for emergency repairs. I have friends who even use it for blisters.

Waterproof watch or cheap pocket watch: Although you may want to get away from it all, knowing the time can be extremely useful once in a while.

A general trip plan discussed with at least one other responsible person: Perhaps the most important item of all.

Essential Equipment List for Knapsacking or Camping in Alaskan Wilderness

A good tent, preferably freestanding, with a fly and plenty of stakes: Carry a big sponge, small whisk broom, and a scrap of canvas for a "front porch."

Extra line

Sleeping bag: Down or synthetic.

Air mattress or pad

Backpack

Small day pack: Brightly colored.

Plastic bags: They keep clothing dry and easy to find.

Toilet kit: Small and light.

Sunburn lotion and sunglasses: Believe it or not!

See also lists for Twenty Necessities for Alaskan Adventuring, above, and Optional but Useful Items of Clothing and Equipment, below.

Optional but Useful Items of Clothing and Equipment

Light underwear	*Shorts*
Light shirt	*Wetsuit*
Broad-brimmed hat	*Bathing suit*
Dental floss	*Waterproof notebook*
Nail file	*Waterproof pen*
Sleep shade	*Binoculars*
Jeans	*Magnifying lens*

I make these last two optional reluctantly; they will add so much to your experience.

The Compass

The farther north you travel, the more the needle on your compass will point upward—at Fairbanks it will be only 11 degrees from vertical. The magnetic force centered in the North Pole will also skew your needle to the east of north. Thus, in Southeast Alaska, your compass needle will point to between 28 and 31 degrees east of true north. If you're using a U.S. Geological Survey (USGS) map, this difference between magnetic north and truth north, or declination, will be shown for the area the map covers; look at the bottom of the page and use your compass accordingly. In the Arctic, the distortion will be even greater.

14. Traveling in Small Boats

Before the Great Flood, the Koyukon people believe, the rivers in the world ran both upstream and downstream, like two-way highways, and it was possible to travel them in both directions. But after the Flood, Raven took a good look at things before restoring order. He decided that humans had been having too easy a time of it, so he directed the rivers to flow in only one direction, as they do today.

There is no better way to experience the ultimate beauty of Alaska than to travel its waterways in a small, motorless boat: a canoe, a kayak, or perhaps an inflatable raft. As the buoyant waters cradle and carry you, you become an integral part of this great land and move with the flow of the river or with the rhythmic motion of the tidal waters and their current. Or else you propel yourself naturally, dipping your paddle or oar into the water, and, as you lift the blade, watching the drops fall like small crystal worlds to float briefly before they disappear. The shore slips by, sometimes deeply forested, sometimes a bare sharp cliff or wedge of earth, sometimes a drape of tundra. The air smells clean, perhaps fragrant with lupine or, near the coast, with the faint pungent scent of salt.

The silence of your passage may be broken by the sudden, distant roar of rapids—the pure sound of adventure—or the soft sigh of waves meeting the shore may invite you to land and explore unknown territory. You may hear the elemental crash of an iceberg as it leaves its parent glacier or an avalanche of earth crumbling from a riverbank. If the river you travel is glacial, the sibilant hiss of silt against your craft will sound like the cool rustle of silk.

On a clear river, there will nearly always be a mother merganser to race ahead of you with her brood, at first traveling immense distances in an effort to escape you and then, finally, giving up and huddling near the riverbank as you sail by. Eagles may soar above you—or osprey or peregrine, rough-legged hawks, or perhaps a rare great horned owl. On any river, you are likely to find shorebirds of one kind or another who have come, like yourself, from a distant place. They will dip and bow, performing deep knee bends on the sandbars. A bear may amble along the shore unconcernedly until, abruptly aware of you, it bolts into the nearest brush. You may pass the neatly constructed lodge of a beaver or see a mink scoot sleekly through the water. Near the coast, you may watch a whale blow, then arch powerfully but easily as it sounds.

To really enjoy traveling by small boat in Alaska, you should be familiar with the kind of craft you'll be using and know what you are doing. Can you right a boat that has capsized—or gotten hung up in midstream—especially if the water is cold and rough and the current is swift? Do you know how to get back into your righted boat quickly under such circumstances? If you are kayaking, can you do an Eskimo roll? Can you avoid sweepers in a hurry? Does swift water faze you? If you're traveling in tidal waters, can you read a current table as well as a tide table? You can find almost any kind of a small-boating experience you want in Alaska, since Alaskan waters vary enormously. The moods of these waters, and the Alaskan weather, however, are not predictable. Even the slowest stream or the most placid stretch of a lake or a channel can be suddenly roiled and roughed up by winds or a storm. Therefore this is really not the place for neophytes or would-be small-boaters to venture out for the first time on their own. If you're not experienced in such things as I have mentioned, consider learning about them (whichever ones apply to the kind of boating you have in mind) before you go to Alaska. If this is not possible, then go with someone, or several people, knowledgeable about small-boating in Alaska. Or you can go with an organized commercial outfit; there are some excellent small-boat outings now being conducted in many parts of Alaska that can introduce you to the wonders of this great land in a small, silent craft. (See references throughout this book.)

Some Thoughts About River Travel

Alaska's rivers are still the most magnificently wild rivers remaining in the United States, and there is extraordinary variety among them. You should be able to get a broad overview of them, as well as some idea of the many river-running possibilities they offer, from this book. For further information, you can write the state or federal agency administering any area you are interested in and ask for details about its riverine system.

Alaska has rivers that are deep and crystal clear, so clear that plants can fasten themselves to the riverbed and thrive on the sunshine coming through the water. These rivers are a particular delight to travel. Alaska also has rivers that are dense with gray glacial silt and therefore difficult to read. It has other streams, like the Yukon, that are fed by such a mix of waters from such a variety of watersheds that, like the Mississippi, they are "too thick to drink but not thick enough to plow."

Like proper rivers anywhere, Alaska's rivers have characters of their own, and they're also very changeable. In high winds, their waves can slow you down, and, if the wind direction is upstream, you may feel that you're actually traveling backwards. Summer weather, whether it's heat or storm, can also change rivers radically, particularly in streams flowing over impermeable land—be it rock or permafrost. Such waterways can flood dramatically in a remarkably brief time from either the meltoff of snow in their headwaters, from rainfall, or from both combined. I once traveled the Alatna River, usually as clear blue as a fine aquamarine, through a day of rain. That night we made a very late camp on an island at a place that was at least 4 feet above water level. The next morning, the river was lapping at our tent doors; in a matter of a few hours it had risen a good 4 feet, doubled in width, and engulfed the lower riverbanks, drowning the mouths of smaller streams. Indeed, it looked something like the Mississippi: majestic, roiling with mud, with flotillas of foam and tree branches sailing down it.

This kind of flooding (described so well by Bob Marshall—see Suggested Reading) can pose problems for your safety and should always be taken into account on Arctic and Interior rivers when there is rain or meltoff. It can also be a nuisance as far as drinking water goes. True, you can let the mud and grit in the water settle out, but it takes time, and the taste is not likely to be wonderful.

Braided rivers—there are many of them in Alaska—pose other problems. You need to travel the main channel if you don't want to get hung up on barely covered river bars. The explorer Frederick Schwatka told hilarious accounts of many such happenings when he explored the Yukon in a large homemade sailing raft. Even experienced river people can be fooled by braided glacial waters, and you should be prepared to get in and out of your small craft many times when you travel in low water on such a stream. Glacial streams are often swift flowing and always cold; they need to be treated with respect and good sense.

15. Bear Essentials

If you are very lucky you may get to see one or more of the great Alaska Brown Bear. What a fascinating creature he is! So very human, so concerned with "face." So playful. Watch one climb repeatedly up a steep rocky slope in order to slide on his butt down a snowfield. Watch a sow teaching her cub how to fish in a stream, catching one in her jaws to show how it is done, then carrying the fish ashore to demonstrate that delicious eating and the fun of fishing are closely related. Watch a sow discipline a disobedient cub with a spank which may send it flying through the air. Watch two boars telling each other off.

But aren't bears frightfully powerful and dangerous? Powerful: oh my yes. A bear's great muscles move so smoothly that he seems to flow, and he can run maybe twice as fast as a fast human runner. Dangerous, of course. Dangerous like a car hurtling along the highway. People who cannot accept the chance of meeting sudden death on the road have no choice but to stay out of cars and off the road. People who cannot tolerate the probably more remote chance of being mauled by a bear can simply stay out of the bear's country. No problem at all.

The single most important rule for moving safely in bear country is to let the bear know you are there, bearing in mind always that it is his country; you are the intruder. If you want to see and watch bear, however, then you must move quietly, thereby somewhat increasing the chance of an unexpected encounter. But not to panic. In a secret bear-watching spot where we take people we have several times, while watching bear in a river bottom out in front of us, discovered that there was a people-watching bear behind us having as much fun as we were.

Jack Calvin, Sitka

Almost anywhere you travel in Alaska, you will be sharing the rightful territory of one or more wild animals—great animals like wolves, wolverines, Dall sheep, deer, lynx, Arctic foxes, mountain goats, bears, moose, and caribou. This is a rare experience that cannot be duplicated in many parts of the world. Treat these animals and their habitat with respect. As Alaska becomes more and more developed, these animals will become increasingly threatened, and you will not want to add to the pressures being put on them. In certain heavily visited areas, limitations on human use of the animals' habitat have been initiated by federal and state wildlife agencies; these, of course, must be observed. If you plan a wilderness outing elsewhere, you should also check with the appropriate agency to find out if there are sensitive wildlife areas where you plan to visit; avoid these areas. Walk lightly where you do travel; keep your distance, and you may be privileged to see—and to coexist with—some of the most magnificent wildlife remaining on earth. Always travel with caution but never with fear. Most of Alaska's wild animals, like the wolves and wolverines, lynx, Dall sheep, and deer, are more anxious to stay out of your way than you are to stay out of theirs. Chances are they will do their best to avoid a face-to-face meeting with you at any cost. (How many times have I framed a perfect wildlife shot in my camera, inadvertently made some small sound, and watched my subject leap from sight.) A small animal like the ground squirrel or even a fox may not be so spooky and will probably even pose for a portrait. Caribou, especially the males, are not notably timid either. On more than one occasion when floating an Alaskan river, I have watched a fine caribou bull watch me, first with curiosity, then with indifference.

Moose and bears, however, are another matter. When encountered at close quarters, both of these great animals can be dangerous. It is up to you to stay out of their way. Moose are so large and frequently make so much noise that they can usually be easily avoided. The idea is not to get close enough to be kicked or charged. They are also often found in places that are wetter and sloppier than you would probably want to travel through. Females, especially when they have a calf or calves with them, are very protective, but they are also anxious to get away from you as soon as possible.

Bears demand special respect. Remember that they are the top predator in this particular wild-animal community. Although they are seldom the active aggressor against a human being, they are unpredictable. Unwanted encounters with bears can occur when the bears are surprised or when their territory is intruded upon.

I learned this firsthand one late June afternoon on West Chichagof Island. Five of us had been traveling by boat along the coast of this magnificent wilderness island, and we had come ashore for a stroll through

Brown bear (Ursus arctos); *the grizzly is considered to be the same species. Range: throughout Alaska. The smaller black bear* (Ursus americanus) *is more abundant and is the most widely distributed bear in Alaska. Its color ranges from jet black to brown or cinnamon, with the blue or glacier phase found rarely.*

an area that had been logged a few years before. It was a soft, rainy afternoon, a little misty and mysterious, with big old stumps looming out of the fog. We fell silent as we spread out along the road, musing over the way the forest had been removed or simply thinking our own thoughts. I was second in line, walking behind a young man of considerable strength and size who had a longer stride than I, and he soon disappeared from sight ahead of me. After rounding a bend in the road, he suddenly reappeared, racing toward me and yelling "Bear—get out of here." Then he disappeared as he sped back down the road.

Without thinking, I turned and sprinted after him, passing his wife who, in turn, followed me. Down around another curve, the only Alaskan in our party was standing with my husband in the middle of the road waving his arms and yelling a stream of imprecations that quite surprised me, even in my state of shock, for he was one of the most gentle-spoken people I have ever met. My husband was doing a good imitation of him. Stopping to join them and the other two in our party, I looked back and saw the bear.

It was a brownie, a creature so large that I thought he was standing on

his hind legs until I realized that he had halted on all fours to survey the
situation. He was making sounds that, to me, sounded like the roaring of
a lion. (I have since learned that bears are properly said to "woof" or to
"bellow.") The two men were making a real racket by now, and finally
the bear grew quiet. After what seemed an eternity, the bear turned and
ambled off in the opposite direction. We made a quick and quiet retreat
to the boat and, thoroughly shaken, congratulated ourselves on being
alive.

We were, of course, lucky to have escaped unscathed from such a face-
to-face encounter with a brown bear, but the incident took place only because of our own thoughtlessness. We were the intruders, the uninvited
guests in the bear's territory, and we had made a serious mistake: we had
failed to make our presence known. The first member of our party had
come unexpectedly upon the animal. Walking quietly around the bend in
the road, he had met the brownie practically head-on—and he had made
the mistake of running. Two other members of the party (including myself) had compounded this mistake, quite understandably, because there
was no place to hide, no tree to climb. (Bears, incidentally, have been
clocked at speeds of over 35 miles per hour—never try to outrun one!)
Except for the presence of mind and the bear expertise of our Alaskan
friend, who was an old hand in the Alaskan wilderness, we could easily
have had at least one serious injury among us. (Recent studies also suggest that a large group has a better chance of alerting a bear and so
avoiding a face-to-face meeting—another reason not to travel alone.) We
learned our lesson and added another bear story to the Alaskan anthology of bear encounters with happy endings.

The lesson was, of course, that you must announce your presence
when you travel in bear country and cannot see or be seen easily. Make
some kind of noise as you walk. Some old-time Alaskans strap a tin can
half full of pebbles onto their packs; others tie a bell to their belts or bang
on a tin can as they walk. (A Sierra Club cup makes a good loud clang,
especially when struck with a spoon.) You can lace bells onto your boots
or you may want to sing, or even play your harmonica. Field biologists
working for the Alaska Department of Fish and Game (ADFG) have
been known to set off firecrackers when they are working in areas with
high bear concentrations along salmon streams. You can also, when possible, walk with your back to the wind. This gives the bear the added
warning of your scent. Whistling is not recommended since it may inadvertently suggest that you are another wild animal.

If you are traveling cross-country, as you will be in most wilderness
areas of Alaska, choose where you walk with care. Avoid willow patches
and other brushy places, especially along salmon streams when the

salmon are running. Keep a sharp eye out in rolling terrain where there are berry patches. A browsing bear can be invisible in a hollow while feasting on blueberries. Also, beware if you smell decomposing meat; avoid the source of the smell, for it is likely that any bear in the vicinity will be at work on the carcass.

Travel with care on any game trail through brushy country or through forests or any other area where you cannot be easily seen. Never, never make your camp on a game trail; this simply invites disasters. Game trails used by bears are easily identifiable. They are likely to run along the banks of rivers and every now and then down to the stream. There are almost always several near salmon streams. These trails may also lead into berry patches, and they frequently cross the low points of ridges. Bear trails usually have been worn into two well-traveled lanes, about the distance apart of a bear's legs, and you may find occasional large bear footprints, as bears, like many animals, like to step in the same place over and over again. There are bear prints in Southeast, in fact, which biologists believe have had 10,000 years of continuous use!

When you camp in the wilderness, you should pitch your tent downwind from any evidence of bears, such as scat or dug-up earth. The most effective bear insurance of all for campers is to keep an immaculate camp. Despite what you have been taught in the Lower Forty-Eight, do clean your fish into the stream or river in Alaska, being sure the offal gets into the current and is carried away. (Decomposing fish contribute important nutrients to Alaska's fast-running streams.) Burn or pack out any garbage you have left after eating, and wash your dishes well. The USDA Forest Service says that improper waste disposal is a primary cause of "problem bears."

Never keep food inside your tent, and never leave food lying around. If there are trees nearby, wrap your supplies in double plastic bags; if you have a heavy cloth or burlap bag, use that too for added strength. Tie this bundle on a rope and sling it over a branch out of the reach of bears. If there are no trees, wrap your food as described and stash it as far away from your tent as is practical. Well-packaged dehydrated or freeze-dried food and canned food are less attractive to bears than fresh food and meat. The National Park Service advises campers to cook and eat 200 feet or more away from their tents, and many parks supply—and require—bearproof containers.

If you camp in a frequently visited area where the bears have become relatively tame and accustomed to being fed, your bear problems may be worse than when you are in the wilderness. Keep in mind that in Alaska it is illegal to feed bears (and other wild animals). It is also extremely dangerous—both to yourself and to the bear. Expecting food and being inadvertently provoked, a bear may injure you and end up being shot for the "offense." If you care about your own safety and the animal's right to survival, don't treat a bear like a pet. It is a wild animal. It is particularly important to avoid close encounters with a female bear (sow) that has her cub or cubs with her. These charming animal families are safely viewed only from a long way off—through your field glasses or the telephoto lens of your camera. Never make the mistake, which has cost more than one eager photographer serious injury or even life, of trying to get a close-up of bear cubs. In Denali National Park one summer, I nearly witnessed an eager seasonal ranger being badly mauled when he stalked a bear family too closely. If you're into wildlife photography, keep in mind that a good telephoto lens is a lot cheaper than a stay in the hospital.

If, despite all precautions, you do surprise a bear at close range, try not to panic. A startled bear will frequently simply let out a *woof* and run. (If this sound reminds you of a dog, remember that dogs are evolutionary relatives of bears.) The bear, however, may stand its ground, rear up on its hind legs, and swing its head from side to side; this is an effort to try to see what or who you are. This is the time to talk to the bear in your normal voice, and wave your arms. Bears may not see as well as humans, but they can readily distinguish motion, and they have sharp ears as well as a keen sense of smell. Sometimes a bear will turn sideways and pose, as though showing off its muscles. This is supposed to intimidate you (it undoubtedly will), and it is a signal that you should leave. Another signal is when a bear pops its teeth or lets out a series of loud *woof*s in a sound that is routinely described as being "like air being forced out of a bellows." Never "woof" or bellow back at a bear, and do not imitate its actions, which may well be body language indicating hostility. *Do not run*. Bears have a critical "personal space," or territory, which may range up to 50 yards; avoid it if you possibly can, or back slowly out of it, always facing the bear. Or, if it's a grizzly or brown bear, climb a tree, if one is handy and you have time. (Black bears are tree climbers.) If there is no place to go and the bear comes toward you, stop, hold your ground, make as much noise as possible, and wave your arms. Should all your cool-headed efforts fail to deter the bear, and it actually reaches you, drop flat onto your stomach or curl up into a ball, clasp your hands behind your neck to protect your head, and stay as still as possible. Play dead. Bears that attack when they feel threatened usually won't bother someone they think they have killed.

If you are familiar with guns, you may consider packing one with you to protect yourself against bears when you travel in Alaska's wilderness. There are two distinct schools of thought among Alaskans about carrying weapons into the bush. One school argues that a gun is not only heavy and dangerous but also unnecessary. Our Alaskan friend who fended off the bear on West Chichagof Island shared this opinion. He believed that by the time you can get ready to shoot a charging bear, for example, it will probably be too late. If you succeed in only wounding the animal, you will be in an even more serious situation, with a wounded, infuriated bear for an adversary. Those who do not tote guns also point out that too many bears are killed needlessly by trigger-happy people who are unfamiliar with these great animals. There is the further chance that people not thoroughly used to high-powered weapons will kill or injure themselves or another person instead of the bear.

In the opposite camp, there are many Alaskans who would not think of going into the bush, or at least into known bear country, without a gun. These people feel that a firearm not only gives them control over many risky variables in potentially dangerous situations, but it adds greatly to their confidence—an important factor, since body language may influence how a bear will act. They feel, too, that in camp situations in which a bear chooses to invade human space in search of food, a gun is essential. On long, cross-country treks, they point out, the loss of your food supply could be disastrous. They grant that guns are cumbersome and potentially dangerous but argue that knowing how and when to use a gun can effectively remove the hazards. They recommend a twelve-gauge shotgun loaded with either oo buckshot or rifled slugs, rifles larger than 30-06, or pistols chambered for .357 magnum or larger cartridge. And they emphasize being familiar with your firearm and understanding how to use it.

If you do decide to carry a gun for protection, you will not need to get a hunting license in Alaska. (You are not permitted, however, to carry a pistol in Canada, and some national parks in Alaska prohibit firearms; check ahead.) If you should be forced to kill a bear to save your or someone else's life, do not just leave the dead animal. Alaska law requires that you turn over the skin and skull of a bear killed in self-defense to the Alaska Department of Fish and Game.

All public land agencies in Alaska are anxious to help you avoid a human-bear encounter. Consult them when you travel Alaska's wilderness. The pamphlet *Bear Facts*, published cooperatively by these agencies (and the Alaska Natural History Association) is highly recommended reading: it is available from any Alaska Public Lands Information Center, as well as from the above agencies.

With all these warnings, it is important to remember that you are far less likely to be injured or killed by a bear in Alaska's wilderness than you are by driving on an Alaskan highway. Odds of being in a serious auto

accident in Alaska are fifty times greater than those of being in a serious
bear encounter, and Alaska's highway accident rate is lower than that of
many other states. While a bear incident makes headlines all over the
country, an auto accident is usually just one more statistic. As noted earlier, be cautious in Alaska's wilderness, but do not be afraid.

16. The Bush

Alaskans refer to the great roadless area that comprises most of their
state as "the bush" and to small, isolated communities as bush communities or bush villages. (The federal government actually classifies the entire state of Alaska except for Anchorage as "rural"—Fairbanks and the
capital, Juneau, notwithstanding.) The bush is homeland to most of
Alaska's Native people and to many sturdy emigrants who have homesteaded (in past decades), mined, or acquired land by other means,
choosing to leave the pressures of urban life to adopt an elemental
lifestyle.

You will find some of Alaska's most interesting residents living in the
bush, be they Native (see Visiting Native Villages, below) or non-Native.
Some of the latter may have migrated from universities or businesses or
simply have been ambitious and rugged individualists who succeeded in
making it on their own in an extraordinarily beautiful if difficult and demanding environment. (It's too bad that there isn't enough of Alaska to
go around for all the people who might have the same idea!) People in
the bush are routinely strong, independent, and careful—or they would-
n't survive. Many are also extremely ingenious and add many gracious
amenities to their basic subsistence in the midst of the wilderness.

Many bush families make their living by being outfitters, professional
guides (hunting or otherwise), or bush pilots, or by operating wilderness
lodges. If you stay at a wilderness lodge, therefore—say, at Thayer Lake
Wilderness Lodge on Admiralty Island or at the Coles' Camp Denali in
Denali National Park—you will have a chance to get acquainted with the
uniquely Alaskan bush way of life. (See sections on these areas for how
to contact these outposts.) This can give you insights into Alaska and a
feeling for it that you otherwise could not have. It is highly recommended
if you can afford it.

17. The Alaskan Bush Pilot and His Remarkable Flying Machine

In the wonderfully vast roadless area that is most of Alaska, the way people get around is by air, frequently in a small airplane. This explains why Alaska sets records for small-plane use in the United States on several scores. Of any state, Alaska has the highest per capita ownership of small planes; there is one plane for approximately every fifty-four Alaskans. It has the greatest percentage of pilots, by far; as many as one out of every forty Alaskans is a licensed aircraft operator, some twelve times the national average. Alaska has the greatest number of floatplanes (planes equipped with pontoons rather than wheels). Lake Hood in Anchorage is not just the busiest floatplane base in the United States, but in the world, and Merrill Field in Anchorage, used by small wheeled aircraft, may have more than 225 takeoffs and landings a day. Merrill, in fact, ranks among the nation's most heavily used airports. Small wonder that if you stand on an Anchorage corner on a clear summer day, you will probably see a small plane almost anywhere you look in the sky.

From all of this, you will gather that most Alaskans, particularly those who live in the bush or find their recreation in it, get in and out of small airplanes as casually as you do your own automobile or the corner bus. If you're to do any off-the-track travel (or even on-the-track travel, in places) in Alaska, you too will have to go by small plane. If you have not flown much in such planes, it might take some getting used to, but it's worth it. Small planes can not only take you where you want to go in the wilderness and bring you back, but they can also give you the opportunity to view the country from a relatively low altitude, traveling at a relatively slow speed. You can see the grandeur of the country much more intimately than you would from a jet, and you can also put things into a manageable perspective. Furthermore, flying in a small plane offers you chances to see animals like bears and moose, as well as nesting pairs of trumpeter swans and other birds, which you might not see as comfortably on the ground—or might not see at all. (It's pretty exciting, too, to fly with and past a bald eagle, as you very well may do.) I fly in a small plane in Alaska whenever I have the chance; flights in small aircraft have given me some of my most memorable views, and best photographs as well. Although Alaska's small planes may look fragile and as if they have been around for a long time (they probably have), they are usually sturdy, reliable vehicles. As noted, many are on floats, which lets them land on Alaska's many lakes and wider rivers throughout the state, and some are amphibious. But even when they are equipped only with wheels, they can and do land in a remarkable variety of places under a truly remarkable variety of conditions.

If you are any kind of a small airplane buff, you'll have a field day in Alaska. You'll find Widgeons, Beavers, Otters, Grumman Goose, Beechcraft, Cherokees, Cessnas, Piper Cubs, and Supercubs routinely. D-C3s— among the greatest airplanes ever built—still fly in a few places, and not all that long ago an old PBY bomber from World War II was carrying passengers in its bomb bay on scheduled flights in the Southeastern part of the state.

In the Arctic regions, you'll find that most of the small planes, even those used for scheduled flights, have a single engine. This is because it takes less time (and is cheaper and easier) to warm up one engine in minus-50-degree weather than it does to service two. Single-engine planes haul around a lot besides people: furniture, groceries, cases of beer, game. I once was the next passenger after a moose in a Piper Cub, and I still haven't figured out how the pilot got the moose into and out of a plane so small it crowded even me. Sometimes you will see various things strapped on the outside of small planes, but large items such as canoes are generally taboo (according to Federal Aviation Administration regulations, that is). Be sure to check with your bush pilot, now frequently known as an air-taxi pilot, if you need to transport this kind of gear.

Chances are that you will find your bush pilot—particularly if he has been around for a while—an especially interesting Alaskan. Alaska's bush pilots are members of a legendary fellowship and hold a special place in Alaskan history.

The first civilian bush pilot to arrive in Alaska was Roy F. Jones, a World War I aviator for the U.S. Signal Corps. After the war, he picked up a surplus Curtiss flying boat and outfitted it in Seattle with a 90-

Merrill Pass, near Anchorage, the kind of landmark pass crossed routinely by Alaska's bush pilots. Source: National Park Service.

horsepower Hispana Suiza engine, christening it the *Northbird*. In 1922, he flew the *Northbird* up the Inside Passage, and, on July 17, he landed it on the waters of the Tongass Narrows, right outside of Ketchikan. Without knowing it, Jones thus initiated a new and colorful mode of travel in Alaska. (Little could he foresee the difference it would make.) The *Northbird*'s battered, brass-feathered propeller still hangs on the wall of Ketchikan's air terminal.

During the next decades, the bush pilots—often flying for the U.S. Fish and Wildlife Service or on other federal missions—explored Alaska's territory as it had not been explored before. They were the first to see what today has become commonplace for the thousands who fly around Alaska. They saw the immensity of the frozen land and how intricately the frost action had patterned it—pitting and pocking it, drawing it into scallops on steep slopes, and fracturing it into laceworks of polygons. They discovered the vastness of the Southeastern snowfields, the beauty of hanging glaciers cupped in dark ragged rock, the incredible size of the

Malaspina Glacier with its pattern of black and white stripes. They were the first to see the extent of the Kobuk and Koyokuk dunes: sand dunes that lie far inland from the ocean. They saw the thousands of lakes that dot the Arctic Slope and the wind-blown silt from Arctic rivers like smoke against the pale skies. They saw the slow rivers of the Interior winding across the land in sinuous curves. They flew in every kind of weather, by moonlight, through darkness (carrying a lantern to mark their location should they lose their way and a friend need to find them), and past erupting volcanoes when the cinders rained around them like hail. Of necessity, they flew by the seat of their pants, for there were no maps and no weather reports to guide them; they followed the great rivers—the Yukon, the Porcupine, the Kuskokwim, the Copper, the Yentna—even as earlier, wingless explorers had.

Bush pilots flew to the most distant and smallest Native communities, performing amazing takeoffs and landings and using any near-level spot they could find. They brought not only access but change everywhere they went. Early on, they began to carry the mail, ending the legendary dog-team mail service in Alaska. They hauled in not only mail and food supplies, but also missionaries and doctors, some of whom became bush pilots themselves. They brought, often for the first time, news from around the world—along with sport hunters and many other people from Outside (even as they do today).

From the early twenties until the mid-fifties when the Distant Early Warning Stations (DEW line) went in (with time out for World War II), the bush pilots seemed to own Alaska. There were almost no rules and regulations to check their adventures, and they could fly where and very much how they chose. They became folk heroes of a sort, and rarely have there been more romantic heroes. Expert flyers, they wove tenuous lifelines into the bush and were often willing to risk their lives for the people who lived there—daring to land in the most inaccessible places to rescue a stranded hunter or to save the life of a dying child. Many died, themselves, as a result.

The stories about Alaska's bush pilots are legion. Noel Wien, one of the greatest, refused to use a map even when maps were finally available: he carried the physiognomy of Alaska around in his head until he died. Archie Ferguson from Kotzebue loved to fly, and yet he never learned how to land a plane: "Every landing he made was a controlled crash." During World War II, when the army took over in Alaska and tried to lay down the law, Ferguson flew merrily into Nome, which was off limits. When the control tower challenged him, he replied hoarsely: "I got only one engine," and they let him land. He always flew, of course, a single-engine plane. Jay Hammond, the third governor of Alaska, broke both ankles landing a Piper Cub at King Cove, rather than endanger children skating on a frozen lake that was the landing field.

Over the years, many pilots homesteaded land and patented hunting and fishing camps in some of Alaska's choicest wilderness. They made their living in part as hunting and fishing guides, and some still do. In the process, they managed to more or less divide Alaska up into their own territories: thus if you flew out of Kotzebue in the 1930s, chances are you would have flown with a Ferguson (and you still might); if you flew out of King Salmon in the 1950s or 1960s—or even the 1970s—you would likely have flown with Dick Jensen or Jay Hammond. The tradition continues, particularly in the more remote parts of the state.

Whenever I can, I fly with an old-timer, for there are still quite a few of them around. (There are old pilots and bold pilots, the saying goes, but no old bold pilots.) Pilots like Jay Hammond are so familiar with their country that they know where they are even when the fog is so thick you can't see ground. There are many good newer pilots, of course, flyers who have gotten bored with piloting jets, or who are fresh from the armed services, or who have simply fallen in love with Alaska. Sooner or later they learn their way around the bush, but it may take a while. I once flew in a helicopter with an ex-marine who had just arrived from Texas. He got lost the minute he left the road between Fairbanks and Circle, which is where the road ends. Heading for the Charley River, we flew instead within sight of the Wrangell Mountains and had to set down on hillsides twice to lay out the maps—and eat blueberries—before we finally ended up using the Yukon River for navigation.

Experienced bush pilots may fly in conditions that may petrify you if you have not flown before in Alaska. However, they will usually know what they are doing, and you have to respect their judgment (and remember that they, too, want to keep on living). Accidents happen most often when the pilot is pushed too hard. People have lost their lives trying to keep a particular engagement that seemed more important than dangerous flying conditions. When you travel in a small plane, don't be in a hurry and do keep your schedule flexible. If your pilot doesn't want to fly because of one reason or another, abide by his decision.

When you fly around Alaska in the summer, expect to wait at both ends of your trip. Bush pilots do most of their year's business during the summer season, and they try to pack in as much as possible. This usually works fine if the weather is good. Poor flying conditions, however, can cause major delays. I once waited for days in Kaktovik when a wintry storm hit the area in early July—but I was lucky. There were twenty people stacked up behind me who waited even longer. We went out in our proper order, and our party finally took off one midnight and flew to the headwaters of the Kongakut River in the very early morning, delighted that we could make it. You are even more likely to wait on the other end of your trip. Don't worry if your pilot fails to show up on time, and rejoice if he does. Carry extra food, a pack of playing cards, or an extra paperback or two, just in case. He'll make it when he safely can.

If you're laying out the logistics of an Alaskan wilderness trip on your own, plan to fly commercial as far as you can before you charter. Try for a scheduled mail carrier to more remote places. You will want to rent the smallest air taxi you can that can still handle your gear. If you have a lot of gear, balance the cost of a larger plane versus two trips in a smaller plane—assuming, of course, that your air-taxi operator gives you a choice. (Air taxis are not cheap.) Keep in mind that you will have to pay for a round-trip unless you're lucky enough to find passengers to take your place on the return trip.

In many parts of Alaska, you'll need to carry your own stove because of lack of wood. It is, however, against federal regulations to carry gasoline on any commercial flights; so choose your cooking equipment accordingly if you're flying a scheduled carrier on any leg of your Alaska trip.

Chances are you'll travel in a floatplane on most of your air-taxi journeys into the bush. If you're in a Beaver for the first time, don't panic when, at takeoff, the plane appears to be going underwater; this is only an illusion. If you're not wearing hip boots on such an outing (and you probably won't be), expect to get a ride, piggyback, on your pilot's shoulders from the plane to the shore if you land in fairly deep water. (Bush pilots of floatplanes routinely wear hip boots.) This is standard practice when the plane cannot be brought close enough in to a reasonably dry landing spot.

Enjoy your travels in Alaska's small planes. They can provide you with some of the best memories—and best stories to tell—of your wilderness adventure. Even though times are changing in Alaska, the bush pilot, with his remarkable flying machine, still plays a very special role in the Alaska experience.

If you're visiting public lands, the agency administering them—the National Park Service people, for instance—can cue you in to current air-taxi rates and give you a list of qualified pilots.

18. Who Takes Care of Alaska's Lands

Your travels in Alaska will take you for the most part through lands administered by the federal or state government. These lands have until recently been the subject of much, and often bitter, contention. Indeed, public land ownership and administration in Alaska have been primary concerns and frequent and lively topics in the news media and in a good deal of conversation. You may still hear mutterings about the "feds' big lock-up" or see old signs in a village like Eagle telling members of a federal land agency to go away—but not so politely—and how the freedom of the hills is a thing of the past. The following will provide some background for understanding what this has all been about.

Historically, the Native people of Alaska had a sense of territory, but the land in general was looked upon as a kind of vast commons—nobody owned it. The Europeans who started appropriating Alaska in the mid-eighteenth century had, of course, a very different land ethic, but they failed to make any treaty with the Natives spelling out just how different that ethic was. Nor did the United States make any final land settlement with the Natives when it acquired Alaska in 1867—beyond guaranteeing them their "historic rights." Thus the 375 million acres of Alaska purchased by the United States simply became part of the "vacant and unappropriated" public domain, and—although nobody thought about it that way—the stage was set for the eventual subdivision of these acres.

A few communities, homesteads, mining claims, and trade and manufacturing sites (5-acre parcels) took a nibble here and there out of the whole, but no major federal land withdrawal from Alaska's public domain occurred until the national forests were roughly delineated and set aside, soon after the turn of the century. Further withdrawals continued during the following decades with the establishment of the first national parks, the Navy Petroleum Reserve (Pet 4) in the Arctic, military reservations, Indian reservations, the U.S. Fish and Wildlife Service refuges, and large power withdrawals. By the time statehood was decreed for Alaska in 1959, the disposition of the land had come this far:

Alaska Land Ownership, 1959

Lands	Acres
Federal Land Reserves	
National forests	20,700,000
National parks and monuments	6,900,000
Wildlife refuges and ranges	7,800,000
Navy Petroleum Reserve No. 4	23,000,000
Power reserves, etc.	27,400,000
Indian reservations, school reserves, etc. (BIA)[1]	4,100,000
Military reservations	2,300,000
Other	200,000
	92,400,000
Private ownership, patented and certified	700,000
Unperfected entries	600,000
Vacant, unappropriated public domain lands (BLM)[2]	217,800,000
Total Alaska land:	*365,500,000*[3]

1. Bureau of Indian Affairs.
2. Bureau of Land Management.
3. From: *Alaska, A Challenge in Conservation* by Richard A. Cooley. Estimates of total land acreage vary. Note: At the time these acreages were compiled, significant portions of Alaska had not been surveyed, so the individual entries do not add up to the total as given.

The Statehood Act gave Alaska 104 million acres, to be selected out of this enormous reservoir of public domain, as well as the rights to all tidelands (35 to 40 million acres) and navigable waters (another 8 to 12 million acres). The first state selections, however, ran head-on into Native resistance, and the Native people in turn began to lay claim to land that they identified as belonging to them historically and legally, in light of the failure of Congress to settle their legitimate claims. (At one point during the 1960s, because of overlapping claims, more than 375 million acres of Alaskan land had been spoken for by the Natives.) In 1966, Secretary of the Interior Stewart Udall froze all land disposition in Alaska pending settlement of the Natives' claims. Among other things, this brought an end to homesteading, which—based as it was on land laws drawn up with the east coast of America in mind—had always been an incongruous, frequently destructive, and prohibitively expensive method of acquiring Alaskan land.

In 1971, the Congress passed the Alaska Native Claims Settlement Act (ANCSA), and a huge step was taken in the subdivision of Alaska. Under terms of this exceedingly complicated act (which has helped make Alaska a lawyer's paradise), the state was divided into twelve Native regional corporations, each of which would receive acreage according to its historic land use and the number of its corporate members. One region, Doyon, in the Interior, ended up with over 12 million acres, the largest corporate holding in the United States. (A thirteenth Native regional corporation, representing the approximately five thousand out-of-state Natives, was also established and received $56 million in 1976, but no land.) Every Native village was also mandated to be a profit-making or non-profit-making corporation (or both), which would receive from one to three townships of land according to the number of its stockholders— that is, its Native villagers. (To qualify as a "Native," one had to be born before December 1971 and have at least one Native grandparent.) In all, some 44 million acres would pass into Native ownership—as private property—as would nearly $1 billion from the federal government and from state oil royalties.

The terms of this act also decreed, under Section 17:d-2, the setting aside of at least 80 million acres of "national interest" or conservation lands for the protection, more or less, of their unique and superlative values. (These are the "d-2 lands," or National Interest Lands.) Congress implemented this measure in December 1980, after nine years of struggling to identify these lands, with the passage of Public Law 96-487, the Alaska National Interest Lands Conservation Act (ANILCA). The land situation in Alaska now looks something like the table at the top of page 94—subject to final conveyances under ANCSA and ANILCA.

Each federal agency that administers land in Alaska (and elsewhere) has a different charge and a different emphasis in the way it handles its lands. Thus the U.S. Department of Agriculture (USDA) Forest Service is dedicated to "multiple use" (harvesting timber, protecting watersheds, recreation, wilderness, wildlife, and other uses, such as mining, hunting, and gathering firewood). The National Park Service is dedicated to the preservation of its lands "in perpetuity" and, simultaneously, to making the lands available for the use and enjoyment of the general public. (This dual purpose has led to many conflicts in land administration, and the National Park Service has been charged with both overprotection and overdevelopment.) Hunting, mining, and the use of motorized vehicles off the beaten track are traditionally prohibited in national parks; how-

Alaska Land Ownership, 1997

Lands	Acres
Federal land reserves	
National forests	22,430,000
National parklands	54,709,000
Wildlife refuges and ranges	75,261,000
Wild and scenic rivers (3,152 river miles)	1,200,000
Military reservations and other federal holdings	2,100,000
	155,700,000
State selections[1]	104,500,000
Private ownership	
Native selections	44,000,000
Other	1,000,000
Vacant, unappropriated public domain lands (BLM)[2]	70,000,000
Total Alaska land	*375,200,000*

Acreages are approximate.
1. Does not include tidelands (completed, but not yet conveyed).
2. Bureau of Land Management.

ever, the legislation placing some 48 million more acres of Alaska's lands into the National Park Service has established numerous "preserves" that allow sports hunting and, in places, the use of snowmobiles, and all of the new National Park Service lands in Alaska allow subsistence use by Alaskans where it has been established historically.

The U.S. Fish and Wildlife Service is charged with the management and enhancement of the habitats of the fauna living on its lands. (The state manages the fish and game per se, except for sea mammals, which are under the protection of the U.S. Departments of Commerce and the Interior.) The Fish and Wildlife Service also allows hunting and mining under its regulations. The Bureau of Land Management (BLM), which for so long administered most of Alaska and had almost no strings tied to the use of the land under its aegis, has less stringent land use restrictions than any other federal agency, although, under the terms of its 1975 Organic Act, it has powers and opportunities for protecting as well as managing the public domain. (For years, many Alaskans used and considered BLM lands their own, and some still do.) All of these agencies—except for the USDA Forest Service, which is part of the Department of Agriculture—are under the Department of the Interior.

Note that while the acreage of the National Park Service has increased about sevenfold in the past few years, the BLM-administered public do-

National Wildlife Refuges in Alaska

Refuge	Acres	Wilderness Acres
Alaska Maritime NWR	3,548,956	2,576,302
Alaska Peninsula NWR	3,500,000	
Arctic NWR	19,351,300	8,000,000
Becharof NWR	1,200,000	400,000
Innoko NWR	3,850,000	1,200,000
Izembek NWR	320,893	300,000
Kanuti NWR	1,430,000	
Kenai NWR	1,970,000	1,350,000
Kodiak NWR	1,865,000	
Koyukuk NWR	3,550,000	400,000
Nowitna NWR	1,560,000	
Selawik NWR	2,150,000	240,000
Tetlin NWR	700,000	
Togiak NWR	4,105,000	2,270,000
Yukon Delta NWR	19,624,458	1,600,000
Yukon Flats NWR	8,630,000	600,000
Total	77,355,607	18,936,302

National Forests in Alaska

Forest	Acres
Chugach	5,900,000
Wilderness	0
Tongass	16,800,000
Wilderness	5,650,000

Acreages are approximate.

National Parks in Alaska

Park	Acres
Aniakchak National Monument and Preserve	600,000
Bering Land Bridge National Preserve	1,000,000
Cape Krusenstern National Monument	659,000
Denali National Park and Preserve	6,000,000
Gates of the Arctic National Park and Preserve	8,400,000
Glacier Bay National Park and Preserve	1,300,000
Katmai National Park and Preserve	4,000,000
Kenai Fjords National Park	669,000
Klondike Gold Rush National Historical Park	12,990
Kobuk Valley National Park and Preserve	1,700,000
Lake Clark National Park and Preserve	4,000,000
Noatak National Preserve	6,500,000
Sitka National Historical Park	106
Wrangell–Saint Elias National Park and Preserve	13,200,000
Yukon-Charley Rivers National Preserve	2,500,000
Total	50,341,096

Acreages are approximate.

main has shrunk to about a third of what it once was. This is one thing that has upset certain Alaskans, who feel they should be able to use "their" land however they want to, as they have in the past. Of course, all public lands are the property equally of every United States citizen.

Add to the federal public lands in Alaska those administered by the state itself. Although the state has a Forestry Department and a Department of Fish and Wildlife, the outdoor traveler will more than likely be concerned with the state park land. There are over 3 million acres of land in Alaska state parks, some of them in exceptionally beautiful areas. The primary use of these lands is, of course, recreation.

Each of the agencies described above also has recreation as one of the primary, specific uses of its lands. As you adventure in Alaska, you can get a great deal of information and help from the federal or state agency administering the land you visit. The legislation setting aside National Interest Lands called for the establishment of federal-state interagency centers to answer questions and supply valuable information to the recreationist. With the development of these interagency information centers (the state of Alaska joined with the federal agencies to establish

National Wild and Scenic Rivers in Alaska

River	Federal Agency	River Miles in NWSR System
Alagnak	NPS	69
Alatna	NPS	83
Andreafsky	FWS	100
Aniakchak	NPS	31
Beaver Creek	BLM	111
Birch Creek	BLM	126
Charley	NPS	100
Chilikadrotna	NPS	65
Delta	BLM	62
Fortymile	BLM	392
Gulkana	BLM	181
Ivishak	FWS	60
John	NPS	30
Kobuk, Upper	NPS	120
Koyukuk, North Fork	NPS	120
Mulchatna	NPS	215
Noatak	NPS	300
Nowitna	FWS	245
Salmon	NPS	55
Selawik	FWS	207
Sheenjek	FWS	200
Tinayguk	NPS	50
Tlikakila	NPS	43
Unalakleet	BLM	65
Wind	FWS	70

BLM=Bureau of Land Management	Total BLM:	968
NPS=National Park Service	Total NPS:	1,281
FWS=Fish and Wildlife Service	Total FWS:	882

Source: American River Management Society and BLM.

them) in key locations in Alaska—Anchorage, Fairbanks, Ketchikan, and Tok—you will have ready access to almost all you need to know about adventuring on federal or state land. The USDA Forest Service also has set up an interagency information center in Juneau. These centers not only provide helpful pamphlets and brochures, but have interesting exhibits, videos, and computer-based question-and-answer facilities. Since much of the Alaskan land that you will likely visit is under public administration—and thus really belongs to you—you should avail yourself of these facilities if possible. And, it goes without saying, you should also do your part to take care of Alaska's wild and beautiful lands. If you cannot visit one of these centers, you can write, instead:

Alaska Department of Natural
  Resources Public Information Center
3601 C Street
Anchorage, AK 99503

Alaska Public Lands Information Center
605 West Fourth Avenue
Anchorage, AK 99501

Alaska Public Lands Information Center
250 Cushman Street
Fairbanks, AK 99701

Alaska Public Lands Information Center
Box 359
Tok, AK 99780

Forest Service Information Center
101 Egan Drive
Juneau, AK 99801

Southeast Alaska Visitor Center
50 Main Street
Ketchikan, AK 99901

If you know which state or national park or forest you want to visit, you can contact the superintendent or regional forester directly—addresses are included in discussions of the different units throughout this book. They can supply you not only with the details about their park or forest but with the names of accredited guides, outfitters, air taxis, and other services and suppliers.

This book tells of many of the superlative recreational opportunities you will find on these publicly administered lands. It may, however, be necessary for you to pass through Native-owned private property or to fly into or out of Native-owned villages to reach these lands. You should, of course, respect the property rights of these landowners as you would those of anybody else. Permission to use Native lands should be requested. (See Visiting Native Villages, below.)

19. Visiting Native Villages

One summer afternoon a few years ago I was in Fort Yukon when a flying club from the Lower Forty-Eight arrived—twenty-eight planes strong —on an unannounced sightseeing visit. One after another, the little Cessnas and Pipers landed on the small airstrip, and their passengers, amounting to fifty-six or more people, jumped out and took off for the village. Roaming the dirt streets in crowds, they gawked at the little log cabins (some only one room in size), wondered out loud where the toilets were, stared at the Native people (whom they almost outnumbered), photographed them without the least thought of asking permission, and muttered audibly: "Imagine living like this!" After a cursory once-over of the town's eating place, no purchase of the really beautiful beadwork done by the Athabascan women who live in Fort Yukon, and scarcely a word, friendly or otherwise, to anyone in the village, the crowd trotted back to the airstrip en masse and took off. It is small wonder that this kind of rude visit—too often typical of thoughtless tourists—has left a lingering bad taste in many Alaska villages.

Add to this the fact that Native people in villages have, historically, been the subject of other kinds of unannounced, and often unwelcome, visits. In recent years, as a friend of mine once said: "People just dropped down out of the sky all the time and started asking us what we eat, how many teeth we have. Or what we wear under our parkas. Or how come our kids have runny noses." Many such visits were made—and to virtually every village—by government agencies with the best of intentions. Or they may have been made by anthropologists or other scientists who were sincerely concerned about their subjects. But the Natives were rarely consulted beforehand; their permission was simply taken for granted and they were, in fact, treated arbitrarily.

With the passage of the Alaska Native Claims Settlement Act (ANCSA), the situation has, of course, changed. The Native villages are now privately owned, and the village corporation must be consulted before any outside agency takes actions affecting the residents. You, too, should get permission before staying for any length of time in a small village or using village-owned facilities.

Also keep in mind the fact that Alaska's Natives are presently in a period of major and profound change. Although the impact and influence of white cultures have been felt for over two centuries, many traditional ways have survived until recently. In recent years, however, these ways have been more strongly challenged than ever before. As each village has made the quantum leap from a more or less traditional enclave to a corporate entity, new ways of looking at things and doing things have had to be incorporated into a deeply rooted lifestyle. Inevitably, there have been difficult choices and conflicts in values; for many of Alaska's Native people, this has not been an easy time. (There are some seventy thousand in-state Natives.)

Subsistence hunting, a cherished way of life, has become a particularly sensitive subject as new uses have been spelled out for the land. The federal Alaska land laws allow for established subsistence use throughout all public lands, including the new federal reserves; anyone traveling in Alaska should respect the Natives' (and non-Natives') rights to pursue it. This means that you should not intrude when subsistence hunting or fishing is taking place, and you should never touch a fish net, fish wheel, traps, or any other subsistence gear that you might come across. (Natives on the Kobuk River have been appalled—and outraged—to find that their set nets had been removed by kayakers who were trying to help keep the wilderness clean.) Of course, you should never occupy a vacant fish camp . . . it belongs to someone; and do not walk in, uninvited, on one in use. A friendly wave is in order.

Another sensitive point to some Natives is the increasing number of people who are using land that historically has been used by themselves. The idea of boundaries is not easy to accept in a culture that has lived so long without them, and it is hard for some people to see the difference between a group of backpackers (nonconsumptive and noncompetitive recreational users) and a wealthy foreign hunter out for a prize trophy. If you should encounter hostility on your travels, a friendly approach and discussion of why you are there can usually clear the air and can certainly help establish long-range good relations at a time when many attitudes are taking shape.

All of this should make it clear that you should never descend, unannounced, upon a small Native village that has limited facilities—if any—

In subsistence use, every part of the animal is utilized. This Eskimo is trimming seal intestines. Source: National Park Service.

and expect to be welcomed with open arms. Also, it will pay you to do some homework, as well as to exercise courtesy, with regard to any village you wish to spend some time in, or whose land you wish to pass through or over. Some communities, like Kotzebue and Point Barrow, are on the tourist circuit, and there you will routinely be treated like a tourist if you travel like one. Other villages may have less in the way of tourist accommodations and may not be interested in tourist development. You can get background information on any Alaska village by writing the *State Department of Community and Regional Affairs,* 333 West Fourth Avenue, Anchorage, AK 99501; this information should convey some flavor of the particular village and show what lands it owns and what its particular interests are. Further, if you are going to be traveling through village lands or if you want to spend any time in a village, you might want to write ahead and ask permission or inquire about accommodations. (The Appendices include a list of Alaska zip codes; address the village president.) If you do not receive a reply, your letter—and your courteous intent—will be on the record. (Note: The *Alaska Wilderness Guide* contains community profiles, maps, and more detailed travel information than the scope of this book allows; see Suggested Reading.)

When running a river, it is good wilderness manners to keep a low profile. Not only does this respect the rights of others in the area, it gives you a much better chance to experience the wilderness fully. If you spread out your gear all over a river bar, you will not only offend any people around you but will scare off any local wildlife. If you feel it necessary to carry a gun (and many do not—see Bear Essentials, above), do so discreetly. If your route passes several villages, it will make your trip more pleasant to advise the village presidents of your plans. Easements for public camping have been established in areas of private property and should be used accordingly. (Along some rivers you may find "Private Property, No Trespassing" signs; observe them. You are free to camp on river bars below the high-water mark.) The agency administering the river you run can advise you of the status of land ownership along your route. (You can expect a good commercially run river trip to take care of all of this.) When in a Native village, keep in mind that you are in the home community of people whose ancestors settled Alaska many millennia ago. Their way of life may be different from yours, but it has succeeded in a particularly difficult environment. Please respect it, and respect the people who have learned to get along under conditions that might easily have long since done you in. The great majority of these people will return the friendship that you offer them.

20. Tanana Moon Calendar

The year begins with October, is 13 months long, and there are 29 days, 12 hours, and 44 minutes in a month. Not to worry if there are more than 365 days in a Tanana year: the day of the month need not be exact.

Month 1	Moon when the bull moose ruts
Month 2	Moon when the sheep ruts
Month 3	Hook Game month (a time of games and social activities)
Month 4	Moon when the sun appears again after long sleep
Month 5	Moon when days grow longer
Month 6	Moon of the cold winds, or Eagle Moon
Month 7	Hawk Moon
Month 8	Moon when snow is soft by day and freezes by night
Month 9	Moon when young animals are born
Month 10	Moon when moose comes down off the hill
Moon 11	Moon when the moose fat is ready
Moon 12	Moon when the animals take on their winter coats
Moon 13	Moon when the leaves turn red

With thanks to Neil Davis of the Geophysical Institute, University of Alaska.

PART II

Southeast

21. Introduction

The Southeast is a very special part of Alaska. Stretching from the Portland Canal in the south to Icy Bay in the north and arcing gently from southeast to northwest, it is a long (540 air miles), narrow (140 air miles at its widest) area of land and water lying between roughly the 55th and 61st parallels north latitude. Geographically, it consists of a slender strip of mainland territory and, except at its northern end, of an extraordinary assembly of countless islands—the Alexander Archipelago—which account for the impressive mileage of the Southeastern coastline. Although its acreage comes to about the size of Massachusetts, New Hampshire, Connecticut, Delaware, New Jersey, and Rhode Island put together, the Southeast comprises only about 6 percent of the state and is a relatively small and compact area compared with the rest of Alaska. Southeastern Alaska is also more intimate, and its wilderness is more readily accessible.

Delineated on the west by the Gulf of Alaska, its eastern boundary runs along the tumultuous crest of the tallest coastal mountains on earth, a section of the two-continent cordillera that approaches its most splendid northern climax here. This section is tied to the main body of Alaska by only a sliver of land that at one point stretches less than 11 miles from the coast to the Canadian border. The Southeast is frequently called Alaska's panhandle, and it is a world of its own. Not only are its scenery, climate, and biota distinctive, but its way of life is as well. This is a place of flower-filled alpine meadows, shining glaciers, island-studded channels, waterfalls, dark green forests, and clear, cold ocean waters. It is a place of soft rain and brilliant sunsets, of snow stained the color of ripe apricots by the winter sun, of fishermen and poets, and of people with a culture so ancient it predates the coming of white men by millennia. It is a place for those who love bird song, snow, silence, storms, small deep blue lakes, wetness, and wilderness. (It should be noted that similar country extends west along the coastal mountain area around Prince

William Sound and on the Kenai Peninsula and easternmost Kodiak Island.)

Despite its many intimate qualities, the Southeast is put together on a scale that's overwhelming. Consider the uplift of the mountains that rise almost directly from the sea. In places they brush the 20,000-foot level. Snowy peaks of 10,000 feet appear as mere foothills next to giants like Mount Fairweather and Mount Saint Elias. When seen from the sea, such mountain complexes fill up half the sky.

This remarkable upthrust of the earth's crust is currently believed to be related to the massive collision between two major tectonic plates— the Pacific and the North American plates—which occurred and is continuing to occur in this part of the world. In this area, the Pacific plate is presently moving generally northwest, and from Yakutat to the north it is plunging—being subducted—under the continental, or North American, plate. As it does this, it acts like a giant bulldozer, heaping the land up higher and higher. Evidence indicates that in the past the Pacific plate was being subducted in a more northeasterly direction, so that it bulldozed up the great mountains of the Southeast. However, the present tectonic action seems to be dragging the Pacific plate along the continental margins in this area in a series of strike-slip faults, which would account for earthquakes like the one that wracked Lituya Bay in 1958.

Geologists continue to study the Southeastern coastal region for further answers, as many questions remain and new information keeps surfacing. (See Geology, in Part I.) For decades, for example, many geologists were puzzled by the curious disparity between vast chunks of Southeastern rock formations. Earlier theories had explained these disparities in terms of more or less stable and definable landmasses, which might rise and sink but didn't go anywhere. More recent ideas suggest that blocks of Southeastern Alaska have been "rafted" in from distant areas of the Pacific, being swept up and carried along by the moving crustal segments of the planet. One such block has been christened Wrangellia (after the Wrangell Mountains); Wrangellia matches regions in British Columbia and the Queen Charlotte Islands, and the Hell's Canyon region of Oregon and Idaho. Another block, christened Stikinia, has fossils associated with China, Japan, and Indonesia. It is now believed that this area was transported across the oceans and pinned against the North American continent. The evolving science of paleomagnetics, which identifies the direction of the earth's magnetic field that has been locked into certain rocks at times past, helps to confirm these new ideas.

The mountains of the Southeast, in places, contain rocks that date

Southeast Alaska

back to Paleozoic times. It seems likely that the forces of uplift, erosion, and downthrust have created many landscapes here that have been worn away, drowned, or long since lost in time. Today's rugged terrain has been—and is still being—actively uplifted over a span of time much shorter than the age of the older rocks that formed it.

Along with the vigorous and continuing earth movements in the Southeast, the immense powers of water and ice have helped to shape this land. Mighty rivers—the Alsek, Stikine, Taku, and Unuk—drain the coastal and Interior mountains. Gathering and carrying along enormous volumes of water, they have worn the earth into great canyons and valleys and have formed vast deltas and marshlands along the coast. Working with them and contributing to the profile of this unique landscape as much as any single earth force have been the glaciers.

Glaciers

The Southeast's glaciers rise from some of the world's most impressive ice fields, which are cradled among the high ridges and peaks of the coastal mountains. They clothe hundreds of square miles, and, when you fly in a small plane over the shimmering high landscape, you can get some idea of how the North American continent must have looked during the millennia of the great ice ages when snow and ice engulfed everything except the highest peaks and pinnacles and the open sea itself. There may be remnants of these ancient glaciers buried deep beneath Alaska's present ice fields, but the snow and ice you see blanketing the land today are estimated by geologists to be much younger, at most 3,000 years old. Because these ice fields are being constantly renewed and replenished, they constitute a sort of small-scale living ice age and offer a bonanza for scientists studying glacial phenomena.

Glaciers require a particular set of meterological and geographical circumstances for their formation and continuing existence. Interestingly enough, extreme cold is not a prerequisite, and while heavy precipitation is required, it is not sufficient by itself. A delicate climatic balance is needed. It must be just cold enough and just wet enough, the average summer temperature must be just low enough, and there must be just enough average persistence of cloudiness so that over a long period of time more snow and ice will accumulate in an area than will be lost through melting and evaporation (and the calving of glaciers). There must also be, of course, terrain on which snowfields can form and grow, and over which glaciers can flow. The unique landscape and climate of Alaska's Southeast fulfill these special requirements, as do only a few places on this planet. Even a minor climatic change could disrupt the present dramatic glacial conditions.

The Japanese current is primarily responsible for the amount of precipitation that falls in the Southeast. This great stream of warm water surges into the Gulf of Alaska, and, kept in strong motion by the Coriolis force, it heats the cool water and causes warm, wet air to rise. Borne by offshore winds against the immensely high wall of the coastal mountains, the warm, moist air condenses, falling as frequent and often steady rain and becoming heavy snow at about the 5,000-foot level year-round. (In winter, you can watch the snow level inch down the Southeastern mountains, storm by storm—sometimes hour by hour—until it touches the water and all the world is white.) The 1,500-square-mile Juneau Ice Field, which rises to 6,000 feet above Juneau, may receive more than 100 feet (1,200 inches) of snow a year. The long hours of sunlight during the summer months can cause heavy melt, but the high altitude acts as a refrigerant and slows the melting. Added to this, in winter frigid air masses formed in the sunless Arctic region flow across the continent to be stopped by the rim of the high coastal mountains. Pressing against this mountain barrier, the intensely cold and heavy air mounds up into a dome. Ultimately, it must breach the mountain passes and pour through as fierce cold gales called Taku winds. Takus have been known to blow away the anemometers set up to measure their speed—after registering wind speeds of more than 100 miles an hour near Juneau. (At Wrangell, these winds are known as Stikines; at Prince Rupert, as Skeenas.) The Takus race through the mountains and set the snow streaming off the high peaks in glittering white banners, but these frigid winds also send the temperatures plummeting at every level of altitude.

As the snow piles higher and higher in the ice fields, certain phenomena occur below the surface. At a depth of about 200 feet, the immense weight of the overburden brings about structural changes in the buried snow. The snow crystals are compressed into extremely hard ice, which, paradoxically, has the ability to flow like viscous water. As it gathers mass, this plastic glacial ice moves of its own weight, being pulled downward by gravity. It can travel at remarkable speed, sometimes several miles a day. It stops only when meltback literally brings it to an end or, in many places in the Southeast, when it encounters the warmer salt water of the sea.

Glacial ice is formed under such intense pressure that air bubbles are completely squeezed out of it and all cracks are obliterated. The resultant dense ice can admit light but absorbs the reds and yellows of the spectrum, its prisms reflecting only the shades of blue: hence, the marvelous intense blues that you see in crevasses and on the faces of many of Alaska's glaciers, especially when they have just "calved," or dropped large chunks of ice.

A glacier is actually a river of ice, and, like any proper river, as it travels it follows the lines of least resistance in the terrain, bending around areas of tougher rock (though scouring away at them the while), plucking off loose rocks, and wearing away the ground it moves over. In the Southeast, glaciers also gather and transport a great deal of loose dirt and debris from the fractured rocks of this heavily faulted area. This debris gathers along the sides, or lateral moraines, of the glaciers, making black borders. When glaciers flow together and coalesce, as they do frequently in the Southeast, they form a massive river glacier, and the debris from each of them forms a black, ribbonlike stripe. Each stripe originated on and marks a different glacier. On the Malaspina, a vast piedmont glacier, there are multiple stripes that have been curved and formed into intricate and extraordinary designs—a breathtaking sight from the air. You will also have some incredible aerial views if you fly over the Juneau Ice Field on a clear day: thirty-six different glaciers radiate from this great mass of ice and snow.

During earlier ice ages, glaciers were much more extensive than they are today. They covered the Southeast completely, burying virtually all of what is now the Inside Passage under ice and snow. A few places here and there remained ice-free: these were the places of refuge, or refugia, where plants and animals could survive. The sea level was probably some 400 feet lower during these cold eons because so much of the earth's water was locked into ice. During those ice ages, glaciers shaped the unique landscape you see today, including such features as the fjords that incise the mainland (and may, like the Endicott Arm, still have glaciers at their heads) and the cirques and high U-shaped valleys. The long, straight channels in the Inside Passage—for example, Lynn Canal—were also the work of those early glaciers, marking major earthquake faults where the rock was unstable and easily quarried out. The Southeast's myriad islands, too, were carved by ice, being the tops of mountains and nunataks—or islands of resistant rock—that were drowned when the ice melted and the seawaters rose. (You can see nunataks in Glacier Bay today.)

Actually, not many decades ago the Southeastern glaciers were more extensive than they are today. When Capt. George Vancouver visited what is now Glacier Bay in 1793, it was entirely under ice. Mendenhall Glacier, near Juneau, covered much of the forested area below its snout as recently as 1940. (The Mendenhall is the most visited, and the most easily visited, of the glaciers in the Southeast. See Day Hikes, under Juneau.) A recent warming trend in the climate has caused a great many of the Southeast's glaciers to shrink. Despite the fact that they continue to be fed by heavy snowfall and can travel very rapidly, most of them are melting more rapidly than they can grow in their terminal portions. As noted, however, only a very slight change in any of the variables responsible for the formation of glaciers could send one or all of those in the Southeast surging ahead once more—with some interesting results. (Some glaciers are, in fact, presently growing, the Hubbard Glacier above Yakutat, which dammed Russell Fjord in 1986, being a notable recent example.) Imagine the Mendenhall Flats or Glacier Bay once again under ice. It could happen and very well may.

The Forest, the Waters, and the Rain

Because Southeastern Alaska has been formed by such stark and elemental forces, it is pleasantly surprising that it is not entirely a bare and frozen though dramatic land like Antarctica. The lowlands and thousands of islands here are clothed with deep, sweet-smelling forests of spruce, hemlock, and—to the south—cedar. The understory of these dense forests glows with a soft, green light like an underwater scene. (Sometimes it feels like one, too!) Parasols of devil's club (admire but don't get too close to those prickly leaves and stems) and the big, handsome leaves of skunk cabbage fill the shadows, and dwarf dogwood and delicate white saxifrages star the forest floor. Succulent blueberries may reward a hungry hiker in summer but also tempt the resident brown and black bears. Streams lace through the Southeast forests, and the lakes and the wet meadows of muskegs break the dense forest canopy into pleasant openings. In the Southeast the tides are immense, lifting and dropping the channel waters as much as 20 to 25 feet; in many places the tidal water floods the low-lying lakes and streams. These spectacular places of encounter are known as salt chucks. At low tide, you can be sitting next to a silvery cascade of fresh water, but as the tidal waters lift, you may see it drowned before your eyes. (Watch where you sit.)

If you're traveling on the water in a small boat or kayak, you can nearly always find a bay or easy shore for landing in the Southeast. Beaches are sometimes formed of sea-smoothed rock, or they may be cobbled with small, rounded stones and pebbles that are elegantly patterned and make for pleasant walking at low tide. Kelp and other seaweeds festoon the high-tide mark, perfectly outlining the parameter of the last high water. The tidepools hold fascinating sea animals, shelled creatures, brightly colored starfish, sea urchins, and sea anemones.

When flying in a small plane over the Southeast, you'll see swirling patterns of opaque jade and turquoise where silt-laden glacial meltwaters pour into the clear, dark-green channel water. There may also be whole flotillas of small icebergs spewed from the glaciers riding the tides. From the water, you can frequently see seabirds or seals riding the icebergs.

All in all, there are few places on earth that can match the particular beauty of Southeast Alaska. Along with the sheer magnificence of the landscape, there are the changing waters, the lift and sigh of the tides, and always the special quality of the light. On blue days in the summer, the colors—all greens and blues, gold and white—glow with a special intensity. In winter, the late and early sun paints the blank canvas of the snow-covered landscape with orange and rose; the snow shadows are deep blue.

There is also a special magic here on days that are gray. In summer, the air is cool and soft, and the waters shine with a smooth patina like old, well-polished silver. Suddenly the quiet surface of the channel breaks with the rising curve of a whale. A raven cries. Bald eagles spiral overhead and disappear into the low clouds. When the rain comes, it makes music on each leaf and the streams sing louder. Islands loom dark and mysterious in the mist. In winter, snow outlines every bough of every spruce and alder; you can watch a pair of oldsquaw ducks glide past in the dark, clear water, and the glaciers gleam, illuminated from within by a deep blue light.

Because rain and snow are so much a part of the Southeast, it is a good idea to accept the fact that the weather will probably be rainy or snowy or misty for at least part of the time you visit there, whatever the season. May and June, on the average, are the driest and the sunniest months, and the sea, as well, tends to be the calmest during these months. Still, you should always be prepared for wetness, remembering it is responsible for the lush forests, green alpine meadows, and blue-faceted glaciers, as well as for the unique mood of the place. At the same time, the amount of precipitation does vary quite dramatically in different parts of the Southeast. Thus, in places on Baranof Island, rainfall can average over 220 inches a year; in Ketchikan, it is 162 inches; in downtown Juneau, 92. Haines, however, receives an average of only 53 inches and Skagway, just 26.3. Snowfall varies as well: Haines, for example, averages 139.6 inches of snow a year, while Ketchikan catches only 32. Remember the ice field above Juneau, with 100 feet of snow falling in a single winter!

Average Temperature Range

1	2	3	4	1	2	3	4	1	2	3	4	1	2	3	4	1	2	3	4
	May				June				July				Aug				Sept		

1. Sitka   3. Ketchikan
2. Juneau   4. Skagway

22. Traveling by Ferry

Southeast Alaska does not have the usual highway system. While each of its fourteen communities has its own larger or smaller network of streets and service roads, there are no connecting roads. (Juneau has the most extensive system of paved highways—about 54 miles in all, and only 8 miles of it are four-lane, from the airport to downtown.) Therefore, you travel by air or by water, and the grand waterway you travel is the Inside Passage. You can start your voyage up the Inside Passage at Bellingham, Washington, or at Prince Rupert, British Columbia, and go for more than 1,000 miles among forested islands, alongside breathtaking cliffs that tower as high as 4,000 feet above you, and past picturesque towns on the shore. (As of 1998, you can also travel from Bellingham to Seward, on the Kenai Peninsula, via the Inside Passage and Prince William Sound.)

If you have a small seaworthy boat of your own, the lore of the Inside Passage has probably already reached you. Everyone I know who has traveled it in such a craft has had memorable and beautiful experiences. There have also been legendary canoe trips from Seattle up the passage: one—a honeymoon journey—was taken by friends of mine in a hand-made wooden canoe, but such a trip is recommended only for intrepid, enthusiastic, and experienced canoers. Kayaking in various parts of the Inside Passage is superb, but more of this later.

If your time is short and you enjoy organized tours, you have a good choice of well-run tour ships, many offering reasonably priced trips through the Inside Passage. They sail from United States West Coast ports as well as from British Columbia. These tours usually run from one to two weeks with stop-offs at most of the principal towns in the Southeast.

If you can take your time, however, and want a less programmed, more active Southeast adventure—and if you really want to see the country—the way to travel the Inside Passage is by public transportation, that is, to voyage up the "Alaska Marine Highway" on a state-operated ferry liner. Alaska's ferries are, generally, the most comfortable (and always the most fun) of any I have ever traveled on. The large ships, the MV *Co-*

lumbia and the new *Kennicott,* service the Southeast from Bellingham, Washington; the *Malaspina* and the *Matanuska* sail from Prince Rupert, British Columbia. (Alaska's ferry liners are named after glaciers.) In summer, from May through October, these ships travel steadily, stopping at Ketchikan, Wrangell, Petersburg, Sitka, Haines, Skagway, and, of course, Juneau. (Smaller ferries, the *Aurora,* the *Bartlett,* the *LeConte,* and the *Tustemena,* generally make local runs, serving the smaller communities such as Kake on Prince of Wales Island, Angoon, Hoonah, Metlakatla, Hollis, Tenakee, and Pelican—although not necessarily daily.) Incidentally, it costs about twice as much to travel from Bellingham to Skagway as from Prince Rupert, British Columbia, to the same destination. (The *Kennicott*'s route in Prince William Sound and the opportunities it opens up are described in the section on Prince William Sound.)

There are several wonderful things about Alaska's ferries. First of all, you can take aboard for a reasonable charge anything that you can carry. This means that you can tote not only a large backpack but your bicycle, canoe, or kayak. (You will keep your backpack with you aboard, but you can park your bike, canoe, or kayak in a special section.) Second, the ferry liners are not only spacious but also generally comfortable. The berths on the larger ships (the smaller boats have no sleeping cabins) are clean and comfortable, although you may have to share a double or a four-berth accommodation and you must make reservations well ahead of time. There are also banks of lounge chairs where you can stretch out and sleep inside, although these get taken early. Most of the ferries have a solarium or sundeck, where there are deck chairs and a radiant heating system that keeps you cosy even in frigid weather, and this is where I prefer to sleep. (My last ferry trip from Juneau to Haines took place during a lovely December snowfall, and I was almost too toasty in my down sleeping bag sleeping topside beneath the overhead heater.) Unfortunately, the solaria are apt to be very crowded in the summer; if you want a deck chair, you have to board early and mark one for your own. Although I have never been wet in a solarium, I am told that under some conditions they can be "wet above and marshy on the floor."

On the larger ferries, there are two restaurants—one a snack bar, the other a dining room—and there is a bar. On the smaller boats, there's one cafe and a small bar. However, you can bring along your own food as long as you don't mind eating cold.

If you like to bike, the ferries offer you an ideal vehicle to travel to numerous interesting destinations in the Southeast. If you are after a more extensive bike trip in Alaska, the ferry is a great way to start it. You can ferry your bike to Haines and, in summer months, transport it by bus until you're home free on the Alaska section of the Alaska Highway. Or you can take your bike off at Skagway and carry it on the Gray Line or

other motor coach (in the summer) to Whitehorse and from there—again
by bus—back into Alaska. The Alaska Highway is not highly recommended for biking during the summer when it is heavily traveled; there
are many blind curves, and if gravel is sprayed onto you by passing vehicles, it's terrifying. (Gravel on less-traveled Canadian and Alaskan side
roads is not such a problem.)

If you can arrange your time in Alaska out of tourist season, you'll
find ferry-liner travel especially attractive. During peak tourist months—
from mid-June through August—the ships are apt to be full, if not overcrowded, although you will probably have no difficulty getting on with
a car (except for the Southeast Alaska Fair Days in Haines in mid-
August). But in May, September, or early June (before school is out),
you'll find fewer passengers on board. Further, if you like crisp weather
and don't mind some snow, you may be able to take a ferry trip from November through April at a slightly reduced fare, and you are likely to
have the ship more to yourself, although the number of people, even in
December, may surprise you. (If you should be bringing a car along during these months, you will only pay for your vehicle: auto passengers ride
free.) The schedule does slow down during the off-season, with the big
ferries making the long round-trip only once a week. (Anyone sixty-five
or older can travel on the smaller ferries inside Alaska at nicely reduced
rates from October 31 through April 30.)

It is also worth noting that the ferries traveling south are more apt to
be less crowded than those heading north during the summer. If it fits
into your summer plans, you might want to finish—rather than start—
your Alaskan adventure on the ferry.

All of the large, and some of the small, ferries on the Alaskan Marine
Highway in the Southeast, incidentally, have USDA Forest Service ranger-
interpreters aboard in summer. Forest Service movies and slide shows are
routinely shown in the main lounge. Most of the Forest Service people are
well informed, friendly, and helpful. They can give you tips about Forest
Service facilities that you'll find on shore and possibly about road conditions for biking and so on. Ask them for anything you need to know.

Using the Ferry for Your Small-Boat Trip

Almost any community on the regular Southeast ferry run will offer interesting opportunities not only to hikers (see following sections) and
bikers but also to kayakers and canoers. These communities can also be
ideal "roadheads" and "pickup points," using the ferry as your "shuttle
vehicle." For example, you can put your canoe or kayak in the waters in
the Inside Passage at Ketchikan and take it out at Wrangell. Sightsee and
stock up at Wrangell and continue on to Petersburg, and so on, re-
boarding the ferry when you wish. Or you can take the main-run ferry,

say, to Sitka, and then plan a kayak trip to take out at Tenakee—or, if you have more time, at Hoonah—on a day when a smaller ferry calls at one of these little communities. (Either of these suggested trips will be a fine one if you're an experienced kayaker; you will have to cope with a stretch of open ocean on the way.) Or you might take the regular ferry to Juneau, then take the small ferry to Angoon and canoe or kayak across Admiralty to Mole Harbor and have a charter air-taxi pickup to get back to Juneau. (This is another lovely trip that does not call for super expertise, but it does require a strong back for some of the portages.) If you decide to use the ferry this way, it's particularly important that you obtain the schedule, since not all runs serve Sitka, and the service to many of the small villages is less frequent. When planning trips of this kind, you should also write the USDA Forest Service for suggestions on routes and camping spots along the way.

For further information about Alaska's ferries, for the latest fares and schedules, or to make reservations, write *Alaska Marine Highway System,* Box 25535, Juneau, AK 99802-5535; phone 1-800-642-0066 from outside; in Alaska, phone 907-465-3941 or fax 907-277-4829.

When you travel Alaska's ferry liners, keep in mind that, as with all things in Alaska, the time frame is elastic. You may have to wait an hour or so, or possibly longer, for your boat. Sometimes the weather holds things up—for example, fog in the Wrangell Narrows can be a cause of delay. Or a ferry may get flagged along the way for one reason or another, or it may have to wait for a tide. Mechanical difficulties can also slow operations: one year the *Malaspina* broke down so often that some wag suggested it be renamed the *Lemon*—for the Lemon Glacier, of course! However you travel in Alaska, don't bind yourself to a rigid time schedule if you want to enjoy yourself and avoid frustration.

23. Intertidal Life

The intertidal life in the Southeast is a fascinating part of the scene and, happily, it can be observed very easily in many places. The great tides in Bartlett Cove, the Gastineau Channel, and around Admiralty Island, for instance, draw the waters up and down the shore like giant curtains opening and closing on a marvelous vertical stage. If you're camping on the shore of one of these areas—well above high tide, of course—you will have the chance, twice a day, to view the complex cast of strange and beautiful characters that live and die in the intertidal world.

It is a demanding, often dangerous world. Intertidal animals and plants must be adapted to harsh and constantly changing conditions, to strong tidal action, racing currents, and heavy waves. They must be able to survive in the air as well as in the cold, salty water, for at least short periods of time. They must be tolerant of hot sun, of winds, of storms of rain, of snow, and, in many places, of the icy meltwater of glaciers. Some members of the intertidal community are sessile, unable to move once they've chosen a spot to live, and so are forever subject to the whims of the elements. Those that are mobile have certain advantages, but they are also more easily picked up by large predators or swept away in heavy surf. Indeed, life in the intertidal world is never safe or easy.

But, despite its drawbacks, the intertidal world offers intertidal creatures many advantages. Like any "edge" environment, it is biologically rich, with the tides constantly carrying food into the area. Furthermore, the rocks provide protected homes in their cracks and crannies. Muds and sands are good places for burrowers to live, too. And it is a tight-knit community: in curious and interesting ways, the animals and plants of the intertidal zone depend upon one another for their mutual survival. You will find that almost every available bit of space in this forever changing and difficult environment teems with life.

To help you enjoy the living pageant that you can see in the intertidal zones of the Southeast, there follows a brief discussion of some of the animals and plants that are most readily observed and identified. You will find the shores of the Southeast rocky in places, sandy in others, and muddy (very) in still others when the tide ebbs. Perhaps your most rewarding observation points will be in the tidepools of the rocky shores, but you will also want to keep your eye out for signs of interesting life in the sand and mudflats.

When you enter the intertidal world, remember to step carefully; many of the animals are easily destroyed by a clumsy or careless footfall. Do not go in a crowd, which increases the danger, and do not disturb the animals beyond turning over a rock or two (replace them where you find them, of course). Please, never take an animal out of its home. Most of the living creatures can be touched gently, but again, don't overdo it. Keep in mind that even though you're much bigger—indeed, you're top predator here—you're still a visitor. And, of course, keep a sharp eye on your tide table: it will advise you not only of optimum times to view the intertidal scene but of when the tide is going to change and when it's time for you to leave. You don't want to be like the Tlingit boy who was clutched by a giant clam at low tide and drowned in the onrush of incoming waters.

You will find that different species of intertidal animals live generally in different intertidal zones, from the high-tide line to the lowest areas exposed by the tides. In part, the location of a particular species depends upon its ability—or lack of it—to survive out of water over periods of time. Thus, the barnacle can live out of water for as much as three years, as long as it gets a chance to feed underwater once a month. In part, however, the zonation of the animals depends upon predation. The barnacle, it turns out, can also live underwater for extended periods of time, but it is limited to the upper intertidal zones by predators that lurk in the lower waters. To help in identifying the intertidal animals and plants, the following information will give you clues as to where in the tidal zones you should look for the different species.

The *high intertidal zone* is heavily populated but has only a few species living in it, for the animals here must tolerate a great deal of exposure. On the other hand, the animals are the easiest to see, being on view for the longest periods of time.

You'll find the coastal rocks of the Southeast embroidered with intricate patterns of barnacles (*Balanus* spp.). These are among the toughest and most interesting of the intertidal creatures. As noted, barnacles can succeed at any intertidal zone, but the lower you go, the fewer you will see because of the dogwinkles, ribbon worms, and the crafty starfish that inhabit the lower zones and relish barnacles for dinner. As noted also, barnacles can survive out of water for years provided they get submerged once a month.

Barnacles are hermaphroditic—that is, each one is both male and female, and they may mate with their neighbors or with themselves. Their larvae float around for three months or so in the water before, in their final, shrimplike stage, they cement themselves headfirst to a surface of their choice. The adult barnacle feeds by sweeping the water with its legs (cirri) for food, and fans out its wastes. Look for barnacles feeding in tidepools or at the edge of the water: they always remind me of multi-legged bicyclists, pedalling away furiously.

There are several species of barnacles that thrive in the Southeast, some being so highly specialized that they spend their lives on one particular kind of whale—and sometimes on one particular part of one particular kind of whale. One local fellow, for example, lives only on the lower lip of the humpback whale. Barnacles can attain considerable size, and another local species has been measured at 8 inches in diameter, one of the largest known barnacles in the world. Barnacles frequently crowd together—as many as ninety thousand in a square meter—and when every last bit of space is taken they may piggyback onto one another and build up a thin "pencil form."

Along with the barnacles, you'll find many limpets (*Notoacmaea* spp.) in the upper tidal reaches. These are the little snails that wear the familiar "Chinese hat" shells. They keep themselves wet by trapping water between their shells and their bodies, and they have a certain advantage over barnacles because they can move about. Some are so territorial, however, that they return to the exact same spot every night and refuse to budge when challenged; the creatures that do this wear depressions in the rocks, which give protection from the pounding waves. Limpets can also hang on for dear life: it can take as much as 70 pounds of force to pry a dime-size limpet off its rock. These little animals are equipped with a kind of rough, serrated tongue, called a radula, so that they can scrape diatoms and algae off the rocks for dinner.

Another member of the high intertidal community is the periwinkle (*Littorina sitkana*), a true marine snail, having a gill instead of the "lung" possessed by terrestrial and many freshwater snails. It lives on and under the rocks and in algae, and, despite its gill, it drowns if it stays underwater too long. It can, in fact, live quite successfully out of salt water for as many as forty-five days. Periwinkles also have radulas to help clean off the rocks.

The tubular green algae that you will notice on the higher reaches of the shore are *Enteromorpha intestinalis* (also known as sea hair or sea confetti), which do very well in the Southeast. Green algae, by the way, differ from the red and brown in lacking the extra photosynthetic pigments found in those other algae. The greens utilize chlorophyll alone to grab the sunlight.

Hopping about in the algae, much of which drifts up from the lower tidal zones to festoon the upper beaches, are the minuscule scavengers the side swimmers (amphipods), which do a cleanup job on the plants as they decay.

As the tide ebbs lower, you'll find another spectrum of sea life coming into view: the *middle intertidal zone*. The small dogwinkle or dog whelk (*Thais* spp.) is a prosperous member of this community, and it does particularly well around barnacles and mussels, which are its favorite foods. The dogwinkle is able to use its radula as a drill; it makes a neat little round hole in the shell of its victim, pours in some digestive enzymes, and then sucks out the ready meal through its proboscis. Notice the round holes you'll find frequently in empty mussel shells. If you turn over a rock in this middle zone, you may find a tan or white cigar-shaped capsule containing hundreds of dogwinkle eggs. The dogwinkle adult is not above eating these eggs, either, and the first whelk that hatches in an egg capsule will almost certainly finish off the rest of its potential siblings.

The rocks of the middle and lower intertidal zones are often thickly encrusted with the beautiful blue-black shells of mussels *(Mytilus edulis)*. Being sessile, mussels are ready prey for the dogwinkle and other wily predators such as the ribbon worm. However, mussels come in large numbers and, along with providing meals for other creatures, they seem to proliferate quite successfully themselves. (This may be because a female mussel often produces several million eggs.)

Mussels often congregate in such immense numbers that they overgrow their neighboring friends, the barnacles, which, being unable to eat, then perish.

Mussels attach themselves to rocks with a kind of thread, and their crowded communities, which tend to hold water when the tide ebbs, provide shelter and protection for many other, miniscule sea creatures. Like the barnacles, mussels are capable of surviving very well in lower tidal zones, but the predatory worms and especially the starfish of the lower reaches keep them in their place in the middle intertidal region.

Mussels are filter feeders and use their gills to strain plankton—the microscopic animals and plants that float around unseen—from the clear Southeast waters. These little shellfish are, in turn, succulent food for people, except during the summer months when they retain (sometimes for as long as a month) the poisonous dinoflagellate *Gonyaulax:* a single heavily contaminated mussel can kill a person.

Among the most interesting animals of the middle intertidal zone are the various worms. The ribbon worms, which may be as long as 18 inches and can extend their proboscises another 9 inches, come in dark green *(Emplectonema)*, purple *(Paranemertes)*, and white *(Amphiporus)*. These worms are equipped with poison glands and stinging barbs, which they use something like poisoned arrows. They can paralyze an open, feeding barnacle in a flash and even knock out the powerful-jawed mussel worm. When picked up, a ribbon worm may break into pieces, each one of which is capable of regenerating into another worm.

The mussel worm *(Nereis* spp.) is a very long, segmented animal—as long as 3 feet—which normally has a pair of little paddles on each segment to facilitate its crawling around. Once a year, however, the rear segments of the worm swell enormously with either eggs or sperm, the paddles enlarge so that the animal becomes a swimmer instead of a crawler, and the female turns a brilliant red. Then both males and females surge toward the surface to release their eggs and sperm, which unite to start new mussel worms. Then, spent, the adults become food for birds and fish. As the name suggests, the mussel worm is very fond of eating mussels, and uses its strong jaw to dispatch its prey. This worm has been known to bite a person who molested it, as well.

At least three kinds of chitons live in the middle and lower intertidal zones. These are curious animals that are oval, quite flat, and armored with eight leathery plates down their backs. *Katharina tunicata* is the large dark one, which grows to be several inches in length. *Mopalia ciliata* is the hairy chiton, having a fringe of hairlike growths. *Tonicella lineata* is small and colorful: look for it in channels where there are strong currents.

The brown alga commonly called rockweed (*Fucus* spp.) is the one you'll find in great abundance in the middle intertidal zone. It is luminescent golden brown and can be seen attached to the rocks with a "holdfast" that looks like a root, but isn't, since it is a mechanical device only, providing no nourishment to the plant. The tips of the rockweed branches appear to have grapes embedded in them, but these are gas-filled sacs that act as flotation chambers to hold the plants erect when underwater, and thus closer to the sun.

The *low intertidal zone* is populated by all sorts of fascinating creatures. Some of them may tantalize you with only a glimpse of themselves, or they may stay hidden from you completely. But you can look for and find many others, and almost always you can find clues to the hidden animals. One of the most attractive is the feather duster worm, one of the polychaetes. This animal builds itself a parchmentlike tube to live in and then fans out its beautifully colored tentacles to filter food from the water. (Some of these worms look like carnations dropped on the sea bottom.) Let even your shadow touch the feather duster and it will disappear into its tube before your startled eyes. Another polychaete, the *spirobid,* uncurls its tiny white calcareous tubes to form minute spirals on the undersides of rocks: you can look for the tufts of scarlet tentacles, which make minuscule polka dots.

In the sands and muds exposed at low tide, there are whole colonies of creatures that you may not see. These are the burrowers, like the worms and the clams. (There are cockles and littlenecks among those that send up silvery geysers of water here.) Many of these underground dwellers have permanent guests residing with them: tiny crabs live inside the various tubes and shells and clean up the wastes of their hosts. You might see a live Dungeness crab *(Cancer magister),* but chances are that you will see, instead, bits and pieces of its molted shells: adults molt once a year, but the youngsters molt a half a dozen times. If you come across what looks like a large fat slug at a very low tide, it will likely be a moon snail *(Polinices lewisii).* This odd creature completely envelops its shell with its body when it is feeding.

You should keep an eye out for sponges on the low intertidal rocks. The bread crumb sponge (*Halichandria* spp.) is fairly common, looks yellowish to greenish, crumbles easily and—so it's said—smells like garlic. Sponges are very primitive animals, being no more than a group of different specialized cells. They feed by pumping water through one set of cells, digesting the indrawn organic matter with another set, and ejecting the wastewater out of still another. Simple indeed, but very efficient.

Look also for the sea anemone *(Tealia),* typically red and tan and with large translucent tentacles. It sits and waits for food to be carried over it by the currents, and relishes such treats as snails and mussels and sea urchins when they happen to float its way. Along with having carnivorous tastes, it is one of the most beautiful of the low intertidal zone animals.

Sea urchins themselves may be found in areas exposed by minus (lower than average) tides, usually in prodigious numbers. Relatives of the starfish, these thorny creatures *(Strongylocentrotus droebachiensis)* are vegetarians and use their spikes to spear algae. They play an important role in determining which algae grow where.

You will almost certainly find a big varicolored starfish on any visit to the intertidal region in the Southeast. Although the mottled sea star, *Evasterias troschelii,* is a resident of the low intertidal zone, it moves around freely. This handsome animal, which usually has five rays and may be brightly colored, is quite unlike its vegetarian cousin the sea urchin. It is one of the most influential predators in these intertidal waters. The starfish is especially fond of mussels and barnacles and, to eat them, it everts its stomach through its mouth (which is on its underside), then projects its stomach into the open shell of its victim and digests its dinner outside of its body. On their topsides, starfish have tiny little pinchers, which they use to clean themselves, to signal aggression toward other starfish, and to prevent predation on themselves, as well. You can feel these pinching organs if you place the back of your hand on their upper surfaces.

There are several large brown algae, or kelps, found in the low intertidal zone in the Southeast—*Alaria* spp., *Laminaria* spp. (known, respectively, as split and sugar kelp), and *Costeria costata* (known as seersucker kelp) among them. When you find a large bed of large kelp, look for the bulb kelp *(Nereocystis luetkeana),* which has a big leathery, balloonlike bladder and a very long stipe like a big, smooth rope. This is one of the fastest-growing plants on earth, sometimes increasing its length by a foot a day. You may also find the delicate sea lettuce (*Ulva* spp. or *Monostroma* spp.) on tidal flats, its vivid green near-transparent fronds glowing like neon.

Before you leave the low intertidal region, look for fish in the tide-pools. They may hide under rocks or bury themselves partially in the sand. The tiny brown fish with a huge head, wide mouth, and long tail is the sculpin: it is usually less than 2 inches overall. The eel-like fish that may throw itself into a tantrum when disturbed is one of the gunnels or pricklebacks commonly called "blenney eels."

If you don't want to get your feet wet, you can also look for intertidal life on the floats and docks that you'll see around the more civilized areas of the Southeast. The underwater surfaces are often festooned with algae or with the quite spectacular hydroids, which spread out their translucent tentacles like creamy plumes. Hydroids actually lead fairly complicated lives, going through two distinct stages of existence: in one, they are the asexual, sessile polyps you will see; in the other, they are free-swimming jellyfish-like creatures, which are male or female.

Once you have admired the complex intertidal communities in the Southeast, you may come to better understand the extraordinary way the plants and animals interact among themselves. Predator, prey, protector, guest, producer, scavenger, or consumer, each has its own special role to play in maintaining this unique and dynamic environment.

24. Traveling in Southeastern Waters

The great tides of Southeast Alaska are a part of the magic of the place. To experience their lift and fall in a small boat and to be carried by them is a special and elemental experience. Understanding these tides and some of their effects can add to the dimensions of that experience and also help you to enjoy it safely.

Tides are caused by the gravitational pull of the celestial bodies closest to the earth, our sun and moon. Tides vary according to the distance of these bodies from our planet, so that when the moon, for instance, is closest to us—at perigee—the tides will be subjected to greater pull and will be higher; when the moon is farthest away—at apogee—its effects are less forceful. Tides are also affected by the size of the body of water in which they occur, by the depth of the water, and by the configuration of the land that surrounds the water. Thus, in midocean, where the waters are vast and very deep and there is no immediately constraining landmass, the tides are little noticed. Along the shores, however, the tides make themselves felt to one degree or another, and they can vary markedly within a fairly narrow range. In Alaska, the tides reach extremes: some of the greatest recorded tides on earth occur in the Cook Inlet (36 feet), and some of the weakest (less than 1 foot) occur along the Arctic Ocean. In northern Alaska, the tides occur only once a day; in the Southeast, they rise and fall twice a day (on a twenty-five-hour cycle). They can exceed 25 feet in range in narrow channels distant from the sea.

Such tides require your respect and a strict observance of their rhythm. Even a 1-foot tide can wash away gear left too close to the tide line: you will have to think in terms of much higher tides in the Southeast. When you camp, or even when you stop for a brief exploratory wander along the shore, keep in mind the tidal schedule. (You can get a tide book at any sporting goods store in the Southeast and in other stores as well. It is among the most-read publications in the region.) Obviously, you should make your camp well above the tide line; you should tie your boat securely; and be sure that all of your gear is stowed out of danger. (Note: Grasses fringe many Southeast beaches, making the territory look safely above salt water—but it isn't. Tidal waters frequently invade this part of the shore. It's best to park your boat and gear among trees whenever possible.) You will also want to take the tides into account when planning the put-in as well as the take-out of your boat. There's no point in hauling your craft up and down the beach if the tide can do it for you.

Apart from their effects on the shorelines, the Southeast tides have a powerful effect on the speed, volume, and character of the water. A great deal of the ocean is pulled back and forth irresistibly through some very narrow channels in this area, and the resulting currents can build up to what my friend Jack Calvin of Sitka described as "furious torrents." That is why you may come across a number of boats of various shapes and sizes waiting just short of certain narrows. If you do, by all means wait with them for slack water or a favorable current. As Calvin put it: "Swift-water narrows must be traversed 'by the Book,' and the book is not the tide tables; it is the *Current Tables of the West Coast of North and South America* (of the current year), published by the National Oceanic and Atmospheric Administration (NOAA). I believe that *Current Tables* should head the equipment list of anyone traveling by boat in the Southeast."

Along with paying attention to and enjoying the tides and currents in

Icebergs, Tracy Arm. Source: USDA Forest Service.

Southeastern waters, there are a few other things to be aware of. At least part of the time, you will probably be traveling through glacial waters, and they are really cold, particularly so in fjords and inlets where the terrain tends to contain the water that is pouring from ice. In such places the water temperature ranges between 34 and 42 degrees Fahrenheit. Dress to keep yourself snug in your small boat and try to keep your boat upright. These are waters you don't want to spend any time in.

Ice can be gorgeous, whether in glacial or iceberg form, but it is also unpredictable. Do not get too close to a tidewater glacier; the National Park Service advises that a half mile from the glacier's face is a safe distance to observe. A tidal glacier can "calve"—cast off a huge building-size chunk or chunks of ice from its snout—most unexpectedly, particularly at low tide when its lower ice is exposed and melts more readily. Tons of ice smashing suddenly into inlet waters that have no place to go can cause waves that can easily swamp your boat. (Waves 30 feet high have been recorded under these circumstances.)

Along with the tidal range, keep the above in mind when you stop or camp along the shores of an inlet. Your gear can be drenched or washed away if it is left too close to the waterline and a nearby glacier suddenly decides to calve. Your kayak, too, is vulnerable; be sure it is secured. In other words, always keep a safe distance from the terminal faces of glaciers, on land as well as in the water; don't linger too close to the water's edge with unstashed gear; and make your camp well above high-water level.

Icebergs pose other, equally interesting, problems. While little boats can make their way through smaller pieces of ice safely, larger bergs can be hazards and should be avoided if possible. Don't leap onto one to get your picture taken! They are unstable and can tip over without warning, taking you with them. They can also disintegrate with extraordinary suddenness. Keep an eye out, as well, for icebergs just below the surface of the water. Sometimes they're so heavy with glacier silt that they travel around slightly submerged and out of obvious sight.

Once in the water, ice moves almost continuously. Tidal action carries it back and forth. A good, stiff wind can push an iceberg around even as it can a small boat. Sometimes, ice floes will jam up to block your passage. Since you don't want to be inside an inlet when such a thing happens, pay particular attention to your tide schedule and wind direction when you're venturing around.

Winds and weather in general are as unpredictable as the ice in Southeastern waters. Mornings can start out with the water as smooth as a well-waxed table, but around eleven o'clock or noon, the winds can rise, and the going can get much less comfortable. (Traveling early in the morning is good technique, and early morning is a beautiful time to experience the water world of the Southeast.) Sudden squalls can also occur on blue days when the water is calm and there is absolutely nothing to give you a warning. A squall can be particularly dangerous if you're close to a glacier and the wind slams you into it—another reason to keep your distance from the tidewater glaciers.

Keep in mind that the climate in the Southeast is maritime and apt to be damp. This, too, is part of the magic of the place. You may travel through rain and fog with near-zero visibility (and a wonderful sense of mystery) for hours at a time—and then the weather can clear with total unexpectedness, and the beauty of the day will almost stun you. By the same token, on a crystal-blue day, a sudden storm can roar in from the Gulf of Alaska. (High drama!) You should be prepared for anything. (See Equipment, in Part I.)

Although seals can be the most enchanting of animals as they watch you with their round black eyes and their sleek wet heads dipping into and out of the water, try to keep your distance from them. When they need to make a quick getaway from a predator, they have been known to clamber aboard a kayak as though it were an iceberg or a tiny island. Take care, as well, when approaching or traveling among whales or sea lions; any large mammal can inadvertently upset a small boat. (Be sure to keep your eyes out for sea otters—these enchanting animals are returning to some Southeastern waters.)

Numerous large cruise ships sail the Inside Passage during the tourist season. They have—and take—the right of way, and you surely don't want to argue with them. In narrow stretches of water, they usually travel down the middle, so you can chart your course accordingly.

As always in Alaska, don't try to keep a tight schedule. Be prepared to wait out bad weather, take time to repair a paddle or whatever, or especially to linger in a place you find particularly lovely. Allow for at least a day or three extra when you plan a small-boating trip, and take along enough extra food to let yourself enjoy it. An alternative, of course, is to use the fish and shellfish of this richly endowed region of Alaska for at least part of your subsistence. Bottom fish are plentiful, and you can jig for them from your boat. In season, salmon practically leap onto your hook. Abalone, sea snails, limpets, and crabs are all delicious and easily gathered. Clams and mussels should be taken only during safe months; check with the National Park Service or the Forest Service to be sure that there are no red tides before you risk a feast on these filter feeders.

What kind of small boat will serve you best in the Southeast? If possible, use one that you can carry on and off the ferry. That way you can go least expensively, and you will have the greatest mobility. This means, of course, that you will choose a lightweight canoe, a kayak, or a rubber raft. The National Park Service recommends a touring kayak with a spray cover or a closed-deck canoe. A raft that will take oars is also a good choice.

The Forest Service can steer you to locations of boat facilities and public recreation sites in the Tongass and Chugach Forests. Write: *Forest Service Information Center,* 101 Egan Drive, Juneau, AK 99801; phone 907-586-8751; fax 907-586-7928.

25. Hiking and Backpacking

Although caveats apply to many of the trails in the Southeast, they should not discourage strong hikers and backpackers from trekking in this area. You should be prepared for some of the realities and eventualities you can encounter if you decide to explore in the Southeast on foot. It takes strength, skill, and good sense to get around in this country. The rewards, however, can be great. The forests are lovely to walk through; the meadows are full of wildflowers; the muskegs are very special places; and the views from high places are breathtaking. Where else would you have the chance to so readily explore among major and gorgeous glaciers, look for mountain goats, perhaps see a wolf or brown bear? And where else can you hike (or ski) from a downtown area into superb wilderness in a matter of minutes?

If you do decide to go it on foot, start with the fact that the number of maintained trails in the Southeast is limited, which means that so are your opportunities for a relatively easy backpack. You will be traveling generally over wet and fragile terrain that is not suited to the building, or the maintenance, of trails. Trails erode easily, quickly turning into stretches of soggy and slippery mud. Not infrequently they develop potholes that are potential ankle breakers. During heavy rainstorms, trails are more like waterways than passages over land.

The USDA Forest Service, which administers most of the land through which you will hike in the Southeast, is confronted with the choice of boardwalking trails through continuously wet areas (thus detracting from the wilderness experience), damaging the land by building a regular trail, or just not building a trail at all (in the past, this has too often been the choice). The Forest Service is further confronted with the fact that maintenance must be constant to be effective, and this is costly. One major problem of maintenance is the rapid regrowth of underbrush in this lush country. Trails can choke up in a matter of weeks, it seems, particularly if they are not heavily used, and some are not. There is also frequent windfall; in fact, you'll find whole blocks of forest that have been leveled by what are locally known as williwaws—sudden, localized, brutal windstorms.

Animals can also add to the difficulties of trail maintenance. Along with hiking in different places on Admiralty Island, I have taken two of the better known cross-island routes. The first is a canoe trip that involves portages between several lakes across trails where one slips and slides through mud and climbs in and out of potholes. (Despite this, I recommend this trip most highly.) The second is a foot trail that travels less than 2 miles from the east side of the island to Hawk Inlet on the west. The last time I took this route we found that beavers had dammed up a creek and flooded out a sizable section of the trail, which wasn't in the greatest shape to begin with. The water was deep enough for a small boat, so we had to hike around the beaver pond through heavy brush and tangles of fallen trees, all of which slowed us down considerably.

Some of the better trails are old logging roads, routes of old tramways, or abandoned mining roads. Along mining roads, you may be tempted to wander off and explore the ghostly weather-beaten buildings that may still be standing in places. Keep in mind that they can be unsafe, and, just as dangerously, they can obscure the location of mine shafts located around them. Watch your step, literally as well as figuratively, in such places. Preferably, stay on the trail.

In the lowlands, you'll be hiking primarily through forests (or cutover land) and muskegs. Note that there is considerable sameness to the forest. The Southeast forest species are, in fact, limited, although each one thrives in this habitat. (You will find gorgeous skunk cabbage, for instance, much larger and lusher looking than that of the northwestern Lower Forty-Eight states.) It is not easy to establish good landmarks even along the trail through many forests; once off the trail, it can be extremely difficult to get back on. Stay on the trail unless you are in the company of an Alaskan who knows the terrain through which you are traveling. Bushwhacking is also difficult and not recommended, even if you carry a machete. Not only is the heavy growth a formidable barrier to progress on foot, but willow and alder stands are places where bears like to relax and snooze.

Muskegs—or peat and sphagnum bogs—are quite extensive throughout the Southeast and are especially interesting parts of the terrain. They are prime wildlife habitat for many animals and are used by several species of birds for nesting and feeding grounds. They are also fragile and easily damaged, and they can be difficult to travel through, since they are wet and sloppy, possibly leading to drenched boots, socks, and feet. (They can also, in places, have areas of quicksand.) For all these reasons, watch where you step. It may be possible to find your way on the higher ground in and around muskegs, or, if there is a boardwalk, stay on it.

Beach walking in the Southeast can be a particular pleasure. There are tidal meadows and glacial forelands as well that may offer good wildlife viewing. But, watch the tides!

While the alpine country in the Southeast may be open and a delight to travel through, it is also quite often extremely steep. The grass can be unbelievably slippery, and many of the drop-offs are literally deadly. People have lost their lives when they have lost their footing, or their balance, and have fallen nonstop down one of these precipitous slopes. A good friend of mine, and an excellent mountaineer, was killed on Mount Juneau when he tried to help another hiker across a slippery exposed spot. The other hiker made it safely, but my friend's boots did not hold on the grass, and he plummeted to his death. These two people were off the trail, traveling cross-country, and so are many of the people who get into trouble on steep grades in the Southeast. If there is a trail, stay on it. If you reach a spot that makes you uneasy, turn back. If there is no trail, you're better off in the company of an experienced Alaskan who knows that part of the country, or else you should have a very clear idea (from your Alaskan friend or from Forest Service or National Park Service people) about what you're getting into.

Rock slides and avalanches are also dangers in alpine country. Move quickly and carefully across the obvious paths of rock slides if you must traverse them at all. If you are cross-country skiing during the winter or in spring, watch out for areas of snow avalanches. Even in summer, you will find patches of snow in many places at higher elevations: these may not pose avalanche problems, but they may be extremely slippery, and you will find that an ice ax is useful.

Even if you plan a day hike only, be prepared for the contingency of staying overnight. Essentials in your backpack include: waterproof matches, topo map, flashlight, first aid equipment, compass, bug juice, extra food, knife, enough warm clothing, rain gear.

If you are a seasoned hiker in good shape and want the adventure of backpacking in the Southeast, it is a good idea to write the appropriate state or federal agency before you plan your trip. If you have not visited the Southeast before, do not plan on a cross-country trip. Even if you're a dyed-in-the-wool loner, don't backpack alone; it's a lot easier to have one or more friends help carry the weight, and it's immeasurably safer.

Once your plans are made and you arrive on the scene, check with the local agency people again to get last-minute information and advice on your proposed itinerary. If this all seems too much trouble, why not take a hiking or backpacking expedition with an organized group? This way, on your first Southeastern outing, you'll save yourself a lot of headaches as you learn the ropes and prepare yourself for future adventuring on your own. You can start with *Alaska Discovery,* 5449 Shaune Drive, #4, Juneau, AK 99801; phone 907-780-6226 or 1-800-586-1911; fax 907-780-4220 (kayak rental as well as guided trips). Or try the *Forest Service Information Center,* 101 Egan Drive, Juneau, AK 99801; phone 907-586-8751; fax 907-586-7928.

26. Muskegs

As you travel through the countryside of Southeast Alaska, sooner or later you will come upon a muskeg. Muskegs, like glaciers, are unique and interesting natural phenomena that are common in the Southeast. These open peat or sphagnum bogs may occur in the midst of forested land, on more or less level areas throughout the subalpine terrain, and even on slopes as steep as 60 degrees. Actually, they are quite complex small ecosystems that scientists are still exploring.

The Southeast muskegs form in areas of heavy rainfall (where precipitation is generally greater than evaporation), where the substrate is uneven, with dips and declivities, and where there is poor drainage; that is, the substrate is either composed of hard bedrock or of impermeable soil that can hold water like a big saucer. Over the centuries, bogs form in the depressions and build up layer by layer. Muskegs can become as much as 40 feet thick, as one plant community succeeds another.

Since conditions for the formation of muskegs are so frequently ideal in the Southeast, these lovely landforms are abundant. Rainfall and snowfall nourish them year-round. They rest in the deep or gentle depressions that past glaciers have scooped out and paved in many places with water-laid glacial flour or compacted till; through the millennia, they have become as hard as concrete.

Muskegs have, in fact, been around in the Southeast for a long time. When a muskeg plant community reaches its climax of growth, it may give way to invading conifers, and what was once a thriving peat bog will become a forest. The Forest Service estimates that about 10 percent of the forest land in the 16.8-million-acre Tongass National Forest was muskeg in the recent geological past. (Perhaps another 10 percent of this forest is presently living muskeg.) Interestingly, it is also suspected that mature spruce forests can eventually degenerate into muskegs, which makes this unique landform unusual ecologically as well as aesthetically.

Muskegs come in various shapes and sizes and vary greatly in appearance. (Scientists identify four quite different types in the Southeast.) You may come upon one that looks like a dying lake choked with sedges and rushes or another that you think is only a thick patch of blueberries. More frequently, you will see something that looks like a floating community of several different kinds of plants. Typically, the water level of muskegs is at or very close to the surface, and there are many little pools of standing water—hence the illusion that things are afloat. Actually, the muskeg plants are fastened into a layer of drenched sphagnum moss, which may be 4 to 12 inches thick. The plants may include, among many others, such familiar ones as Labrador tea, bog rosemary, skunk cabbage, highbush cranberry, salal, marsh marigold, shooting stars, and sundew. Here and there may be a small grove, or scattered individuals, of lodgepole pine, mountain hemlock, or—more rarely—of the graceful yellow (Alaska) cedar, those trees having found precarious footholds and assumed a shrubby growth. If you're fortunate to find a muskeg where spruce has taken hold, you will enjoy a Japanese-print-like scene of exceptional loveliness—totally unlike the black spruce–tamarack muskegs of the North Woods or those of Alaska's Interior. Sometimes a single plant species will dominate a part of the muskeg. I once explored a muskeg near Thayer Lake on Admiralty Island that was so thickly studded with sundew (*Drosera rotundiflora,* one of the carnivorous, insect-eating plants) that in places it looked as though splotches of rose-colored paint had been splashed onto it.

Underlying the sphagnum moss in a muskeg there will probably be layers of older moss and woody peat. Here the air has been pressed out, and the soils have become highly acidic, but even in this strange, dark anaerobic world, there are forms of life that have adapted. The peat layers, incidentally, may be between 4 and 40 feet deep. They will be resting, of course, on a base of hard glacial till, or silt, or bedrock.

Muskegs provide important habitats for several species of animals as well as plants. You might surprise a black bear or a Sitka black-tailed deer as you hike past a muskeg, or see the quick flash of an ermine, wolf, or even a wolverine. Birds such as the greater yellowlegs and the northern shrike can often be seen among the sedges and rushes that surround the little muskeg pools or in the shrubby or grassy areas that surround the muskeg. (The northern shrike will typically breed in Interior muskegs and come south for the winter; even as a hibernal visitor, it may sing for you.) Or you could hear the pleasant call of a pine siskin as you pass by or the lilting, finchlike song of the Lincoln's sparrow. Try to put up with the mosquitoes that may also be part of the muskeg community and take the time to look and listen. (Also, be sure to keep your feet dry.) The Southeastern muskegs are unique, important, and fragile parts of the landscape, definitely worth a few moments of careful observation. You won't find anything like them in the Rockies or the Sierra Nevada!

27. Ketchikan

The name *Ketchikan* is Tlingit, but just what it means or where it came from is unknown. Perhaps it honors a Tlingit fisherman named Kitschk who found a superb salmon run in the creek (*hin* is "creek" in Tlingit), settled here, and left his name behind him. Or perhaps it means "eagle wing river" and was given because a particular bend near a particular waterfall in Ketchikan Creek looks like an eagle with outstretched wings. No matter. *Ketchikan* today means a small Alaskan city with a certain character and charm all its own. It means lush Southeastern forests of spruce and hemlock and superb Southeastern scenery in general—to which it is a major gateway. It once also meant an unequaled salmon fishery and was known as the salmon capital of the world, but, by 1977, its fish catch had become only a third of what it once had been. And, surely, *Ketchikan* means water, whether it's falling from the sky, rushing in streams or waterfalls, lying at your feet in the Tongass Narrows, or keeping you afloat in your kayak. Ketchikan gets measurable precipitation for 224 days of the year, on an average. (In one record year, 1949, it received 202 inches!) For another 100 days, it's apt to be cloudy. But for 42 days, it has clear skies, and if you're lucky enough to be there then, you'll see the beautiful snow-streaked mountains that form this city's backdrop. The people who live in Ketchikan are not bothered much by the wet weather (as a Ketchikan friend once told me: "Southeastern Alaskans don't tan, they rust") and you'll enjoy the place more if you adopt the same attitude.

You can get to Ketchikan by ferry liner or by commercial air service. Appropriately enough, even if you travel by air, you'll have to make your entrance into town across water. Ketchikan and its airport are on adjacent islands with a five-minute ferry ride across the Tongass Narrows, which separates them. The Ketchikan Airport on Gravina Island, incidentally, is one of the more interesting jet airports in the state. It has a runway that doubles back on itself to get you downhill from your point of touchdown to the air terminal.

Gravina Island was named in 1792 for a Spanish naval officer, Federico Gravina, by the explorer Jacinto Caamaño, who was among the first Europeans to sail through this area. Ketchikan's home island is 700,000-acre Revillagigedo (ruh-vee-yah-guh-gay-do); it is larger than Rhode Island and got its Spanish name from Capt. George Vancouver in 1793 when he chose to memorialize the then-viceroy of Mexico, Count Revilla Gigedo. Today, most people simply call the island Revilla and anglicize the pronunciation. Revilla is separated from the mainland and encircled by the Behm Canal, also named by Vancouver in 1793. (Magnum Carl von Behm, in the service of Russia, helped out the 1779 Cook expedition.) This 150-mile canal is one of the most breathtakingly scenic waterways in Southeastern Alaska and a paradise for fishermen. Part of its eastern section is now properly within the boundaries of Misty Fjords National Monument.

The short ferry ride from the airport on Gravina Island to Ketchikan sets you down about 2.5 miles from downtown. This doesn't begin to give you the overall view of the town that the ferry liner or a tour boat does. Although Ketchikan is only a few blocks wide—at most ten—it strings along the water for several miles. Its colorful houses and buildings, many of which are built over the water on pilings, come in a variety of styles and vintages, offering photographers many interesting shots. Along Ketchikan Creek, the town climbs up the lower part of Deer Mountain, which rises 3,001 feet above it. (There is a local saying that if you can't see the top of Deer Mountain, it's raining, and if you can see it, it's about to rain.) You'll notice that a number of the houses are perched on the mountainside and can only be reached by stairs.

Ketchikan is called "Alaska's First City" and so it is, physically, being the first large community you encounter north of the Dixon Entrance as you travel the Inside Passage. It was actually settled, however, several years later than Juneau and did not get its post office until a decade after

Juneau did. Although it likes to call itself Alaska's third largest city, it is in fact the fourth.

Until the mid-fifties, Ketchikan was primarily a fishing town with first a saltery and later, canneries and cold-storage facilities for salmon and halibut. In 1954, the USDA Forest Service initiated serious (and over-committed) logging in the Tongass Forest in Southeast Alaska, and Ketchikan became a center for it; that year, the Ketchikan Pulp Company completed and opened one of the largest dissolving pulp mills in the world. Louisiana Pacific Company acquired and operated this mill for many years. But economic conditions and deteriorating equipment cut profits, and Louisiana Pacific was unable to meet the pollution standards required by the Forest Service; the company closed the mill in 1997. Presently, local Native corporations continue to engage in logging operations around Ketchikan, exploiting their patrimony.

Commercial fishing remains an important part of the Ketchikan economy, and articulate fishermen are fighting to preserve and restore the once-fabulous fishery habitat of the area. If you're going Outside directly from Ketchikan during the fishing season, it's worth trying to find a fresh salmon or halibut to take with you. If you don't meet up with someone who can help you do this, inquire at the Visitors Bureau (see below).

Ketchikan is a most pleasant place to wander around in. You can pick up a map of the town at the ferry dock or at the Visitors Bureau on the downtown dock where the cruise ships drop anchor. Unless you decide to go uphill on Deermont, you'll find yourself taking a long stroll along the waterfront, sometimes on boardwalks. It's likely to be misting a light rain, and, as you pass the old houses along Creek Street, you can get the feeling of stepping back in time. In fact, there is lots of history, Alaskan as well as Indian, in Ketchikan. The town was a major supply center for sourdoughs heading north during the gold-rush periods around the turn of the century. Look for the site of Fort Tongass on the bluff above Creek Street; this is a relic of one of the earliest United States military outposts in Alaska. The area around Ketchikan was also the heartland of Tlingit and Haida country, and there are many traces remaining of these peoples' rich culture. If you're interested in fine Native crafts, you may be able to find a contemporary handmade spruce-root basket here—expensive, but worth it. A good place to look for contemporary Native work is at the Totem Heritage Center, up the hill at 601 Deermont Street. The selection here may be limited, but you might find the beaded vest you've always wanted. You can also see a number of totems that are stored here for preservation. The Totem Heritage Center is open every day, including Sunday afternoon, during the summer.

The largest collection of totems in Alaska (indeed, worldwide) can be seen in and around Ketchikan. Totems greet tourists near the cruise ship dock, and there are more on Creek Street. At Totem Bight State Park, about 10 miles north of town, there are many brightly painted and completely intriguing totems that tell Tlingit stories and legends. There is also the replica of a Tlingit community lodge. Less than 2 miles south of town there is another display of totems at Saxman Village in its Totem Park. Many local people think that this park has the more interesting totems; for instance, you'll find the famous Abraham Lincoln totem here. I recommend visiting both parks, as well as the Totem Heritage Center, if you have the time. At the Saxman Tribal Community, you can see Native artists carving new totems and canoes. You may also be able to see a display of Native dancing. There is a small gift store here, too. Photographers with an interest in older Tlingit art will have fine opportunities; the totems at Totem Bight and Saxman are restorations of old totems brought in from such places as Tongass Island and Old Kasaan. (*Kasaan* is a Tlingit word meaning "pretty town," and it was given to that village, which happens to be Haida, because of its many beautiful and ornate totems.) The restoration work was done under the direction of the Forest Service during the 1930s in an attempt to gather together and preserve local Indian artwork. Most of the people working on the project were members of the Civilian Conservation Corps.

You might also like to visit the Ketchikan Centennial Museum and Library, which is downtown near Ketchikan Creek on Dock Street. There are Indian artifacts here as well as local history items. Another museum (private) is Dolly's House on Creek Street; it is filled with the memorabilia of a near-legendary Ketchikan madam. Note the many restored buildings in this area.

Ketchikan's hotels and restaurants are not remarkable, although they are clean and generally reasonable. If you have wheels of any kind, however, there's very pleasant, if limited, walk-in camping about 6 miles north of town at Ward Lake Recreation Area, a Forest Service facility. The whole town uses this area, as it's particularly good for picnicking; along with four campsites, it has two large shelters where you can cook over an open fire and stay reasonably dry if it's raining. The Forest Service also maintains a rainforest nature trail here, which makes for a pretty 0.7-mile walk. Last Chance Campground, at the Ward Lake Area, has nineteen units, and Signal Creek Campground has twenty-four. These Forest Service campgrounds all charge a modest fee. Check at the **Southeast Alaska Visitor Center** at 50 Main Street for the current charge. The Visitor Center is run by the Forest Service, and you'll find information there about all public lands in Alaska. You might enjoy the out-

Sun and Raven totem. Saxman Park, Ketchikan. Source: USDA Forest Service.

standing displays, and, if you're spending time in the area, you can also pick up a Forest Service map and other material to help you plan your trip. There are another nine units at Settler's Cove Campground (managed by the state) at Mile 18.2 of the North Tongass Highway south of town. This is a beautiful site, and there's good berry picking in August. There is also a twelve-unit private campground at Clover Pass, 12 miles north of the ferry terminal, which has almost all the comforts of home—water, restrooms, tables, grates, showers, and even a laundromat.

Ketchikan offers you the chance to take your own walking tour, or to hike from downtown to the top of a mountain, and although Deer Mountain is not quite so high as Juneau's backdrop peaks, it's still a good hike that enables you to experience the beauties of the Southeastern spruce forests very close to civilization. It will also take you through a magnificent stand of Alaska cedar. The trail takes off at the end of Deermont Street and has stretches of boardwalk and several switchbacks. There's a fine view from the 1,500-foot elevation. You can continue to the top of the mountain without technical difficulties, and, if you want to make your trek into an overnight or two- or three-day trip, you can stay at a most attractive Forest Service cabin on Deer Mountain. The distance up Deer Mountain is 3 miles one way; elevation gain is 3,000 feet.

There is another beautiful and more strenuous outing you can take from Beaver Lake, about 14 miles south of town, up Twin Peaks, but you will have to get yourself to the roadhead. There are also short hikes out of the Ward Lake Recreation Area that are very lovely and that will give you a good sampling of the local flora and fauna. There's a loop all the way around the lake, and there's a stroll up the Perseverance Trail that takes you to Perseverance Lake. This is a less-than-2-mile hike, one way, and is easy walking in the summer, being largely over boardwalk.

Ketchikan offers some good opportunities for bikers as well as hikers. There are several miles of paved highway around the town, and traffic is light. It is also a good place for kayakers to put their boats in the water for trips into the Behm Canal and through other local waters.

Ketchikan is the takeoff point for a large number of Forest Service cabins. If you're on wheels, you may want to take advantage of the ferry service from Ketchikan to nearby Prince of Wales Island, where there are several of these unique cabins accessible by car or by bicycle. There are also lodge accommodations in the village of Craig on Prince of Wales Island. Prince of Wales Island also offers good camping. You might work out a kayak trip around the island to tie into the ferry schedule (but you might also want to close your eyes when you see the clear-cut logging).

The Forest Service can provide you with up-to-date information about these and the numerous other recreational opportunities available out of Ketchikan.

Some Useful Information About Ketchikan

Zip code: 99901. Area code: 907

Ferry

Runs daily in summer. The ferry terminal is some 3 miles north of downtown and adjacent to the Ketchikan Airport ferry-taxi.

Airport Ferry and Bus Service

The ferry departs every half hour (every fifteen minutes during the summer season), at fifteen and forty-five minutes past the hour from the ferry port. City airport buses serve the ferry port from downtown, departing on the hour and half hour; they drop you at the airport parking lot on the city side of the channel. Remember, if you miss your bus, you'll lose a half hour on your flight departure time, so be sure to allow enough time for the bus ride and the ten-minute ferry ride. Phone 225-2800. There's a long (at least two blocks), quite steep ramp from the Gravina ferry terminal to the airport terminal where you will check your baggage. If you have heavy bags, you can avoid this ramp by taking the private *Airporter Shuttle;* this will give you door-to-door service from your hotel; phone 225-5429.

Taxi

Alaska Cab: phone 225-2133. *Sourdough-Ingersoll:* phone 225-5544. *Yellow:* phone 225-5555.

Car Rental

Available at the airport. *Avis:* phone 225-4515. *Alaska Car Rental:* phone 225-5000 (another office is at 2828 Tongass).

Air Service

Alaska Airlines provides regular jet service inside and outside of Alaska; phone 225-2141.

Air Charter Service

Ketchikan Air/Ketchikan Travel: write 1600 Airport Terminal Building, Ketchikan; phone 225-6608 or 1-800-656-6608; fax 247-0008. *Taquan Air/Alaska:* write 1007 Water Street, Ketchikan; phone 225-8800 or 1-800-770-8800; fax 225-0522. Both charter services serve local Forest Service cabins as well as provide sightseeing flights.

Hotels

(There is a room and sales tax.) *Clover Pass Resort:* Mile 15 North Tongass; write Box 7322, Ketchikan; phone 247-2234. Lodge and cabins on the water, restaurant, trailers, and campers, reasonable fishing package. From April to October. *Gilmore Hotel:* across from cruise ship dock, 326 Front Street; phone 225-9423. Downtown, reasonable, year-round, with restaurant, room service, courtesy shuttle from airport. *Best Western Landing:* across from ferry terminal, 3434 Tongass Avenue; phone 225-

5166. Year-round, moderate, with restaurant. *Ingersoll Hotel:* downtown, 303 Mission Street; phone 225-2124. Year-round, moderate. *The Cedars Lodge:* downtown, 1471 Tongass Avenue; phone 225-1900. Views, hot tubs, jacuzzis, exercise room. *Super 8 Motel:* near ferry terminal, 2151 Sea Level Drive; phone 225-9088 or 1-800-800-8000. Moderate, year-round, with pets allowed; courtesy shuttle from ferry terminal. *New York Hotel:* 207 Stedman; write Box 9112, Ketchikan; phone 225-0246. *Ketchikan Bed and Breakfast:* write Box 5015, Ketchikan; phone 225-8550. Check with the Visitors Bureau (see below) regarding the *Youth Hostel.*

Wilderness Lodges

The ones near Ketchikan include *Yes Bay Lodge, Misty Fjords Resort, Unuk River Post, Floating Fishing Lodge, Humpback Lake Chalet.* Air taxi needed. Inquire at the Chamber of Commerce or Visitors Bureau, or consult the *Alaska State Vacation Planner* (see Suggested Reading).

Campgrounds

Signal Creek, Three C's, and *Last Chance* Campgrounds at Ward Creek Recreation Area off Ward Lake Road north of ferry approximately 5 to 7 miles; Forest Service administered. *Settler's Cove:* Mile 18.2 North Tongass Highway; Alaska State Division of Parks administered. *Clover Pass Resort:* private (see Hotels, above).

Boat Tours and Rentals

Alaska Cruises: write Dale Pihlman, Box 7814, Ketchikan; phone 225-6044; fax 225-8636. Misty Fjord day trips; cruise/fly back; historical waterfront cruises. *Southeast Exposure:* write Box 9143, Ketchikan; phone 225-8829. Kayak rentals and tours.

Fishing Charters

Folks looking for fish to take home should inquire at the Visitors Bureau (see below) or at one of the cold-storage plants.

Laundromats

At 2703 Tongass, at the north end of town, is the *Highliner Laundromat;* phone 225-5308. At the south end of town is *The Mat,* 989 Stedman; phone 225-0628.

Swimming Pool

There's a pool and sauna in the *Ketchikan High School;* phone 225-2010 for hours when they're open. There's also a smaller pool at *Valley Park Elementary School;* the same phone number will give you open hours.

Useful Names and Addresses

Chamber of Commerce: write Box 5957, Ketchikan; phone 225-3184. *Ketchikan Visitors Bureau:* write 131 Front Street, Ketchikan; phone 225-6166. Located on the downtown dock where cruise ships come in. Check with these friendly people if you're interested in a local tour or a visit to the totem parks. *Forest Service:* write c/o Federal Building, Ketchikan; phone 225-3101. The Forest Service also operates the *Southeast Alaska Visitor Center* on the waterfront. Its beautiful green-roofed building houses several exhibit rooms: one explains Southeast Alaska's seven ecosystems; another is a replica of a temperate rainforest; a third shows a traditional Native fishing camp, with material explaining Native traditional life (this room was planned with a group of Native elders from Ketchikan); yet another describes Southeast Alaska's commercial fishing, logging, mining, and recreation industries. There is also a trip planning room (open in the summer) stocked with videos, maps, cabin, and other information you can use to help plan your trip. In addition, there's an award-winning multimedia slide show, "Mystical Southeast." The Southeast Alaska Visitor Center is open all year: from May 1 to September 30, seven days a week; 8:30 A.M. to 4:30 P.M.; in winter, Tuesday through Saturday, 8:30 A.M. to 4:30 P.M. There's a small admission fee, but be sure to take advantage of this terrific resource. Write 50 Main Street, Ketchikan; phone 228-6214. The *Alaska Natural History Association* runs a bookstore in the Visitor Center, a good source for maps, trail guides, and other material to help you plan your trip. The address is the same as the Visitor Center; phone 228-6233 for a flyer describing available material. For information about Forest Service cabins, ask at the Visitor Center or write: *Forest Service Information Center,* 101 Egan Drive, Juneau, AK 99801; phone 586-8751; fax 586-7928. To make cabin reservations, call *Forest Service Reservation Center* at 1-800-280-2267; or write Box 900, Cumberland, MD 21501-0900. It's best to telephone this centralized reservation number for information on availability and rates for these popular cabins once you know when and where you want to visit. There is a small nonrefundable reservation fee. The *Misty Fjords National Monument* office is at 3031 Tongass Avenue, Ketchikan; phone 225-2148.

Misty Fjords National Monument. The cliffs rise higher than those in Yosemite Valley. Source: USDA Forest Service.

28. Misty Fjords

Ketchikan is the gateway to Misty Fjords National Monument, a magnificent wilderness (2,142,907 acres) complex of fjords and mountains rising sheerly from the water, with dense rainforests, wild rivers, waterfalls, and high alpine lakes. You get there by boat or air taxi; you can charter either. En route, you may see seals or whales, and you're sure to see many bald eagles.

Even if the weather doesn't cooperate entirely, you'll also see—and feel—some of the most superb country in the Southeast in this monument. Sometimes you can travel through rain into blue-sky weather, so don't give up. When Henry Gannett wrote the following in 1902, he could have had Misty Fjords in mind:

> There is one other asset of the territory not yet enumerated; imponderable and difficult to appraise, yet one of the chief assets of

Alaska, if not the greatest. This is the scenery. There are glaciers, mountains, fjords elsewhere, but nowhere else on earth is there such an abundance and magnificence of mountain, fjord, and glacier scenery. For thousands of miles, the coast is a continuous panorama. For one Yosemite of California, Alaska has hundreds.

Recreational use of Misty Fjords National Monument is presently restricted largely to boat use or to fly-in campsites, but trails may be put in by the Forest Service or further camping opportunities may be developed. (There are several Forest Service cabins in the monument.) The future of the molybdenum mine in the heart of the monument—about a 150,000-acre piece of land that may be disastrously developed—will also determine the use of a sizable area of this extraordinary place.

For further information, contact the Monument Manager, *Misty Fjords National Monument,* Tongass National Forest, 3031 Tongass Avenue, Ketchikan, AK 99901; phone 225-2148.

29. Wrangell

Wrangell lies about six hours north of Ketchikan as the ferry sails and is located close to the mouth of the Stikine, a great river that rises in Canada and has been an important—and spectacularly beautiful—waterway for people for many millennia. Northwest Indians probably used the Wrangell area extensively as long as 8,000 years ago; the legends they carved into the argillite along the waterfront are believed to date back that far. When the Russians found the place in the early 1830s, they considered it important enough to build Fort Saint Dionysius there to prevent trespassing by the Hudson's Bay trappers who were after otters. The Americans gave the town its name in honor of Baron Ferdinand Petrovich von Wrangell, a vice admiral in the Imperial Russian Navy and governor of Russian America from 1830 to 1835. Many other nearby place names, including Woronkofski, Mitkof, and Kupreanof Islands, also reflect the region's Russian history.

In 1839, the British managed to lease the area from Russia and to rechristen the town Fort Stikine. After the United States acquired Alaska in 1867, it established a military post known as Fort Wrangell, which survived about a decade. Later, sourdoughs bound for the Klondike and the Cassiars headed through Wrangell up the Stikine, and the town became a busy supply and trading center.

John Muir made Wrangell his headquarters for his 1879 adventures in Southeastern Alaska, traveling from there to Haines (then known as Chilkat) by canoe with his missionary friend S. Hall Young and a party of Tlingit Indians. Of Wrangell, Muir wrote:

> No mining hamlet in the placer gulches of California, nor any backwoods village I ever saw approached it in picturesque devil-may-care *abandon*. It was a lawless draggle of wooden huts and houses, built in crooked lines, wrangling around the boggy shores of the island for a mile or so . . . without the slightest subordination to the points of the compass or to building laws of any kind.

This last part of Muir's comment would apply to many towns in Alaska for many decades afterward as well.

Wrangell has become far more orderly and circumspect since Muir made his visit. It has orderly streets and houses. It has played a significant role in the economy of Southeast Alaska as the site of canneries and sawmills along with being a busy port. It has wonderful, accessible petroglyphs and is the takeoff point for twenty-two Forest Service cabins. And it is the beautiful place Stikine river runners see both going and coming.

The ferry stopover in Wrangell is usually only a half hour, but the tides may stretch the time you'll have in town. If you visit the Wrangell Visitor Information Center (see below), you can get a local *Visitor's Guide*. This will contain a city map, which is very useful. (You can also get this guide in the ferry terminal.) Since there are twenty-two USDA Forest Service cabins in the Wrangell Ranger District, you might also want to stop by the Forest Service office at 525 Bennett Street to inquire about them. If you want to buy some local shrimp (excellent), ask at the Visitor Information Center or the ferry terminal. If you stay around the terminal when a ship comes in, you'll likely meet the local children selling garnets from the nearby Garnet Ledge. This claim was willed to the town's children and the Boy Scouts of Southeast Alaska by a resident miner. For more local color, you can admire the totems that ornament the town.

If you have a few hours to spend in Wrangell, you can enjoy a couple of strolls from the ferry terminal or from the town. A mile-and-a-half round-trip walk can show you the best of the Indian petroglyphs. It is illegal to use chalk on the petroglyphs to outline the designs or to deface the carvings in any way. They should of course be treated with respect.

Wet or dry, however, they are good subjects for your camera, and, perhaps even more interesting, you can make beautiful rubbings of them if you carry along paper and charcoal or crayons or even a pencil. (Rice paper is available in a local gift store.)

Another stroll in Wrangell will take you to Chief Shakes Island, less than a mile south from the ferry terminal. Ask at the Visitor Information Center (see below) for directions for these worthwhile outings.

If you have longer to stay in Wrangell, you might want to visit the museum on Second Street (open during the summer, Monday through Friday, 10 A.M. to 5 P.M.; Saturday, 1 P.M. to 5 P.M.) or, if you're feeling more energetic, you could hike a mile up Mount Dewey to see the view. You start up from Second Avenue and Mission Street. If you have your bike, you can ride south down the Zimovia Highway. The traffic is light, and the road hugs the shore most of the time. This is also a pleasant road to walk along. Look for whales and shorebirds. There is a free campground at Shoemaker Bay Recreation Area (Mile 4.6) with tent and vehicle camping and a Forest Service trail up to Rainbow Falls. The trail is through about a mile of forest and much of it is wet, so wear good boots or your Southeast sneakers, if you have a pair. The views are lovely on this trail, and you'll likely hear bird song as you walk. You may even see a black-tailed deer or a black bear along the way. This walk should take less than two hours.

The Stikine River, which rises in Canada, pours its swift-flowing waters through the Coastal Range and into Alaska, spreading into a beautiful tangle of braids as it forms its delta near Wrangell. It is navigable for a good 150 miles upstream and is considered to be the fastest-flowing (6 to 8 miles per hour) navigable river in the United States. River runners should avoid an incoming tide at the mouth of the river; it once took our party in an oar-powered rubber raft more than three hours of steady rowing—battling the surging tide—to make the short passage to land.

The Stikine passes through some exceptional Southeastern scenery. Its grand canyon, which is over 100 miles long and has cliffs that soar upward over 4,000 feet, reminded John Muir of Yosemite when he visited there in 1879. He wrote, "The majestic cliffs and mountains forming the canyon walls display an endless variety of form and sculpture, and are wonderfully adorned with glaciers and waterfalls while throughout almost its whole extent, the floor is a flowery landscape garden. . . ." Although a swift-running river, the Stikine presents no major difficulties for an experienced river runner. The put-in at Telegraph is a short flight from Wrangell and, as noted, air service is available.

Note: There's good black bear viewing out of Wrangell; inquire at the Visitor Information Center (see below).

Some Useful Information About Wrangell
Zip code: 99929. Area code: 907.

Ferry
Runs daily in summer.

Air Service
Alaska Airlines: serves Wrangell year-round; phone 772-4255.

Air Charter Service
Sunrise Aviation: write Box 432, Wrangell; phone 874-2319.

Taxi
Service is provided by *Star Cab:* phone 874-3622.

Car Rental
Practical Rent-A-Car: phone 874-3975.

Hotels
(There is a room and sales tax.) Hotels include: *Hardings "Old Sour-dough Lodge"* (and charter service): boarding-house type of accommodation; fishing and photographing opportunities by charter; seasonal, moderate; write Box 1062, Wrangell; phone 874-3613. *Roadhouse Lodge:* year-round, reasonable, with courtesy car; write Box 1199; phone 874-2335. *Stikine Inn:* downtown, moderate; write Box 990, Wrangell; phone 874-3388. *Thunderbird Hotel:* year-round, clean and reasonable; write Box 110, Wrangell; phone 874-3322.

Laundromat
In the *Thunderbird Hotel,* five blocks from the ferry on Front Street. Open seven days a week.

Boat Charters
Ask at the *Visitor Information Center* (see below).

Useful Names and Addresses
Chamber of Commerce and Visitor Information Center: 107 Stikine Avenue (in the Stikine Inn); write Box 49, Wrangell; phone 874-3901 or 1-800-367-9745. *USDA Forest Service:* write Box 51, Wrangell; phone 874-2323. Ask about nearby cabins.

30. Petersburg

Located on the tip of Mitkof Island and at the northern end of the Wrangell Narrows, Petersburg lies about halfway between Ketchikan and Juneau. It is tucked between the almost 10,000-foot snowy mountains on the mainland and the much lower but green-forested mountains of Kupreanof Island. The neat Norwegian-style wooden buildings of Petersburg make a picture-postcard scene in the midst of this magnificent setting.

Petersburg was named for Peter Buschmann, a Norwegian who founded the town in 1897. He selected the site because of its superb fishery, its forests, and its good harbor. After building himself a saltery, he anticipated later generations by building a sawmill. The LeConte Glacier (which was named for Joseph LeConte, a University of California professor of geology and founding member of the Sierra Club) lay conveniently just across Frederick Sound from Petersburg and provided the new little town with plenty of ice. LeConte ice was also exported by ice ships south to the burgeoning city of San Francisco until the early twentieth century. The LeConte, incidentally, is the southernmost tidewater glacier on the North American continent. It is very lively and launches many icebergs into Frederick Sound, some of which you can see from the ferry.

Petersburg today is a thriving community with the largest home-based halibut fleet in Alaska. It is, as well, a principal fish-processing port for the Southeast, handling all five kinds of salmon—silver, pink, chum, king, and sockeye—along with crab, shrimp, herring, and halibut. (It is famous for its succulent shrimp.)

Petersburg celebrates its Scandinavian heritage with a three-day Little Norway Festival that includes dancing, costumes, Viking ships, and delicious food and is held every year around May 17, Norwegian Independence Day. The colorful Norwegian influence of its founders permeates the houses and gardens as well as the boats of the town.

There are two beautiful hikes accessible from Petersburg, but you will have to find a boat or an airlift to get across the Wrangell Narrows to Kupreanof Island. One trail will take you along Petersburg Creek to Petersburg Lake, a distance of 5.5 or 6.5 miles one way, depending upon where you start. The elevation gain is only 200 feet, there is excellent and varied fishing along the way, and you are likely to see lots of bald eagles; this is their home territory. The second trail, up to Petersburg Mountain, is considerably more strenuous but will give a strong hiker some unmatched views of the Wrangell Narrows and, on a clear day, of the spectacular mountains and ice fields on the mainland. This is a 5-mile round-trip, with an elevation gain of 2,888 feet. You should allow a full day for either of these hikes and take along your lunch. On the Petersburg Mountain Trail, it is also wise to carry a canteen. Ask the Forest Service people (address below) about further details as well as current trail conditions.

If you're traveling in your own small boat, you can make the run across the Wrangell Narrows yourself. (Whosever boat you travel in, dress warmly for this short—twenty minutes or so—but chilly crossing.) Be sure to check the tides; and check with the Forest Service about this adventurous trip. Watch for humpback whales, sea lions, and porpoises on the way, and keep your eyes out for deer along the shore.

If you have your bicycle (or your car) with you and want to spend some time around Petersburg, the Mitkof Highway runs south for 35 miles, and there are three Forest Service sites along it: Blind Slough Recreation Area at Mile 17.5, Ohmer Creek Campground at Mile 22, and Summer Strait Campground at Mile 26.8.

Experienced mountain climbers with proper equipment may want to investigate the climbing possibilities on the mainland near Petersburg. It is the takeoff point for the Devil's Thumb and other peaks. Check with the Forest Service for details.

Some Useful Information About Petersburg

Zip code: 99833. Area code: 907.

Ferry

Runs daily in summer. Dock is at south end of town. Phone 772-3855.

Air Service

Alaska Airlines: daily jets, serves Petersburg year-round; phone 772-4255.

Air Charter Service

Consult the Chamber of Commerce (see below).

Car Rental
Avis Car Rental: phone 772-4716. *All Star Rental:* phone 772-4281.

Taxi
City Cab: phone 772-3003.

Boat Charters
Inquire about boat rentals and other charter operators at the Chamber of Commerce (see below).

Hotels
Scandia House: write Box 689, Petersburg; phone 772-4281. *Tides Inn:* write Box 1048, Petersburg; phone 772-4288 or 1-800-665-8433. For other hotels, campgrounds, and bed and breakfasts, check with the Visitor Information Center (see below).

Showers
LeConte RV Park: Fourth and Haugen Streets (also laundry).

Useful Names and Addresses
Chamber of Commerce: write Box 649, Petersburg; phone 772-3646. At First and Fram Streets. *Petersburg Visitor Information Center:* in the same building; phone 772-4636. The *USDA Forest Service* office is above the post office on Nordic Drive; write Box 1328, Petersburg; phone 772-3871.

31. Juneau

All of Southeast Alaska's communities share essentially the same geography, flora, and fauna, but the weather in each one varies and so does the character. Ketchikan, Alaska's southernmost "port of entrance," for instance, has the flavor of a fishing and logging community, while its fine totems tie it vividly to its Indian heritage. Petersburg has a distinctly Norwegian atmosphere, and the Russian influence in Sitka is inescapable. Skagway has kept enough of its gold-mining history intact to have most of its main street designated as a national historical park. Juneau is not only the picturesque population center of the Southeast and full of Alaskan history, it is also a cosmopolitan little city.

Juneau was the first American settlement in Alaska that succeeded; for many years it was the first port of call north of Seattle. (It is still an active port.) Juneau started out as a mining town, has been a center for local commercial fishing of salmon and halibut (in 1936, there were fourteen salmon canneries in the area), and has become today the home of some of Alaska's most creative people—artists, writers, scientists, and scholars. It has been the state capital for nearly one hundred years and the heart of Alaska's political arena, and is the place where the state of Alaska does much of its business with Washington, D.C. In 1974, Alaskans voted to relocate their capital to a site to be chosen somewhere between Anchorage and Fairbanks. However, three years later, they voted down the bonds for a capital move and, in 1982, they rejected Willow as a site and nullified the 1974 vote. To date, Juneau remains the capital.

Juneau is the city where, at one time or another, for one reason or another, most of the people involved in Alaska's present, and future, will come. If you stand around in the lobby of the Baranof Hotel, which is located a couple of blocks down the hill from the capitol building, chances are you can rub shoulders with Alaskan decision makers such as the governor and members of his cabinet; Native leaders; directors of major oil companies; businessmen from home and abroad; experts in the fields of geology, fisheries, finance; and more. If you happen to be around when the legislature is in session, you will be able to see a good sampling of Alaska's population—not only the lawmakers themselves—who may be prospectors, hunting guides, fishermen, construction workers, lawyers, or writers—but also people from every part of the bush. In summer, of course, you'll encounter tourists from all over the world; they pour in by the thousands from cruise ships. (The Forest Service estimates that 500,000 people—equal to the entire population of Alaska—visit the Tongass National Forest every summer.)

If you're interested in adventuring in the out-of-doors, Juneau is the point of departure for some of the best country in Southeast Alaska—Admiralty Island, West Chichagof Island (also see Sitka), and Glacier Bay National Park included. It is also the gateway to some of the finest Southeastern waters for canoeing and kayaking. In the winter, Juneau is close to one of Alaska's major downhill skiing facilities, Eaglecrest (just 12

Mendenhall Glacier, near Juneau. Source: USDA Forest Service.

miles from downtown), and the cross-country skiing opportunities around it are fabulous. Many people simply ski cross-country from their back doors. And where else can you hike from a downtown corner through forests and fields of wildflowers to the top of not one, but two nearly 4,000-foot mountains and some of the loveliest views anywhere? For all of these reasons, if you are able to visit only one of Alaska's three principal cities, I recommend Juneau.

Juneau began life as a tent city that was located as close as possible to the site of the 1880 strike on Gold Creek in Silverbow Basin. (Gold Creek now flows encased in a concrete culvert through the center of town.) In terms of good weather, this was not the optimum location, and the tents are said to have been flattened at least twice by Taku winds before more permanent buildings could be erected. Only a few miles north of Juneau, on the Gastineau Channel, the climate is more moderate, the winds are less fierce, and the total precipitation is 36 inches a year less. Despite its less-than-ideal climate, Juneau has a set-

ting that turned out to be superlative. Situated on the shore of the
Gastineau Channel, it has a backdrop of two snow-topped mountains,
Mount Roberts (3,819 feet) and Mount Juneau (3,516 feet). Dark
spruce forests streak their precipitous slopes, and long, white streamers
of waterfalls sway through their avalanche canyons. In summer, the
slanting sunlight backlights the trees and makes the high green-napped
meadows glow like the best velvet.

It was John Muir, founder of the Sierra Club, who is credited with
having initiated Alaska's first gold rush when he was indirectly responsible for sending Joe Juneau and Richard Harris to their find in Silverbow
Basin. Muir was on his second trip to Alaska, traveling with S. Hall
Young, and from his geological know-how suspected the possibility of
gold in the area. This information was conveyed to Juneau and Harris,
and the hunt was on.

Joe Juneau's claims paid off handsomely; he sold them for so much he
is said to have worried that he would never live to spend all the money,
but he did. The gold content of most of the ore in Mount Roberts, however, proved to be too low grade to be profitable for prospectors. In
1897, the Alaska Juneau Company bought up the twenty-three lode
claims that covered the most promising area and began an extensive low-
grade mining operation that lasted until 1944. During that time, it reduced the cubic footage of Mount Roberts by an estimated 88.5 million
tons of rock and netted about $77.6 million worth of gold. Some of the
old AJ Company buildings still stand on the slopes above Juneau, but
they are now unsafe. In 1881, another low-grade operation commenced
on Douglas Island, directly across the channel from Juneau; in thirty-six
years, John Treadwell, a San Franciscan, is said to have taken out $66
million in gold. In 1917, a major cave-in and subsequent flooding of the
Treadwell mine by seawater closed down the operation.

As the town of Juneau took shape, the first obvious place to go was
up. The early builders fitted their homes, stores, hotels, and saloons into
and onto the lower slopes of Mount Roberts, taking advantage of every
small natural shelf. Much of their work still stands, and older Juneau is
as colorful as many small European cities. The best way to see this part
of Juneau or, indeed, all of Juneau, is on foot: the Juneau Visitor Information Center, located in the Log Cabin at Third and Seward Streets, will
provide you with maps and a suggested self-guided walking tour. You'll
find the narrow streets that wind up- and downhill past the well-kept
Victorian houses don't always have sidewalks, but the traffic is usually
light—Juneau has all of ten traffic lights, which is more than twice the
total in the rest of the Southeast. When the slopes get too steep, there are

long wooden stairways built more than half a century ago for substitute thoroughfares, and these will take you to some of the best viewpoints in town.

Juneau's suburbs reach north and south for many miles and include Auke Bay and the Mendenhall Valley. Territorially, Greater Juneau is, in fact, one of the largest cities in the United States. Its 3,100 square miles stretch from the grand ice field above the town to the west side of Douglas Island and encompass several mountains and glaciers as well as the city of Douglas itself, which is linked to Juneau by a bridge across the Gastineau Channel.

Juneau has been enlarged considerably through the years by fill, much of it supplied by the Mount Roberts AJ Mining Company tailings. This has expanded the waterfront area and provided for more building space. Today, you'll find that many important Juneau buildings stand on filled land—for instance, the Federal Building and the excellent Alaska State Museum. A principal food and service shopping mall is also in this part of town.

Spanning the two main levels of the city vertically and being fitted into the hillside in the process is Juneau's largest structure, the State Office Building (sometimes referred to as the SOB). This building has its main entrance on Fourth Street up the hill and its basement entrance eight floors below on Willoughby Street. (The main floor is numbered the eighth, and the basement is the first. There are actually eleven stories in this building.) If you stay around Juneau any length of time, you'll find it convenient, especially on rainy weekdays, to use the SOB elevator to get yourself from "uptown" to "downtown" or vice versa. The state library, an excellent one, is located in the State Office Building on the main (eighth) floor; it has a great deal of Alaskana on its shelves, should you feel like browsing on a rainy day.

Although Juneau has been the official state capital since 1900 (the actual move from Sitka was not completed until 1906), it had few official buildings until 1912. That year, Congress made Alaska a proper territory with its own, elected legislature. (Its executives were federal appointees.) The event was celebrated by the construction of the Governor's Mansion up the hill on Calhoun Street. The mansion fronts so directly onto Calhoun Street that people sometimes walk the few steps from the sidewalk to peer through the curtained windows, ring the doorbell, or even open the big front door if someone has forgotten to lock it. If you become so tempted, please refrain. Although Alaska is probably the most informal of the fifty states, and the governor and his family are easy to see around town, they are entitled to a little privacy. Incidentally, to illustrate

Saint Nicholas's Church, Juneau. Source: Mike Miller.

Alaska's small-town atmosphere, every Christmas the governor holds an open house to which everyone in the state is welcome; cookies are served literally in the thousands. And up to a few years ago, the mansion's telephone number was listed in the Juneau phone book.

Not far from the Governor's Mansion, on Fourth Street, is the State Capitol Building, which was erected by the federal government in 1931 at a cost of $1 million. The building is a monument to the decade of the thirties. This massive period piece with its pillars is worth a visit, if only to see how lavishly marble was used in its construction. Brought in from Prince of Wales Island, marble covers many of the walls. As you walk through the halls of the capitol, keep in mind that Alaska was so small when it was constructed that this building housed the entire Alaskan governmental operation; within these six stories were the territorial legislature, the U.S. District Court, twenty-five federal and seven territorial departments as well as the Alaska Historical Library and Museum. Now the capitol building is occupied only by the state legislature and executive branches. (Judicial is across the street.) If you are in Juneau during the legislative session, which runs from January to May (and may continue into June), try to find time to sit in on the assembly or the senate when one or the other is in session. There are few better ways to get a feeling for what Alaska is all about. Unfortunately, there isn't much of a gallery for either house of the legislature, but you may get a seat if you're lucky. (If you know anyone in the legislature, don't be surprised if you get introduced to everyone present.) Up the hill from the capitol at 326 Fifth Street is Juneau's small and charming Russian Orthodox Church, Saint Nicholas's, which has visiting hours in summer. Farther up the same hill is a fine totem erected by the Juneau Rotary Club and sometimes called the Rotary Totem. Unfortunately for photographers, neither of these unique city ornaments can be photographed easily because of interfering telephone wires or poles.

If you plan any outdoor adventuring on your own starting from Juneau, you'll want to talk to the National Park Service or the USDA Forest Service people in the Centennial Hall Information Center, 101 Egan Drive. This is where you get firsthand information and printed material about the camps, trails, Southeast bird life, and so on, within their bailiwick—including Glacier Bay and Admiralty Island.

Not far from Centennial Hall is the Federal Building (Willoughby and Ninth Street), which houses a post office and various federal agencies, including the Bureau of Indian Affairs. And nearby on Whittier Street is the Alaska State Museum: hours during the summer are 9 A.M. to 6 P.M. Monday through Friday; 10 A.M. to 6 P.M. Saturday and Sunday. This is one of Alaska's most interesting and comprehensive museums, so allow plenty of time to visit it. You'll find historical exhibits, including the replica of a gold assay office, Russian memorabilia, and good collections of Native artifacts—Eskimo, Athabascan, and Tlingit-Haida. (Unfortunately, so much of the Aleut culture was lost early on that this Native group is not well represented here or anywhere else in Alaska's museums.) There are a couple of excellent wildlife dioramas that will give you an idea of what some of Alaska's animals look like. (The animals in the dioramas and elsewhere in the Alaska State Museum have been provided by the Alaskan Department of Fish and Game (ADFG), and most of them were killed accidentally; ADFG has a policy not to kill specimens for display only.) And there's an "eagle tree," a real tree, which shows off the eagle and the bear in their natural habitat. There are also changing exhibits of contemporary artists: a number of these artists live in Alaska—some in Juneau. (The Museum Store has a small, but excellent selection of Native crafts. If you're interested in acquiring a good piece of Native art, I suggest your looking here.)

Since Juneau is a waterfront city with an active harbor, you'll want to spend a little time in the marine park and along the wharf. You'll find boardwalks for strolling and watching the traffic in the channel. In sum-

Common raven (Corvus corax principalis). *Range: throughout Alaska.*

mer, there will probably be big white tour ships in dock. (You are apt to encounter crowds of tourists from the cruise ships downtown. In summer as many as eleven thousand people—almost a third of Juneau's population—may crowd into the city in a matter of days.) Small boats, including sailboats and fishing boats with their big cerise-colored halibut buoys, come and go, and you'll see small planes taking off or landing. Incidentally, the waters of the channel can be more dangerous on absolutely calm days, especially when the sun is very low, than when they're ruffled by a light wind: the smooth, luminous surface requires exceptionally good depth perception on the part of pilots. Be sure to look for whales and porpoises and a variety of waterfowl; in winter, a pair of oldsquaw ducks can provide hours of good watching. Don't forget to look up, down, around, and everywhere for bald eagles, particularly when you first get to Juneau. Later on, the bald eagles will be a familiar, always welcome part of the Southeastern scene, especially when you get farther away from built-up areas. The other big bird to become acquainted with is the raven, so much a part of the Indian cultures. The

Average Temperatures: Juneau

	Daytime High (F°)	Nighttime Low (F°)	Monthly Average (F°)
Jan.	28.3	17.2	22.8
Feb.	33.5	21.9	27.7
March	37.6	25.2	31.4
April	46.1	31.3	38.7
May	54.9	38.0	46.5
June	61.4	44.2	52.8
July	63.7	47.2	55.5
August	62.4	46.3	54.5
Sept.	55.9	42.4	49.2
Oct.	46.8	36.4	41.6
Nov.	37.0	27.3	32.2
Dec.	31.6	22.2	26.9

raven thrives not only in the Southeast but all over Alaska, and is a great aerobatic performer as well as avian conversationalist.

There is a good bookstore in downtown Juneau, the Hearthside, at 254 Front Street. It has a nice selection of Alaskana and encourages browsing. If you're hungry for good food instead of literature, you'll find a wide variety of places to eat in this part of town (and other parts, too). Shoppers have numerous stores and wares to intrigue them, but, as mentioned above, beware the crowds on the days that cruise ships drop anchor.

Note: Juneau is the home of many well-known artists, including Rie Muñoz, whose imaginative and charming prints can be found in her shop across from the waterfront, and R. T. "Skip" Wallen, whose beautiful bronze bear (down the hill and across from the SOB) and *Gang of Four* (also of bronze and of bears, and in front of the Fish Hatchery on Egan Drive) are Juneau's special pride.

Day Hikes You Can Take from Downtown Juneau

There are over two dozen Forest Service trails described in the USDA Forest Service brochure *Juneau Trails*. Four of these can be reached on foot from downtown Juneau. For Mount Roberts (a nearly 4,000-foot climb), you take the wooden stairway at the end of Sixth Street and continue upward. For the other three—Perseverance, Mount Juneau, and Granite Creek Trails—you follow Gold Street up the hill to Basin Road and cross Gold Creek to commence your climb. In good summer weather, you may encounter Juneau people on the Perseverance Trail during lunch hour. The other trails make for more strenuous outings. Any of these trails will quickly acquaint you with typical Southeast hiking conditions.

Because of the great diversity in natural habitats these trails travel through, there are many different birds along them, and, in June and July, the bird song is a delight. Listen particularly for the fox sparrow, which introduces its song with a liquid whistle and then warbles its melody. At twilight, you may hear the gray-cheeked thrush alone or in charming duet with a Swainson's thrush.

You can also take a tram from the middle cruise ship dock on Franklin to an 1,800-foot ridge on Mount Roberts, halfway up the mountain. The Mount Roberts Tramway was constructed in partnership with Goldbelt, the local Juneau Native corporation, and has many Tlingit cultural elements. The upper-level terminal complex has a gift shop, a fifteen-minute film on Tlingit history and culture, a restaurant, and a nature center with books, maps, and pamphlets for sale. You can take several different walks from the nature center—from a stroll along a $1/8$-mile nature trail to a hook-up with the main Mount Roberts trail, which leads to the top of the mountain. The view from the ridge, and especially from the summit of Mount Roberts, is spectacular. Look for wildflowers from mid-May through June, and also keep an eye out for deer and bear. The tramway is open seven days a week, 8 A.M. to 10 P.M., from mid-April through early October. For further information, write **Mount Roberts Tramway,** 490 South Franklin Street, Juneau, AK 99801; phone 463-3412; fax 463-5095.

At least six other interesting trails can be reached from downtown Juneau by bus. These include the Mendenhall Glacier trails, which range from a 1.5-mile loop to longer trails that offer a chance to view mountain goats as well as ice fields. The **Forest Service Visitor Center** at Mendenhall Glacier has information on these; phone 789-0097.

Other trails are the Lemon Creek Trail, which is fairly easy, but a scramble in places, and runs through lovely forest; the Salmon Creek Trail, a scramble, but with fine berry-picking in season; the Spaulding, which is easy if steep in places and leads to good muskegs as well as to the John Muir Cabin, built by the local Sierra Club group; the Mount Bradley (Mount Jumbo) Trail, which is difficult but has magnificent views and wildflowers in season; and the Dan Moller, or Kowee Creek, Trail, which is a former ski trail and is described by a Juneau friend like this: "The loveliest readily accessible subalpine forest and meadow around Juneau are up Kowee Creek. The trail has a boardwalk through its lower muskegs and ends up, unlike other local trails, in an exquisite subalpine bowl. It can be hiked after supper on long summer evenings,

Mountain goat (Oreamnos americanus). *Range: the alpine zone in Southeast and Southcentral Alaska.*

but it is good at all seasons, although you do cross, briefly, several avalanche tracks. There are wonderful wildflowers in summer and bird song in June and July."

You can buy a copy of *Juneau Trails* for a modest sum at the **Forest Service Information Center** in Centennial Hall at 101 Egan Drive, or at the **Visitor Information Center** at Third and Seward.

Some Useful Information About Juneau

Zip code: there are several in the Juneau area, included with addresses below. Area code: 907.

Ferry

The state ferry liner runs daily during the summer. Note that it does not dock at the downtown pier—used by cruise ships—but about 14 miles to the north, at Auke Bay. Between the downtown terminal and the Auke Bay terminal, the Mendenhall and Lemon Glaciers pour out so much silt and sediment that the Gastineau Channel is too shallow to accommodate large boats. Hence, Auke Bay is used primarily for travel to and from the north, avoiding the shallow areas. Ships docking at the downtown terminal travel out around Douglas Island to reach the deeper waters. If you're on foot, you may have to use a taxi or hotel courtesy van for transportation downtown. (There is also bus service: see below.)

The larger ferries serve the larger communities and carry the most tourists. Smaller ferries, like the *LeConte,* serve the smaller villages, and, primarily, the local people (good for exploring locally). Phone 789-7453.

Air Service

There is daily interstate scheduled service by *Alaska Airlines* and, in summer, *Delta Airlines.* Your agent can give you the latest schedules and tariffs. Interstate flights to Haines, Skagway, and so on are provided by several local airlines (see Air Charter Service, below).

Air Charter Service

L.A.B. Flying Service: write Box 2201, Juneau, AK 99801; phone 789-9160. Amphibious or wheeled air-taxi service. Scheduled flights to Haines, Skagway, Gustavus, and Hoonah. *Wings of Alaska:* write 1890 Renshaw Way, Juneau, AK 99801; phone 789-0790. Scheduled flights to Haines, Skagway, Hoonah, Gustavus, Angoon, and other nearby communities. The following three services are located in the Terminal Building, Juneau Airport: *Ward Air:* phone 789-9150; charter service. *Glacier Bay Airways:* phone 789-9009. *Skagway Air Service:* phone 789-2006. A flightsee over the Juneau Ice Field will give you views unparalleled in the world. *Temsco Helicopters:* at 1650 Maplesden Way, Juneau, AK 99801, on the Juneau side of the airport; phone 789-9501. Helicopter tours land you on the Mendenhall Glacier for twenty-five-minute guided walk; longer tours, with two landings, to the Juneau Ice Field.

Bus Service

Mendenhall Glacier Transit (MGT) serves downtown Juneau, the airport, and the Auke Bay Ferry, traveling as far as DeHart's Grocery at Auke Bay. The bus also makes a loop run up the Mendenhall Valley to within 1¼ miles of the Mendenhall Glacier and 2 miles of the Mendenhall Lake Campground, and certain buses travel to Douglas Island across the Gastineau Channel. Runs hourly from 6:50 A.M. to 11:36 P.M., Monday through Saturday. Bus schedules are available at the *Visitor Information Center* on Third and Seward.

Car Rental

Available at the Juneau Airport: *Hertz:* phone 789-9494. *Avis:* phone 789-9450. *Budget:* phone 789-1386. *National:* phone 789-9814. The following provide free pickup service: *Payless:* phone 780-6004. *Rent-A-Wreck:* phone 789-4111.

Taxi

Taku Glacier Cab: phone 586-2121. *Capital Cab:* phone 586-2772.

Boat Charters

Ask at the *Visitor Information Center* on Third and Seward.

Hotels

(There is a hotel and sales tax.) *Alaska Bed and Breakfast Association:* write 369 South Franklin, No. 200, Juneau, AK 99801; phone 586-2959. Also handles B & B's in most other Alaskan cities and communities. (Check ahead if you have a pet with you—some homes will take pets.) Reservations are suggested. Check with the Visitor Information Center on Third and Seward for other good B & B's.

Juneau has more than a dozen hotels. Among them, *The Alaskan Hotel* (167 South Franklin Street) and *The Bergman* (434 Third Street) are both old enough to be classified as historical monuments, which give them a certain charm. The tariff in these hotels, as well as in the *Inn at the Waterfront* (55 South Franklin) and the *Silverbow Inn* (120 Second Street; smoking allowed only in Smokers' Lounge; good restaurant), is reasonable, and you can experience some of the old Alaska atmosphere in any of these four. *The Alaskan,* the *Driftwood Lodge* (435 Willoughby Street), and the *Baranof Hotel* have housekeeping units. The *Baranof* (127 North Franklin Street), right downtown, is the center of many local activities, and local people as well as tourists pass through it a great deal. The food and the rooms, however, are expensive. The same is true for the *Westmark Hotel,* at 51 West Egan Drive. The *Breakwater Inn,* 1711 Glacier Avenue, is moderately expensive but has a good view and restaurants. It is reasonable. You can write any of these hotels in Juneau, AK 99801. There is a *Travelodge* at the airport.

Campgrounds

There are two Forest Service campgrounds near Juneau, one at *Mendenhall Lake,* 13 miles from downtown, and one at *Auke Bay,* about 16 miles from downtown. These facilities have a modest fee. You can take the MGT bus from downtown to within 2 miles of Mendenhall Lake, but the Auke Bay Campground is nearly 4 miles from where the bus line ends at DeHart's store at Auke Bay. Incidentally, if you plan to hitch with your backpack, don't despair if several cars pass you by; some Alaskans are still quite conservative about hitchhikers. On the other hand, you will find most Alaskans to be the friendliest people in the world, and sooner or later you will get a ride.

Storage

Inquire at the Juneau Airport. Most hotels and bed and breakfasts will keep your gear for short periods of time, especially on your day of departure.

Showers

Available at the **Harbor Wash Board** (see Laundromats, below), and at *Augustus Brown Swimming Pool* (which has a sauna, too), 1619 Glacier Avenue.

Laundromats

Harbor Wash Board, 1111 F Street, off Glacier Avenue, behind the Alaska Laundry. The *Dungeon Launderette* at Franklin and Fourth is open daily 8 A.M. to 8 P.M. Also inquire at the Visitor Information Center (see below).

Special Events

The Gold Creek *Salmon Bake* is a traditional all-you-can-eat Juneau fish feed that is held from mid-May to mid-September at the end of Basin Road in Last Chance Basin. Hours are 5:30 to 9:00 P.M. Prices are reasonable, and it's an easy, if steep, 2.5-mile walk from downtown, or you can catch a lift in the courtesy bus that makes pickups at the Baranof Hotel. You'll find lots of local people eating at this open-air—under a roof—special dining event, which says something about how good the food is.

Local Outings

The *Juneau City and Borough Park and Recreation Department* (155 South Seward Street) sponsors day outings every week of the year. These are open to everyone and include local hikes and cross-country ski trips in the winter. Inquire at the Park and Recreation Department for information or telephone 586-5226. These outings give you a good chance to meet local people.

Other Basic Sources of Information

Check with the cruise shop *Information Kiosk* at Marine Park next to Merchant's Mall on the Wharf (open in summer), or with the *Visitor In-*

formation Center on Third and Seward Streets. The *Foggy Mountain Shop* (134 North Franklin; phone 586-6780) may be able to give you up-to-the-minute tips on local hiking and kayaking out of Juneau. Also inquire at *Alaska Discovery* (see below).

Useful Names and Addresses

Juneau Visitor Information Center: write 134 Third Street, Juneau, AK 99801; phone 586-2201. Free brochures and ready advice about what to do and see in the greater Juneau area. *Alaska State Division of Tourism:* write Box 11801, Juneau, AK 99811-0801; phone 465-2010. You can get your free copy of the *Alaska State Vacation Planner,* a helpful source of information for travelers in Alaska, by writing this agency. *Forest Service Information Center:* 101 Egan Drive, Juneau, AK 99801; phone 586-8751; fax 586-7928. You can make Forest Service cabin reservations here. *National Park Service:* write Box 1089, Juneau, AK 99802; phone 586-7137. *Alaska Travel Adventures:* write 9085 Glacier Highway, Juneau, AK 99801; phone 789-0052. This outfit conducts daily outings. *Alaska Discovery:* 5449 Shaune Drive, #4, Juneau, AK 99801; phone 780-6226 or 1-800-586-1911; fax 780-4220. Guided and outfitted kayak, canoe, and whitewater rafting trips of one or more days. *Alaska Up Close* offers sensitive nature excursions and birdwatching outings; write Judy Shuler, Box 32666, Juneau, AK 99803; phone 789-9544. If you have only a short time in Juneau, it's worthwhile contacting any one of the last three outfits. (Note: Alaska Up Close requires prior bookings.)

Environmental Organizations

Southeast Alaska Conservation Council (SEACC): write 419 Sixth Street, Suite 328, Juneau, AK 99801; phone 586-6942. This group is concerned with protection of sensitive environmental areas in the Southeast.

32. Admiralty Island

Over a million beautiful acres in size—the island is nearly 100 miles long and close to 30 wide—Admiralty Island is a wonderfully representative and relatively untouched sample of Southeast Alaska. Surrounded by salt water, it has nearly 700 miles of coastline, which is intricately incised with bays and inlets, aproned with tideflats, and ornamented with islands. Admiralty rises high enough, over 4,500 feet, to cup snowfields as well as two glaciers. It has idyllic lakes, white waterfalls, and lively streams, some of which tumble directly into the sea. The tidal waters make for unique salt chucks, and it is an extraordinary experience to watch an inland lake drop dramatically as the waters rush through its outlet at low tide. The land of Admiralty Island is densely clothed with a typical Southeast rainforest. Great old spruce and hemlock shadow a lush understory of devil's club, skunk cabbage, dwarf dogwood, and ferns—all of which will delight the heart of a photographer.

The wildlife of Admiralty Island is rich and diverse. Humpback whales cavort in its coastal waters; sea lions use its islands for their rookeries. Fishing is good, a fact attested to by the prodigious number of bald eagles. In fact, according to the USDA Forest Service, there are more bald eagles on Admiralty than there are crows, and in springtime the eagles congregate in the Seymour Canal, which cleaves Admiralty, in numbers unequaled anywhere on earth. Sitka black-tailed deer use almost all of the island from the uplands to the tidelands, staying in front of the snowline as it inches down from the heights in autumn. Admiralty Island is also one of the last remaining large bastions of the great brown bear.

Tlingit Indians have lived on Admiralty Island and used its resources for their subsistence for many millennia. Sealaska, the Native Regional Corporation, has identified several historic sites and cemeteries on the island and has selected and requested land conveyance—under the terms of the Alaska Native Claims Settlement Act—of five locations, including the Chatham Strait pictographs. The village of Angoon, population about six hundred, the Native community on the island, has an interesting history. About a century ago, it was shelled by the revenue cutter *Corwin*—one of the few incidents where firearms were used against Alaska's Native people by the United States. (The incident involved the killing of a Native by a whaler's gun, and the subsequent seizing of a white hostage by the Natives.) Angoon was a fishing center for many years and also the site of salmon canneries. The people were known as "Hootzenoowoos," a name that has become "Kootznoowoo" and has been taken by the village corporation.

Admiralty Island has been administered by the USDA Forest Service since 1909. Under the aegis of this agency, the island has been managed for multiple use. There has been sporadic mining, and attempts to "harvest" the island's magnificent "mature" forests. In 1970, conservationists challenged the Forest Service on a logging contract that would have turned most of the island's trees into commercial timber. A landmark court decision resulted in the abandonment of the contract. This made possible

Tidal flat in Admiralty Island National Monument. Source: USDA Forest Service.

the subsequent establishment of the near 1-million-acre Admiralty Island National Monument by Congress in 1980. Twenty-three thousand acres of the monument were awarded the Native corporation Shee-Atika as part of its entitlement under ANCSA and are therefore not included in the wilderness status of the rest of the monument. Do not be surprised to see clear-cut areas that Shee-Atika has logged. The Forest Service is managing the rest of the monument as a roadless area, with emphasis on wilderness, cultural, educational, recreational, and scientific values.

Admiralty Island has some of the finest canoeing I have enjoyed in Alaska. A trans-island route takes you from Mole Harbor on the east to Angoon on the west. You paddle the length of one after another beautiful lake, portaging (alas) between them. (I remember only one portage, however, as being literally, as well as figuratively, a drag.) Forest Service cabins en route provide restful layovers and welcome shelters from the frequently rainy weather. The tidal flats around Angoon are gorgeous and should, of course, be treated respectfully. The high-low tidal phenomenon here is also noteworthy and requires special caution by kayakers. (See Traveling in Southeastern Waters, above.)

Some Useful Information About Admiralty Island

Zip code: 99820. Area code: 907.

How to Get There

Scheduled air service goes only to Angoon, and then only by mail plane: inquire at the Juneau Airport for the schedule. Other air access is by charter: see Juneau and Sitka information for the names of local air-taxi operators. Limited ferry service also serves Angoon.

Where to Stay

Thayer Lake Wilderness Lodge on Thayer Lake is a beautiful, small, privately owned and reasonably priced wilderness lodge. If you can afford this kind of accommodation, a stay here will offer you a wonderful (and very comfortable) way to experience some of the magical qualities of the Southeast. During summers, write *Thayer Lake Wilderness Lodge,* Box 5416, Ketchikan, AK 99901; phone 225-3343 or 789-5646. In winter, write Box 8897, Ketchikan, AK 99901; phone 247-8897. The *USDA Forest Service* has several recreation cabins (including some of its most beautiful) on Admiralty Island. These are on a first-come-first-served basis, and reservations are essential. See USDA Forest Service, below, for further details. Or contact the *Admiralty National Monument* office in Juneau (8461 Old Dairy Road, Juneau, AK 99801; phone 586-8790) or the *Forest Service Information Center* in Juneau (101 Egan Drive, Juneau, AK 99801; phone 586-8751; fax 586-7928) to get up-to-date information.

Motels in Angoon include *Kootznahoo Inlet Lodge:* write Box 134, Angoon; phone 788-3501. For fishermen: *Whaler's Cove Lodge,* Box 101, Angoon; phone 788-3123. There is also the *Favorite Bay Inn Bed and Breakfast,* which has canoe rentals, guide service, and evening meals available: write Box 101, Angoon; phone 788-2123 or 1-800-3123; fax 788-4104.

Boat Tours and Rentals

Consult *Alaska Discovery* (5449 Shaune Drive, #4, Juneau, AK 99801; phone 780-6226 or 1-800-586-1911; fax 780-4220) for information about canoe trips across Admiralty Island.

Useful Names and Addresses

The village of Angoon is interested in quality tourism: write *Angoon City Office,* Box 189, Angoon, for information. The original Native beadwork of the village women is beautiful; ask about its availability at *Ramona's Restaurant and Gift Shop.* Also note the totems near the Community Center.

33. Sitka

Sitka (Shee-Atika) was named by the Tlingit Indians: the word may mean "by the sea," which is appropriate enough since Sitka is only a few islands away from the blue Pacific Ocean. Some claim that this was the spot where Alexei Chirikof arrived in the *Saint Paul* on July 15, 1741 (the day before Bering landed on Kayak Island), and so is the site of the Russian discovery of America. Others, however, insist that Bering was the first on the American scene. In any event, there is no disagreement that this is the place where Alexander Andreevich Baranof located his headquarters in 1808. (Six years earlier, the Tlingits had burned out the first Russian outpost in the Southeast, a few miles to the north. The Russians had retaliated by burning the Tlingit village and locating another settlement on what was the choicest site in the area.) Novoarkhangelsk, or New Archangel, was the name of this new Russian America capital.

New Archangel was an interesting place, indeed. For nearly a half a century, it was far more important than the little mission town of San Francisco, and it early came to boast flour mills, tanneries, and sawmills, as well as becoming a major trading center, port, and shipbuilding center. (It also had a cultured—and vodka-devoted—population, which caused visitors to complain that it was difficult to survive the Russian hospitality.) The town was sophisticated enough to be called the Paris of the Pacific.

The iron foundry established in Sitka is said to have cast bells for the California missions, but—alas—this nice idea cannot be verified. It did, however, cast steam-engine parts. By 1860, twenty-five seagoing vessels had been constructed in Sitka, including the first steam-powered ship to be built on the Pacific Coast.

In 1841, Bishop Innokenti Veniaminof (a great friend of the Aleuts) established an observatory here to study the earth's magnetic field. (Although now considered to be not ideally located, it is still a key magnetic observatory in the worldwide network of stations; Sitka is now also the site of a seismic station.) By 1861, New Archangel had two important institutes going: one zoological, as well as the one devoted to the study of terrestrial magnetic phenomena. (This latter was by now supported by the British as well as the Russians.)

When the United States purchased Alaska from Russia in 1867, the ceremonies sealing the exchange of the territory took place on an October day in front of the governor's house in New Archangel. It is reported that the wife of Prince Maksoutof, who was governor at that time, could be heard sobbing from the second-story window of the house throughout the ceremony. The United States rechristened the place Sitka. Within a week, two saloons, a restaurant, and two ten-pin bowling alleys were operating in a new American capital. The population of Sitka that year was about twenty-five hundred, but, with the departure of the Russians, it dwindled rapidly, and a dozen years later it was less than a thousand. The saloons, restaurants, and ten-pin alleys were gone, along with most of the town's erstwhile glory. However, Sitka was the operating capital of Alaska until 1906. (See Juneau.)

Today, most of the original Russian buildings, including the governor's house, have long since decayed or burned. But the beautiful old Saint Michael's Cathedral, which burned to the ground in 1966, has been lovingly restored, and the doors, icons, and many other items are from the original building. (Saint Michael's is open when cruise ships are in, in the summer; a small donation is requested from visitors.) The Russian presence in Sitka also persists strongly in other ways. There is the old cemetery with its elegant Russian Orthodox crosses, the Russian Bishop's House—the second oldest building in Alaska (the oldest, built in 1793, is located on the island of Kodiak and is presently a museum)—and the street plan of the older part of town, which remains today so much the way it was laid out that Russian maps can still help you find your way. Another aspect of Sitka's Russian heritage is preserved by the New Archangel Dancers, who perform Russian folk dances regularly in the Centennial Building downtown; they are well worth seeing. You can find out their schedule at this building. You will also probably enjoy a visit to the (contemporary) Russian-American Company in the wharfside shopping center; the store has a fine collection of Russian crafts.

Baranof showed good taste when he chose the site of Sitka for his capital. The small city sits behind a chain of picturesque tree-tufted islands that hold the Pacific surf away from its snug harbor. A sensational backdrop of mountains encircles the area to the east, some rising as high as 3,350 feet. On the west of Kruzof Island, the classically shaped volcano Mount Edgecumbe stands watch with its cape of glittering white snow. This extinct volcano is often compared to Mount Fuji for the perfection of its silhouette. It was christened Montaña de Jacinto by the Spaniards and, later, Gora Sviataga Lazar'a, or Mount Saint Lazarus, by the Rus-

Sitka black-tailed deer (Odocoileus hemionus sitkensis). *Range: Southeast Alaska and, through transplanting, Kodiak Island.*

sians. Captain Cook gave it its present name, which is believed either to honor the earl of Edgecumbe or to commemorate a mountain with the same name at the entrance to Plymouth Sound. In this lovely setting, Sitka has attracted many artists, and it is the home of cultural activities that are unique in Alaska. In June, a festival of chamber music attracts people from Outside as well as many Alaskans. Art classes are frequently conducted here. There is an excellent workshop that teaches Indian arts at the Sitka National Historical Park. You can enjoy Tlingit artwork—and perhaps observe a workshop teaching it—at the Sitka National Historical Park, where the (original) Russian-American Company people, led by Baranof, defeated the Tlingits. And there is a fine museum of Alaska Native artwork, the Sheldon Jackson State Museum, just before you get to the park.

With so much going for it, Sitka would seem like an ideal place to live. Ah, but there is the ever-present Southeast rain. Once I visited this lovely small town in the company of cruise ship passengers. It was a glorious June day with the sun pouring down on the lush green forests, the quaint buildings, and the sparkling sea. Everyone agreed that this was the prettiest place the cruise ship had dropped anchor, to date. I said nothing but noted as I visited the Old Harbor Book Store a sign reading: "Please Do Not Drip on the Books." It had been raining for twenty-three days straight and had only stopped the night before we arrived.

Sitka is situated on Baranof Island (which memorializes the shrewd old Russian governor-trader) and is a natural gateway for anyone wanting to canoe or kayak along the shores of Chichagof Island (named after another Russian gentleman, Vasilii Yakov Chichagof, who explored the Arctic in the mid-1760s). These waters offer some of the finest small-boat recreation in Alaska, and the bays and coves of West Chichagof Island offer some beautiful snug harbors. The extraordinary wilderness of West Chichagof and its beauty have prompted major efforts to give the area wilderness protection under the USDA Forest Service, which administers it. Congress recognized these wilderness values in part by designating the Pacific side of West Chichagof as a wilderness area in 1980; much of the southern half of Baranof Island is also classified as wilderness.

If you plan to do some sea kayaking in this area, you can make good use of the ferry. From Sitka, you can schedule your boating trip to meet the ferry at, say, Pelican, where it makes scheduled stops (check the schedule), or you can go farther to meet it in Angoon on Admiralty Island and continue on board to Juneau. If you're even more ambitious and have more time, you can travel to Juneau all the way in your small craft or continue to Glacier Bay. If you want to make a place like Elfin Cove your goal, you may be able to "hitch a ride" out of it on a fishing boat; ask around at the docks. Or you can, of course, charter a boat or a plane to pick you up. Larry Edwards, owner of **Baidarka Boats** in Sitka (see below for address and telephone), can give you good advice on planning any small-boat outing in this area; he can also rent or sell you a kayak.

Expert kayakers will find the most exciting part of a trip along Chichagof Island when they feel the force of the Pacific Ocean from Salisbury Sound around the Khaz Peninsula. Remember, this part of Southeast Alaska is not a place to learn to kayak by yourself. The waters around Sitka range from well protected all the way to fully exposed. If you plan any boating on your own, you must know what you're doing. (See Traveling in Small Boats, in Part I.)

There are several lovely hikes that you can take directly from Sitka or from close by. If you like to stroll, it's a pleasant ¾ mile or so from town to the Sitka National Historical Park, which marks the site of the Tlingit village where the Russians asserted their superior strength in 1804. (The Tlingits are fond of noting, however, that they are still around, whereas the Russians are not.) There's a trail through the park that takes you into open forest and then along the beach, and there's also a picnic area if you want to take your lunch. You'll see many totems. (Assembled for the Louisiana Purchase Expedition of 1904, these totems were gathered from villages throughout the Southeast. They were placed in Sitka in 1905. Some are duplicates of deteriorating originals, now stored.) You can also visit the Native Arts Workshop noted above. Along the way from town, you'll pass Sheldon Jackson College, once a school for Native Alaskans and now looking Outside for students. This is the legacy of an early missionary who had great influence in Alaska's preterritorial days.

If you want a little more strenuous activity, you can climb Gavan Hill (Harbor Mountain) directly north of Sitka, starting from downtown. This is a round-trip of about 6 miles with an elevation gain of close to 2,700 feet, so you should allow the better part of a day for it. Although there are no particular difficulties on this trail, like many in the Southeast, it requires you to be a good hiker. This climb gives some superb views, and it has enough good camping places along it to offer backpacking opportunities, but you'll need to carry a stove.

Two other interesting trails are easily reached from Sitka. One will take you to the top of Mount Verstovia, which is named not for a person but for a Russian unit of measure—a *verst*, which equals 3,500 feet. This is about the height you will gain on this trail, and you will get some even more wonderful views than from Gavan Hill, but this trail requires even more stamina and hiking expertise as well. Take care when you reach the final summit of Mount Verstovia. As Margaret Piggott (see Suggested Reading) warns, a false step could land you more than 3,000 feet below. Don't attempt the summit if snow lingers on it.

The other interesting trail will take you along nearby Indian River— a less difficult outing, although it's a good 10-mile round-trip and will be even longer if you walk the mile from town to the trailhead. This is a charming hike with an elevation gain of about 1,300 feet. You will see Southeastern forest, muskeg, a beautiful river, and lots of wildlife. The trail also opens up in places to splendid views of the Sisters and Gavan Hill.

The Sitka Parks and Recreation Department has information about local hikes. Ask for it at the city offices on Lake Street; any resident can tell you where the city hall is. Visit the Forest Service or the National Park Service people for further information about these trails and other local hiking opportunities (see below for addresses).

While you're in Sitka, you might want to visit the Alaska Pioneer Home, a stop on locally operated bus tours. This is the large building downtown that occupies part of what was once the parade ground of both the Russians and the early American garrisons that were stationed in Sitka. The old-timers in Sitka's Pioneer Home are full of Alaskan history, and if you have a chance to talk with any of them, you will probably find yourself enchanted by some of their tales. Many of them brought dreams to Alaska that never came true, but they like to talk about all the reasons they didn't. The state of Alaska is kind to its older citizens, providing housing and medical care for older residents who have not provided for themselves.

The National Park Service is in charge of the Russian Bishop's House, located one block from downtown. The house was first occupied by Father Ivan Popov Veniaminof (who took monastic vows and became Bishop Innokenti).

Until recently, Sitka was known not only as a historical treasure, but as the site of one of Alaska's two original pulp mills, the Japanese-owned Alaska Pulp Corporation. People who pitched their tents in the Sawmill Creek Campground got a strong shot of "perfume" since the mill was close by. Hikers on Mount Verstovia were also treated to the fumes. However, in 1993, the corporation defaulted on its 1950s contract with the Forest Service by closing down the mill. The Forest Service therefore canceled the contract. The mill may be closed, but it's hard not to notice the clear-cut areas of forest that fed this mill over the years it was operating. Many of them are all too obvious as the ferry approaches Sitka.

Note: Sitka is known nationally for its Chamber Music Festival, held in June. Top professionals from all over the country come to perform. This is a very popular event, so if you want to attend, it is best to make reservations well in advance. Contact the Sitka Visitor Bureau (see below) for further information.

Some Useful Information About Sitka

Zip code: 99835. Area code: 907.

Ferry

There is good ferry service in summer. The ferry terminal is about 7 miles north of town, and there is bus service into town. (If you have a bike, this is a good place to use it.)

Air Service

Alaska Airlines to Anchorage, Juneau, Petersburg, Ketchikan, and Seattle; phone 966-2266.

Air Charter Service

Paquan Air: write 485 Katlian Street, Sitka; phone 747-8636. *Mountain Aviation* at Sitka Airport: write Box 2487, Sitka; phone 766-2288.

Bus Service

Sitka Tours, phone 747-8443.

Tours

Sitka Tribe of Alaska conducts tours with a Native perspective; phone 747-7290 or 1-888-270-8687.

Taxi Service

Arrowhead Taxi: phone 747-8888. There are others; check with the Sitka Visitor Bureau (see below).

Car Rental

At the airport: *Baranof:* phone 747-8228. *All Star:* phone 966-2552. *Avis:* phone 966-2404.

Boat Charters

Nature Cruises: For wildlife charters: *Steller Wildlife and Exploring:* phone 747-6157. *Ravens Fire, Inc.:* phone 747-5777. Several boat operators are available for boat rentals and various kinds of waterborne (and land) outings; also flightseeing. Consult the Sitka Visitor Bureau (see below).

Sea Kayak Rentals, Instruction, Tours, Sales, and Advice

Baidarka Boats: write 201 Lincoln Street, Sitka; phone 747-8996. Owner Larry Edwards handles folding boats and fiberglass sea kayaks for a good price and can arrange for delivery anywhere in the United States. He is a sea kayaking expert, and he offers year-round service.

Hotels

There is a 4 percent hotel tax and a 4 percent sales tax. (If you're old enough to carry a Medicare card, and have it with you, you're excused from both taxes.) *Potlach House* (motel): reasonable, between ferry and town; with courtesy car service, restaurant, view; write 713 Katlian Street, Sitka; phone 747-8611. *Westmark Shee Atika Lodge:* in town, moderate, with restaurant; write 330 Seward Street, Sitka; phone 747-6241 or 1-800-544-0970. Check with the Sitka Visitor Bureau (see below) for other hotels, bed and breakfasts, and other unique lodging. There is a *Youth Hostel*—see Appendix E.

Elderhostel

Elderhostel is an international educational and hosteling program open to anyone who is 55 or older or whose spouse qualifies. It describes itself as being for those "on the move—not just in terms of travel but in the sense of reaching out to new experiences." Under Elderhostel auspices, participating universities and colleges, both large and small, offer weekly summer classes on a variety of interesting subjects. The cost is remarkably low and includes both tuition and board.

In Alaska, the Sheldon Jackson College in Sitka and other institutions of higher learning offer Elderhostel classes. You can choose from such courses as "The Ecology of Alaska," "Between Alaska Tides," "A Festival of Alaska Films," and so forth. The campuses are lovely and provide a unique and inexpensive way for elder citizens to get to know Alaska.

For dates of courses and further details, write: *Elderhostel,* 75 Federal Street, Boston, MA 02110. Note: Elderhostel does not make travel arrangements.

Campgrounds

The USDA Forest Service's *Starrigavan Campground* (Old Harbor) is 0.7 mile north of the ferry terminal. This is the best place to camp. It is also the site of the first Russian settlement, Mikhailovskii Redut. *Sawmill Creek:* 1 Blue Lake Road, past the ALP mill; 14 miles from the ferry terminal; no water. (The city and borough of Sitka has RV facilities; phone 747-3439.)

Laundromat and Shower

Duds and Suds: 908 Halibut Point Road; phone 747-5050.

Useful Names and Addresses

Chamber of Commerce: write Box 638, Sitka; phone 747-8604. *Sitka Visitor Bureau:* write Box 1226, Sitka; phone 747-5940. *National Park Service:* write Sitka National Historical Park, 106 Metlakatla Street, Box 738, Sitka; phone 747-6281. *USDA Forest Service:* write Box 1980, Sitka; phone 747-6671.

34. Hoonah

The village of Hoonah lies a little off the beaten track, which adds to its charms. While it is not served by the large ferries, the smaller ships provide a pleasant short voyage from Juneau several times a week. (Check your ferry schedule.) It is also possible to reach Hoonah by air: there are several scheduled flights daily; but a trip on the mail plane is the most reasonable way to fly. (Check at the Juneau Airport for schedules of mail deliveries.) Once in Hoonah, you will find comfortable Native-operated accommodations, and it is possible to make a tour to Glacier Bay from this pleasant spot. There is also the Hoonah Indian Association Culture Center to visit. The Native people at Hoonah are interested in tourism, and you will be welcome. For further details, write *City of Hoonah,* Box 360, Hoonah, AK 99829; phone 945-3663 or 945-3664.

A Southeastern kayaker notes: "For a nice five- or six-day kayak trip, ride the ferry from Juneau to Hoonah and paddle south to Port Frederick. Portage the isthmus and you enter Tenakee Inlet. (Try for a 16-foot-high tide or better!) Then paddle on down to Tenakee Springs for a good soak in the hot springs. Then return to Juneau on the ferry." For more information—including possible renting of your kayak for this trip—contact *Alaska Discovery:* write 5449 Shaune Drive, #4, Juneau, AK 99801; phone 780-6226 or 1-800-586-1911; fax 780-4220.

35. Haines

When you travel up the Lynn Canal, you traverse part of the Chatham Strait–Lynn Canal fault, which delineates a major separation in the earth's crust and is considered one of the world's most spectacular fault systems. Movement along this fault through the millennia has shattered the rocks in the region. The great glaciers of the various ice ages quarried out the rock debris along the fault lines and flooded the deep cleft that remained in the landscape with their icy meltwater. This country is still restless, with major tectonic activity possible at any time. The snowy descendants of those earlier glaciers—vast ice fields and new glaciers—lie glittering and waiting on the mountain peaks as well, their meltwater pouring out in turbulent streams and rivers that still nourish this part of the Inside Passage.

You will notice a change in both the landscape and the climate in this northern part of the passage, which makes for pleasant variety as you travel on the ferry. The island-studded channels of the southern reaches of the passage give way to a cleaner sweep of water that gradually narrows between rising peaks. The influence of the ocean is diminished at Haines, although storms can and frequently do barrel in from the south.

The dark spruce and hemlock forests are softened here by deciduous trees that change with the seasons. In winter, the bare branches of the birches and cottonwoods are a delicate smoky brown; in spring and summer, their light-green leaves tuft the landscape; in autumn, their leaves blaze a tawny gold that illuminates the dark stands of conifers, as though by sunlight, and the leaves of small maples flame a brilliant red, a particular delight on gray days. As you approach the interior of the continent, the gray days are fewer; the winds, however, are more frequent and stronger, flowing in torrents through the high passes of the Coast Mountains, which rise above the canal.

The Lynn Canal has historically served as a major passageway into the interior of the continent from the coastal waters of the Southeast. At its

Bald eagle (Haliaeetus leucocephalus). *Range: Alaska's forested shores.*

northern end, it divides into two fingers. One, the Chilkoot Inlet, leads due north into the famous Chilkoot Pass, gateway to the Yukon. (It also provides access to White Pass.) This was the exclusive pathway of the Chilkoot Indians, who guarded the pass zealously, using it for trade with the Tagish Indians of the Interior. (See Skagway.) The other finger of the Lynn Canal leads northwest, opening a way up the Chilkat Valley to Chilkat Pass. This was once the route of the old Dalton Trail, now largely gone back to wilderness. It is more or less the present route of the Haines Highway, which provides access to Whitehorse, Yukon Territory, and Fairbanks, Alaska. The town of Haines, located on the Chilkat Peninsula, guards the terminus of both these well-traveled routes.

As you approach Haines on the ferry, you may leave some of the whales behind you, but not the bald eagles. In fact, in the fall and early winter, the eagles congregate in great numbers in the valley of the Chilkat River near Haines. Warm springs beneath the gravel outwash of this riverbed keep the water relatively ice-free well into the colder months, and the chum salmon continue their run. Eagles by thousands, literally, crowd after them to Chilkat. Once on a November morning, when the sun stained the snowy mountains of the Chilkat Range a deep orange pink and snow outlined each bare branch of the cottonwood trees along the river, I heard the early morning conversation of a great gathering of these birds and watched them as they fished on the blue-black waters. It was an unforgettable experience. The state of Alaska has recognized the unique qualities of this area by setting aside a 48,000 acre Alaska Chilkat Bald Eagle Preserve. (For brochure, write *Division of Parks and Outdoor Recreation,* Box 430, Haines, AK 99827; phone 766-2292.)

The town of Haines has a recorded history that dates back to 1878, a year before John Muir and his friend the Reverend S. Hall Young made their first visit here. (The man who preceded them was George Dickinson, an agent of the Northwest Trading Company, who was scouting out fur-trading possibilities with the Chilkats.) Muir and Young were traveling in a large canoe manned by Indians from the Wrangell area, and Young was bent on converting the Chilkats. As they approached what was known as the village of Chilkat, they came into sight of the Davidson Glacier, which Muir described in his *Travels in Alaska* as "a broad white flood reaching out two or three miles into the canal with wonderful effect." Muir wanted to camp beside it, but a strong headwind held them back. (To Muir's annoyance, Young had refused to travel the previous day, when the wind was perfect, because it was Sunday.) The next morning, however, Muir wrote with typical exuberance:

> The wind was fair and joyful . . . and away we glided to the famous glacier. In an hour or so we were directly in front of it and beheld it in all its crystal glory descending from its white mountain fountains and spreading out in an immense fan three or four miles wide against its tree-fringed terminal moraine.

You can still visit the Davidson Glacier, which has retreated considerably, by taking the Mud Bay Road out of Haines.

Muir and Young found the Chilkats an independent but friendly people, and Young preached to them valiantly. They preferred, however, to listen to the more charming John Muir and required that he be given equal time. If taken aback, Young was not defeated; to carry on his efforts a couple of years later, he sent the Reverend and Mrs. Eugene Willard back to the village. They managed to establish a mission (although it took quite a while to convert the Chilkats), and it was the Willards who named the town Haines, in honor of Mrs. Francina Electra Haines of the Presbyterian Board of Home Missions.

Haines took its place in gold-rush history as the starting point of the Dalton Trail, which was much safer than the Chilkoot Trail, but it led in too long and circuitous a manner to the Yukon country, which was the pressing goal of the sourdoughs. The Dalton Trail was used largely for animals. More attention was paid to Haines in 1903, when the U.S. Army located there and built Fort William H. Seward, which still stands.

Haines is visited by many tourists who travel the Haines Highway and the ferries, and it is also the site of an annual Southeast Alaska Fair. It has had its share of salmon canneries, local mining efforts, and logging operations, but the town is far enough off the beaten track to have retained much of its own particular Southeast flavor. (If you are interested in Native American artifacts and pioneer history, you might want to check out the Sheldon Museum and Cultural Center on the main street of the town.)

In the opinion of many visitors, Haines vies with Homer and Valdez for being the most beautifully situated community in Alaska today. The Chilkat Mountains form a dazzling and constantly changing display on the horizons around the town, and the mostly good (though windy) weather lets you enjoy the view. On quiet blue days, the water of the Lynn Canal reflects the fishing boats floating in its small harbor as though they were painted on it.

There is good day-hiking around Haines, and the Visitor Bureau (see below) can give you good information. You can also climb from downtown Haines to the top of nearby Mount Ripinski and gain some stunning views of the snow and ice peaks that line the Lynn Canal and separate the Chilkat Valley from Glacier Bay National Monument. (Above treeline, the Mount Ripinski Trail is a wonderful place to watch the storms sweep in from the south.) This is at least a day's hike, with an elevation gain of 3,563 feet, but the trail is good and is well maintained by local people.

Haines is also the place you'll use as a takeoff point for one of Alaska's finest river experiences, the run of the Tatsenshini and Alsek Rivers. When I first made this river trip it was relatively unknown, but in the past several years it has been publicized and much advertised by commercial river runners. If you would like to go with a guide, you can contact the *Chilkat Guides:* write Box 170, Haines, AK 99827; phone 766-2491. Or get in touch with *Alaska Discovery:* write 5449 Shaune Drive, #4, Juneau, AK 99801; phone 780-6226 or 1-800-586-1911; fax 780-4220. This outfit runs several trips every summer down the Tatsenshini and Alsek, putting in at Dalton Post (close to Mile 150 up the Haines Highway) and providing all necessaries, including food, equipment, and their river-running expertise.

If you decide to make this river trip on your own, plan to arrange for wheeled transportation from Haines to the put-in point below Mile 107 on the Haines Highway: contact the Haines Visitor Bureau (see below). You will also need an air-taxi pickup at the end of your trip in Dry Bay—see Air Charters below. Once you've reached Yakutat by air taxi, you can fly on a scheduled airline, either north or south.

One of the best things about this river run is the variety of wilderness waters you will encounter. You start in a fairly intimate clear-as-glass river (although soon after your put-in, you come to a rapids that the natives call, perhaps accurately, "the falls"; you may want to portage this one), then fast-flowing glacial streams pour in their silvery silt, and, finally, you find yourself in a broad, mighty river—one of the great drainages of the North American continent, the Alsek. Along the way, you'll also have gorgeous scenery, including stupendous views of the north side of the Fairweather Range (which you see from the south in Glacier Bay)—if the weather is good, that is. Do not, under any circumstances, follow the Alsek River when you see it is going to swing toward the Alsek Glacier on the back of the range: it could cost you your raft or kayak, and possibly your life, if you do, for the glacier may engulf the river during most of the year. As you approach the Alsek Glacier, stay along the right bank of the river and take your boat out as you reach the base of a large nunatak (see Glaciers, in Introduction to Part II) that looms directly ahead of you. You may have to make a short portage then to the lagoon that leads eventually back into the Alsek after it has emerged from the glacier, but this is a short haul at most and poses no problems. When we ran this section of the Alsek, it seemed to me that the wild, joyous character of the upper Alsek vanished into the glacier, as though it had been captured; a broad, more dignified river emerges from under the ice and moves rather sedately—though still at a good rate of speed—carrying flotillas of icebergs downstream for many miles. (Happily, the Tatsenshini and Alsek Rivers have been protected in a Canadian national park.)

The Alsek is heavily fished in its lower portion, being a particularly fine salmon stream, and, when the salmon are running, you can expect to encounter motorboats from the Alsek Glacier on. You will also probably see fish-processing scows at work, parked in sloughs along the way.

Some Useful Information About Haines

Zip code: 99827. Area code: 907.

Ferry

Runs daily in summer. Inquire about a Haines layover if you're going from Skagway to the south and want only a few hours in Haines; there is often a couple of hours' wait on the regular southbound run. There is baggage storage at the ferry terminal (about 4 miles north of town on Lutak Inlet) and bus service into town.

Water Taxi

Haines-Skagway Water Taxi runs round-trips between Haines and Skagway daily; phone 766-3395. Reasonable.

Air Charters and Scheduled Flights

L.A.B. Flying Service: write Box 272, Haines; phone 766-2222. *Wings of Alaska:* write Box 1829, Haines; phone 766-2030. *Haines Airways:* write Box 470, Haines; phone 766-2646.

Car Rental

Eagle's Nest Motel and Car Rental: phone 766-2891. *Avis:* Hotel Halsingland; phone 766-2000. *Captain's Choice Motel Car Rentals:* phone 766-3111.

Taxi

Haines Shuttle and Tours: phone 766-3138. *New Other Guys Taxi and Tours:* phone 766-3257.

Hotels

(There is a sales tax.) Interesting accommodations are available in buildings once used as officers' quarters in historic Fort Seward in Port Chilkoot, just south of town: *Hotel Halsingland* (phone 766-2000), reasonable, seasonal (March to December), sixty rooms with bath, seafood restaurant, car rental, bus service; *Fort Seward Condominiums* (766-2425), furnished, available year-round, and reasonable; and *Fort William H. Seward Bed and Breakfast* (766-2856), seasonal (April to October), moderate. Other accommodations include *Captain's Choice Motel* (766-3111), downtown, year-round, moderate, with executive suites; *Eagle's Nest Motel* (766-2891), 1 mile out of town, year-round, reasonable, with free transportation; *Mountain View Motel* (766-2900), adjacent to Fort Seward, year-round, reasonable, with ferry shuttle; and *Thunderbird Motel* (766-2131), downtown, year-round, moderate, with some kitchenettes. There is also a Youth Hostel: *Bear Creek Camp and Hostel* (766-2259), seasonal (June to September).

Campgrounds

Chilkoot Lake: 5 miles from the ferry terminal, 10 from town. *Portage*

Cove: 2 miles from town on Beach Road; 7 miles from ferry. Attractive but small. *Mosquito Lake Campground:* Mile 27, Haines Highway; 32 miles from ferry. *Chilkat State Park:* Mile 7, Mud Bay Road. Large facility of Alaska State Parks; phone 766-2292. These are all public, with small fees. There are also private campgrounds; check with the Visitor Bureau (see below).

Useful Names and Addresses

For all kinds of Haines information—resources, attractions, facilities, and services—write the *Haines Visitor Bureau* (at Second and Willard Streets), Box 530; phone 766-2234 or 1-800-458-3579.

36. Skagway

You can step back into history when you walk up Broadway from the ferry in Skagway. This was the gateway to the Yukon in 1897 and the staging point of the great Klondike gold rush. If you listen carefully, you can almost hear the frantic, hurrying footsteps of thousands of men and women echoing on the boardwalks that border the street. Theirs was a poignant story: teachers, lawyers, con men, farmers, bank clerks, prostitutes—they were infected with the fever for gold that spread like the plague once it became known the precious metal was there for the taking in the Yukon. Seeking their fortunes, many of them found instead defeat, disaster, and, too often, death. Almost none found gold, for by the time they learned of the strike on Rabbit Creek (gold was "caught between the rocks like cheese in a sandwich"), the best claims had all been staked.

Now, in the Klondike Gold Rush National Historical Park, the National Park Service has memorialized the thousands of Cheechakos (non-Alaskans) who poured through Skagway bent on reaching the Yukon. The town of Skagway has cooperated enthusiastically with re-creating the scene much as it was more than a century ago. The National Park Service has its headquarters and Visitor Center in the old depot of the White Pass & Yukon Route Railroad at the corner of Second and Broadway. This building along with such places as the Arctic Brotherhood Hall and the Red Onion—now a saloon and gift shop but once the small city's "house"—have been carefully restored to give you an interesting look into Skagway's bawdy past. The Chilkoot Trail (out of the ghost town of Dyea, a few miles to the south) has also been revived, with the cooperation of the Canadian government, giving it a unique international significance. This trail beckons any backpacker who has a sense of history and adventure—and a strong pair of legs and a good heart, for the Chilkoot is a tough pull; it is a testament to the courage, determination, and perhaps the foolhardiness of the "ninety-eighters," who would lock arms to pull one another over the summit.

The name *Skagway* probably comes from the Tlingit word *sch-kawai*, which means "end of the salt water," although it is also close to *skagua*, another Native word, meaning "home of the north wind." Both names are appropriate to the place, which marks the northernmost arm of the saltwater Lynn Canal and is also frequently buffeted by gales. The first white settler, who named the community, was a seventy-four-year-old former steamboat captain, William Moore, who surveyed for Canada and found a route across the Coast Range through White Pass. He figured that a port would thrive at the tidewater terminus of his route where the Skagway River poured its water into Lynn Canal. Moore homesteaded there in 1887 and, with his son, constructed a wharf and settled in to wait for the railroad to be built over White Pass.

The Moores had in mind that Skagway would become a gateway to the Yukon, for, as early as the 1870s, hopeful miners had been prospecting in the streams along the great river to the north. When the great rush did come—it took almost a year after the initial strike on August 16, 1896, for the stampeders to reach Skagway—the Moores found themselves completely overwhelmed. The sourdoughs simply took over, threw up their shacks, and rigged their tents wherever they could find a spot of vacant ground. From a handful of people, the population of Skagway briefly burgeoned to ten thousand unruly souls. John Muir, who visited the place with the 1899 Harriman expedition, called it "a nest of ants taken into a strange country and stirred by a stick."

Steamer followed steamer up the Lynn Canal the autumn and winter of 1897, hauling people, their tools, food, horses, and cattle into the rough new town. Among those who came was Jefferson "Soapy" Smith, who brought his gang along with him and bullied his way to control of Skagway, turning it into what was called "the roughest place on earth." When the town grew tired of his ruthless despotism, more sober citizens called a meeting of vigilantes to oust him. Smith confronted the group and in an ensuing duel mortally wounded the town's surveyor, Frank Reid, who died a couple of days later. Reid, however, had killed Soapy instantly with a single shot from his pistol. Now the two rest not far from one another in the Gold Rush Cemetery. Soapy left a legend, but Reid—

the real hero of the incident—only left his name on a charming waterfall not far from his grave and the legacy of a neatly laid out town.

On July 10, 1900, William Moore's dream was fulfilled and a 110-mile-long railroad linking Skagway to Whitehorse was completed. By then, however, the gold fever had waned, and Skagway was on its way to becoming a more respectable little ghost town.

The construction of the White Pass & Yukon Route Railroad was a saga in itself. Although it was backed by a British financier and a Canadian railroad builder, when the Alaska-Canada border was finally established, the railroad turned out to be the first in Alaska. It was also an American, George Brackett, who had blasted out a toll road over White Pass during the gold rush and had unwittingly laid the bed for the narrow-gauge tracks.

For decades, the White Pass & Yukon Route Railroad and the ferry were Skagway's lifelines, but in the late 1970s a road from Carcross to Skagway was completed, and in 1982 the railroad suspended operations, thus interrupting service on what was a wonderful train ride. The railroad reopened in 1988, providing passenger service between Skagway and Fraser, British Columbia, and a track car to pick up Chilkoot Trail hikers at Lake Bennett. Buses now travel the highway route that traverses some breathtakingly beautiful country, traveling from the rainforest zone with its thick stands of spruce and hemlock through mixed stands of birch, cottonwood, and alder (all second growth here, since the hillsides were stripped during the gold rush); it continues to the subarctic alpine tundra zone above the 3,000-foot level, where lichens, low-growing willow, dwarf birch, mosses, and heathers grow. On the Canadian side, you will move into a drier climate since the Coast Range catches most of the rain. There, the sparser boreal forest takes over with its alpine fir, lodgepole pine, spruce, cottonwood, and aspen.

You can drive to Carcross year-round; 20 miles south of Whitehorse, Yukon, you can pick up the Alaska Highway and continue on to Interior Alaska (or head back south). A ride on the bus, however, will let you relax and enjoy the fabulous scenery. There is regular motorcoach service from Skagway to Fairbanks, from whence you can take off on many Interior adventures.

If you want to explore the area around Skagway on foot, there's a choice of interesting and beautiful trails. Once again, you can walk from downtown directly into wilderness, and there are opportunities for a short stroll or a major outing, depending on how much time you have. If you only have a few hours, go to the National Park Service Visitor Center on Broadway (only a short walk from the ferry dock) and ask about the trail to Lower Dewey Lake. You can make a 2½-mile circuit with an elevation gain of 600 feet (time, about an hour and a half) to a lovely lake that is fine for swimming in the summer. (If you're there in the winter, it's also a good place to go ice skating.) There are good views along the way.

If you want a longer, more strenuous outing, you can continue from Lower Dewey Lake to Upper Dewey Lake. You can make this a day's outing or an overnight trip, since there is good camping as well as a cabin at the upper lake. It is a round-trip of 7 miles from town, and you'll have to climb over 3,000 feet before you're through, but there are views along the way, and Margaret Piggott (see Suggested Reading) describes the lake as "a gem captured in a bowl of 5,000 to 6,000-foot peaks which back onto the Skagway ice fields; its overflow spills almost directly into the beautiful fjords below, by a series of cascades."

If you visit Upper Dewey Lake, you'll probably want to go on another three-quarters of a mile or so to the Devil's Punchbowl, which is 700 feet higher up. There are incredible views of Skagway on the way, as well as of Taiya Inlet and the spectacular peaks that surround it.

Another short hike will take you from downtown to the Gold Rush Cemetery, for a view of the graves of Soapy Smith and Frank Reid, and then you can stroll to Lower Reid Falls, which are highly photogenic, especially when they are frozen in the winter. This is an easy 5-mile round-trip walk that will make up a pleasant afternoon. If you have a car, you can visit the area in an hour or so.

On the way from Skagway to Dyea, there is another area that is lovely for hiking: the Skyline and AB Mountain trail. To reach it, you can take the bus to Dyea and get off at Mile 3. Again, you have a choice of a short stroll, with a good viewpoint, or you can climb 5,000 feet to the top of AB Mountain. This is not a trail for tenderfeet. (The name *AB* refers to the rough outline of the letters *A* and *B* that late snow forms on the face of the mountain.)

The USDA Forest Service maintains trails to Denver Glacier and to Laughton Glacier. The Forest Service cabin, which sleeps six, on the way to Laughton Glacier is recommended. Contact the **Forest Service Information Center** in Juneau (101 Egan Drive, Juneau, AK 99801; phone 586-8751; fax 586-7928) for information about these glacier trails and the use of the cabin. Of course, the trail with the greatest challenge of all is the Chilkoot.

Hiking the Chilkoot Trail

The National Park Service advises you to allow at least four days to hike the Chilkoot Trail. It is 33 miles from its takeoff point at Dyea to Bennett, British Columbia. You will gain 4,700 feet if you take the trail from

Skagway; 2,500 feet if you travel it north to south. Remember that the use of handguns is prohibited in Canada, and you are not permitted to carry assembled firearms on the United States portion of the Chilkoot Trail. (You can check your guns at the Skagway Police Department, or, if you're hiking from Canada south, with the Royal Canadian Mounted Police at Carcross or Whitehorse.) On your return to Skagway, you must check through U.S. Customs at the border.

Before you make the Chilkoot Trail hike, you should check into the National Park Service Visitor Center at Skagway (see below) for the latest information about the trail. Parks Canada may charge a fee to hike the Canadian portion and may limit the number of hikers over Chilkoot Summit. You will need a permit to camp along the trail; this, and current trail regulations, are available at the Dyea Ranger Station, ½ mile from the trailhead. During the summer you will find park service rangers at Dyea, Sheep Camp, and Lindeman along the way who can provide you with further information or assistance if you need it.

Equipment for this long hike requires a camp stove and fuel (there's no wood in places); warm clothing (wool, please) and good rain gear; good hiking boots; a freestanding lightweight tent with fly; a first aid kit; and plenty of food plus extras in case of emergency.

You will find historic artifacts all along the Chilkoot Trail. The park service requests that you not disturb or remove them. Actually, the old wagon wheels and iron scraps and other bric-a-brac that you'll see beside the trail are mute testimony to the extraordinarily arduous trip the sourdoughs made getting to the gold country of Canada. There was a weigh scale at the summit of the pass, manned by the Royal Canadian Mounties, and every person entering Canada was stopped and required to produce 1,500 pounds of food supplies and equipment adequate to last a year. This near-ton of necessary supplies had, of course, to be transported up and over the pass. Enterprising operators built tramlines up the steep slopes, but those who couldn't afford to pay the going rate had to relay their gear, piece by piece—and many did just that during the coldest parts of the bitter winter of 1897–98. (It is 16.5 miles from Dyea to the summit. At 60 pounds a single haul, it would have taken thirty-three round-trips—about an even 1,000 miles—to get the required food and equipment to the weigh station.) It is estimated that, one way or another, over twenty thousand rugged souls managed to get across Chilkoot Pass and to the Yukon River headwaters between the winter of 1897 and the fall of 1898.

Although four days is the recommended minimum for hiking the Chilkoot Trail, if you are in top shape and enjoy backpacking, you can do it in three—provided you get a really early start on the first day. But this allows for no lingering along the way and no unexpected delays. Seasoned Alaska hikers point out that the Chilkoot Trail is subject to all the vagaries of any Southeastern Alaska trail. Stretches of it can be boggy; there are avalanche hazards in winter and spring in the upper elevations; and snow rests in the summit area for much of the year and can make for slow, soggy, and difficult travel. And the weather is unpredictable; many people have crossed the summit in fog, rain, or snow, grateful for rock cairns and the old tramway cable to guide them. Winters (when a snow-shoe trip can be beautiful, especially from the Canadian side to the south) often bring 30 feet of snow to pile up on the summit. Almost any time of year, storms can come barreling in from the south to smash against the summit area. In the words of an Alaskan friend, "When the weather's good, you can plan on making 3 miles in an hour; but when it's bad it may take you three hours to make a mile." (If this prospect sounds ex-hausting, take note that rufous hummingbirds fly all the way from Mex-ico to cross the summit of the Chilkoot Trail. If you carry a red pack, one may even accompany you on your way.)

Furthermore, there's a lot to see along this historic route, and you're bound to miss some of it if you hurry your trip too much. Not only does this trail have unique historic value (remember, it was used by the Indi-ans in their time), but it also rises from sea level to cross a major divide. Here you have the opportunity to experience the full spectrum of zones in the Southeast, from sea level through the lush rainforest to the open subalpine, then the more forbidding alpine. To top it off, when you gain the rugged summit, you move into a wholly different ecological commu-nity. The Canadian side of the pass is much drier, being in the rain shadow of the coastal mountains. The country is softer, smoother, and more open, and there are lovely lakes and streams. Forests of lodgepole pine and subalpine fir greet you with their wonderful fragrance. One hiker, stepping into the forest one day, took a deep breath of the per-fumed air and exclaimed: "Ah, Wyoming!" (The stampeders used trees like these to build boats for the lake and river portions of their journey northward.)

For all these reasons, I recommend allowing plenty of time for this trek—at least five or six days, if you can. And remember not to box your-self in too tightly with commitments on the other end. You can get an ex-cellent publication, *The Chilkoot Trail Guide* (put out by the park services of the United States, Canada, Alaska, Yukon Territory, and British Columbia), from the **National Park Service** in Skagway, in person or by writing them at Box 517, Skagway, AK 99840. You can make arrangements for a pickup (of one kind or another) at the Canadian ter-minus of the trail. Check with the National Park Service Visitor Center (see below) for details on transportation options.

You can get from Skagway to the trailhead for the Chilkoot Trail in

Dyea by car, taxi, or bus. While you're in Dyea, you will probably want to visit the Slide Cemetery, where rest forty-five men and women who were killed on an upper slope of the Chilkoot Trail in the Palm Sunday avalanche of April 3, 1898—the worst of many disasters the stampeders encountered.

Some Useful Information About Skagway

Zip code: 99840. Area code: 907.

Ferry

The year-round ferry runs daily during the summer and docks almost downtown at the south end of Broadway; phone 983-2941. Also check *Haines-Skagway Water Taxi;* phone 983-2083.

Railroad

The *White Pass & Yukon Route,* Box 435, Skagway; phone 983-2214 or 1-800-343-7373.

Air Service

L.A.B. Flying Service and *Wings of Alaska* (see Juneau). *Skagway Air Service:* write Box 357, Skagway; phone 983-2218.

Air Charter Service

Temsco Helicopters: write Box 434, Skagway; phone 983-2900. A helicopter tour over Dyea and the Chilkoot Trail follows Klondike gold rush history and lands you for a twenty-five-minute guided walk on the West Creek Glacier; longer "pilot's choice" tours, with two landings, to nearby glaciers.

Bus Service

Daily, from mid-May to mid-September, the *Gray Line* provides motor coach—and train (Alaska Railroad)—service from Skagway to Whitehorse, Fairbanks, Anchorage, and points en route and south. Write 300 Elliott Avenue West, Seattle, WA 98119; phone 1-800-544-2206 or, in Skagway, 983-2241; fax 206-281-0621.

Taxi

Most hotels have courtesy pickups at the ferry, airport, and train station. Numerous individuals provide taxi—and local tour—service; check with the Convention and Visitors Bureau (see below).

Car Rental

Avis: phone 983-2247. *Sourdough Car Rental:* phone 983-2523.

Hotels

Most hotels in Skagway are within a half mile plus or minus of the ferry depot, and on or just off Broadway. Included are the *Golden North* at Third and Broadway: thirty-four rooms, gold-rush decor, a restaurant, and so on (plush); phone 983-2451 or 983-2294. The *Westmark Inn* is on Third between Broadway and Spring; large, with a large restaurant, expensive; phone 1-800-544-0970. *Miner's Cache and Gifts,* on Broadway at Sixth, was built in 1899; gold-rush atmosphere, reasonable; phone 983-3303 or 1-800-764-7670. Consult the Convention and Visitors Bureau (see below) for other accommodations, including bed and breakfasts.

Campgrounds

There is primitive and limited camping at Dyea, 9 miles from Skagway. *Hanousek Park,* at Broadway and Fourteenth Avenue, has modern facilities, is city owned, and reasonable. Check with the Convention and Visitors Bureau (see below) for other city facilities.

Guide Service for Chilkoot Trail

Consult *Alaska Discovery:* write 5449 Shaune Drive, #4, Juneau, AK 99801; phone 780-6226 or 1-800-586-1911; fax 780-4220.

Useful Names and Addresses

Visitor information: *Skagway Convention and Visitors Bureau:* write Box 415, Skagway; phone 983-2855. *Klondike Gold Rush National Historical Park Visitor Center:* in the old Railway Depot, Broadway and Second Avenue. Write Box 517, Skagway; phone 983-2921.

Note: When the White Pass & Yukon Route Railroad revised its service, it left empty one of Skagway's most interesting old buildings—the Depot. *The National Park Service* has taken it over and restored it. Their *Visitor Center* is a good place to start in Skagway to get any information you might need. The National Park Service also conducts interesting walking tours.

37. Glacier Bay

In Alaska, as in few places on our planet, you can observe great earth forces actively at work and see their effects directly on the landscape. Volcanism, mountain building, frost action, avalanches, erosion, and deep-seated earth movements along with glaciers, floods, and mighty and swift-flowing rivers—all constantly change the face of Alaska's land, frequently before your eyes. More subtle but just as exciting, the rapid evolution of the living landscape can be witnessed throughout Alaska. Nowhere in Alaska can you see both earth and life forces in action more easily and dramatically than at Glacier Bay National Park.

Glacier Bay is across Icy Strait from Chichagof Island, about 60 miles north and west of Juneau. Its icy waters are fed by some nine dazzling tidewater glaciers that surge from the precipitous high mountains rising from its shores. The bay is a recent feature of the landscape: only a little over two hundred years ago, when Capt. George Vancouver sailed through Icy Strait, it was hardly more than a slight indentation in the shore choked with the towering blue walls of a great glacier. (This explains why Glacier Bay is one of the few places in the Southeast that was not named by Vancouver—it wasn't there when he traveled by: Glacier Bay was named in 1880 by Capt. Lester Beardslee of the U.S. Navy, and the Beardslee Islands in Glacier Bay were, in turn, named for the good captain.) When John Muir visited the area a little over a century after Vancouver, however, Glacier Bay had not only come into being but had already grown to be some 48 miles long. Thus, in little more than a dozen decades, the warming period that began around 1750 had caused a spectacular retreat of glaciers in this region—the most rapid ever recorded, in fact—and the consequent birth of a respectable body of water. Meltwater has continued to feed Glacier Bay during the past century, and the bay has now reached nearly 62 miles in length. Should the warming period hold and glaciers on the Fairweather Range continue to thaw, this could pose an interesting international situation: the shores of Tarr Inlet at the northwest point of Glacier Bay National Park are al-

Yellow dryas (Dryas drummondi).

ready close to the Alaska-Canada border, and they could end up in British Columbia, which would be happy to have this extra territory. As it happens, however, the Johns Hopkins and the Grand Pacific Glaciers at the head of Tarr Inlet (already in Canada) have—for reasons only generally understood—been slowly advancing since the 1920s.

As the earth around Glacier Bay emerged from beneath the ice, life pressed forward onto it. A fascinating process of plant colonization has occurred, with a sequence of ever more complex plant communities taking over. You can see this evolution of the living landscape—as though in some huge scientific laboratory—at Glacier Bay National Park. Starting at the head of the bay, you can observe how lichens take hold in the bare rocks: these primitive plants help fragment the rocks into soil. Then notice the soft tinge of green color made by the tough but inconspicuous mosses and primitive plants like the *Equisetum,* or horsetail. Then you can see how the first pioneer flowering plants, the magenta-stained dwarf epilobium and the creamy-blossomed dryas, push up bravely from the harsh, newly exposed, and rocky terrain. These modest plants will bloom intensely through their brief summer, their root systems helping to stabilize the raw land.

When cold weather comes, the decaying bodies of these plants will provide nutrients to the soil so that other plants can follow. As you proceed down the bay, you can see these other plants growing in orderly succession. The various species—the willow, the alder, the cottonwood—indicate the length of time the land has been available for plant life to succeed upon it. At the mouth of the bay, you can go on to experience the beauty of the vigorous spruce-hemlock forest, with its lush understory and groundcover. This represents the climax community of this particular succession. (If it remains ice-free long enough, the moister parts of this forest may give way to muskeg, and, indeed, Pleasant Island near Gustavus is clothed in muskeg.) Then you can appreciate that, although it may only take you a few hours to travel the length of Glacier Bay, you have in effect moved in time through hundreds of years of plant succession—from a living ice age world into the present.

As the current warm period persists—though no one knows for how long—forests like those in Bartlett Cove are slowly taking over the areas where you now see the willows, alders, and cottonwoods, and even the dryas and epilobium. Forests have, in fact, grown the length of Glacier Bay many times in the past and then been engulfed in ice- and stream-carried sand and gravel; this is evidenced by the ancient tree trunks and branches—known as interstadial wood—that are found here and there along the shores. These may be thousands of years old. You can see many specimens of interstadial wood around Morse and Forest Creeks and just north of Fingers Bay. (Interstadial wood burns easily, and the National Park Service asks that you stay well away from it should you build a fire during your travels. Of course, you should also not take or use it for your own purposes—leave it where it is.)

As the plant communities came to provide livable habitats, birds and animals in prodigious numbers also came to live in and around Glacier Bay. At any season you visit the park, you can expect to see a spectacular panorama of life. This is the way the National Park Service overviews it:

Spring and early summer: Snow persists, especially in the high country, and ice fills the inlets in the upper part of the bay. Mountain goats are down low, birds are returning north, and the plants are beginning to turn green again.

Midsummer: Whales are gorging on herring in the bay, and the birds are raising their fledglings. The seabirds can be seen in variety and abundance. Wildflowers in vast array color the landscape. It is also time for insects to prosper.

Late summer and early fall: Snow is all gone from the ridges and low peaks, but the rain and winds increase. Berries are abundant and the salmon migrate into the rivers. Vegetation shows off its splendor of fall colors. Whales and summer birds begin to leave. The aurora borealis appears during starry nights.

Horned puffin (Fratercula corniculata). Range: rocky cliffs of Southcentral Alaska and offshore islands. Source: U.S. Fish and Wildlife Service.

If this sounds inviting, here is a glimpse of some of the other wildlife you can expect to encounter on a visit to Glacier Bay Park during the months of May through September. From Bartlett Cove, in the evenings or in early morning, your chances are good of hearing the song of coyotes on the nearby isolated Beardslee Islands. Wolves have become even more common than coyotes, with the increase of the moose population in the lower bay. Black bear and brown bear roam the wilderness throughout the park. As snow and ice melt under the summer sun, the mountain goats clamber ever higher among the cliffs and mountainsides. The birds are everywhere—especially from May through July—seabirds, shorebirds, and landbirds. More than two hundred species have been found in the park. Many are particularly easy to see and identify when you travel by boat.

On the steep rocks that rise above the fjords and inlets and on the remote islands, you can sometimes observe pigeon guillemots, tufted and horned puffins, and glaucous-winged and herring gulls where they have tucked their nests and eggs. A puffin is a particular delight to watch in the water. One always wonders if it will fly; the answer is, of course. Although its short, whirring wings seem barely adequate to get its fat little body airborne, they actually work very well. Kittiwakes, among the loveliest and most prolific of Alaska's winged coastal residents, lift in moving clouds from their nests when disturbed. So do the terns. Dark little marbled murrelets and the rare Kittlitz's murrelet fly vigorously above the water, racing to keep up with the traveler who shares their territory. Parasitic jaegers like to chase the fleet but vulnerable terns, while the beautiful pelagic cormorants wing their arrow-straight way above the water.

May, June, and July are crucial months for hatching and rearing young birds in Glacier Bay. If you visit the park during this period, the nesting bird colonies on the islands and along the shores will be off-limits, closed by regulation. The National Park Service also closes seal-pupping areas, and kayakers should never get too close to icebergs with female seals and pups on them lest the family become separated. Best to watch and photograph quietly from a good distance.

On the land, you may find the willow ptarmigan (the official Alaska state bird), common redpolls, and snow buntings near the retreating glaciers, while yellow warblers and gray-cheeked thrushes wing among the alder thickets and the cottonwoods. And everywhere there are the barn swallows, ravens, and bald eagles, which are not above taking on the terns, and vice versa. Young eagles can cavort in aerial battles that put the most skillful stunt fliers to shame.

As of this writing, commercial fishing is allowed in Glacier Bay, which accounts for the presence of the red-buoyed halibut boats you may notice here and there during the halibut season. You can also hope to see humpback whales, and you will certainly see harbor seals.

Glacier Bay is obviously a paradise for naturalists or would-be naturalists, which is reason enough for wanting to visit it. It is also a place of exceptional beauty. On a blue day, the waters may be as still and shining as a polished mirror; a motorboat leaves a wake that fans out into a wide ruffle that seems to float on the glossy, motionless surface. Against the north and westward sky, a panorama of snow-shining mountains, the Fairweather Range, rises to over 15,000 feet. (If you should raft the Tatsenshini and Alsek Rivers, you will see the other face of these tall mountains filling the sky to the south.) Around your boat, icebergs looking like small floating castles drift by, catching the sunlight and shattering it into a thousand flashing crystals. The intricately crevassed faces of the tidewater glaciers glow blue. On clear evenings at sunset, soft shades of rose and tangerine flood every white, gleaming surface in this world of ice; and, on gray days, there is a special sense of mystery and wonder.

The beauty of Glacier Bay is best experienced from the water, whether you're on the deck of a large ship, a smaller tour boat, or, better yet, in a canoe or a kayak, or even camped close to the shore. (After you have rigged your tent, you can sit for a moment to let the silence—broken, perhaps, by the thunder of the moving glaciers or the crash of ice into the water—seep into you.) Except for the open glacial terrain and the area around Bartlett Cove, this is not ideal hiking country, and the park service has not developed a trail system through it. Backpacking is made difficult and sometimes chancy by the unstable and slippery terrain, the rockfalls, the heavy thickets of alder that must be beaten through, and the glaciers, which may require ice work. If you do decide to hike, be prepared for major scrambling. Unless you're a very surefooted and experienced hiker, keep in mind that your own discomfort (especially when bushwhacking) and the noise of rocks set rolling by your boots can be real distractions to your own full enjoyment of this very special place.

For many years, the Glacier Bay tour boats have been dropping off kayakers on their daily trips up the bay. (The cost is the same as the regular boat fare plus a reasonable drop-off or pickup charge—there is no extra charge for the kayak.) This is a unique service that can make for a fine on-the-water outing on Glacier Bay. If you decide to try this (please, not alone, unless you really know your way around in Southeastern waters), you can check with the tour boat operators (see below) to find out when and where they can deposit you and pick you up.

You can rent a kayak at *Glacier Bay Sea Kayaks* in Gustavus (write Box 26, Gustavus, AK 99826; phone 697-2257) or from *Sea Otter Kayaks* (write Box 228, Gustavus, AK 99826; phone 697-3007). *Alaska Discovery* (5449 Shaune Drive, #4, Juneau, AK 99801; phone 780-6226 or 1-800-586-1911; fax 780-4220) conducts kayak outings on Glacier Bay.

Whether you are camping or kayaking, be sure to check with the National Park Service at Bartlett Cove before taking off. You can also get your required backcountry use permits here. The park service people can give you pertinent information about current conditions and help you plan your trip as well as your camping experience. (There is a park campground in Bartlett Cove.) They can also cue you in on what to look for and where to look for it, providing in-depth information that can add immeasurably to your outing. Leave your proposed schedule with them; then, should you get yourself lost or into any other trouble and not show up when expected, they will (sigh) come look for you. Be sure to check back when you return from your trip. Also, be sure to carry out your garbage. Note: Bears, both black and brown, are present in the park (see

Bear Essentials, in Part I). Bear-proof cannisters are required if you're going to be camping in the back country; they're available from the National Park Service.

A Few Final Tips

Guns are not allowed in the park; if you're carrying one, you can check it with the park service. State fishing licenses are required if you want to supplement your food with Glacier Bay fish: you can get a license at the Glacier Bay Lodge (see below).

If you decide not to hassle with bringing your own kayak, you can join a kayak trip run by a local guide (see below).

Remember that cruise ships have the right of way, and that there are a lot of them that travel Glacier Bay. Check with the National Park Service for their anticipated schedules. Some biologists suspect that heavy boat travel may be having an impact on the local marine life: the number of humpback whales in the park has dwindled. Attempts to cap or reduce the number of cruise ships have not been welcomed.

There are limited storage facilities for gear at Bartlett Cove. If you want to camp at Bartlett Cove, there is a good campground there and a spiffy food cache against bears. If you decide to venture farther afield, consult the park service; also check with them regarding camping regulations.

Keep in mind that the tides in Glacier Bay can fluctuate as much as 25 feet, and it goes without saying that you should be prepared for rain and that you should have both sunglasses and bug juice along, although the colder areas are more likely to be insect-free.

Hikes You Can Take from Bartlett Cove

There are two lovely and easy hikes you can take if you're staying at Bartlett Cove; even a nonhiker might enjoy them. Neither involves any major elevation gain, and both can be extended if you want a longer, more strenuous hike. You can do the Forest Trail in a half hour or so, but allow a couple of hours for a Bartlett River outing.

Beach and Nature Trail

The park service conducts a 1-mile round-trip walk daily along the beach and through the forest along the shore. If you are able to join a group with the ranger, it's worthwhile. However, it is easy enough to take this short, charming walk yourself; inquire at the lodge or at park headquarters for directions and information.

If you're a good hiker and enjoy making your way along a sometimes muddy, sometimes slippery, but always beautiful beach, you can continue on the beach southward to Point Gustavus (7 miles). Check the tide before you start out; a high tide may force you into a forest scramble. And expect to see many black bears around Point Gustavus.

Bartlett River

You can make this a morning's or an afternoon's stroll or a whole day of wandering beside a beautiful river. However you take it, the trail will offer you many joyful sights and sounds. You will pass through mossy forests along the shore, and, of course, alongside the river itself. Expect to hear bird song and the scolding of red squirrels. When you reach the river (less than 1.5 miles from the Gustavus Road), look for bald eagles, great blue herons, waterfowl, coyotes, and possibly a bear. In season, the wildflowers should be lovely, with mimulus studding the grassy and wet places you pass through. Check with the National Park Service people (see below) for further details.

Note: Although Glacier Bay National Monument was enlarged by Congress in 1980 and redesignated Glacier Bay National Park and Preserve, valid mining claims still exist within its boundaries. These pose periodic—and long-range—threats to the integrity of this national treasure.

Some Useful Information About Glacier Bay

Zip codes: as listed. Area code: 907.

How to Get There

There is a scheduled air service out of Juneau to Gustavus, and bus and taxi service to Bartlett Cove, which is about 10 miles distant. Air-taxi service is available in Juneau, Haines, Sitka, and Skagway. (If you can afford a flightsee over Glacier Bay on a blue day, don't miss it. It could give you one of your greatest travel memories.)

Many tour ships include the bay on their Southeastern itineraries; the ferry liners do not.

Where to Stay

The *Glacier Bay Lodge* at Bartlett Cove is beautiful, but heavily used. Reservations are essential. Best to contact your travel agent or call the lodge at 1-800-451-5952. The *Gustavus Inn* in Gustavus has been run by the same family for many years, and it is a delightful place to stay. This is also too often booked full, but you can try writing ahead. Although it's 10 miles from Bartlett Cove, the Inn makes airport pickups (and drop-offs), or you can take the bus, or you can pedal one of the bicycles provided by the Inn or hike the level (and lovely) road if you're going back and forth. The Gustavus Inn sets a family-style table; the food is legendary. Write Box 60, Gustavus, AK 99826; phone 697-2254 or 1-

800-649-5220. Reservations required. Another charming place to stay is the *Glacier Bay Country Inn,* where the hospitality is warm and you can enjoy home-baked breads, local seafood, and fresh vegetables from their bountiful garden. Write Box 5, Gustavus, AK 99826; phone 697-2288. Seasonal. Opened in 1997 and specializing in fishing, whale watching, and photography, Glacier Bay's *Bear Track Inn* offers a luxury Alaska experience. Write 255 Rink Creek Road, Gustavus, AK 99826; phone 697-3017. There are also a number of bed and breakfasts in Gustavus; check with the National Park Service (see below) or the *Gustavus Visitor Association* (write Box 167, Gustavus, AK 99826; phone 697-2358; fax 766-3155) for further accommodations.

One of the special things to do if you're staying in Gustavus is to go whale watching in a small tour boat such as the *Sea Wolf.* You might even be able to kayak with the whales from the boat—but get no closer than 100 yards, please. The people at Gustavus Inn can give you further information, or ask the Gustavus Visitor Association.

Useful Names and Addresses

There are numerous package tours available from Juneau to Glacier Bay. For starters, you might try one of the following: *Alaska Discovery:* write 5449 Shaune Drive, #4, Juneau AK 99801; phone 780-6226 or 1-800-586-1911; fax 780-4220. *Alaska Airlines* also runs a short see-it-all tour. Other boat charters and tours and flightseeing trips are operated out of Gustavus. Excursion boats sail from Bartlett Cove for a day's—or several days'—exploratory trip up the bay. For further information, check with the National Park Service people (see below), the *Juneau Visitor Information Center* (134 Third Street, Juneau, AK 99801; phone 586-2201), or the Juneau *Forest Service Information Center* (101 Egan Drive, Juneau, AK 99801; phone 586-8751; fax 586-7928).

The *Glacier Bay National Park and Preserve* is headquartered in Gustavus (write Box 140, Gustavus, AK 99826; phone 697-2230). Note: Park service naturalists accompany daily tour boats as well as provide walks and talks in Bartlett Cove.

38. Yakutat

The village of Yakutat is midway between Southcentral and Southeastern Alaska and is one of the only sizable coastal villages that cannot be reached by ferry. There are good reasons, of course, why this is so: the turbulent open waters of the Gulf of Alaska through which the ship would have to pass, for instance, and the fierce storms that batter this unprotected portion of the coast. Winds here can be even worse than at Valdez, where children have been tied together for safety to get them home from school. Yakutat is also the longtime site of violent tectonic activity, with a history of quakes that's enough to shake anybody up. Perhaps the worst seismic events occurred in 1899, when on September 3 the village was wracked by a quake measuring an estimated 8.3 on the Richter scale and just a week later was slammed by one estimated at 8.6.

Nearby Lituya Bay to the south has also been the center of some spectacular joltings. On July 10, 1958, one of the worst generated a wave 1,740 feet high—the biggest splash wave ever observed anywhere. It scoured the hillside above the bay bare. This same temblor hit Yakutat as well and caused spectacular "sandblows" on the Yakutat forelands, which lie between Yakutat and Lituya Bay. The sand below the surface of the forelands was shaken down and consolidated, which caused it to fissure and erupt loose sand and water in spouts that rose several feet high in volcano-like fashion. In this same shake, a piece of Khantaak Island (about half a million cubic yards in size) in Monti Bay near Yakutat was swallowed by the bottom of the bay in a great dark boil of water. Three unfortunate people who were on the island were never seen again. For several years thereafter, sailors avoided Monti Bay.

If you can manage a trip to Yakutat on a clear day, however, you will find it to be another seemingly serene place of beauty. Backdropped by snowy peaks, it has two wonderful, accessible ocean beaches that you can walk along for miles. It also has comely forests of mossy trees and, in the Yakutat forelands as well as other areas, some of the most beauti-

Lituya Bay. Source: National Park Service.

ful flower gardens in all Alaska. (I have been on Dry Bay on a cloudy July day when a mass planting of blooming yellow paintbrush seemed to light up the world as though with sunshine.)

The country around Yakutat is the primary home of the blue bear— or glacier bear. This magnificent animal is a rare color phase of the black bear and has a surmised evolutionary history that is intriguing. Blue bears are believed to have been isolated from the rest of the local black bear population during the ice ages and to have adapted to a treeless situation where their pale bluish color gave them protection. Their heads are also shaped differently from those of black bears, and their teeth are not as differentiated; but, now reunited with their fellow black bears, they interbreed with them readily. Scarce even around Yakutat, the blue bears are threatened by increased logging, possible oil development, and habitat destruction of their relatively small primary range.

There are many pleasant things you can see and do around Yakutat.

You can reach Harlequin Lake by road. This is a large, spectacular glacial lake that is rimmed with flower-filled meadows. You can charter a skiff to wind your way among islands and then past a beach (where you may see a blue bear) on into a wide, bowl-shaped bay surrounded by 12,000- to 18,000-foot peaks. Some people who know Alaska well call this the most impressive glacier-viewing spot they have seen. Or you can charter a wheeled plane to fly you above the nearby Malaspina Glacier, which is certainly one of the great sights of the earth. Other, very short charter flights can take you to remote beaches that are ideal for camping. The beach to the north is part of the Wrangell–Saint Elias National Park and Preserve. Behind this beach, you can walk to ponds overlooking the Malaspina Glacier, or you can wander through half-mile-long meadows that, in early summer, are full of wildflowers "not excelled in Alaska," according to a friend. Also accessible is the Situk River, a short, intimate, gentle stream, with excellent fishing. This offers an ideal one-day (or overnight) paddle down to a saltwater lagoon.

The bird life around Yakutat is fabulous. Another friend once saw 150 trumpeter swans on a pond in April when the snow was still on the ground. This is also the southernmost nesting area of the Aleutian tern, which can sometimes hold its own very well against the predatory bald eagles that find it here. (It is wonderful to see how the small birds gang up to chase the marauders away from their nesting grounds.) This is a favored area of snow geese as well, which can congregate here by the tens of thousands.

Alaska Airlines makes regular scheduled trips to Yakutat, weather permitting. There are several places to stay, including the *Glacier Bear Lodge* (write Box 303, Yakutat, AK 99689; phone 784-3202) and the *Yakutat Lodge at the Airport* (write Box 287, Yakutat, AK 99689; phone 784-3232). Air-taxi service is available from *Gulf Air Taxi* (write Box 367, Yakutat, AK 99689; phone 784-3240. You can contact this service for pickup if you run the Tatsenshini and Alsek Rivers: see Haines.) Icy Bay, just north of Yakutat, offers a kayak trip that rivals those on Glacier Bay—for experienced kayakers only.

┌── 39. USDA Forest Service

For many decades, virtually all of Southeast Alaska was the exclusive do-main of the United States Department of Agriculture (USDA) Forest Ser-vice, the Tongass National Forest comprising some 16.9 million acres (originally more than 20 million) of land, an area larger than West Vir-ginia. (Alaska's other national forest, the Chugach, is discussed under Anchorage as a Gateway, in Part III.) Under the terms of statehood, how-ever, the state was given 400,000 acres to be selected out of this forest, and under the terms of the Alaska Native Claims Settlement Act (ANCSA), Southeast Natives were granted more than 500,000 acres of Forest Service land in settlement of their aboriginal claims. Not surpris-ingly, the areas selected for state and private property have included some of the most valuable commercial timber stands. Since the Forest Service unfortunately overcommitted the commercial timber of the Tongass For-est in long-term contracts let during the 1950s, the state and Native se-lections have had a major impact on its resource management program.

Added to this, the 1980 Alaska National Interest Lands Conservation Act (ANILCA) called for a total cut of at least 450 million board feet every decade in the Tongass Forest and authorized major appropriations ($40 million per year) to help guarantee this cut. (Environmentalists mounted a campaign to alleviate the further destructive pressures this put on the forest.)

At the same time, ANILCA also increased the size of the Tongass For-est by some 1.45 million acres—largely of ice and snow and including the Juneau Ice Field—and it established two wilderness national monu-ments, Admiralty Island and Misty Fjords, in the Tongass Forest and des-ignated some dozen more wilderness areas.

In November 1990, Congress recognized the increased pressures on the Tongass called for under ANILCA and passed the Tongass Timber Reform Act (TTRA), which eliminated the mandated cut and the $40

Tongass National Forest

Wilderness Area	Acres
Established by ANILCA (December 2, 1980)	
Kootznoowoo Wilderness	988,050
(Admiralty Island National Monument)	
Coronation Island Wilderness	19,232
Endicott River Wilderness	98,729
Maurelle Islands Wilderness	4,937
Misty Fjords National Monument Wilderness	2,142,907
Petersburg Creek–Duncan Salt Chuck Wilderness	46,849
Russell Fjord Wilderness	348,701
South Baranof Wilderness	319,568
South Prince of Wales Wilderness	91,018
Stikine-LeConte Wilderness	449,951
Tebenkof Bay Wilderness	66,839
Tracy Arm–Ford's Terror Wilderness	653,179
Warren Island Wilderness	11,181
West Chichagof–Yakobi Wilderness	265,529
Established by TTRA (November 28, 1990)	
Chuck River Wilderness	74,990
Karta Wilderness	39,894
Kuiu Wilderness	60,581
Pleasant–Lemusurier–Indian Islands Wilderness	23,151
South Etolin Wilderness	83,371
Total Acreage	5,788,657

Source: Acreages as reported to Congress with official boundary maps. These acreages may change over time as mining claims or state and Native land selections are patented. These wildernesses include only the public lands above mean high tide.

million annual appropriation. This act also established five new wilderness areas and a dozen roadless areas totaling some 1,027,461 acres.

The closure of the Southeast's two pulp mills in the mid-1990s (see Ketchikan and Sitka) was the result of lower demand—and lower prices—for the kind of pulp these mills produced. As of this writing, the Tongass National Forest has come up with a new forest management plan for allowable cut and pollution requirements. Environmentalists are highly critical of the plan, believing the allowable cut is too large and the opening up of untouched forest areas is unacceptable. Whether they can effect any changes in the plan remains to be seen.

The table on page 205 describes what are now the congressionally designated wilderness areas of the Tongass National Forest.

The USDA Forest Service maintains a unique system of wilderness cabins that are located principally on wilderness lakes or along wilderness shores. These cabins—some 150 in the Tongass National Forest, 42 in the Chugach National Forest, and quite a few in the two national monuments—can be rented for a modest sum. Most have eight bunks, and many are charming A-frames with good wood stoves and other amenities of comfortable wilderness homes. (No electricity or running water, of course!) Those located on lakes generally have their own skiffs, thanks to local sportsmen (who also help maintain the cabins). You will have to fly to most of these cabins (notable exceptions are those on Prince of Wales Island and one near Cordova, which are accessible by road), but they still provide wonderful places for a family or a group of friends to enjoy an Alaskan adventure for a minimum cost. They must be reserved in advance (see below).

When traveling in the Southeast, keep in mind that the Forest Service is still the principal land administrator and is pledged to serve the needs of the public, including the recreationist. Do not hesitate to call upon the service to provide you with information or to help you plan an outing in this part of Alaska. It has some excellent (free) material, including maps, interpretive brochures, and a good checklist of Southeastern birds. For this material, and for information about the cabins and making reservations, write: *Forest Service Information Center,* 101 Egan Drive, Juneau, AK 99801; phone 586-8751; fax 586-7928.

PART III

Southcentral
and Southwest

40. Anchorage

The Setting

Located at the head of Cook Inlet, the Anchorage bowl forms a wide, roughly triangular plain of outwash gravel delineated on the east by high mountains and on the northwest and southwest by long embayments of the inlet, the Knik Arm and the Turnagain Arm. The bowl is part of a larger and unique region in Alaska, the Cook Inlet–Susitna Basin, a place where major and magnificent features of the landscape converge. Here the Chugach Mountains curve in from the southeast and continue southward along the Kenai Peninsula and Kodiak Island; the Alaska Range sweeps down from the north to meet the Aleutian Range; and the Talkeetna Mountains form a high mountain divide separating these ranges.

Into the basin formed by these great mountains great rivers flow: the Susitna drains the Talkeetnas and then reaches deep inland to drain a distant segment of the Alaska Range; the Matanuska marks the divide between the Talkeetnas and the Chugach Mountains and drains both ranges; the Yentna, the Chakachamna, and the Drift flow from the Alaska-Aleutian Ranges; the Knik, the Eagle, Ship Creek, and other swift streams drain the Chugach. Filling the shallows of this basin and washing its shores are the waters of the Pacific Ocean, which race in here with some of the greatest tides on earth.

During the Pleistocene ice ages, the Cook Inlet–Susitna Basin was filled to its brim with an immense flood of ice as much as 4,000 feet deep. So widespread and thick were the glaciers and snowfields there during this period that they actually spilled over from the Copper River basin to the northeast into the headwaters of the Susitna and Matanuska drainages. Massed in the valley of the Susitna was a monstrous tongue of ice with a south-trending lobe estimated to be at least 50 miles long; pouring into it from the Knik Arm and Turnagain Arm was more ice spilled from the Chugach Mountains. What would become the Cook

Inlet and the lowlands you see today lay 4,000 feet beneath this icy burden.

As the last great ice age drew to a close and the glaciers began to shrink, the topography of the present landscape slowly emerged. The resident rocks of the mountains had been deeply sculpted. V-shaped valleys were dredged out into U-shaped, steep-walled canyons. Valleys were left hanging thousands of feet high, sometimes with cascading waterfalls. Loose rocks had been quarried out into immense quantities of rubble, which were piled on the lowlands in irregular heaps and looping ridges. Because the area is underlain by a resistant floor of sedimentary rocks, the lowlands drained poorly, and many lakes, tarns, and marshes were formed by the meltwaters.

Throughout the many millennia during which this glacial landscape was forming, ash showered onto it repeatedly from the nearby volcanoes of the Aleutian Range. Unquiet earth forces lifted and lowered the land at will, swallowing portions of the tidelands and marshes and forever evolving new landforms, for this is a highly unstable portion of the planet. It is the meeting place not only of these major landforms but also of tectonic plates that are in active and ongoing encounter. In the middle of this turbulent landscape, already crowding the margins of the Anchorage bowl, sprawls the city of Anchorage, Alaska's metropolis.

The City

If you talk to almost any Alaskan who doesn't live in Anchorage, the chances are you'll be told what a terrible place the city is. It's the Los Angeles of the last frontier, your friend may say—overpriced, overcrowded, and overbearing. It's a scourge on the face of the wilderness, a disgrace and a disaster. Or you may hear the old joke that goes something like: "The only good thing about Anchorage is that it's so near Alaska."

Talk to somebody who lives in Anchorage, on the other hand, and you may get a different story. True, Anchorage does have its share of problems—rush-hour traffic jams, urban sprawl, lack of adequate zoning, flag-flying used-car lots, too much plastic, too many fast-food depots, and tourist-jammed hotels—but it has many urban amenities as well. Its bike paths, for example, total more than 120 miles throughout the city, and they're well kept, well located, and quite beautiful in many places. It has a public transportation system, the People Mover, which does a remarkably good job despite the city's sprawl. Anchorage has its own symphony orchestra and a community chorus that ranks high nationwide. It has opera, dance, chamber music, and theater, two university campuses, a number of good art galleries and restaurants, well-stocked sporting goods stores, a zoo, and an excellent historical and fine arts museum (with, incidentally, one of the fine gift shops in the state for Native artwork). Although it is not served by state ferry, Anchorage is used by tour ships and is one of Alaska's principal commercial marine ports, and it is readily accessible by air, rail, and paved highway.

The scenic location of Anchorage, moreover, is one that almost any city might envy. The great tides that wash it on the northwest and southwest put on constantly changing and spectacular shows, at one time revealing beautifully patterned wetland, and then providing exciting views of tidal bores. And everywhere you look around the city, you see those encircling mountains. To the east, the Chugach—with names like Williwaw Peak, Mount Magnificent, Temptation Peak, Wolverine and Suicide Peaks, the Wedge, the Ramp, Mount Muir—lift upward as much as 7,800 feet directly from sea level. To the north rise the Talkeetnas, which can be viewed from high points in the city. To the west and south as far as the eye can see are the great peaks of the Aleutian Range—Spurr (11,670 feet and Anchorage's resident active volcano), Redoubt (10,197 feet, and also an active volcano), and—visible from the south of the city on clear days—Iliamna (10,016 feet). Little Susitna (only 4,366 feet) seems almost an insignificant nubbin directly across the inlet. Clear weather also reveals the dreamlike shape of McKinley with Foraker on its shoulder—the high points of the Alaska Range—shimmering against the pale sky to the north. In good summer weather, you'll be struck by the brilliant greens of the nearby mountain swards, the dark, deep-colored rock, and the dazzle of white snow against blue sky. On rainy or hazy days, the mountains blur into soft gray, silver, and black like a fine photograph.

Along with its spectacular setting, Anchorage enjoys one of Alaska's more moderate climates, although it has its share of cloudy days and somewhat unpredictable seasons. Some winters, the temperature can plummet, and it will seem and be even colder when the wind blows. In frigid weather, every branch of every tree can be etched with rime ice, and the city will look like it's decorated for Christmas, whether or not the month is December. (On December 21, Anchorage has just five hours and twenty-nine minutes of sunlight.) On the other hand, winter temperatures can be remarkably mild: one notable year, the coldest day's minimum in Anchorage through the end of February was identical to the coldest day's minimum in Dade County, Florida—17 degrees above zero. Another year, a used-car dealer kept a palm tree alive and happy outside all winter long. In the summer, the weather can vary equally; you should be prepared for temperatures in the 50s and gentle drizzles, as well as for pleasantly warm and sunny days.

Anchorage has another unique advantage; it lies in the heart of coun-

Southcentral and Southwest Alaska

try that is not only magnificent but wonderfully hospitable to all sorts of outdoor recreation. As in Juneau, you can start your adventuring almost downtown; you cannot climb a mountain from a street corner, but you can run quite a respectable stream (Campbell Creek) right through the city. As noted above, you can also bike through some very pleasant urban terrain, and you can birdwatch on urban lakes and in publicly protected marshlands in and on the edge of town. What's more, it is only a few miles from downtown to the Chugach Mountains and a gorgeous, nearly half-million-acre state park where hiking, backpacking, rock climbing, and cross-country skiing are par excellence. Travel just a few hours to the south, and you can be in superb canoeing and kayaking country in the Kenai National Wildlife Refuge. Take a slightly different direction, and you will reach the waters of Prince William Sound, which are ideal for sailing as well as kayaking. In winter, there is fine downhill skiing near the city at Alyeska, more skiing to the north on Hatcher Pass, and even good cross-country skiing, night and day, in Anchorage's municipal parks. (See Downhill and Cross-Country Skiing, under Anchorage as a Gateway, below.)

All of this outdoor pleasuring is readily available, of course, to visitors as well as residents, and since you don't have to leave the ground to reach these outdoor playgrounds, it is relatively inexpensive to enjoy them. But bear in mind that Anchorage is the population center of Alaska, and most Alaskans love the great out-of-doors. If you do your Alaskan adventuring in places readily accessible to Anchorage, you should be prepared to share your experience with a few, or many, people. The more popular recreation spots around Anchorage can be crowded, just as similar areas are in the Lower Forty-Eight.

There is one more important plus for Anchorage: it is the gateway and point of departure for more distant wilderness and wildlife areas, including some of Alaska's most superlative wild places.

When you visit Anchorage, you may have to look for its Alaskan flavor, but it is there—in old clapboard cottages, in the few log cabins still standing and occupied downtown, and in certain events like the Fur Rendezvous ("Rondy") and the Iditarod Race, which take place annually in the city. Anchorage is a young city that is still making its history.

Among the first people who used the Anchorage area were the Chugachimiut Eskimos and Tanaina Indians, and archeological digs at such places as Beluga Point on Turnagain Arm reveal that there were settlements here at least 6,000 years ago. Captain James Cook was the first European to immortalize the region. He charted the waters here in 1778 and named Turnagain Arm for obvious reasons. (Cook Inlet was named for him posthumously by his patron, John Montagu, first lord of the

Average Temperature: Anchorage

	Daytime High (F°)	Nighttime Low (F°)	Monthly Average (F°)
Jan.	20.0	3.5	11.8
Feb.	26.6	8.9	17.8
March	32.8	14.6	23.7
April	43.8	26.8	35.3
May	55.2	37.2	46.2
June	62.9	46.2	54.6
July	65.6	50.1	57.9
August	63.8	48.0	55.9
Sept.	55.7	40.4	48.1
Oct.	41.8	27.8	34.8
Nov.	28.3	13.9	21.1
Dec.	20.6	5.3	13.0

British Admiralty.) The Russians left little evidence of passing this way, although there is an interesting Russian church not far from Anchorage in Eklutna. Sourdoughs, however, crisscrossed the Anchorage bowl extensively around the turn of the century, looking for gold. They left a few old mining towns, like Hope, which was once a bustling place of five thousand souls but is now gone ghost with only a couple of dozen names listed in the phone book. In 1907, the United States government moved in and established a forest reserve, the Chugach, with somewhat vague boundaries, which included the Anchorage bowl within its 11 million acres (today, the Chugach National Forest is closer to 6 million acres in size). A decade later, the government entered the scene again and sited a construction camp for the building of the Alaska Railroad on one of the bowl's better drainages, Ship Creek, so named because ships found good harbor at its mouth. At that point and in that place, Anchorage was rooted, albeit inadvertently, an offshoot of one of the first major federal projects in Alaska.

Like many Alaskan towns, Anchorage had an early series of booms and bursts, but it ended up as the repair center and headquarters for the Alaska Railroad. By the mid-1930s, it had settled down into a small town with a population of just over 2,000 people, while Fairbanks (the northern terminus of the railroad) had about 2,100, and Juneau had over 4,000. But the advent of World War II brought major changes to Anchorage. The military moved in in force, building two major bases, Fort Richardson and Elmendorf Air Force Base, nearby. (Military personnel

Fourth Avenue after the 1964 Good Friday earthquake. Source: Bob Olendorff.

still constitute a healthy percentage of the city's population.) Anchorage became linked directly to the world Outside with the construction of what would become the Alaska Highway. By the end of the war, the city had emerged as the state's principal transportation center, and it had been discovered by thousands of people. In the 1950 census, Anchorage had a population of 40,000, and the discovery and development of oil on the nearby Kenai Peninsula and in the Cook Inlet during the late 1950s and early 1960s clinched a pattern of continuing growth and expansion.

Good Friday in 1964 fell on March 27, a day that was to become the most memorable—and certainly the most dramatic—in the history of Anchorage to that date. That afternoon at 5:36 P.M., an earthquake measuring between 8.4 and 8.6 on the Richter scale—the strongest quake ever measured on the North American continent and one of the strongest ever recorded in the world—devastated large areas of Anchorage, including the residential area of Turnagain Heights. The earthquake left nine dead in the city. Statewide damage was estimated overall at between $300 and $400 million, with much of it centered in Anchorage. Within months, the federal government had funneled $406 million in disaster aid to the stricken areas, and Anchorage was on its way to a massive rebuilding effort.

The bringing in of oil at Prudhoe Bay in 1968 and the subsequent construction of the oil pipeline in 1974 flooded Anchorage with more people and brought a renewed transportation, construction, and business boom. Most of the oil companies and unions involved in the Prudhoe Bay development chose Anchorage for their headquarters. Then banks, savings and loan companies, and other businesses moved in to service them. After the passage of the 1971 Alaska Native Claims Settlement Act and the establishment of Native regional corporations, more Alaskan Native activity came to be centered in Anchorage. And in the late 1970s, a local Native regional corporation, Cook Inlet Region, Inc., erected a glass-walled headquarters building that has become one of the city's major landmarks.

The greater Anchorage area counts a population of over a quarter of a million people, some 50 percent of the state's population.

What to See and Do in the City

If you enjoy strolling along city streets, you can explore Anchorage and its somewhat meager but always charming history quite pleasantly on foot. Downtown Anchorage is generally level, and it's easy to find your way around. Running east-west are the avenues, which are numbered, with First Avenue being the nearest to and paralleling Ship Creek on the north. The north-south-trending streets are arranged alphabetically on either side of A Street; those to the west are lettered B, C, D, and so on through W Street, while those to the east are named Barrow, Cordova, Denali, and so forth, until the pattern is interrupted at Orca by Merrill Field, the airstrip used by small aircraft.

A good place to start exploring Anchorage is at the Railroad Depot, which is so much a part of the city's beginnings. Walk north on E Street until it dead-ends at First Avenue to reach the terminal. The railroad was almost completely rebuilt in the late 1940s, and this building survived the 1964 quake, although it was severely damaged. Inside, you can get information for the state ferry, which leaves from Whittier, as well as the railroad schedule. Across from the terminal stands old Engine Number 1 of the Alaska Railroad, flanked by two handsome totems. (This engine is not, in fact, Engine Number 1; that piece of equipment got scrapped along the way. But it is one of the railroad's original switch engines, a hand-me-down from the Panama Canal construction endeavor, and it did yeoman service in its time and makes an appropriate monument.)

You can walk from the depot across Ship Creek and upstream to a small dam where, during the summer, you may see salmon thrashing their way upstream to spawn. During the winter, the water impounded by this dam steams like a fumarole, being warmed by the discharge water from a nearby power plant. Many birds use this open water, which makes it a fine place for hibernal birdwatching. Two blocks north of the Railroad Depot, the C Street Overpass crosses Ship Creek and leads westward to the Port of Anchorage.

From roughly E Street to A Street and from Fourth Avenue north to Ship Creek, there is a region of highly unstable ground that turned to jelly during the Good Friday earthquake, sinking 8 to 10 feet in places and devastating many of the buildings then standing there. Major efforts have gone into attempts to stabilize this section of the city, known as the buttress area, and to make it safe for the reconstruction of buildings. Notice what look like smokestacks along the sides of the streets in part of this area; these are ventilating devices designed to help the moisture escape from the water-retentive ground. Also note that many new buildings have gone up, most of them since 1969. Among them is the Sunshine Mall on Fourth Avenue, an enterprise that is owned jointly by the Chugach Natives, Inc. (Prince William Sound, Copper River delta, and lower Kenai Peninsula Natives) and Kotzebue's Native Kikiktagruk Inupiat Corporation. Next to it is the Post Office Mall. There are several good eating spots here.

On returning to the downtown area, you can enjoy the summertime flower beds that ring the block around City Hall, located between E and F Streets and Fourth and Fifth Avenues. (At 343 West Fifth Avenue you'll find Laura Wright Alaskan Parkys, which are extremely well made, reasonable, and beautiful; telephone 274-4215.) If you stop in the Visitor Information Center office in the log cabin on the corner of Fourth and F, you'll find an abundance of literature and information concerning almost all aspects of Anchorage and its recreational opportunities. You will also want to stop by the Alaska Public Lands Information Center on Fourth Avenue between F and G Streets.

Then look for the Wendler Building on the corner of Fourth Avenue and D Street. A restaurant for many years, this is one of the oldest buildings in Anchorage; it was constructed in 1915. Across the street, at 413 D Street, there is Cyrano's "Off-Center Playhouse," a unique combination of small live theater, bookstore, and cafe (the baked goods are freshly baked on the premises).

If you walk to I Street and follow it to the south, you'll come to Delaney Park and more summertime flowers. The park runs all the way from A Street to P Street and from Ninth Avenue to Tenth and is Anchorage's in-city playground. It began life as Anchorage's first airstrip and was used by early bush pilots until Merrill Field went into operation in 1930. The strip served as a firebreak as well, protecting the town from what was then the wilderness to the south of it. In a remarkable burst of community effort, the strip was constructed in a single weekend in 1923. (That was the year President Warren Harding visited Alaska to drive the spike completing the Alaska Railroad.)

At the west end of Delaney Park, there is an attractive residential area of the city. (One resident here grows over 200 species of native Alaska flowers.) At the other end of the park you'll find the local cemetery, which is worth at least a few moments of your time. There you can see the tombstones of people from many denominations, including Russian Orthodox. Many of the inscriptions sum up with wonderful conciseness the history or character of the person resting below. Look for my favorite marker, which reads simply "Here Lies Lucky And Always Will Lie."

Not far from the cemetery is the Anchorage Historical and Fine Arts Museum, located on the corner of A Street and Sixth Avenue. There are interesting permanent Native and historical exhibits here as well as rotating art exhibits that sometimes feature the work of contemporary Alaskan artists. The Museum Gift Shop is a good place to look for (or at) Native crafts; it is very expensive. (If you are interested in Native crafts, a trip to the Alaska Native Health Center Gift Shop might be worth your while. It's located at 4315 Diplomacy Drive, off Tudor Road, and is open 10 A.M. to 2 P.M. weekdays; phone 719-1122.)

Across from the museum to the south is the Federal Building, which has a good scientifically oriented reference library as well as a reasonable cafeteria that is open to the public.

The city of Anchorage maintains an extensive trail system for walkers, bikers, and runners. (Delaney Park is one of the popular running areas and is also convenient for visitors. The park's perimeter is about 1.7 miles.) You can access the coast and travel along it on municipal pathways for over 17 miles; start this ambitious trip at Third Avenue and L Street and you can stay along the waterfront all the way past the Anchorage International Airport to Point Campbell. (During the winter, the city maintains cross-country ski trails, too.) Resolution Park, at the foot of Third Street, is a charming and easy little park to visit, and it affords a good view of the Knik Arm and the grand mountains across the Cook Inlet (when it's clear, that is). There is a statue of Capt. James Cook here that is identical to the one in Witby, England, one of Anchorage's several sister cities. Here, at low tide, you can get a good look at the marshes with their beautifully sculpted wetlands and their extraordinary tidal range. Tides in the Cook Inlet can fluctuate up to 30 feet or more, and are exceeded worldwide only by those in the Bay of Fundy. Note: The inviting tidelands of Cook Inlet can be treacherous because of the real danger of quicksand and the swift onrush of tidal waters—which can, at times, be seen as a high "tidal bore"—and hikers should be wary. For more detailed information about the city's parks and recreation facilities, write Anchorage *Municipal Division of Parks and Recreation,* Box 196650, Anchorage, AK 99519.

Annual Events

Every February, the Fur Rendezvous helps speed the long wintertime along in the city. Begun as an annual celebration after trappers had finished auctioning off their furs, the "Rondy" still has a fur auction but has many other events as well. These include the world championship sled-dog races and the world championship dog weight pull; a Saint Bernard set the record in 1976 by pulling 5,220 pounds of weight. There are also balloon races, snowshoe events, and the Miners and Trappers Ball.

March is the month for the Iditarod Race, which sees dog teams start from Anchorage on a 1,000-mile pull to Iditarod (the race ends in Nome). They follow the historic trail that originally started on the Kenai Peninsula (see The World of the Chugach and Kenai Mountains, under Anchorage as a Gateway, below) and then went over mountains, rivers, and tundra to reach the mining area around the Iditarod River, which flows into the Innoko and from there into the Yukon. (The Iditarod is a National Historic Trail and is administered by the Bureau of Land Management [BLM].)

In June, the city puts on a Renaissance Faire. This is a weekend-long celebration that features medieval costumes, Shakespeare, music, and feasting.

Some Useful Information About Anchorage

Zip code: varies and is noted in addresses below. Area code: 907.

Air Service

Since Anchorage International Airport is one of the major refueling stops on the polar air route, it is served by numerous international air carriers, and you can see aircraft from all over the world on the runways. Interstate passenger service to Anchorage is provided by *Alaska, Delta,* and *United;* these all fly out of Seattle, the principal air gateway to Alaska. Within the state, *Alaska Airlines* and *ERA* serve the principal cities and bush communities, with *Reeve Aleutian Airways* linking Anchorage to the Alaska Peninsula, the Aleutian Chain, and the Pribilof Islands. There are other, smaller carriers that serve various parts of the state from Anchorage as well. Air charters are too numerous and too often in states of change to list in full. For latest information, you can inquire at Anchorage International Airport or write the Log Cabin Visitor Information Center (see below).

If you fly into Anchorage during the tourist season, you'll find the airport the scene of considerable commotion. The several money exchanges take care of a growing number of foreign tourists who are visiting Alaska, and the airport restaurant is apt to be crowded around mealtimes. While you're waiting for your baggage, you might want to stroll around and see some of the displays of mounted animals there; this will give you a chance to get an idea of the size and beauty of a variety of Alaska fauna: polar bear, brown bear, glacier (blue) bear, muskox, wolf (shown snarling, alas, thus embodying the obsolete idea that this animal is a varmint), moose, trumpeter swan, and bald eagle. There is good locker service in the airport, and you can store large items. The people here are used to taking care of the equipment of miners, geologists, and engineers. The price is not cheap, but you can leave your belongings for up to thirty days.

There is van and cab service from the airport into Anchorage. The cab costs approximately twice what the van does, and if you can share your ride into town with another person, it will be worth the extra you'll pay for a tip. The municipal bus, the **People Mover**, also runs to the airport: it stops on the lower level; phone 343-6543.

Bus Service

Scheduled bus service to Anchorage is offered by **Gray Line of Alaska** (745 West Fourth Avenue, Anchorage, AK 99510; phone 277-5581 or 1-800-544-2206), which runs between Prince William Sound and Seward to the south. Although bus service has been discontinued north of Anchorage, you can visit Denali National Park on Gray Line's McKinley Explorer, in dome cars pulled by the Alaska Railroad (see below). Gray Line also runs to Skagway, Whitehorse, and Haines to connect with the Alaska state ferry.

It is also possible to visit Anchorage by bus from Seattle, Portland, and other points south. If you are interested, ask your travel agent to check the possibilities.

Highway System

The Alaska highway system ties Anchorage directly to Seward, Kenai, and Homer to the south, and to Fairbanks and the Dalton Highway to the north. It also links Anchorage with the Richardson Highway to Valdez and the Alaska Highway to Canada at Tok Junction. A good highway guide is *The Milepost* (see Suggested Reading).

Railroad

The *Alaska Railroad* (Box 107500, Anchorage, AK 99510; phone 1-800-544-0552 or, in Anchorage, 265-2494) runs daily during the summer between Anchorage and Fairbanks, with stops at Talkeetna and Denali National Park. It runs between Portage (where you drive) and Whittier (where you get the ferry) from mid-May to mid-September. For the rest of the year, passenger service between Anchorage and Fairbanks operates on weekends. The railroad also operates local service between Anchorage and Hurricane Gulch on Thursdays, Saturdays, and Sundays. If you visit Anchorage during the daylight months, try to ride the Alaska Railroad. It will give you a feeling for Alaska that you can't get any other way, and, if the weather is clear, you'll get matchless views of Mount McKinley (there are a glass-domed car and tour guides on the express train). Highly recommended. Note: It is a long ride from Anchorage to Fairbanks on the regular run, twelve hours in summer and ten and a half hours off-season. During the dark months, you lose much of the view, and it can seem like an endless trip; the cost, however, is about half the price of flying. A summer-only express stops once at Denali National Park, and takes only eight hours. Also inquire regarding service to Seward.

Public Transportation

The main *Bus Accommodation Station* (the *People Mover*) is at Sixth Avenue and G Street, and you can get information about schedules there; phone 343-6543.

Taxi

Checker Cab: phone 276-1234. *Yellow Cab:* phone 272-2422. *Alaska Cab:* phone 563-5353.

Car Rental

The Anchorage phone book lists about three dozen car rental outfits, including all the well-known companies. Check with your travel agent.

Hotels and Other Lodgings

Anchorage has more than its share of hotels. Your travel agent—or the Anchorage Convention and Visitors Bureau (see below)—can give you detailed information. Most larger hotels offer typical tourist accommodations, comfortable and more or less expensive—usually more—and there's not much choice. Among the higher priced, you might consider the *Sheraton* (phone 276-8700), which has a fine Alaskan jade stairway; the *Westward Hilton* (272-7411); or the *Captain Cook* (276-6000). I always stay at the *Voyager* (501 K Street; phone 277-9501, or 1-800-247-9070 outside Alaska), a small hotel that is relatively reasonable, quiet, and well located downtown. Each room has a kitchenette equipped with utensils; there are also nonsmoking rooms for nonsmokers only. The *Anchorage Youth Hostel* is located at 700 H Street; rates are very reasonable; phone 276-3635. You can also find many reasonable and informal bed and breakfasts; inquire at the *Log Cabin Visitor Information Center* at F Street and Fourth Avenue; phone 274-3531.

Campgrounds

The *Centennial Camper Park* has hot showers and trees all around and is serviced directly by the People Mover bus; it is highly recommended. Campgrounds are also located in *Chugach State Park* and the *Chugach National Forest,* but they require wheels to reach them. Inquire at the *Alaska Public Lands Information Center,* located in the old Federal Building, 605 West Fourth Avenue, Suite 105, Anchorage, AK 99501; phone 271-2737.

Municipal Swimming Pools

Pools are available for public use at the following locations: *Bartlett Pool,* 25-500 Muldoon Road; *Dimond Pool,* 2909 West Eighty-Eighth Avenue; *East High Pool,* 4025 East Twenty-Fourth Avenue; and *West High Pool,* 1700 Hillcrest Drive. For further information, contact *Cultural and Recreation Department,* Division of Parks and Recreation, Box 196650, Anchorage, AK 99519; phone 343-4476. You can also get complete details of the municipality's other recreational facilities from this source. *YMCA* showers and pool are at 5353 Lake Otis Parkway (zip 99507); phone 563-3211.

Canoe Rentals

Check with the Alaska Public Lands Information people (see below) to see if canoe rentals are available. They may be able to refer you to the *Knik Kayakers and Kanoers,* the local small-boaters' association (whose address and telephone number change with its current officers); these people will have the most up-to-date information for you regarding the local canoeing and kayaking scene.

Library

The *Loussac Public Library* at 3600 Denali (phone 343-2975) has video presentations; a fine, extensive catalog of Alaskana; and helpful computer-supplied information. This is a beautiful, sumptuous building worth seeing on its own; it also makes a nice place to relax, listen to music, and read.

Environmental Organizations

Alaska Center for the Environment, 519 West Eighth Street, Suite 201, Anchorage, AK 99501; phone 274-3621. This is worth a visit if you would like to learn some of the environmental issues Alaskans are grappling with. It also has a good and growing library. *Sierra Club,* 241 East Fifth Avenue, Suite 205, Anchorage, AK 99501; phone 276-4048. This organization has an active membership and many local outings. *Trustees for Alaska,* 725 Christenson Drive, Anchorage, AK 99501; phone 276-4244. *National Audubon Society,* 308 G Street, Suite 217, Anchorage, AK 99501; phone 276-7034. *Greenpeace,* Box 104432, Anchorage, AK 99510; phone 277-8234. *Alaska Conservation Foundation,* 750 West Second Avenue, Suite 104, Anchorage, AK 99501; phone 276-1917. *The Wilderness Society,* 430 West Seventh Avenue, Suite 210, Anchorage, AK 99501; phone 272-9453. *National Parks and Conservation Association,* 329 Frank Street, Suite 208, Anchorage, AK 99501; phone 277-6722. *Alaska Wildlife Alliance,* Box 202022 (600 Cordova, Suite 3), Anchorage, AK 99520; phone 277-0897. *National Wildlife Federation,* 750 West Second Avenue, Suite 200, Anchorage, AK 99501; phone 258-4800; fax 258-4811. *The Nature Conservancy,* 421 West First Avenue, Suite 200, Anchorage, AK 99501; phone 276-3133; fax 276-2584.

Useful Names and Addresses

The Anchorage Convention and Visitors Bureau's *Airport Information Center* is located in the main terminal building of Anchorage International Airport. The *Airport International Visitor Information Center* is located in the international terminal of Anchorage International Airport. The main office of the *Anchorage Convention and Visitors Bureau* is at 524 West Fourth Avenue, Anchorage, AK 99501; phone 274-3531. The bureau's *Log Cabin Visitor Information Center* is next door at the corner of F Street and Fourth Avenue, Anchorage, AK 99501; phone 274-3531. It has the latest thing in computer-supplied information: you have only to touch the screen to get an answer to your question, and printouts are available. There is also the *Visitor Information Phone Line* with recorded messages of current visitor attractions and events in the Anchorage area; phone 276-3200. *Anchorage Municipal Division of Parks and Recreation:* 120 South Bragaw Street; write Box 196650, Anchorage, AK 99519; phone 343-4474. *Alaska Convention and Visitors Bureau,* 524 West Fourth Avenue, Anchorage, AK 99501-2212; phone 276-4118. *Alaska State Information Center,* 3601 C Street, Anchorage, AK 99501; phone 269-8400. *Alaska Public Lands Information Center,* 605 West Fourth Avenue, Suite 105, Anchorage, AK 99501; phone 271-2737.

41. Anchorage as a Gateway

Anchorage is the immediate gateway to the mountain worlds of the Chugach-Kenai Mountains and the Talkeetnas. It is the takeoff point for the wonderful waterways and shores of the Kenai Peninsula and, via the Alaska Railroad and the state ferry, for the beauties of Prince William Sound. It is also the jumping-off place to more distant and inaccessible places that beckon lovers of true wilderness: the Lake Clark region, Aniakchak National Monument and Preserve, the Wood-Tikchik State Park, Katmai National Park and Preserve, the Pribilof Islands, Kodiak, the Wrangell–Saint Elias Mountains, the Kenai Fjords, and the wild rivers of Alaska's Southcentral and Southwestern regions.

Many of these areas are in public hands, state or federal, although the Pribilof Islands are a special situation (see below). The Alaska State Division of Outdoor Recreation and Parks administers nearly 3 million acres of superb state parkland, including the Wood-Tikchik State Park and Chugach State Park (which is directly outside of Anchorage). The USDA Forest Service is in charge of the near 6-million-acre Chugach National Forest, which embraces Prince William Sound and its numerous islands as well as the northeastern portion of the Kenai Peninsula. The U.S. Fish and Wildlife Service administers wildlife refuges on the Kenai Peninsula, in Kodiak, and in areas to the west. The National Park Service looks after the Kenai Fjords, the Lake Clark region, Aniakchak National Monument and Preserve, Katmai National Park and Preserve, Wrangell–Saint Elias National Park and Preserve, and the rivers that flow through these units. What's left of federal public land is administered by the Bureau of Land Management (BLM). Use these agencies to help you in your travels (see below).

Public Agencies Administering Recreational Land Around Anchorage

(Remember, the area code for all Alaska phones is 907.) The *Alaska Public Lands Information Center* (605 West Fourth Avenue, Suite 105, Anchorage, AK 99501; phone 271-2737) represents and handles information for all the Alaska public land agencies—federal and state. However, should you want to contact one of these agencies directly, the following contact information should be helpful. *National Park Service:* 2525 Gambell, Anchorage, AK 99503; phone 257-2690. *USDA Forest Service:* 3301 C Street, Suite 300, Anchorage, AK 99503; phone 271-2500 (for cabin reservations, phone 1-800-280-2267; you will reach the National Forest Reservation Center in Maryland, which handles these reservations). *Bureau of Land Management:* 222 West Seventh Avenue, Anchorage, AK 99513; phone 271-5960. *U.S. Fish and Wildlife Service:* 1101 East Tudor Road, Anchorage, AK 99503; phone 786-3487. *Alaska Department of Natural Resources Public Information Center,* 3601 C Street, Suite 200, Anchorage, AK 99503; phone 269-8400 (handles general questions).

The World of the Chugach and Kenai Mountains

If you fly between Juneau and Anchorage on a clear day, the snowy peaks you admire along the eastern horizon for most of your trip will belong to the Chugach, or, more properly, the Chugach-Kenai-Kodiak Mountains. This flyby is a good way to get a slight overview of this extremely rugged and impressive mountain system that is an approximately 500-mile-long segment of the Coast Range, which curves around the Gulf of Alaska. Varying in width from 30 to 110 miles, the Chugach Mountains sweep north and westward from Mount Saint Elias and then, where they reach their greatest height (over 13,000 feet), they bend abruptly to the southwest. Marching the length of the Kenai Peninsula, they are known as the Kenai Mountains. After they plunge beneath the waters of the Gulf of Alaska, they finally emerge as the mountains of Kodiak Island, which are only 2,000 to 4,000 feet high. This great feature of the Alaska landscape is the scene of major earth activity. The epicenter of the Good Friday earthquake of 1964 was in the heart of the Chugach Mountains where they embrace Prince William Sound; portions of the entire range were displaced by the tremor.

The Chugach and Kenai Mountains are notable for their immense relief: valleys may have almost mile-high walls; peaks can lift directly from the sea to soar thousands of feet. Another of their notable features is the great burden of glaciers they carry. The word *burden* is deliberately cho-

Autumn in the Chugach Mountains. Source: Pete Martin.

sen; the immense weight of the snow and ice in large glaciers actually depresses the land, a fact that is graphically illustrated in areas that have recently become ice-free and are now springing up as much as an inch a year—more than 8 feet a century. (See Glacier Bay, in Part II.) Spectacular ice fields sprawl between the high spires and ridges of both the Chugach and Kenai Ranges. The Bagley Ice Field in the eastern section of the Chugach is the largest ice field outside those of Antarctica and Greenland. Fed by the Bagley Ice Field, and augmented by the great Saint Elias Mountains to the south, the Bering Glacier is the longest glacier on the North American continent: it is also one of the most rapidly receding. During the past century, it has retreated 7 miles and lost one-fourth of its depth in meltwater. Scientists cite this as an example of what global warming is doing.

The ice fields on Mount Witherspoon in the central Chugach and the Harding Ice Field on the Kenai Peninsula also rank among the greatest on the North American continent. Radiating from these snow and ice masses are dozens of other great glaciers, many of which flow directly

Nootka lupine (Lupinus nootkatensis).

into tidewater. One of these, the Columbia Glacier, provides a fine spectacle for travelers on the ferry from Whittier to Valdez. Many smaller and almost more beautiful tidewater glaciers make the Kenai Fjords a unique area where you can watch and hear the rivers of ice as they plunge into the sea.

Sealed into the rocks of the Chugach-Kenai-Kodiak Mountains is the record of a restless and sometimes violent history. There has been immense earth movement at the junction of tectonic plates in this region during the last 100 to 150 million years. This has resulted in intermittent volcanism, submersion of the land beneath the sea, great uplifts of the land, and long periods of erosion. The geology of these mountains fits the theory of continental drift to a fine degree. Anyone with an interest in geology will find travel through these mountains interesting, especially if it is done on foot. Roads through both the Chugach and the Kenai Mountains also offer interesting geological observation points, and there are lots of places where you can park and get out to explore.

Rising thousands of feet as they do from tidewater, the Chugach and Kenai Mountains offer an extraordinary variety of Alaskan landscape for anyone who travels through their different life zones. You can start in marshlands, pass through dense and fragrant forests, slosh across lush bogs, boulder-hop over joyous white-water streams (or get your feet drenched wading through them), make your way up ridges into meadows of heather and dry alpine tundra, and finally enter a world of perpetual ice and snow—all within a few miles. If this is not enough, along the way you may pass a glacier or a dazzling waterfall, or find lakes as lovely as jewels.

Sweeping in from the southeast as these mountains do, they also carry with them a sampling of both flora and fauna that may reach the north-ernmost and westernmost limits of their ranges here. And because they come together with other major features of the Alaskan landscape—such as the Talkeetna Mountains—this range also shares in the flora and fauna of other regions as well. Thus you will find in these mountains a rare overall sampling of Alaska's birds and beasts, as well as flowers, trees, and other plants.

As you hike through this terrain, you can hope to see the more com-mon species of fauna—black bear, moose, ground squirrels, maybe a brown bear or wolverine—but you may also have the unique opportu-nity of seeing both Dall sheep (not found in the Southeast) and the more elusive mountain goat (not found north and west of here). You will also see many different species of trees, and you may be able to identify all three varieties of spruce that grow in Alaska—the Sitka spruce (a tree of the Southeast forests that approaches its northern and western limits here), the black spruce (not found in the Southeast), and the white spruce (a tree of the Interior and the Alaska Peninsula); only in this gen-eral region do the ranges of all three of these trees overlap.

The wildflowers bloom in profusion in these mountains and in ex-ceptional variety. You can look for and find everything from the ubiqui-tous but always beautiful fireweed to rare species of orchids. In between, you can enjoy the shy plants of wet forests as well as the lupine and po-tentilla and polemonium (Jacob's ladder) of more open places, and the anemone and wild geranium. Look where you least expect to find a show, and there one may be. One summer afternoon I found the most gorgeous mass planting of dwarf dogwood I have ever seen within easy strolling distance of an access road out of Anchorage. Also, keep your eye out for berries; there are all kinds here, from wild raspberries to suc-culent high-bush cranberries, low-bush cranberries, currants, and, in the hills, crowberries and blueberries. The last named can make even the roughest scramble worth it, for they can be as sweet and juicy (and seem as big) as grapes. Incidentally, it is the leaves of the alpine bearberries that color the landscape such a gorgeous crimson in the fall.

The Chugach Mountains form, of course, the splendid ridge over which the sun rises to shine upon Anchorage. They are close enough and accessible enough to Anchorage for the people there to look upon them as their own private mountains. In fact, to the east and to the north of Anchorage, over 300,000 acres of these mountains form the Chugach State Park, administered by the Alaska State Division of Outdoor Recre-ation and Parks. This parkland offers a wonderful spectrum of outdoor activity almost all year round.

Canoeing and Kayaking in the Anchorage Area

River	Distance (miles)	Time	Class	Open Canoes	Hazards	Put-Ins (PI) / Take Outs (TO)
Campbell Creek	6–8	1–3 hrs.	I	Yes	Tight bends, sweepers	PI: Folker St. PI: or TO: Lake Otis, Old Seward Hwy. bridge, Dowling Rd., Arctic Blvd., Dimond Blvd. bridges.
Upper Eagle River	13	3–5 hrs.	I, last mile II–III	Yes	Sweepers, log jams; last mile rocky rapids, last rapid III; open canoes should TO at power line	PI: 10 miles up Eagle River Rd. where tributary is along road. TO #1: Eagle River Loop Rd. (canoes); TO #2: state park campground just above Glen Hwy. bridge.
Lower Eagle River	8	2–3 hrs.	II–IV	No	Many rocky rapids	PI: state park campground above Glenn Hwy. bridge. TO: Route Bravo bridge on Eagle River flats—take Artillery Rd. off Glen Hwy. Contact U.S. Army base at Fort Richardson for access; phone 384-0437.
Upper Kenai River	11	2–3 hrs.	I–II	Yes	Swift water in places, some rocks; best in spring when low	PI: Sterling Hwy. bridge at Kenai Lake. TO: Sterling Hwy. bridge at Resurrection Trailhead; Jim's Landing boat launch.
Kenai River canyon	6	1–2 hrs.	III	No	Large standing waves	PI: on Skilak Lake Rd. TO: hike out 1.5 miles on Hidden Creek Trail from mouth or go down Skilak Lake 7 miles to Upper Skilak Campground on road; danger of strong wind and waves

River	Miles	Time	Class	Canoeable	Hazards	Access
Lyons Creek/ E. Fork Sixmile River	9	2–3 hrs.	II above first Hwy. bridge; then I	Yes	Swift water, sweepers, log jams in upper part	PI: in higher water, Lyons Creek bridge just south of Turnagain Pass; usually better at Bertha Creek Campground off Seward Hwy. TO: just below Silvertip Hwy. camp where river is next to road; no canoes beyond here! River changes rapidly.
Portage Creek	6	2–3 hrs.	I	Yes	Brush, logs, possibly jams, some shallow water	PI: outlet of Portage Lake near Forest Service Visitor Center. TO: Seward Hwy. bridge near Portage Glacier Rd.; Mudoy at low tide.
Glacier Creek	3	1–2 hrs.	I–II	Yes (experienced only)	Very swift glacial water; sweepers and log jams common	PI: bridge just before Alyeska ski lodge. TO: Seward Hwy. bridge just south of Aleyska Rd.
Little Susitna	17	1 long day or 2 short	I	Yes	Log jams in upper part	PI: bridge crossing off Shrock Rd. 10 miles out of Wasilla. TO: Parks Hwy. bridge (Mile 58).
Fish Creek	13	4–5 hrs.	I; last mile II	Yes	Last mile swift, brushy, jams possible	PI: Big Lake Rd. bridge at Big Lake outlet. TO: Knik Rd. bridge, 14 miles south of Wasilla.

WARNING: Don't trust this guide. People have gotten into trouble on the "easiest" of rivers. Water levels can alter conditions radically—and rapidly—seasonally and even daily. New "sweepers" and log jams can occur anytime. Wear life preservers, scout unfamiliar water, and line or portage when in doubt—no one ever drowned on a portage! Constant cold water temperatures can make even a class I stream into class II. *Compiled by Patrick Pourchot.*

Chugach State Park

Chugach State Park is well described by its administrators as being an accessible wilderness. From the city of Anchorage, there are four ready entrances you can drive to and leave your car at before taking off into the backcountry: Prospect Heights, Upper O'Malley (difficult in winter), Upper Huffman (winter only), and Glen Alps (very steep and difficult in winter). Upper Huffman is the central point of access for a number of summer trails (but is too heavily used for you to safely leave your car there in summer) and is the access for snow machines in winter. Check at the *Alaska Public Lands Information Center* regarding possible public transportation to these trailheads. (It's in the old Federal Building, 605 West Fourth Avenue, Suite 105, Anchorage, AK 99501; phone 271-2737.)

North of Anchorage, there are also access roads and campgrounds at Eagle River and Eklutna Lake. South of Anchorage, there are a number of improved trailheads, a picnic site, and a campground at Bird Creek. You can pick up a good map of the Chugach State Park at the Alaska Public Lands Information Center (see above); the *Alaska Department of Natural Resources Public Information Center* (3601 C Street, Suite 200, Anchorage, AK 99503; phone 269-8400); or at the *Chugach State Park headquarters* at the Potter Section House (Box 8999, Indian, AK 99540; phone 345-5014).

The best way to explore this accessible wilderness is, of course, on foot, and there are many hiking opportunities on developed trails and easily identifiable cross-country routes. There are also a number of mountains that are delightful to climb in the summer. Thus, you can suit your schedule and your mood and take anything from an afternoon stroll to an alpine scramble or a week-long backpack trip. A major bonus of any hike you take will be the magnificent views you'll get as you gain the heights of these mountains. You can choose your route to get a panorama of the Alaska Range, the spectacle of changing tides in Turnagain Arm (and maybe the sight of a beluga whale), or all of Anchorage at your feet; or you can simply find yourself a superb vista of snow-filled cirques and rugged spires. The subalpine birch woodlands here, incidentally, are probably unique in North America, a biologist friend of mine tells me, and, with their grassy floors and picturesquely shaped trees, are particularly charming. Note: Keep your eye out for bears, with whom you share this wilderness. (See Bear Essentials, in Part I.)

Some of the trails through Chugach State Park were originally blazed by miners and other early settlers of the area. Since the mountains rise so precipitously from the water in places, most of these routes took the easiest passes through the peaks. Many were winter trails and were traveled by dog teams and rugged drivers carrying the mail or news to the Interior. The Crow Pass Trail (best entered at its southern terminus through the Chugach National Forest), Johnson's Pass, Indian Pass, and the Iditarod Trail are all full of history. Other trails have been more recently developed for cross-country skiing in winter and hiking in summer and are pleasant and often easy pathways across the landscape.

A wilderness as accessible as Chugach State Park is bound to attract not only a lot of foot travel but also pressures for the use of off-road vehicles. Dedicated to meeting the wishes of the public, the Chugach State Park people have set aside several areas for four-wheel-drive vehicles, and certain areas of the park are open to snowmobiles in the winter. There are, however, other areas that are closed to motorized use, and you can enjoy them with only the sounds of the mountains around you. Hunting and trapping in specific areas of the park are allowed in season, between September 3 and April 15. If you're going to travel the park during the hunting season (September 3 to March 31), it's wise to wear a bright-colored cap or carry a bright-colored pack. Several species of animals are protected in the park, including grizzlies, mountain goats (the taking of Dall sheep is permitted under regulation), beavers, wolves, and wolverines. You should report any poaching to the park headquarters. The use of firearms is limited to hunting in season; target practice and the use of guns for trapping are both prohibited. There is a fee for vehicle use and for camping. Open campfires are not allowed in the backcountry, and you should plan to carry your stove if you're staying overnight or want a spot of tea during your park outing.

The northern portion of Chugach State Park is roughly delineated by Knik Arm, and the lovely Eagle River valley lies within it (in the exact geographic center of the park). The valley holds the Eagle River Campground (fifty sites) as well as the Eagle River Nature Center, the park's principal visitor center. To get there, you take an easy 13.4-mile drive north of Anchorage on the Glenn Highway and a 12.7-mile park road (the deepest into the park of any road at sea level) east to the valley. During the summer months, the Chugach State Park puts on several programs at the *Eagle River Nature Center.* There are daily guided nature hikes, longer overnight adventures, and special programs. Phone 694-2108 for further information and for a schedule of current park events. The center also has displays, local nature trails that you can wander, and good salmon watching when the salmon are running. There's a good trail from the valley up Peters Creek, and Mount Rumble lifts about 5,000 feet above its headwaters; the mountain is a dazzling snowy sight to see.

Chugach State Park Trails: Hillside Area

Destination	Access	Distance in Miles	Elevated Gain	Rating	Comments
Flat Top Mtn.	Glen Alps	3.5	1,550 ft.	Moderate to difficult	Some steep rock scrambles. Fine views: Anchorage, Alaska Range, Kenai Peninsula. Classic alpine plant communities.
Little O'Malley Peak	Glen Alps	7.5	1,937 ft.	Fairly easy	Fine mountain scenery, wildflowers, berries.
Wolverine Peak*	Prospect Heights	10.5	3,380 ft.	Fairly easy	Good views: Anchorage, Alaska Range, Cook Inlet. White spruce, birch, mountain hemlock.
The Ramp The Wedge	Glen Alps	11	Ramp: 3,182 ft. Wedge: 2,602 ft.	Fairly easy	Dall sheep in summer. Berries in fall.
Knoya and Tikishla Peaks	Prospect Heights	K: 13 T: 15	K: 3,525 ft. T: 4,075 ft.	Moderate to difficult	Portions of route are cross-country; for experienced hikers.
McHugh Peak	McHugh Creek	5.7	1,551 ft.	Fairly easy	Highly scenic. Cross-country travel above brushline.
Rabbit Lake McHugh Lake	McHugh Creek	5	300 ft.	Easy	Exquisite alpine lake, set in high tundra beneath scenic Suicide Peaks. Short hike to McHugh Lake.
Williwaw Lakes	Glen Alps	13	742 ft.	Fairly easy	Exquisite alpine lakes backdropped by Williwaw Mountain (5,445 ft.). Most scenic hike in Campbell Creek drainage.
Iditarod Trail	Crow Creek Rd. Chugach N.F.	27	2,500 ft.	Fairly easy	Backpack. Historic route. Fine Alaska countryside: glaciers, high tundra, mountain passes, spruce forests, bogs, open meadows, wildflowers. Forest Service cabin at Mile 3. Avalanche danger.

*Good for winter use. Extensive cross-country skiing in the Chugach State Park: check with park. Hiking plus water activities in the Eklutna Lake region, and it is possible to run the Eagle River. *Note:* State parks people are developing a bike trail (from Indian to Girdwood) and a scenic overlook trail system at Bird Point. Check if open.

Eagle River Valley is also the place where you want to go if you plan to run the upper part of Eagle River—class I and II. Consult the *Chugach State Park headquarters* (phone 345-5014) or the *Alaska Public Lands Information Center* in Anchorage (phone 271-2737) for details about the run. Note: The last mile of Upper Eagle River is class III.

The Eklutna Lake basin, a little farther north, is less than an hour's drive from Anchorage (25 miles). There are a dozen trails out of this basin into backcountry that is described by one knowledgeable resident of Anchorage as being "among the most beautiful in all Alaska—you can walk 5 miles into it and be in superb wilderness." The lake itself is milky blue with glacial till, and very cold. The lower-altitude countryside is heavily wooded, with white spruce and birch forests and cottonwoods that glow gold in autumn. The autumn coloring is spectacular, and the spring wildflowers equally so. The peaks of the high country are brilliant with snow, there are dazzling waterfalls, and there's even a glacier within walking distance. Some of the highest mountains in this part of the Chugach Range are here—mountains with names like Bold Peak (7,522 feet), Bashful Peak (8,005, the park's tallest), and Baleful Peak (7,900 feet). In season, the berrying is excellent.

There is a natural mineral lick north of Eklutna Lake that is one of the few places in Chugach State Park officially designated for wildlife viewing. If you hike in the higher altitudes, you can also expect to see both Dall sheep and mountain goats. Expect lots of company, as well, in the Eklutna Lake and Eklutna River region; this is one of the most heavily used parts of the Chugach State Park.

There are several beautiful hikes that commence at Eklutna Lake, with such destinations as East Twin Peak, West Twin Peak, the East Fork of the Eklutna River, and Hunter Creek Pass. There is also a pleasant hike that climbs up to the Peters Creek Valley. Another interesting, but strenuous, outing you might want to consider in this part of the country is a trek up Ship Creek through Arctic Valley and out at Indian Creek—this is an old winter trail used by dogsledders. (Note: This is not a maintained trail and should be attempted only by experienced backcountry hikers.) Ask the state park people (phone 345-5014) for more thorough details and descriptions of the many trails in this region of Chugach State Park, or consult Nienhauser and Simmerman's *55 Ways to the Wilderness in Southcentral Alaska* (see Suggested Reading).

Note: The road around Eklutna Lake, blocked by landslides several years ago, must be hiked, and this adds several miles to any journey starting from the lake. The road is open to all-terrain vehicles (ATVs) Sunday through Wednesday only. Hikers and bikers can use it any time.

The only canoeing or kayaking opportunities in the Chugach State

Park are on the Eagle River or on Eklutna Lake. It is also possible to run this fine river through military lands, but permission must be granted; check with the *Alaska Public Lands Information Center* (605 West Fourth Avenue, Suite 105, Anchorage, AK 99501; phone 271-2737) for details.

Chugach National Forest

The Chugach National Forest adjoins the Chugach State Park on its southeast corner and embraces more of the fine alpine terrain of the Chugach and Kenai Mountains. Along the length of the eastern Kenai Peninsula, however, the mountains lose elevation as they trend southward in their gentle descent to the sea. With close to 6 million acres, the Chugach National Forest is the next to the largest unit of the United States Forest Service, being second only to the Tongass National Forest, which comprises so much of Alaska's Southeast. This is also one of the oldest units of the United States Department of Agriculture (USDA) Forest Service. The precursor of the present service was established in 1891, and, in 1892, President Benjamin Harrison designated Afognak Island, just off Kodiak, as a fish and forest reserve. Afognak was incorporated into the Chugach National Forest when it was formally established under Teddy Roosevelt in 1907. (Under the terms of the Alaska Native Claims Settlement Act, Afognak has become Native property.) Originally, the Chugach Forest boundaries took in a much larger area and included both the Anchorage bowl and the Kenai National Wildlife Refuge, which adjoins it on the west. The boundaries presently encompass the northeastern shoulder of the Kenai Peninsula and the land bordering Prince William Sound, as well as the islands in it all the way to Cape Suckling in the south. This amount of territory gives the national forest an extraordinary range of terrain that includes some of Alaska's loveliest coastal scenery; some of its most beautiful forests and forelands, mountains, and glaciers; as well as areas that are exceptionally rich in wildlife, like the Copper River delta.

Recognizing recreation as a primary use of the forest, the USDA Forest Service has developed and maintains more than 200 miles of backcountry trails in the Chugach National Forest, many of which are in the Kenai Mountains and readily accessible from the Seward or Sterling Highways. Some of these trails are meant for a short stroll to admire the particular features of the area (as at Portage Glacier; see below); others are meant for more serious hikers and backpackers. Many of the backcountry trails are closed to horses and motorized vehicles during April, May, and June, and most of those in the high country are likely to be subject to dangerous avalanche conditions during the winter. The Chugach

Chugach Forest Service Trails

Destination	Access	Distance in Miles	Elevation Gain	Rating	Comments
Lost Lake	Lost Lake Subdivision at Mile 5, Seward Hwy.	7	1,820 ft.	Good family trail	Fine views. Access to high country and good cross-country hiking. Salmonberries near Miles 4 and 5 in August. Carry stove if camping.
Ptarmigan Lake via Ptarmigan Creek	Mile 23, Seward Hwy. (Ptarmigan Creek Campground)	3.5	255 ft.	Easy	Good chance of seeing sheep and goats. Carry insect repellent. Avalanche hazard in winter.
Crescent Lake via Crescent Creek	Mile 3.5, Quartz Creek Road off Sterling Hwy., Mile 45	6.2	864 ft.	Easy	Good trail; two cabins at Crescent Lake. Closed to motorized vehicles May 1 through November 30. Avalanche hazard in winter.
Carter Lake	Mike 34, Seward Hwy.	3.3	986 ft.	More difficult	Primarily used by hunters; steep in places. Makes possible loop with Crescent Creek Trail.
Russian Lakes and Cooper Lake	Mile 52.8, Sterling Hwy. (Russian Lake Campground)	Lower Lake: 3 Upper Lake: 12 Cooper Lake: 21	100 ft. 290 ft. 768 ft.	Easy to fairly easy	Three cabins. Good fishing. Brown bear country. Avalanche hazard in winter above Lower Lake.
Johnson Pass Trail	Mile 64, Seward Hwy.	23	Approx. 1,000 ft.	More difficult	Historic. Great views. Brown bear country. Good access to cross-country alpine hiking. Avalanche danger in winter.
Resurrection Pass (and trail system)	Hope and Seward	75	1,900 to 2,400 ft.	Easy backpacking	See Note, below.

For Chugach National Forest trails, contact USDA *Forest Service*, Box 390, Seward, AK 99664; phone 224-3374; phone 277-1500 x2398 for snow conditions. For cabin, phone *Forest Service Information Center* in Juneau at 586-8751. For cabin reservations, call 1-800-280-2267. The 75-mile Resurrection Pass trail system includes the Resurrection River, Russian Lakes, and Resurrection Pass Trails. Contact the *Forest Service* at the above address; phone 277-1500 x2398. Or write *Alaska Public Lands Information Center*, 605 West Fourth Avenue, #105, Anchorage, AK 99501; phone 271-2737.

Forest Service Trails chart on page 237 offers a sample of some of the more popular trails—you can get detailed information about these and other Forest Service trails from the *Alaska Public Lands Information Center* (605 West Fourth Avenue, Suite 105, Anchorage, AK 99501; phone 271-2737), or any Forest Service district office (Seward, Girdwood, Cordova, etc.).

Gold panning is another kind of recreation offered by the Chugach National Forest, which, like all national forests, is managed overall for "multiple use." There is what the Forest Service calls "geology highly favorable for the discovery of mineral deposits . . . lead, zinc, gold, molybdenum, antimony, and copper" within the forest, and there are about five thousand established mining claims (many of which are inactive). Virtually all the active claims are for gold, and most of these involve placer operations (with their concomitant equipment, such as dredges) on the Kenai Peninsula. There are also creeks, streams, and rivers that attract the recreational miner with a gold pan. If you want to try your luck at finding some "color," check possibilities—and regulations—with the people at the Alaska Public Lands Information Center in Anchorage (see above), or write the Chugach National Forest; there is a booklet entitled *Recreational Gold Panning, Chugach National Forest* that should prove helpful. Keep in mind that any patented mine is off-limits without the permission of the owner, and that it is illegal to tamper with mining equipment or to disturb a mining operation in any way and, of course, to jump a claim. Keep in mind, too, that even recreational mining can have an impact on streams that are important to anadromous fish, and on what is often fragile country, as well.

The Chugach National Forest also contains more than three dozen recreational cabins for public use, about half of which are on the Kenai Peninsula. As in the Tongass Forest, these cabins are accessible largely by foot, small plane, or boat only. A seven-day limit is the general rule, but the hike-in cabins have a three-day limit from May 15 to August 31. The cabins have bunks to accommodate four or more people and either a wood or oil stove. You should check to see which; if it's the oil type, 5 gallons of kerosene or one of stove oil will stoke it for about forty-eight hours of continuous summer use. Some of the cabins located on lakes have their own skiffs, provided by the Forest Service. United States Coast Guard regulations require that each person using such a small boat have an approved flotation device (not provided by the Forest Service). Small outboard motors are permitted if you can haul them in. The cost of these cabins, as in the Southeast, is minimal, and one of the better buys in Alaska. Remember to carry out what you carry in. Remember, too, that summer temperatures in this part of Alaska will range from 30 to 80 degrees, and you should, as always, be prepared for rain. Cabin reservations can be made up to six months (180 days, to be exact) in advance, on a first-come, first-served basis. Since hunting and trapping are permitted throughout the national forest, and since snowmobiling and cross-country skiing, along with backpacking, are excellent in areas around some of the cabins, they get well used year-round; you should get your name in early if you want to enjoy one. (A few of the cabins are so much in demand that they are reserved in special drawings only, during the months of August and September.) You need to enclose your check or money order with your request for cabin reservations. For information regarding these cabins, write: *Forest Service Information Center,* 101 Egan Drive, Juneau, AK 99801; phone 586-8751; fax 586-7928. For cabin reservations, write *Forest Service Reservation Center,* Box 900, Cumberland, MD 21501-0900; phone 1-800-280-2267. It's best to telephone for information on availability and rates for these popular cabins, then either pay by credit card or mail your check or money order to the above address. There is a small nonrefundable reservation fee.

One of the many interesting features of the Chugach National Forest is the Begich, Boggs Visitor Center at Portage Glacier, some 50 miles southeast of Anchorage off the Seward Highway. Portage Glacier, itself, is notable on several counts: it is 6 miles long and 1 mile wide, flowing into Portage Lake about 3 miles from the Visitor Center; being so close, and producing highly photogenic bergs that come even closer, it offers chances for some fine and unique pictures—you can even get good shots from inside the Visitor Center; and the glacier has honest-to-goodness ice worms. (Ice worms—*Mesenchytraeus solifugus,* or, more simply, tiny annelids—inhabit the crevices between ice crystals near the surface of glaciers; their fare is windborne pollen along with local algae. The Forest Service will take you on a hunt for them on nearby Byron Glacier if you bring your own toothpick and small container.) Added to all this, you can hope to see a few of the one hundred species of wildflowers that have been identified in Portage Valley, or perhaps you'll get a glimpse of a black or a brown bear, a beaver or a moose, or even a bald eagle on your drive from the highway to the Visitor Center. You can also keep your eye out for the three "hanging" glaciers on the sides of the mountains around you.

The Begich, Boggs Visitor Center remembers two U.S. representatives who were lost in a small plane somewhere between Anchorage and Juneau in 1972 while campaigning for Begich's reelection. (No trace of the plane was ever found.) Along with wonderful views of the glacier, the

Visitor Center offers excellent displays on glaciology; interpretive pro-grams, including films and nature walks (have your boots along for the one on Byron Glacier); and the chance to run your fingers through "glacial flour," look at a "living iceberg" (brought into the center), and listen to "the voice of the glaciers." You can also walk through the shim-mering blue interior of a simulated ice cave. During the summer, the Vis-itor Center is open seven days a week, and motor coaches make a day's outing from Anchorage to Portage and back, with a stop off at the Mount Alyeska Ski Resort in Girdwood: inquire at the downtown An-chorage *Log Cabin Visitor Information Center* (F Street and Fourth Av-enue, Anchorage, AK 99501; phone 274-3531) if you're interested. If you have your own wheels—a car or a bike—there are two campgrounds in Portage Valley: Williwaw (thirty-six campsites) and Black Bear (twelve campsites). Portage Creek provides for a canoe or kayak outing in sum-mer months, but conditions are variable; be sure to check with the rangers at the Visitor Center before putting in. Also keep in mind that Portage Pass is one of those classic Alaskan wind tunnels, and if it's a blowy day, strong gusts can knock you off your feet. (A Forest Service ranger working here once watched a 6-foot-2-inch, 200-pound man get out of his car and sail through the air into a nearby clump of alders; no real damage was done, but it was a highly spectacular, if short, journey.) The Alaska Public Lands Information Center in Anchorage (see above) should be able to give you up-to-the-minute weather conditions. Inci-dentally, Portage Glacier is one of the most popular tourist sites in the Anchorage area; it is visited every year by more people than live in all of Alaska.

Note: The Chugach National Forest has several other campgrounds; all are equipped with tables, fire grates, water, garbage pickup, and toi-let facilities (of varying degrees of sophistication). These are generally open during the summer months; some campsites in each campground can be reserved, while others require no reservations. For information contact the Forest Service Information Center in Juneau (see above) or the Chugach National Forest offices listed below. There is a small camp-ing fee. Campfires are permitted throughout the Chugach—unless other-wise posted—but only dead or down wood may be used. If you're backpacking in the high country, carry your own stove since you won't find much wood of any kind. Although trees and tundra may look too soggy to burn, they can be flammable, and a wildfire can spread with alarming speed and be extremely difficult to extinguish.

For more complete information about the Chugach, write or call the Chugach National Forest office in the area you plan to visit. Following is a list of ranger districts with addresses and phones:

Forest Supervisor,
  Chugach National Forest
3301 C Street, Suite 200
Anchorage, AK 99503
Phone 271-2500

Glacier Ranger District,
  Chugach National Forest
Box 129
Girdwood, AK 99587
Phone 783-3242

Cordova Ranger District,
  Chugach National Forest
Box 280
Cordova, AK 99574
Phone 424-7661

Seward Ranger District,
  Chugach National Forest
Box 390
334 Fourth Avenue
Seward, AK 99664
Phone 224-3374

Rivers

The Tazlina River system includes the (glacial) Little Nelchina, Nelchina, and Tazlina Rivers and Tazlina Lake. You can explore 74 miles of these waterways in four to six days. The rivers include class II and III white water, and Tazlina Lake can be dangerous in high winds. A raft or kayak is best: an open canoe is not recommended. Access in is on the Glenn Highway, and the take-out is on the Richardson Highway. Aircraft pickup is possible about midway at Tazlina Lake. Watch for log jams and interesting geological formations along the Little Nelchina. There is a dangerous whirlpool at the outlet of Tazlina Lake. For further information, contact the *Alaska Public Lands Information Center,* 605 West Fourth Avenue, Suite 105, Anchorage, AK 99501; phone 271-2737.

The Upper Tangle Lakes, Middle Fork of the Gulkana River, and the Gulkana River are clear-water lakes and streams that offer several possibilities to a canoer, rafter, or kayaker. You can put in from the Denali Highway and run 76 miles to Sourdough on the Richardson Highway; this is a five- to seven-day trip, and includes lake travel, several portages, possible lining, and white water that varies from class I to, in a few places, class IV. As an alternative, you can put in at Paxson Lake and run the Gulkana River to Sourdough—a two- to three-day trip. From Sourdough, it is possible to travel 35 miles on the Gulkana River to Gulkana, a nice one- to two-day trip. The Gulkana River flows into the Copper here, should you want a really major outing.

These are beautiful waterways, but heavy use dilutes the wilderness experience. For further information, contact the *Alaska Public Lands Information Center* (see above) or the *Bureau of Land Management,* 227 West Seventh Avenue, Anchorage, AK 99513; phone 271-5960. Note: A book (reasonable in cost) that you may find useful is *Alaska Paddling Guide;* inquire about it at the Alaska Public Lands Information Center.

The Delta River has both clear and glacial stretches. It is 35 miles (two to three days) to the first take-out, and 17 miles farther to Black Rapids. Any river craft is suitable for the first 35 miles, but there is a ¼-mile portage across the Denali fault in this stretch and a nice little rapid near the take-out point. The glacial, 17-mile portion of the Delta has some class IV rapids and canoes are not advised. An easy put-in on the Denali Highway and take-out on the Richardson Highway make this a very popular short trip, and here, too, the very heavy use dilutes the wilderness experience. For further information, contact the Alaska Public Lands Information Center or the BLM.

If your time is short and you want a one-day river experience in your kayak or canoe, check with the people at the Alaska Public Lands Information Center: there are at least three class I and II readily accessible streams in the Chugach National Forest on the Kenai Peninsula. These include: Granite Creek (class II), which flows southwest some 8 miles into East Fork Sixmile Creek, is scenic, and parallels the Seward Highway (put-in at Mile 65.5, Mile 68, or the Granite Creek Campground); Portage Creek (class I and II), which has a 7-mile run northwest into Turnagain Arm and can be accessed from the Begich, Boggs Visitor Center; and the longer Quartz Creek (class I, slow and clear, but with the chance of sweepers), which flows northwest 7 miles and then doubles back to the southwest for 10 miles to Kenai Lake, 28 miles northwest of Seward (put-in at Mile 40.8 on the Sterling Highway). Sixmile Creek is a more dashing stream (class IV, with white-water rapids) that rises where East Fork Sixmile Creek joins Canyon Creek and then flows north 9 miles to Turnagain Arm at Sunrise; it is best run before the summer thaws and rains, say, in late April or early May, when it is still at a relatively moderate river stage.

Downhill and Cross-Country Skiing

Alaska's largest and most developed ski resort is Alyeska, just an hour down the Seward Highway from Anchorage. Alyeska is inside the Chugach National Forest and operates under a special use permit from the Forest Service. It has five chair lifts, a snow-play area, and a lodge, and it offers cross-country as well as downhill skiing plus dogsled rides. During the summer, you can take a chair lift to the top for some grand views of the surrounding country.

There's good cross-country skiing at several other Forest Service spots, including the Portage Recreation Area, Twenty-mile and Placer River Valleys (where there's also snowmobiling, snowshoeing, and dogsledding); Summit Lake/Manitoba Mountain (Mile 48, Seward Highway); and Turnagain Pass (58 miles southeast of Anchorage). Inquire at *Alaska*

Public Lands Information Center in Anchorage (605 West Fourth Avenue, Suite 105, Anchorage, AK 99501; phone 271-2737) for further information. (Don't forget that the city of Anchorage also has skiing opportunities for winter visitors.)

Biking

You can bring your own bicycle to Anchorage via ferry and bus (see Traveling by Ferry, in Part II), or you can inquire about the possibilities of bike rentals in Anchorage at the Alaska Public Lands Information Center (see above).

Among the places you can travel locally are, of course, the quite extensive bicycle trails of Anchorage, which can make for a pleasant day's exercise. You might enjoy taking the coastal trail or finding your way out to Earthquake Park, among other nearby places. If you're an ambitious bicycle rider and have more time, there are at least three week-long trips you can make. Each offers excellent possibilities for seeing some of Alaska's best. Each offers, as well, good biking on paved roads and the opportunity for an exceptional adventure. All are highly recommended.

Three Bicycle Trips

Trip One

You can take the Seward Highway south to its junction with the Sterling Highway and continue from there into Homer. This is a long trip, 227 miles, but there are many excellent campgrounds along the way, starting just south of Anchorage with the state park facilities. Check with the state park people about what is available at McHugh Creek, Beluga Point (a beautiful spot with offshore islands and interesting archeological work that places Chugach Eskimos here over 6,000 years ago), Falls Creek, and Bird Point, where you may see nesting bald eagles as well as other raptors and seabirds.

A stop at the Begich, Boggs Visitor Center at Portage is worthwhile to admire the very photogenic Portage Glacier (see above).

There are numerous other very good Forest Service campgrounds farther south along your route, as well as many operated by the U.S. Fish and Wildlife Service in the Kenai National Wildlife Refuge. For details, check with the *Alaska Public Lands Information Center* (605 West Fourth Avenue, Suite 105, Anchorage, AK 99501; phone 271-2737). Once in Homer, you can camp on the famous Homer spit if you can abide wall-to-wall trailers. Despite the crowd, it is a spectacular place. You will probably want to visit Kachemak Bay State Park (accessible by boat) while you're there, and you might also enjoy a trip to Diana

Tillion's studio on Halibut Cove. Tillion is a well-known Alaskan artist who uses octopus ink—a soft sepia color—for her medium. The Kachemak Bay ferry (at the small boat harbor) operates regular boat trips to the Tillions' place, and the whole trip takes about five hours. Tillion's husband is the well-known former state senator Clem Tillion. Their daughter, Marion Beck, operates a popular eating place, The Saltry, in Halibut Cove. This is open from 2 to 9 P.M. during the summer. You get there by the above-mentioned ferry or if you have a boat, by same. Reservations are essential; phone 235-7847.

For a remarkably comfortable, even luxurious, and memorable wilderness experience, you might plan to stay with Mike and Diana McBride at their Kachemak Bay Wilderness Lodge, reached by boat from Homer. The McBrides are dedicated wilderness people who share their love and knowledge of this naturally lovely area, along with fine food and accommodations, with their guests. Write Box 956, Homer, AK 99603.

At Homer, you can put your bike onto the state ferry for as long or short a trip as you like. The seaworthy *Tustamena* plies the waters between Homer, Seldovia, Seward, and Kodiak year-round. Twice a year—in May and late September—it braves the open ocean and travels to Sand Point and King Cove on the Alaska Peninsula. If you're a good sailor and interested in birdwatching, you might check the dates of these trips; they may coincide with outstanding shows of migrating birds. Under any circumstances, you should get a current ferry schedule before you plan your trip. Note that, from Seward, it is just 129 miles to Anchorage.

Trip Two

You can bike down the Seward Highway to Portage, load your bike onto the Alaska Railroad train there, and travel on to Whittier. The Alaska Railroad charges an amazingly low fare for bicycles and is reasonable for people as well. If you bike this stretch of the Seward Highway, plan to take time out at Potter Marsh, just south of Anchorage, to admire the birds. Just south of the marsh itself, is a state and national historic site, the Potter Section House, a 1930s railroad complex that has been lovingly restored. Eighteen layers of paint were removed from the house to get to the original color! The Potter Section House (Chugach State Park Headquarters) is open Monday through Friday; phone 345-5014 for information about it. (You can, of course, enjoy this historic site which re-creates the pioneer Alaska Railroad scene, on any trip south of Anchorage; it's only 11 to 12 miles from town.)

In Whittier, you can take the ferry for a sightsee run through Prince William Sound and a stop at Valdez, where you can pick up the Richardson Highway for a return trip to Anchorage (304 miles) after viewing the pipeline terminus. Or you can continue on the ferry to Cordova, where there are excellent opportunities for birdwatching. (Ask the Forest Service where you can roll out your sleeping bag.) There are reasonably good gravel roads for biking, and you can travel to the Million Dollar Bridge, which crosses the Copper River, or did before the 1964 earthquake, when it was permanently buckled. (You can get across it, but the road ends on the other side.) There are good opportunities for hiking, and look for the (excellent) Forest Service display at Miles Lake. Talk to people at the Alaska Public Lands Information Center (see above) or the Cordova Ranger District office in Cordova (see page 241) for more information. From Cordova, you can, of course, take either the road to Anchorage from Valdez (reached by ferry) or the ferry all the way to Whittier, retracting your original route. This ferry does not service the Kenai Peninsula south of Whittier, or Kodiak, regularly.

Trip Three

You can bike a paved road to Denali National Park (formerly Mount McKinley Park) or carry your bike on the Alaska Railroad (space available) if you prefer. From Denali Park (actually, Cantwell), it is possible to bike the Denali Highway (not paved) into some very different and interesting country, if you have the time. The *Bureau of Land Management* (222 West Seventh Avenue, Anchorage, AK 99513; phone 271-5960) can give you suggestions about camping facilities as well as roadhouses on this 133-mile-long highway, which goes through extensive country above timberline, provides access to lovely mountain lakes, has excellent birding, and, when the weather smiles, spectacular views of Mount McKinley. The BLM has very good brochures on areas that it administers: ask at any Alaska Public Lands Information Center if there is one available on the Denali Highway. See also William Diel and Gina Kruse's book *Rocks, Ridges, and Glaciers: A Geological Tour Along the Denali Highway*, listed in Suggested Reading.

Talkeetna Mountains

The Talkeetna Mountains are about an hour's drive north of Anchorage via the Glenn Highway. A discrete range of their own, they stand between the Alaska Range and the Chugach Mountains, guarding the wonderful lake systems of the Copper River basin to the east. These beautiful rugged mountains reach heights of well over 8,500 feet and, with their granite outcrops, recall the Sierra Nevada to many visitors from the Outside.

The Talkeetnas are heavily used year-round by Anchorage residents.

They offer superb hiking as well as cross-country skiing, and their wild-flowers are renowned throughout Southcentral Alaska. Most of the land in the Talkeetnas is private property or is in the hands of the state or BLM, and has long been prospected and, in places, mined. Roads run through the high country, and the superbly scenic ridges are readily ac-cessible. You can also drive considerable distances through this lovely alpine country; the road to Willow runs through the Talkeetnas, and, while narrow and winding, it makes for a spectacular ride.

A favorite takeoff place into the Talkeetnas is the Independence Mine on Hatcher Pass, about 75 miles from Anchorage. You can park there to start your hiking. (You might want to visit the Hatcher Pass Historic State Park first.) There is also a privately owned A-frame lodge with ac-commodations for fifty to sixty (and the "best sauna in Alaska") that can be rented reasonably for group outings winter or summer. (Ask at the *Log Cabin Visitor Information Center* in Anchorage (F Street and Fourth Avenue, Anchorage, AK 99501; phone 274-3531) for further in-formation. Nienhauser and Simmerman's *55 Ways to the Wilderness in Southcentral Alaska* (see Suggested Reading) gives the specifics of several hikes in the Talkeetnas. A friend of mine who knows the area well sug-gests that you use this book for starters and then just "keep on going." The upper Caribou Creek drainage, in particular, offers exceptional hik-ing opportunities through alpine tundra valleys that are connected by low and lovely passes.

Prince William Sound

Named by Capt. James Cook in 1778, Prince William Sound shares many of the characteristics of Southeast Alaska, although it is a smaller, more compact area. It has lovely fjords and inlets, islands, and lush rain-forested shores. It has stunning tidewater glaciers, and spectacular moun-tains delineate its horizons. The area also has many lakes and streams and cascading ribbons of white water and lots of rain and unpredictable weather (more, in fact, than Southeast). It has a fabulous variety and plenitude of marine wildlife—mammals, fish, and birds. This is a world that has long been best explored from the water, and it continues to be despite the 1989 oil spill (which will go down in the history of ig-nominy). As in Southeast, most of the land in the region is administered by the USDA Forest Service, being part of the nearly 6-million-acre Chugach National Forest.

Unlike Southeast, however, Prince William Sound is readily accessible by highway as well as by train and ferry, and from a nearby metropolis. Obviously there are both pluses and minuses to this fact. Being so easily reached from Anchorage makes it a relatively inexpensive area to visit.

Using a bus or the ferry to get to it and around it, you can explore farther on your bike, or on your own two feet, or in a small boat at a minimum cost. You can also try for one of the USDA Forest Service cabins
in the area—say, one on Hinchinbrook Island—which can be quite reasonable to reach and, as noted, a real bargain for a family or small group
(see under USDA Forest Service, in Part II). (Hinchinbrook Island is
around ten minutes from Cordova in a small floatplane.)

Furthermore, if you want to confine your exploration of Alaska to a
relatively small and manageable area, Prince William Sound can add a
major dimension to your experience. Use Anchorage as your gateway;
the sound lets you sample the environment of the Southeast, and then
you can go on to enjoy that of Southcentral and possibly the Interior—
all within a fairly short time and at a relatively low cost. For example,
you can make an interesting triangular trip by car: drive from Anchorage
to Fairbanks, from Fairbanks to Valdez, and from Valdez back to Anchorage via Whittier (by ferry) and Portage (by train). Or, if you have
more time and like to bicycle, you can get yourself to Cantwell (by train,
if there's space available), then bike the Denali Highway (which has good
BLM camps along the way; contact the *Bureau of Land Management,*
222 West Seventh Avenue, Anchorage, AK 99513; phone 271-5960) to
the Richardson Highway, thence south to Valdez and back to Anchorage
via the ferry, train, and the Seward Highway.

The minus side of the accessibility of Prince William Sound is that a
place so beautiful and easily reached is bound to have heavier use than
more remote areas. The sound is a principal water playground for Anchorage folks, and many of the city's residents keep small boats (motor-
powered or sailboats) available at Whittier or Seward for weekend or
week-long use. This means that you may encounter a good number of
people if you decide to travel by small boat yourself. If you're seeking the
solitude of the wilderness, you may have to travel farther afield. Add to
this the fact that in the very heart of the sound is the busy port of Valdez,
which was once a small, quiet, idyllic Alaska town. This is, of course,
now the southern terminal of the Trans-Alaska oil pipeline, and it has a
battery of enormous holding tanks, each with a capacity of 510,000 bar-
rels (one barrel equals 40 gallons). There is also much coming and going
of numerous oil tankers. This might not be the kind of thing you would
travel all the way to Alaska to see.

However, these drawbacks are minor compared with the wonders of
Prince William Sound, and they should in no way discourage you from
making a visit to this part of Alaska. In fact, the ferry ride from Whittier
to Valdez-Cordova and back is one of the more special short trips you
can take in the state. Near Whittier, there is a spectacular colony of

black-legged kittiwakes that decorates the cliffs and the sky above the harbor; they will give you an unforgettable send-off. Once on your way, you can look for sea otters, sea lions, and harbor seals. Your chances of seeing one or more species of whales are good; killer whales and minke whales travel the waters of the sound in goodly numbers, and there may be more humpbacks here than in Glacier Bay. You can also expect to see many different seabirds. There is a USDA Forest Service naturalist on board the ferry to help you look in the right places for the marine wildlife and to give you interesting highlights of the places you pass. Incidentally, you may find several Anchorage residents on this trip, showing off the scenery to visitors from Outside. The loop through Valdez and back to the city along the Glenn Highway is a favorite local sightseeing trip.

It takes about seven hours on the ferry from Whittier to Valdez and another six hours—plus or minus—to Cordova. (The fare is the same whether you go to Valdez or Cordova.) Cordova is enough off the beaten track that it gets a minimum of recreational use. It is, however, situated very beautifully, with the backdrop of Mount Eccles rising behind it. It has tourist accommodations, but if you prefer to go it on your own, you should check with the Forest Service (see below) about the status of campsites. If you do visit Cordova, try to get up to Miles Lake and the Copper River delta; the latter is one of Alaska's greatest wildlife areas. During the migratory seasons, this region is marvelous for birdwatching. (See Trip Two of Three Bicycle Trips, under Anchorage as a Gateway.) The Copper River itself is one of Alaska's greatest—and most accessible—rivers to run, with vistas and close-ups of grand mountains and glaciers, plus opportunities to view trumpeter swans, and a marvelous berg-filled lake to travel through. (You can also view the old Million Dollar Bridge, which has joined the ranks of ill-fated attempts to span this powerful waterway.) You can drive to a put-in on the Copper River at Chitina, or at McCarthy. (If you want a longer and wonderfully varied river run, get yourself to McCarthy, where you put into the Kennicott River, which flows into the Nizina, which joins the Chitina, which flows into the Copper at the town of Chitina.) A take-out from the Copper is easily accomplished at Cordova, where you can arrange for a pickup by bus. You can get information about running the Copper River from the *Alaska Public Lands Information Center* in Anchorage (605 West Fourth Avenue, Suite 105, Anchorage, AK 99501; phone 271-2737) or from the Forest Service ranger at the Cordova District Office in Cordova (see below). (Note: There are good bed and breakfasts in Cordova.)

If you want to spend some time enjoying Prince William Sound for itself alone, you will want to explore it in a small boat. Again, you have several options as to how you do it. You can go on a commercially operated sailboat for, say, a one- or two-week trip (you may be expected to help sail the boat). Or you can rent a kayak or take a kayak excursion with a local guide (see below). Of course, you can sail or paddle your own boat, if you so prefer. If you do go on your own, you can get detailed information from the Alaska Public Lands Information Center in Anchorage (see above). The following advice from a local kayaker who loves Prince William Sound may also be helpful to you: "There is food everywhere: pink salmon, clams, mussels, rockfish, flounder, and Dungeness and tanner crabs. You can fish from the shore with a line; look for a salmon stream. Or you can bring your own collapsible crab pot. Use herring, sculpin, or other fish for bait, set your pot close to shore (out to a depth of 60 feet), and wait six to eight hours for a feast." Author's note: Best not to count on this wholly on your first trip here.

Camping is a challenge. What looks like a meadow may be a soggy marsh. (Snowmelt is much later here than in the Southeast.) Look for a small tundra-covered knoll. Carry nails with you in case you come across an old platform to which you can fasten down your tent. While much of the coastline is not good for camping, some tidal meadows do have dry areas in their upper portions, and you can usually find a place. Be sure your tent has a dry bottom and a fly, because it rains a lot. Also have good stakes.

Note: Commercial boat guides have fixed campsites of their own that save a lot of time and trouble for people traveling with them. Also, if you travel on your own, keep in mind that you should have at least two boats in your party.

Kayak trips can be made any time between May and September, but, in general, early summer is the best time. Late summer is windier and better for sailing. There are four USDA Forest Service cabins you can tie into when kayaking out of Whittier: (1) Schrode Lake has a nice A-frame that sleeps eight to ten; this requires a 2-mile hike from the shore. (2) Pigot Bay, another spacious A-frame; reaching this one requires a boat. (3) Coghill Lake has great fishing for red salmon; it also requires a short hike from the shore. (4) Harrison Lake is not as attractive as the others but is a good haven in a storm. (There is a *USDA Forest Service* office in Cordova: write Box 280, Cordova, AK 99574; phone 424-7661.)

Paddle as close to shore as possible, and always be prepared for storms. Prince William Sound can have four or five days straight of terrible weather. Then again, it may be so beautiful you'll find it hard to bear. Plan to stay from two days to two months.

Note: Native selections of forested areas around Prince William Sound present a challenge to preservationists. The United States government must buy back these lands (or easements on them) to protect them from being logged. The Exxon *Valdez* settlement money has been put to good use here, with the purchase of 35,000 acres of beautiful forest land from Chenega, its Native owners. The Alaska State Division of Outdoor Recreation and Parks and the USDA Forest Service share in the area's administration, while the Natives retain small inholdings that they may develop. But much more needs to be done.

How to Get There
It is possible to take the ferry from Bellingham to Cordova, Valdez, and Seward, about a 6-day trip in all, which on a blue day will let you experience the beauty of this place. (See ferry information on page 118.) Otherwise, you can use the ferry from Whittier.

Sailing and Kayaking
Alaska Wilderness Sailing and Kayaking: write Jim and Nancy Lethcoe (Box 1313, Valdez, AK 99686; phone 835-5175) for information and bookings. The Lethcoes offer trips from one to several days in duration. They are deeply interested in the natural history of Prince William Sound and in preserving the special qualities of this beautiful area. (See their indispensable *Cruising Guide to Prince William Sound* under Suggested Reading.)

Where to Stay
There are facilities at Whittier, Valdez, and Cordova. Contact *Chambers of Commerce* for information. *Whittier:* Box 607, Whittier, AK 99693; phone 344-3340. *Cordova:* Box 99, Cordova, AK 99574; phone 424-7260. *Valdez:* Box 1603, Valdez, AK 99686; phone 835-2984; fax 835-4845.

Air Charters
Check with the *Alaska Public Lands Information Center* in Anchorage (605 West Fourth Avenue, Suite 105, Anchorage, AK 99501; phone 271-2737) or the *Cordova Ranger District* (Box 280, Cordova, AK 99574; phone 424-7661). Or write the Chambers of Commerce (see above).

The Kenai Peninsula
The Kenai Peninsula is not the place to look for a lonely wilderness experience, although all the warnings about being careful as you venture into the Alaskan wilderness still hold there. (Especially in the winter, you can get into major difficulties on the Kenai if you forget to be prudent.) This region has a remarkable diversity of landscapes and life zones. It is also a place to look for almost any variety of outdoor recreation that you

enjoy, for it seems to have something for just about everyone. It offers fishing, cross-country skiing, hunting, canoeing, day hiking, backpacking, biking, snowmobiling, birdwatching, glacier watching, horseback travel, sailing, kayaking, or simply looking and enjoying. There's even downhill skiing on the way from Anchorage. Being readily accessible (by ground and water transportation as well as air), this unique part of Alaska is not only Anchorage's playground but also probably the most heavily used part of the state, when it comes to recreation.

Providing all these opportunities is the wonderfully varied terrain. Having been shaped and formed by glacial action, the Kenai Peninsula's landscape has a glacial outwash plain filled with lakes and rivers (a paradise for canoers), those splendid Chugach-Kenai Mountains, some very large and beautiful glacial lakes, including Skilak and Tustumena, and even a magnificent ice field (the Harding), from which hangs a whole series of active glaciers. Add to this a lovely coastline and relatively livable climate, particularly for the Southwest. (Backed by the high ridge of the Chugach-Kenai Mountains, the eastern side of the Kenai enjoys all the pluses and minuses of the Gulf of Alaska. Thus Seward gets 67.35 inches of precipitation a year, while the mountains behind it pile up some 80.6 feet of snow; Soldotna, on the west, gets a total of about 18 inches.) Homer, at the southern end of the peninsula, has some of the best weather in Alaska: I once sat for five days in Anchorage in a chilly unpleasant summer rain and, in desperation, drove to Homer and found it warm and sunny.

The Kenai Peninsula was home to Tanaina Indians when the Russians first began to settle on it in the late eighteenth century. The first Russian shipbuilding operation was in what is now known as Resurrection Bay, on which the town of Seward fronts. There are several Russian churches on the Kenai; almost as much as Kodiak (see below), it bears the imprint of these first Europeans. (It is interesting to note that, in the one and a quarter centuries the Russians claimed Alaska, there were rarely more than a total of six hundred Russians living there, and their explorations were limited largely to the coasts.) The Russian Orthodox churches in Kenai and Ninilchik are both interesting, and the one in Ninilchik is easily visited from the Sterling Highway. The church is in the middle of a lupine-filled meadow on a bluff above the Cook Inlet. If you're there on a clear day, you'll have a fine view of the snowy volcanoes across the water.

After the United States acquired Alaska, first Seward and later Whittier became important ports and points of access to the Cook Inlet region and the Interior. Seward enjoyed its heyday as the southern terminus of the Alaska Railroad during the earlier years the trains were running.

During World War II, Whittier took over and enjoyed its brief boom when the railroad was tunneled through the Chugach Mountains to reach a saltwater port with fewer problems. During the war, an eleven-story office building—now called the Begich Towers in honor of Congressman Nick Begich, who was killed in a small plane while campaigning for re-election—was constructed by the United States Army. This incongruous structure sticks up like the proverbial sore thumb and is presently used for apartments and condominiums.

Homer, which has become an artists' colony and is sometimes called the "Carmel of the North," is one of Alaska's most charming towns. Not only is its climate relatively benign (although it does, of course, get its share of storms and winds), but the scenery around it is wonderful. It also has some great tides, superb fishing (its shellfish are legendary), and crowds of people descending upon it during the fishing season.

Almost all of the Kenai Peninsula has at one time or another been in the hands of the USDA Forest Service or the U.S. Fish and Wildlife Service, and most of it still is. Additionally, the National Park Service now has the Kenai Fjords National Park (see page 272). The land in private ownership has skyrocketed in value since the building of the pipeline, when many Outsiders discovered the charms of the Homer area. Now most of the older homesteads—many staked out in the wake of World War II—are being subdivided at prices that might make you gasp.

The Kenai National Wildlife Refuge, administered by the U.S. Fish and Wildlife Service, comprises close to 2 million acres. It takes in the lush wetlands of the northwestern section of the peninsula as well as a section to the south and east that includes most of the Harding Ice Field and Skilak and Tustumena Lakes. The original refuge was designated in the early 1940s by President Franklin Roosevelt when the U.S. Fish and Wildlife Service was first established. (This essentially involved the transfer of federal land from the Department of Agriculture—the Forest Service—to the Department of the Interior.)

The northwestern section of the refuge is some of the best moose habitat in the region. During the 1950s and 1960s, however, it also proved to be an area with great oil potential. A great deal of seismic exploration went on, and now, when you fly over the area in a small plane, it looks as though some strange prehistoric people had inscribed huge hieroglyphics all over the ground. (If you're lucky, you'll see a moose on such an overflight or a pair of trumpeter swans housekeeping their own small lake.) Oil was brought in during the fifties, and presently there are active oil wells, an oil refinery and pipelines, roads, and much activity—with which the moose must coexist. A major fire in 1968 served to refurbish the area with willow and gave the animals a boost.

The Fish and Wildlife Service does its best to protect the refuge for its natural values, to cooperate with oil development while minimizing its impact (there are no more disfiguring seismic explorations going on), and to encourage recreation that is not disruptive. In fact, the wildlife refuge offers some of the most rewarding recreational opportunities on the peninsula. The Swan Lake and Swanson River canoe trails are beautiful; there is hiking in the lake regions; and there are numerous U.S. Fish and Wildlife Service campgrounds and camping spots, as well as four cabins, or shelters.

Where the Fish and Wildlife Service leaves off, in the northern part of the peninsula, the Chugach National Forest picks up. The USDA Forest Service is responsible for a large chunk of the Chugach-Kenai Mountains and maintains a number of campsites, cabins, and more than 100 miles of trails.

How to Get There

You can reach the Kenai Peninsula by the new ferry, by railroad (in summer the train runs from Anchorage to Seward with a stop at Moose Pass), by road, or, of course, by air. You can also use the ferry to explore the coast of much (but not all) of the peninsula: the Cook Inlet presents some discomforting obstacles to passenger ships, including turbulent waters, tides, and storms. The road system is conducive to biking; the Sterling Highway goes all the way to Homer, branching off the Seward Highway a short distance down the peninsula. (See Biking, under Anchorage as a Gateway.) Inquire about bus service at the *Log Cabin Visitor Information Center* in Anchorage (F Street and Fourth Avenue, Anchorage, AK 99501; phone 274-3531). The scheduled air service to Homer uses small aircraft and, on a clear day, offers some dramatic views, including a fine vista of the Harding Ice Field and the Aleutian Range across Cook Inlet. (Note how evenly spaced Spurr, Redoubt, and Iliamna are. They are actually about 40 miles apart; the volcanoes to the south on down the Alaska Peninsula are also nearly equal in distance from one another, being roughly 30 miles apart.)

Where to Stay

Consult the *Chambers of Commerce* in Seward and Homer (and Kenai and Soldotna if interested) for names of hotels. (*Land's End* in Homer is a delightful hotel to stay in, being right on the water.) For *Seward:* write Chamber of Commerce, Box 749, Seward, AK 99664; phone 224-8051. For *Homer:* Box 541, Homer, AK 99603; phone 235-5300. For *Kenai:* 402 Overland, Kenai, AK 99611; phone 283-7989. For *Soldotna:* 44790 Sterling Highway, Soldotna, AK 99669; phone 262-9814. Or consult the Alaska Public Lands Information Center in Anchorage (see below).

The Kenai Peninsula is full of places to camp, especially along the northern part of the Sterling Highway. For information, contact: *Alaska Public Lands Information Center,* 605 West Fourth Avenue, Suite 105, Anchorage, AK 99501; phone 271-2737. (Note: There are twelve state park units with camping facilities that include 230 campsites on the peninsula.) *USDA Forest Service,* Box 390, Seward, AK 99664; phone 224-3374. *U.S. Fish and Wildlife Service,* Refuge Manager, Kenai National Wildlife Refuge, Box 2139, Soldotna, AK 99669; phone 262-7021. *U.S. National Park Service,* Kenai Fjords National Park, Box 1727, Seward, AK 99664; phone 224-3175.

Kenai National Wildlife Refuge offers some of the best—and most popular—canoeing and kayaking in Alaska. You can take almost any length trip you want for a minimum of expense in the canoe system. For information regarding small-boating (including the rental of canoes in Soldotna) and other recreational opportunities in the Kenai National Wildlife Refuge, contact, in Anchorage, the Alaska Public Lands Information Center (see above).

42. Kodiak

Although Alaska has an impressive coastline—over 47,000 miles of it—much of it delineates fjords, bays, and channels or more or less enclosed seas, and it is not easy to find ready access to the wild and wave-washed ocean shore. One of the few places in the state where you can find this and right from a road, too, is on Kodiak Island, which is also a place of many other unique and interesting features. Located southwest of the Kenai Peninsula, Kodiak and its adjacent islands, including Afognak, are an extension of the Chugach-Kenai Mountains, chunks of the earth already detached from the mainland and partially drowned. The area is still sinking slowly beneath the ocean. During the 1964 earthquake, for example, the town of Kodiak subsided over 5 feet. (Following this great shake, the ocean side of Kodiak was also bludgeoned by a huge tsunami, only one in a succession of destructive waves that have historically battered this island.) Although an apron of continental shelf extends from Kodiak beneath the Pacific Ocean, this sea bottom is edged abruptly by the Aleutian Trench; thus Kodiak is immediately adjacent to a region of intense seismic activity.

Kodiak's rugged mountains rise from 2,000 to as much as 4,000 feet above the sea. Totaling about 3,670 square miles of land, the island is so deeply incised by beautiful fjords that there is no point on it more than 15 miles from seawater. Much of the coastline is precipitous, but there are narrow beaches and picturesque stretches of open rocky shore.

Kodiak shows much evidence of massive glacial action as well as the effects of the earth's convulsive movements. During the ice ages, the whole region was buried under ice and snow with only a small area on the island—known as the Kodiak refugium—remaining uncovered. Now lakes lie in ice-rounded basins in the glacially sculpted high country. The rivers are short, and clear, swift streams tumble down steep slopes. There is also evidence of nearby volcanism: Kodiak has been repeatedly smothered with ash from the volcanoes of the Aleutian Range, from which it is separated by the narrow waters of Shelikof Strait. In the road cuts, you can examine the most recent layering of ash sandwiched between glacial till.

The flora of Kodiak is gorgeous. Although much of the island is exposed bedrock, you will probably remember the place as being a glowing green—I do. Alaska's lovely Sitka spruce forest reaches its western limits here and on Afognak Island. It is noteworthy that this forest is very young—from four to eight hundred or so years—and that it is still pressing its way westward. You can see its vanguard of young trees invading the lush meadowland west of Cape Chiniak. This interesting community of grasses, leafy woody plants, and thorny salmonberry is classified as tundra. (It may be beautiful, but it is difficult to hike through.)The wildflowers on the island are spectacular; cinquefoil, wild iris, wild geranium, and other bright blooming plants color the landscape. The alpine tundra has yellow heather, among other unique flowering plants.

Kodiak's fauna is equally outstanding. This is the place where Alaska's great brown bear has reached its maximum size—or so claim the residents of the island—and there is a big statue of the animal in downtown Kodiak. (Sadly, the big brownies here are being pressed by the increasing development that is occurring, with a subsequent loss of wild habitat. Fish and Wildlife biologists note that many of the largest of these impressive bears have been hunted out.) Bear viewing may be possible: check with the U.S. Fish and Wildlife people at the Kodiak National Wildlife Refuge (see below). This is also the westernmost range of the Sitka black-tailed deer, one of the species that has been introduced successfully. Another is the mountain goat. (On Afognak, there is the only population of elk in Alaska, again a successful transplant.) Kodiak is a wonderful place to see and hear red foxes, which are abundant, and the shores are home for many sea mammals. The bird life is beautiful and varied, and the ease of seeing the avian population here makes this an unusually fine area for birdwatchers to visit. Almost any time of year, for example, you can be quite sure of having what an Alaskan birder describes as "fabulous views" of seabirds along the northeastern shoreline—and these from the road. During migration (and in the winter), you are likely to see emperor geese, the elegant harlequin duck, and Steller's eiders. The latter provide a special show as they cavort about in the water as charmingly as buffleheads.

Kodiak was the site of the first Russian headquarters in North America. In 1784, Grigori Ivanovich Shelikof, founder of the Russian-American Company, chose to settle the shores of an inlet he named Three Saints Bay (after his flagship). Eight years later, Alexander Baranof, who had assumed charge of the Russian operation, moved everything to Pavlovsk Gavan or Paul's Bay—later Kodiak Bay—because, a historian notes, it was "higher and drier and . . . was surrounded by the timber to build boats, buildings and better fortifications." Actually, and far more dramatically, Baranof moved because of a particularly severe earthquake and a resultant tsunami that proved disastrous to his group since there was no high ground for refuge. Baranof's new settlement eventually became the town of Kodiak. Although Baranof uprooted a second time in a matter of a few years and sailed off to Sitka (in 1799, having nearly exhausted the sea otter populations nearby), the early Russian influence has persisted on Kodiak. There are place names like Shelikof Strait, Kupreanof Strait, Mount Glotoff, and Olga Bay, and Russian crosses stand in the cemeteries. There is a blue, onion-domed Russian Orthodox church in the town of Kodiak, flanked, unfortunately, by a huge gas storage tank. This was the first Russian Orthodox church (indeed, the first established parish) in the New World, although the original building, like many other Alaskan churches, burned, and the one you see today is a restoration. (Each of the six villages on Kodiak Island—Ouzinkie, Port Lions, Old Harbor, Larsen Bay, Karluk, and Akhiok—has its own Russian Orthodox church.)

The Russians undoubtedly brought Aleuts with them when they came to Kodiak, and a few names—like Ayakulik—attest to their presence here. The people who met these invaders of the islands, however, were Pacific Eskimos, the Koniags, who were longtime residents. Theirs was a highly successful indigenous culture, and it is estimated that their population totaled at least eight thousand when the Europeans found them. Disease and the sometimes cruel domination of the Russians, especially the *promysh-*

leniki (hunters and traders), took a high toll on the Koniags. Most of the place names on the island, however, derive from their language.

After Baranof's departure, Kodiak continued as a center for tanneries and salteries (cod was the first fish to be utilized here). During the 1830s, there were also some minor whaling activities in the water around the island, but most captains took their ships north to the Arctic to hunt the bowheads. The American acquisition of Alaska had little effect on Kodiak until 1882, when the first salmon cannery in the Southcentral region was built at Karluk; at that time the Karluk River was one of the most productive salmon streams in Alaska. This marked the beginning of Kodiak as a major fishery. Today it remains one of the state's major fishing and canning centers, although in recent years much of its fishing depends upon the extensive hatchery system the state has initiated. The town of Kodiak holds a Crab Festival (usually in May and, alas, virtually minus crabs), and its harbor is one of the busiest fishing ports in the area, with canneries lining its shore.

During World War II, the military went into operation on Kodiak, and one of its relics is Fort Abercrombie, now owned by the state. (This is one of the places you can camp on the island; there is a developed campground with fourteen campsites here.) A major U.S. Coast Guard station remains on Kodiak (the largest in area of any in the United States) and is the center for patrol operations to control illegal fishing, as well as for search and rescue missions. A substantial part of Kodiak is now protected in the Kodiak National Wildlife Refuge. (Note, however: The refuge has major problems with private inholdings.)

Placement of a Distant Early Warning Station (DEW line) site (now a communications saucer) on top of 1,270-foot Mount Pillar, just above Kodiak, has resulted in a road that can take you to fine overviews of the surrounding countryside. There are, in fact, several stretches of road (about 100 miles in all) that you can travel—by car, bicycle, or on foot—that spoke out from the city of Kodiak, often following the shore or the valleys between the mountains.

It can be a fine adventure to take the ferry to Kodiak from Homer (thirteen hours) or from Seward (fifteen hours). Along the way, you can enjoy fine vistas of spectacular scenery, if the weather cooperates. Sometimes the ferry from Homer passes among gatherings of sea lions, and you might also be able to see many species of seabirds resting on the water. Windy days seem to bring out more birds, and there are many windy days in this part of the world. (Although the wind averages only 8.7 knots, it often blows nonstop, and it has been known to reach a speed of over 100 knots.)

In the summer, Kodiak is apt to have many mild and cloudy days, enjoying as it does a maritime climate. As in so many parts of Alaska, however, there are miniclimates around the island, and the ranges of temperature and precipitation changes are sizable. Rainfall, for example, varies by as much as 63 inches. A frequent visitor to Kodiak comments that in some places on the island it's wet, foggy, and windy; in other places it's wetter, foggier, and windier—this in spite of the fact that Kodiak residents sometimes refer to their home as the Sunshine Isle of Alaska. The town of Kodiak, where the ferry docks, has temperatures between 45 and 60 degrees during the summer (with a record high of 86) and, typically, only five days will see the thermometer top 70. Winters are moderate as well, with the temperatures sliding between 19 and 45 degrees and a record low of minus 5 degrees. Precipitation, including 72 inches of snow, is right about 60 inches a year. The last two weeks of May are probably the best bet for good weather in Kodiak, but stay away in September when the storms begin to roar in.

There are several motels in Kodiak as well as the state-owned campground at Fort Abercrombie and many good camping spots along the road system. (The state park people are developing more parks in the Kodiak archipelago. Check with the Alaska Department of Natural Resources Public Information Center (see below) for the latest information. In the summer, however, keep in mind that all the facilities can be crowded by the influx of fishermen and cannery workers. You can bicycle or hike many of the roads, or you might want to rent a car for longer trips.

The road south of town to Cape Chiniak and Sequel Point is spectacular. It runs along an area of ocean coast with sea stacks and islets offshore that is evocative of Oregon's shores. The surf here can be memorably beautiful. Look for sea lions along this road—there's a good colony of them just off Cape Chiniak. Also keep your eyes out for shorebirds, including the black oystercatcher, and watch for puffins, cormorants, glaucous-winged gulls, and kittiwakes, which are easy to see on the small islands near the shore. In the winter, there can be thousands of Steller's eiders here, and in the summer this is a nesting area for common eiders. This is also the most accessible place in Alaska where you might be able to encounter nesting Aleutian terns. These lovely birds make their homes in grasslands.

If you'd like a most pleasant and reasonably strenuous hike, there is a trail up Barometer Mountain near the U.S. Coast Guard station. This is roughly a 3,000-foot climb, with a good trail all the way. There are splendid views and a chance to see the alpine tundra. It is also possible to hike, bike, or drive the gravel road over the mountains from Kodiak to Anton Larson Bay. (This is about a two-hour trip by bike.) This part of the island has its own, different charm. Sheltered from the ocean, it has quiet coves and beaches, and the deep red of its rock is set off by the green trees and the dark-blue water. If you want to visit Afognak Island, you will need to charter a boat or a small plane. Note: Afognak has recently been heavily clear-cut. Efforts to protect this beautiful island may, happily, be successful.

Some Useful Information About Kodiak

Zip code: 99615. Area code: 907.

Ferry

The state ferry services Kodiak year-round. Write *Alaska Marine Highway System,* Box 25535, Juneau, AK 99802, for a schedule; phone 465-3941, 465-3942, or 1-800-642-0066. In Kodiak: Box 703; phone 486-3800 or 1-800-526-6731.

Air Service

Scheduled commercial air service is available from Anchorage and Seattle; check with your travel agent.

Hotels

Russian Heritage Inn (some kitchenettes, laundry facilities): 119 Yukon Terrace, Kodiak; phone 486-5657. *Westmark Kodiak* (restaurant): 236 Rezanof, adjacent small boat harbor; phone 486-5712 or 1-800-544-0970. *Shelikof Lodge* (restaurant): 211 Thorsheim Avenue, Box 774, Kodiak; phone 486-4141. Or try *Kodiak Bed and Breakfast:* 308 Cope Street, Kodiak; phone 486-5367. Reservations are essential during the fishing season. For others, write the *Kodiak Island Convention and Visitors Bureau,* 100 Marine Way, Kodiak; phone 486-4782.

Camping Facilities

You can write the *Kodiak Island Convention and Visitors Bureau* (see above) for further information—or just play your luck. The *Alaska Milepost* (see Suggested Reading) notes several undeveloped campsites along creeks in its auto logs of roads out of Kodiak, but there are others as well. For information regarding camping at Fort Abercrombie, write *Alaska State Parks,* Kodiak District Office, S.R. Box 3800, Kodiak; phone 486-6339. The *U.S. Fish and Wildlife Service* has several shelter-type cabins in the Kodiak National Wildlife Refuge. These are available by lottery and can be used by one party for as long as seven nights. Write Refuge Manager, *Kodiak National Wildlife Refuge,* 1390 Buskin River Road, Kodiak; phone 487-2600. These cabins are accessible by air charter from Kodiak. The *Alaska Department of Natural Resources* also has four cabins available on Shuyak Island between Kodiak and Kenai; these are reached via air taxi from either Kodiak or Homer. Write *Alaska Department of Natural Resources Public Information Center,* 3601 C Street, Suite 200, Anchorage, AK 99503; phone 269-8400. (Note: There is a wilderness lodge on Afognak Island that is worth checking out. Write *Afognak Wilderness Lodge,* Seal Bay, AK 99697; phone 486-6442 or 1-800-478-6442.)

General Information

In downtown Kodiak, be sure to visit the *Baranof Museum.* This is the oldest Russian building in Alaska and was erected by Alexander Baranof as a warehouse for sea otter pelts in 1793. It is open to visitors, and a small donation is requested. If you would like to visit the *Russian Orthodox church,* phone 486-3854 for an appointment. Visitors are welcome. Annual events include the *Kodiak Crab Festival,* mentioned above. For further information, write the *Kodiak Visitors Bureau,* 100 Marine Way, Kodiak; phone 486-4782. Also, taxi, car rental, air taxi, and charter boats are available; write the Visitors Bureau if you need information on these facilities before you get to town.

Note: The Kodiak National Wildlife Refuge comprises two-thirds of the island. It is not, however, accessible by road. A fly-in to one of its cabins (see above) can provide an outstanding wilderness experience and, possibly, a good view of a bear. Write the refuge regarding other bear-viewing opportunities.

43. Wrangell–Saint Elias National Park and Preserve

Ask anyone who has traveled widely in Alaska to name the most beautiful part of the state and you're apt to get several answers—or none at all—because the choice is so difficult to make. One well-known Alaskan, however, Ernest Gruening had no problem making up his mind. As long ago as 1938 he singled out the Wrangell Mountains. "It is my personal view that from the standpoint of scenic beauty, it is the finest region in Alaska." Gruening wrote the secretary of the interior that year, "I will go further and state my belief that nowhere on the North American continent is such striking scenery to be seen. It is . . . greatly superior to McKinley National Park . . . this is the finest scenery that I have ever been privileged to see." Other Alaskans are content to call the Wrangells simply the "jewels" of their state.

The Wrangells are an extraordinary group of massive volcanoes that rise to over 16,000 feet. Located in the southeastern portion of the main body of Alaska, this compact immense cluster of mountains measures about 100 by 70 miles, and it rears up to a stunning near 14,000 feet above the 2,500 foot-high Copper River plateau. The snowy summits of Drum, Sanford, Blackburn, Wrangell, and Jarvis can be seen from the roads and highways that skirt the periphery of the Wrangells and from great distances across the surrounding countryside as well. High palisades of dark rose-colored basalt vividly give evidence of past volcanic activity. One of them—Mount Wrangell—is still active, breathing out sulfurous steam and occasionally belching ash from its snowy crater.

The Wrangells are at the heart of the Wrangell–Saint Elias National Park (8,323,618 acres) and Preserve (4,852,773 acres), the largest unit of the national park system. South and east of these magnificent giants, the park boundary embraces other towering icy spires, including Mount Saint Elias (at 18,008 feet the third highest mountain on the North American continent and the zenith of the highest coastal range on earth). At its feet is the great apron of the Malaspina Glacier, half again as large as Luxembourg—which has a population of about half a million people. (Malaspina has none.) To the south and southwest, the parklands include a portion of the Chugach Mountains, taking in the Bagley Ice Field and lakes like Tebay and Rock, which are unmatched for their beauty. Within the park complex, there is a grand total of eight peaks over 14,500 feet high. As Alaskan author Chip Brown puts it, no other area of Alaska surpasses it for "sheer mountainousness." Small wonder that the park has been named a world heritage site by the United Nations Environmental Programme.

Sheer mountainousness, however, is actually only one feature of this park. The geology of the Wrangell Mountains is both complex and interesting; few places show so clearly such a rich diversity of rocks—and such a clear record of uplift, volcanism, glaciation, and other earth processes. (Trips across Skolai Pass have been described as travels "through a geology text.") Furthermore, the flora is extraordinary. With plant communities ranging from those of the moist, warm coast to the high, frigid alpine tundra, almost all of Alaska's vegetation types are represented. The list of animals found here reads like a catalog of Alaska's species (see below); this is one of Alaska's principal wildlife areas. Among these animals are the caribou—three of Alaska's eleven herds use the area—which wander freely through the great sweep of country that is their ancestral territory, unmindful that the Canadian border cuts through it.

Recognizing the significance of this and other wildlife resources and shared scenery as well, Canada established the Kluane National Park in 1972, which transferred upland areas to the already established Kluane Game Sanctuary. The sanctuary, incidentally, permits mining and prospecting but prohibits hunting. These two Canadian preserves together comprise some 6,625,000 acres. They are contiguous to the 13,200,000 acres of the Wrangell–Saint Elias parklands; this means there are nearly 20 million acres of relatively protected land—a true international treasure.

Almost 5 million acres of the Wrangell–Saint Elias complex are ice and snow, making this parkland a glaciologist's paradise, probably the

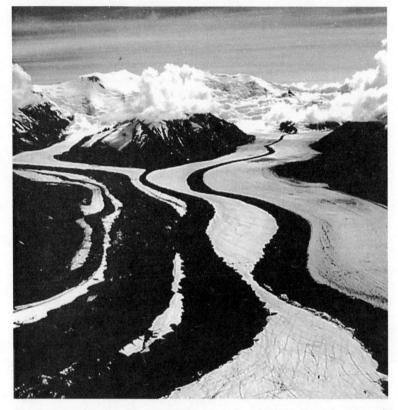

Russell Glacier, Wrangell–Saint Elias National Park. Source: National Park Service.

best place on the North American continent to get an idea, on a broad scale, of what the Pleistocene landscape was like. More than one hundred major glaciers radiate from the massive ice fields on the Wrangell, Chugach, and Saint Elias Mountains. Some of them are so immense that, along the coast, where they meet the sea, they flow underwater. (See Prince William Sound, under Anchorage as a Gateway.) Inland, they pour their meltwaters into powerful, milky, braided rivers like the Chisana and the Nabesna, which eventually drain into the Yukon; and the Tana, Bremner, and Chitina, which empty into the Copper, one of the great rivers of this continent. Blue-watered lakes rest in basins scooped out by the ice, adding to the enormous volume of water that already flows through this region. The amount of raw energy concentrated and circulated through this glacial ecosystem is almost incalculable.

The weather is generally favorable to glacier making, which means that summer days are frequently cool and cloudy, and winters can be very cold, especially in the higher places. It should also be noted that this region is renowned for its great winds at higher elevations and where the Copper River cuts through the mountains near Chitina.

Responsive to the dynamic ebb and flow of glaciers, wild rivers, and a climate that can be cruel, a remarkable spectrum of living communities has evolved here. Creeping from the edges of the ice in high places, the plants of the alpine tundra cling to the raw land—lichens and mosses, saxifrages, louseworts, mountain avens (or dryas), and moss campion. Fingering this fragile tundra world and clothing the lower mountain slopes are dense brush communities with alder and willow, dwarf birch, blueberries, other berries, and shrubs; these are broken up here and there by meadows of bright flowering annuals. Black spruce and white spruce stud the valleys, bearing prodigious crops of cones in the summer to ensure their survival in this rugged country. In wet places, masses of cotton grass edge the lakes and ponds like circles of white clouds; cinquefoil gleams like scraps of sunlight, and the leaves of alpine bearberries splash the autumn landscape with crimson. In places, bogs and tussocky tundra make the going rough for two-legged animals. (To say nothing of the streams and rivers that can suddenly turn to torrents when the sun does shine in the summer; these are actually the greatest barriers to foot travel.)

Four-legged animals have no such troubles with the terrain. Along with caribou, you may encounter moose and bear (the smaller black bears stay out of the way of the great grizzlies; you will want to also). Dall sheep dance over the high crags inland, and mountain goats are frequently seen in places like the south side of the Chitina Valley. Wolves, wolverines, foxes, martens, ermines, river otters, ground squirrels, snowshoe hares, muskrats, beavers, porcupines, and voles are all here. Trumpeter swans nest in the riverine lowlands, loons call from the lakes, and bald eagles soar silently above. If you enter the Saint Elias section of the park from Yakutat, its gateway, you can expect to see many seabirds and sea mammals such as harbor seals, sea lions, and whales. (You will also find Southeastern-type coastal forests around Yakutat.)

Until recently, humans did not succeed so well as other creatures in colonizing this demanding region. The ruggedness of the terrain and the scale of the landscape are almost overwhelming to people. Mile-high cliffs hulking above wild-rushing glacial streams make awesome scenery but hardly a place for settling in. As a consequence, aboriginal people used much of this area lightly. Although a few Eyak Indians and Chugach Eskimos occupied the nearby Copper River delta, where the climate is wet and mild and the wildlife is especially abundant, the population of

The University Range seen from Chitistone Canyon. Source: National Park Service.

Native people inland was confined to the lowlands. Small groups of Nabesna Indians (closely related to the Tanainas) subsisted on the flora and fauna of the valleys of the Nabesna and Chisana Rivers. Along the upper Copper River and its tributaries lived small groups of the Ahtna tribe of Indians, and some five hundred of these people still live in this area. (All of these Native groups have selected lands in this region under terms of the Alaska Native Claims Settlement Act, or ANCSA: some of the Native corporations have logged off some of their lands, and thought twice about doing more.)

Although the Russians made their first landfall in Alaska in 1741 not far down the coast from the parklands and left Mount Saint Elias its name, major explorations of the Wrangell area by white men were delayed for more than another century. In the last decades of the nineteenth century, the search for minerals—and, after 1867, army explorations—got under way and brought adventurous souls into and through some of the most difficult terrain in Alaska. (Rusty stoves are still occasionally found on ice caps where prospectors hauled them and had to abandon them.)

Men swarmed through the Copper River valley, lured by the size of the great copper "shields" that the local Indians had been using in trade. By 1901, when Capt. W. R. Abercrombie of the United States Army made one of his several reconnaissances through the area, he found that "the entire valley, embracing the main and subdrainage of the Copper River, was as well known as that of most any mining district in Montana." The miners' search paid off with the location of an exceptionally rich vein of copper in the Chitina Valley above the moraine of the Kennicott Glacier, named for Robert Kennicott, a pioneer Alaska explorer.

Fired by the reports of the lode and the preliminary surveys, financiers Guggenheim and Morgan formed the famous Alaska Syndicate to get at the copper (as well as coal in other parts of Alaska). At a cost of $23 million, they managed—after some bad weather, bad luck, and bungling—to build a 196-mile railroad from Cordova on the coast up the Copper River to Chitina and thence to Kennicott, the site of what would be the Kennecott Copper Mine. (The misspelling of "Kennicott" as "Kennecott," it is said, was done deliberately to legally avoid the notion that the new community was a "company town," although it was run like a proper one. Recently the correct spelling has been largely reinstituted.) When things went wrong with the locating of the railroad, J.P. Morgan is reported to have banged the table with his fist and bellowed to his colleagues: "Whatever the route, we've got to get that copper out of there."

The railroad was completed in 1911, and mining operations began soon after. Before the mine shut down in 1938, it had paid its owners $200 million. Many of the colorful old mine buildings still stand, testament to a twenty-five-year operation that left the boom towns of Kennicott, McCarthy, Strelna, Chitina, and Cordova nearly ghost towns. (McCarthy and Kennicott together have a year-round population of thirty to forty people, although this number doubles in summer.)

It was the idea of getting another economic base for the stricken region that prompted Ernest Gruening to propose the Wrangell area as a national park. (He was a man ahead of his time.) He was also hoping to divert pressure away from the Rampart Dam proposal—which he espoused, and which conservationists and wildlife experts strongly opposed. While Washington did give consideration to the proposal, nothing came of it. Cordova grew again slowly, but in much of the rest of the region the wilderness began to creep back. With the copper gone, the railroad stopped running, and the last of the wooden bridges that had spanned the Copper River at Chitina went out during spring breakup in 1939. (Inexpensive bridges had been built year after year, only to be swept away by ice and high water.)

Mount Sanford, Wrangell–Saint Elias National Park. Source: National Park Service.

Not until the late 1960s did attention focus again on the area; then both the National Park Service and the Bureau of Land Management (BLM) made studies for possible park and recreational use. The passage of ANCSA brought new explorers into the region, including people who were seeking a better ecological understanding and possible protection for the extraordinary scenic and wildlife resource here. In 1978, President Jimmy Carter recognized the area by establishing the Wrangell–Saint Elias National Monument, and, in 1980, Congress finally decided the long-range fate of the Wrangell–Saint Elias area by establishing the present park-preserve complex.

Rivers

The glacial Chitina River is cold, silty, and heavily braided. You can put into the Kennicott River at McCarthy, float into the Nizina, and then into the Chitina to continue to the town of Chitina, where the river joins the Copper. This 62-mile trip usually takes about two or three days, being mostly class II with stretches of class III water. A raft is recommended; kayaks only for the very experienced. The upper end of the Kennicott River is shallow, and you may have to line. When I made this river run, however (taking out, finally, in Cordova), the Kennicott was in full flood, and, instead of lining, we raced downstream on what seemed like one long class IV rapid into the Nizina; we were drenched, but otherwise it was a great stretch of water. The lower end of the Nizina flows through a narrow canyon with turbulence and tight turns; watch out for the deep eddies. Great caution is required where the Chitina empties into the Copper River at the town of Chitina, particularly if you want to take out at this point. Stay on the right as far as possible as you approach the bridge (the concrete successor to those earlier wooden bridges; this one still stands!): there you may want to take out and line upstream before launching yourself into the great river. This river trip takes you through gorgeous and historic country. The upper Chitina is also accessible by wheeled aircraft. For further information, consult the National Park Service in Copper Center (see below).

The Copper River is one of the continent's great waterways. It is accessible by car at Slana, Chistochina, Gakona, Tazlina, Copper Center, and Chitina, and, as noted, you can continue from Chitina on to a final take-out at Cordova. The section of the river from Slana to Cordova is 244 miles long and will take from seven to twelve days. Rafts are recommended because there are stretches of class II and class IV water and because of the cold water temperature and heavy silt loads. You will pass from Interior to Southeast climate on this run, so be sure you have adequate rain gear. The scenery en route is magnificent and includes glaciers. There is also fabulous birdlife. The Copper is not for novices on their own, but it can be run by almost anyone if there are experienced boaters in the party. For further information, contact the National Park Service or the BLM at the *Alaska Public Lands Information Center* in Anchorage (604 West Fourth Avenue, Suite 105, Anchorage, AK 99501; phone 271-2737) or Tok (see below).

How to Enjoy

Since this is a relatively new unit of the National Park Service, planning for the Wrangell–Saint Elias parklands is still in process. There is no developed trail system. Hiking routes are demanding, following old prospectors' routes and game trails. They will take you into Chitistone Canyon (which could hold several Yosemites), with its fabulous cascade of a hanging river, and into the drainages of Beaver Creek, Jacksina Creek, and the Kuskulana and Kotsina Rivers. You can also hike over Nikolai and Skolai Passes. Be aware that the river crossings will be the major limiting factor to your adventure; they can be lethal. Write the National Park Service in Chitina or Copper Center (see below) for details, or plan a trip with a local guide; the park service can give you names.

Many high mountains in this area offer challenges to mountaineers. Drum, Sanford, Wrangell, Blackburn, Bona, and Saint Elias are among the major magnets, and there are also numerous unnamed and unclimbed peaks. (Saint Elias, incidentally, was first climbed in 1897 by Italy's Duke of Abruzzi. It took over a month just to travel to the base of the mountain.) Most of these are expedition-type peaks, and again you should write the National Park Service for further information about them or go with a local guide. If you are interested in a first ascent, this is a prime area for it.

River running by raft is excellent, and you can find any class of white water that you would like. The Chitina River drains all three of the mountain ranges in the parkland, and you can put in upstream via air taxi. The Bremner rises in the Chugach Mountains and is also reached by air taxi. Note: The Bremner is known as "the River of the Ten B's": brown water, big boulders, bugs, bears, bad rapids, bushes, bad weather, and big bucks. It is not for inexperienced kayakers or rafters, although it has gorgeous scenery, lush vegetation, and plentiful wildlife. Experts consider its three forks "unpaddleable." The Copper River is accessible by car; and you can drive to Chitina to put in and arrange for a pickup out of Cordova. You can also drive to the headwaters of the Kennicott and float the Kennicott-Nizina-Chitina-Copper Rivers (see above).

July is probably the best month to visit the Wrangell–Saint Elias park, but you can't count on good weather even then. In August and September—fall, in this country—the mosquitoes are gone and the river crossings are easier. The season is gorgeous, but it comes and goes at unpredictable times and is all too brief. The first few days of September, give or take a week, usually offer the peak of color.

Some Useful Information About Wrangell–Saint Elias
Zip codes: as listed. Area code: 907.

How to Get There
It is possible to drive to McCarthy usually from late May through Sep-

tember. You can reach Chitina by car without difficulty. From there you cross the Copper River on the Copper River bridge, which was built largely with federal funds to finally replace the succession of old railroad bridges. You continue on a 55-mile road, the old railroad bed, which was upgraded in 1996. There is a final crossing of the Kennicott River (foot traffic only) and a few minutes' walk to McCarthy. It is wise to inquire about road conditions before attempting this trip: contact the Alaska State Department of Transportation (see a local phone book) or inquire at the Chitina Ranger Station; phone 823-2205. Allow three to four hours' driving time from Chitina to McCarthy. McCarthy, by the way, is one of the most scenically situated little towns anywhere—when you can see the scenery around it. If you make it your takeoff point for any expedition, remember that supplies in such a remote place are limited. You should bring your own. (McCarthy people get their ice from the local glacier—the Kennicott.) A jeep road, passable during the summer, goes from Slana on the Tok cutoff into the ghost town of Nabesna on the north side of the park, a privately owned area. (The first half of this road is pretty good, but then you may need a four-wheel drive.) If you prefer to fly in, a good takeoff point is Gulkana Airport in Glennallen, which is served by air from Anchorage and has several air-taxi services of its own. An alternative is to drive to Glennallen or Chitina (or take the ferry to Cordova) and take the mail plane, which flies into McCarthy.

Air-Taxi Service

The National Park Service people (see below) have a list of licensed air-taxi operators for the park. There are more than a dozen of them, based locally and as far away as Anchorage, Yakutat, and Cordova. You might start with *McCarthy Air* or *Wrangell Mountain Air,* both at McCarthy: write Box MXY, Glennallen, AK 99588 (same address for both); phone 554-4440 (McCarthy Air) or 1-800-478-1160 (Wrangell Mountain Air). *Alaskan Air Ventures:* Bart and Rosemary Bartley, float and ski plane, Mile 147 Glenn Highway, Glennallen, AK 99588; phone 822-3905. *Gulf Air Taxi, Inc.:* write Box 367, Yakutat, AK 99689; phone 784-3240.

Where to Stay

As of this writing, there are no developed campgrounds in the Wrangell–Saint Elias park. There are, however, state campgrounds, at Liberty Falls near Chitina and at Dry Creek near Glennallen, and BLM campgrounds at Sourdough, north of Gulkana. These are described as being "rustic," which simply means there is neither electricity nor running water. There are also several private campgrounds. Contact the Greater Copper Valley Chamber of Commerce (see below). There is a privately owned parking lot, camp, bicycle rental, and store at the end of the road to McCarthy, and also several privately owned and operated wilderness lodges within the area. You'll also find comfortable facilities at towns on the highways that skirt the park. Check with the National Park Service in Chitina or Copper Center (see below) or with the Greater Copper Valley Chamber of Commerce.

Useful Names and Addresses

The National Park Service in Chitina or Copper Center (see below) or the *Greater Copper Valley Chamber of Commerce* (Box 469, Glennallen, AK 99588; phone 822-5555) can supply you with detailed information about local accommodations, air taxis, guides, going rates, and so forth. The *Chitina Ranger Station* (Box 39, Chitina, AK 99566; phone 823-2205) is very helpful about the McCarthy region, the Copper River, and other local areas. This ranger station is closed in winter, when you should contact the rangers at park headquarters at Copper Center. If you are traveling on wheels, you can also stop at the *Alaska Public Lands Information Center* in Tok (Box 359, Tok, AK 99780; phone 883-5567); this is a good place to get more details about all the parks in the area. Note: As of this writing, there is year-round bus service from Anchorage and Fairbanks to Glennallen (some buses continue on to Tok and Whitehorse) and, six days a week, from Glennallen to McCarthy during the summer; ask for schedules (and current access information) at the Alaska Public Lands Information Center in Tok (see above) or at one of the park service ranger stations, or call *Backcountry Connections,* 822-5292.

If you're traveling on your own, it's a good idea to get the latest information on this changeable region. (You might be able to rent your river rafting gear locally.) You might also want to leave your itinerary with the National Park Service people, whether you're hiking, climbing, spot-camping, or river running. No need to do this of course, if you're staying at a lodge or are with a registered guide. Write Superintendent, *Wrangell–Saint Elias National Park/Preserve,* Box 439, Copper Center, AK 99573; phone 822-5235. You can get BLM information from the Alaska Public Lands Information Center in Tok (see above).

44. Kenai Fjords

The Alaska coast is to become the showplace of the earth, and
pilgrims, not only from the United States but from far beyond
the seas, will throng in endless processions to see it. Its grandeur
is more valuable than the gold or the fish or the timber, for it
will never be exhausted.

Henry Gannett, 1902

You will find some of Alaska's most beautiful coastline along the southeast shores of the Kenai Peninsula in the Kenai Fjords. Here, dark slate-
gray cliffs soar abruptly from the water's edge, sculpted by ancient
glaciers, storms, and the sea. Blue-iced tidewater glaciers chill the air in
deeply incised bays, announcing their presence by magnificent cannon-
ades of sound when they drop ice into the deep waters. Higher-hanging
ribbons of ice release their meltwaters, which plunge like silvery meteors
into the sea or cascade intricately over the dark rock. Wherever there is
a toehold on the steep slopes, a dusky green spruce tree clings; where the
land is gentler, whole forests stand with mists whirling and smoking
among the tall trees. Kittiwakes nest by the thousands on the high cliffs
and fall into the air like clusters of white flowers at the noise of a boat.
In places, the rocks are tilted to form broad shelves at the water's edge,
and here Steller sea lions crowd to bask in the sun—the great bulls surrounded by their obedient harems bellowing their alarm at a visitor's approach. Overhead, bald eagles ride the thermals, observing the colonies
of seabirds that come here by the tens of thousands to nest and rear their
young. On the jewel-like ice floes that surround your boat, harbor seals
watch you with their great brown eyes. A porpoise might escort you; if
you drift quietly, you might, as I once did, come upon a sea otter sleeping peacefully in the water on its back.

The glaciers that ornament this landscape so gorgeously descend from the Harding Ice Field, a mile-high, 300-square-mile catchment basin that collects the 400 to 600 inches of snow that can fall here in winter and compacts it into ice. As in Southeast Alaska, such prodigious snowfall is caused by the warm ocean currents that send mild, moist air up to condense at higher altitudes into snow. This same current is also part of the process of upwelling that occurs here in the deep waters, which brings an abundance of nutrients to the surface and accounts for the rich communities of living creatures.

The geological forces that formed the Kenai Fjords are unique and fascinating; the southern portion of the Kenai Peninsula is actively subsiding and diving beneath the sea. In the 1964 Good Friday quake, for instance, the land here sank as much as 7 feet in a matter of minutes. Should you visit the Harding Ice Field, you will be able to see graphically how the high terrain slopes off gradually to the south. From the air, you can also observe how the tops of the already drowned mountains still show evidence of ancient glaciation. Where old cirques lay, there are now deep-scalloped bays; where ridges once protruded above the ice, long fingers of land now protrude above the water. The farther out to sea you look, the lower the islands and sea stacks.

The Russians were the first Europeans to explore the region of the Kenai Fjords, but they were looking more for fur-bearing sea mammals than for lovely scenery and interesting geological formations. They found prodigious populations of sea otters and, with their Aleut slaves, they went to work systematically hunting them out of the deep blue waters. There were enough to prompt Alexander Baranof in 1795 to construct a shipyard in the largest of the fjords, Resurrection Bay. There the *Phoenix*, the first sailing ship built in northwest America, was launched to carry the beautiful pelts to Russia. When the sea otters were gone, the Russians moved on too.

Not until 1909 was the coastline to be more systematically explored. That year U. S. Grant and D. F. Higgins of the U.S. Geological Survey traveled the length of the fjords, carefully mapping the geological formations and searching for minerals, of which they found very few. They photographed the tidewater glaciers, produced the first topographical map of the region (published in 1915), and voiced the hope that their report on the Kenai Fjords might gain recognition for "some of the most magnificent scenery . . . accessible to the tourist and nature lover."

It took six decades for that recognition to come nationally. In 1978, President Jimmy Carter established the 580,000-acre Kenai Fjords National Monument. (Sadly, some of its shores were oiled in 1989 by the Exxon *Valdez* spill.)

The following is borrowed from National Park Service descriptions:

What to do and see: Entering the Kenai Fjords by boat is a popular and rewarding experience. Seabirds, sea lions, seals, porpoise, and whales are frequently sighted along the rugged coastline. Tidewater glaciers in Aialik Bay, Harris Bay, and Nuka Bay actively calve huge blocks of ice. Fishing for salmon and bottom fish is usually productive. The terrain is so steep throughout most of the Kenai Fjords that camping and hiking opportunities are limited.

The Harding Ice Field is an awesome and beautiful phenomenon. Air charters out of Seward, Homer, and Anchorage can provide spectacular views of the ice field, glaciers, and the coastline. Crossing the ice field on foot or skis or travel on glaciers is recommended to only experienced and well-equipped mountaineers. Photogenic Exit Glacier is accessible by car and a short walk.

Weather: A maritime climate prevails in the area, bringing abundant rain and snow. The driest month is May; successive months receive increasing amounts of precipitation. Mid-June is the normal beginning of the visitor season, for spring storms have generally passed, and temperatures reach into the 50s and 60s (degrees Fahrenheit). June, July, and August are the best months for boat travel. Warm, sunny days are welcome exceptions. September initiates the usual wet and stormy fall. Snow can occur on the Harding Ice Field during any month.

Clothing: Comfortable wool or synthetic pile clothing is essential, as is heavy, rubber-coated rain gear.

Precautions: The Kenai Fjords are rugged, remote, and exposed to the tempestuous Gulf of Alaska. Strong currents flow past them and few landing sites exist. Visitors are strongly advised to employ an experienced guide and seaworthy craft. Those entering the fjords without a guide should be very experienced and should seek information on landing sites, weather conditions, and navigational hazards from the National Park Service, U.S. Coast Guard, and other knowledgeable parties and sources.

Crevasses and foul weather pose dangers on the Harding Ice Field and its glaciers. Experience, skill, good equipment, and stamina are required for successful ice field and glacial travel. For your further safety, it is wise to leave your itinerary with family or friends.

There is a park Visitor Center at the boat harbor, where you can watch slide shows and videos, pick up brochures, and browse through the bookstore for further helpful interpretive material about the park. There are also ranger-conducted activities in summer at the Visitor Center and at Exit Glacier. For more information, contact *Kenai Fjords National Park,* Box 1727, Seward, AK 99664; phone 224-3175.

Some Useful Information About Kenai Fjords

There is bus service between Anchorage and Seward as well as train and air service. A drive down the Kenai Peninsula on your own, however, is highly scenic, and you can stop when you see a moose, which you are likely to do. You can also take the ferry to Seward, boarding in Valdez or Cordova; or you can take the grand 6-day voyage from Bellingham, Washington.

Seward itself is a highly scenic place, nestled against the mountains at the head of Resurrection Bay. It is the site, come the Fourth of July each year, of an extraordinary race up and down 3,022-foot-high Mount Marathon, which looms above the town. Runners and spectators from all over the world throng to see this contest, which was initiated in 1909 by a bet between two sourdoughs. (That year, the winner did the course in an hour and two minutes, but since then, one speedy racer has done it in an amazing forty-four minutes.) Seward is also the gateway to the Kenai Fjords, and there are wonderful day-long boat trips to be taken among these nearby magnificent waterscapes and landscapes. The *Shaman* is one of my favorite excursion boats. For details about it and other boats, write *Kenai Fjords Tours,* Box 1889, Seward, AK 99664; phone 224-8068 or 1-800-478-8068.

For other boat charters (and there are others), as well as commercial kayak excursions, and for places to stay contact the *Seward Chamber of Commerce,* Box 749, Seward, AK 99664; phone 224-8051. (You might start with the well-located, clean, and friendly *Best Western of Seward:* write Box 675, Seward, AK 99664; phone 224-2378.)

Note: Kenai Fjords National Park is one of the national park system's success stories. The Seward people, skeptical at first about the park's place in their lives, have come to be among its strongest supporters, for the park has been of real benefit to the community and to the local economy. (Check with the National Park Service regarding Native inholdings on the coast.)

45. Lake Clark National Park and Preserve

Towering snowy volcanoes; legions of finely sculpted gray granite peaks; beautifully striated sedimentary formations colored with yellows, grays, and deep browns; and metamorphosed mountains as if painted from an artist's palette with ochre, umber, rose madder, and dark alizarin crimson—these are the Chigmit Mountains. Although they are of modest height by Alaskan standards—most are around 8,000 feet in altitude—they are aptly called the Alps of Alaska. They mark the junction of the Alaska Range with the Aleutian chain in a most dramatic manner.

Once heavily glaciated, many of these mountains still wear living glaciers. The milky meltwaters from these tongues of ice pour into troughs and basins scoured out during the ice ages, thus forming some of Alaska's loveliest lakes. A series of these lakes ornaments the western slopes of the Chigmits like great gems—the Taziminia Lakes, Two Lakes, Telaquana, Twin Lakes, Turquoise, Kontrashibuna, and, the most magnificent of all, Lake Clark. When Stephen R. Capps of the U.S. Geological Survey came upon Lake Clark early in this century, he called it one of the most beautiful bodies of water in the world.

Among the exceptional things about this lake are its color—deep turquoise—the thick, deep-green forests along its shores, and the breathtaking splendor of the snow-streaked, colorful mountains around it. Add a feeling of intimacy that is not a usual feature in Alaskan landscapes as large as this; Lake Clark is 55 miles long. Because it is only 1 to 4 miles wide, however, you can nearly always see across the water to the tree-lined shores. If you go ashore, you will likely walk through a garden of cerise fireweed or perhaps a beautiful tangle of wild roses.

Park-minded people had been trying to gain protection for Lake Clark and the superb country around it for two decades when, in 1978,

President Jimmy Carter proclaimed the Lake Clark National Monument. In 1980, Congress redesignated the area into a 2,439,000-acre national park and a 1,214,000-acre national preserve. Boundaries of the park-preserve, which is located about 100 miles southwest of Anchorage, take in all of Lake Clark and the country lying largely north and east of it. (Certain land around the lower end of the lake is private property, much of it Native owned.)

Almost as much as the Chugach Mountains, this wilderness parkland contains a nearly comprehensive sampling of Alaskan terrain and life zones. It goes from coastlands to the steam-wreathed summits of two high volcanoes—Mount Iliamna and Mount Redoubt; both tower above 10,000 feet. In between there are crowds of peaks, glaciers, lakes, and countless rushing streams and waterfalls. There are silty rivers that braid over the land, and there are rivers so clear that plants grow in them underwater. Forests contain good-smelling white spruce and delicate-looking birches and handsome balsam poplars. There are mountain meadows embroidered with wildflowers, and high, open tundra ridges that accommodate to boots as well as to the hooves of Dall sheep and caribou.

Along the shores of Cook Inlet, the seals and otters play, and you might be able to see a white whale traveling by while a bald eagle watches you from above. The bird life is rich from coast to mountain crest, and most of Alaska's great mammals abound in this wild and beautiful country. (A notable exception is the mountain goat, which is not found west of Kodiak, where it was introduced.) Added to this, Lake Clark is part of the drainage system of Bristol Bay and thus helps support the greatest sockeye salmon fishery in the world.

In good weather, the Lake Clark parklands provide for some of the finest outdoor recreation in Alaska. (But note that Anchorage recreationists and hunters are aware of this.) Many of the lakes are not only lovely to look at but are also gateways to excellent alpine hiking and backpacking. There are challenges galore for mountaineers in unclimbed peaks. Ski touring can be superb in March and early April, though mid-April through late May thaws can make travel difficult. River runners will find some of the world's most beautiful wild rivers in this region.

However, and alas, weather must again be a subject of major consideration. As on the adjacent Alaska Peninsula, it varies on either side of the high mountain barrier, and within the mountains themselves. On the Cook Inlet side, the maritime influence brings average summer temperatures of 50 to 65 degrees Fahrenheit, lots of rain, and low-lying clouds that can limit small-plane travel. The interior and western regions are more apt to be pleasantly dry and warm, though often overcast. (I once rafted the Chilikadrotna and Mulchatna Rivers in western Lake Clark country during weather so hot and sunny we could have traveled happily in bathing suits, which nobody, of course, had considered bringing. We did, however, enjoy a swim in the warm river water. Another time I ran the same rivers and never saw the sun.) The biggest adverse factor in the weather, however, is the classic problem of the Alaska Peninsula winds; they can come roaring in at any time of year and in any part of the Lake Clark area, and they can turn the lakes into small, stormy seas. Since they can also reach hurricane speed through the mountain passes, they add another uncertainty to air-taxi pickups and deliveries. In short, the Lake Clark weather, while milder than in many regions, is totally undependable and unpredictable; you should be well prepared for storm as well as shine. You should also be prepared to wait for your bush pilot at either end of your journey.

Mosquitoes, by the way, can be particularly ferocious in June and early July. If you visit this area then, be sure to take good insect repellent, a secure tent, and a head net; rig your tent high above—and as far away from—swampy areas as you can.

The Lake Clark region lies enough off the beaten track and is well enough guarded by the rigorous terrain of its mountain passes to have remained relatively lightly used until recent times. Native peoples fished its rivers for salmon and took grayling and trout through the ice of its lakes. They also pursued the abundant moose, bear, and caribou. (The Mulchatna caribou herd oscillates in numbers; recently, in a few years, it grew from between forty and forty-five thousand animals to well over one hundred thousand—a spurt that puzzled wildlife biologists. The herd numbers nearly two hundred thousand by the latest estimate at this writing.) The only known traces Native peoples left, however, are relatively recent ones. Archeologists digging on the Stony River, Telequana Lake, and at the site of the former village of Kijik on Kijik Lake have found artifacts of Dena'ina (Athabascan) Indians. But mixed with the Indian artifacts were Russian and English goods, indicating that these camps or settlements date back perhaps only two centuries. Kijik village itself was abandoned in 1902 after a devastating measles epidemic; the Kijik people moved first to Old Nondalton and then, in 1940, to the present town of Nondalton on Six Mile Lake, just below Lake Clark.

The Dena'ina did not welcome the Russians. (The destruction of a Russian trading post, part of the Alaska Commercial Company empire, and the martyring of Father Yacove Federovich Juvenal have been attributed to them, but recent research suggests that they were not involved in these desperate acts of defiance.) Even so, many of them were baptized by Russian priests and ended up with Russian names.

The Americans fared better with the Native people. In 1897, when the eleventh census was under way in Alaska, Alfred B. Shanz (an extraordinary census taker who had led an expedition to Alaska for the *Frank Leslie Illustrated Newspaper* several years before) was much impressed by the hospitality of the people at Kijik as well as by the cleanliness of the village. He, too, noted that the Indians had many Russian trade items. It was Shanz, incidentally, who gave Lake Clark its name, in honor of John W. Clark, head of the Nushagak Trading Post on an arm of Bristol Bay. Clark was supposedly the first white man to discover the beautiful lake.

Around the turn of the century, the lure of gold brought prospectors into the Lake Clark country. They struggled across rough passes, over glaciers, and through the impossible alder thickets to stake their claims early on at places like the upper Mulchatna River basin. In 1908, there was even a small gold rush in this area, but little came of it. About this time, claims were also staked around the head of Lake Clark. Then, in 1911 and 1914, the U.S. Geological Survey entered the scene and did extensive exploration and mapping in the area. Today, there are still sporadic mining efforts going on (hope never dies in a miner's heart). Subsequently, in the impossible terrain of the Lake Clark Pass, where the rambunctious glaciers meet and part like agile boxers, minerals of dubious value prompted serious proposals for a road from Cook Inlet to the summit of the pass.

Although there was some homesteading around Lake Clark before World War II, it was during the years after that war that a modest influx of people arrived to stake out claims along the lakeshore. Some farmed, some built hunting lodges, and some just enjoyed the scenery. Among them were two people who would make Alaskan history. One was Jay Hammond, the Alaska governor who built his beautiful log cabin on Lake Clark in the 1950s and was for many years a big-game guide in this region as well as a well-known bush pilot, poet, and state legislator. The other was Babe Alsworth, who chose a cove on the south side of the lake, married a Native girl, and founded the small settlement of Port Alsworth and something of a dynasty. The best landing strip on the lake belongs to the Alsworths, and Babe's son, Glen, is an air-taxi operator who knows the country as well as anyone and can spot you into and off a river or suggest a special place for you to adventure (see below). Babe and his wife, Mary, incidentally, retired to Hawaii.

If the Dena'ina found the hunting good in the Lake Clark region, so did the sportsmen after World War II. This has been an increasingly popular place for hunting since the 1950s. During the hunting season, the buzz of small planes fills the air over outlying lakes near the park boundary. If you don't hunt, take this into account if you plan a trip into the area. Hunting season for caribou and sheep begins in early August. (As in all national preserves, sport hunting as well as subsistence hunting is permitted in Lake Clark National Preserve; adjacent to this preserve are Alaska state lands also open to all kinds of hunting.)

Rivers

You have a choice of marvelous waterways in the Lake Clark country, both inside and close to the national parklands. Here, for starters, are brief descriptions of seven such rivers (the park service can give you further information on these and others). All require air-taxi service for access.

Crystal clear, swift-flowing, the beautiful Chilikadrotna River offers an excellent white-water experience for the intermediate floatboater.

The Mulchatna is shallow, rocky, and single channeled above Bonanza Hills (The first 22 miles). Downstream, it becomes an easy, leisurely float, wandering through a forest. It is a most pleasant river in its lower stretches. The Chilikadrotna flows into the Mulchatna.

The Copper (Iliamna) is a fast, clear-water flowing through a forest with lovely scenery and seasonally good fishing. Wildlife viewing is good. This makes for a nice, relatively short raft trip.

The Stony is a swift (average 5 miles per hour), silty river flowing through a forest. It offers good mountain scenery upstream from the Necons River and good camping on its gravel bars.

The Telaquana and Necons Rivers are relatively short, moderately swift, semiclear streams that are tributaries to the silt-laden Stony. They are scenic and offer good hiking and seasonally good viewing opportunities for moose, caribou, bear, furbearers, and waterfowl.

The Tlikakila is an extremely fast, small glacial river flowing through a narrow, deep valley. (It has been described as "one long rapid.") You can run it from Summit Lake to Lake Clark in three days. From start to finish, there is a continual array of jagged ice and snow-capped peaks, glaciers, waterfalls, caves, perpendicular rock cliffs, and glacial cirques to be seen from the river. The view at the river's end of Lake Clark and the surrounding mountains is a fine climax to the already enjoyed scenery. The valley floor is covered by alpine tundra around Summit Lake but is heavily forested with white spruce and paper birch along the river. The river offers superb scenery and a rewarding, enjoyable float experience.

Some Useful Information About Lake Clark

Zip codes: as listed. Area code: 907.

How to Get There

There is scheduled air service to Iliamna, and from there you can air-charter into your destination in the Lake Clark country. You can also charter from either Homer or Kenai for a direct flight across the Cook Inlet; this will mean flying through one or another of the passes into the region. (Note that there is limited bus service to Kenai or Homer.) Or, you can charter from Anchorage; it only takes an hour to an hour and a half to fly from there.

For a fine overview, I highly recommend a flight in a small plane from Anchorage to Lake Clark. (Glen Alsworth of Lake Clark Air flies from Anchorage to Port Alsworth; see below.) If you make this flight, you will fly above the waters of Cook Inlet and may see the oil platforms flaring gas like strange, flaming nautical candles. You will pass over the wetlands on the west where the drainage patterns twist and branch in intricate and seemingly infinite designs. To the south, snow-clad Mount Redoubt (10,197 feet) will loom larger and larger against the horizon; a wisp of steam may be visible from its summit area. Then, at Trading Bay, you will head west through one of the most scenic and geologically fascinating passes in Alaska, Lake Clark Pass. Here the mountains, chiseled and molded by past glaciers, are festooned with blue-crevassed hanging glaciers that overflow the high cirques. Avalanche tracks streak down the rock slopes with waterfall after waterfall plummeting between them. Above, the dark peaks brood, made darker and more brooding by the dazzling whiteness of snow and ice around them.

On top of Lake Clark Pass rests small, shallow Summit Lake, whose existence is subject to the whims of the glaciers that feed it. In colder periods, when the ice surges forward (as it has in very recent times), the eastern outlet of the lake gets damned up, and the lake enlarges and deepens. Then its waters flow westward into the Tlikakila River, thence into Lake Clark, and eventually into Bristol Bay and the Bering Sea. When the glaciers are in retreat, as they are at present, the dam disappears and Summit Lake gets little meltwater. What it does get drains both east (into Cook Inlet and the Pacific Ocean) and west. Because of its "unique display of numerous hanging and valley glacial features," Lake Clark Pass has been proposed for national landmark status.

There are as yet no developed National Park Service campgrounds, but camping is permitted throughout the park-preserve.

Air Charter Service

Lake Clark Air: write Glen Alsworth, Port Alsworth, AK 99653; phone 781-2212 (or 278-2054 in Anchorage) or 1-800-662-7661. Check with National Park Service people (see below) for others.

Lodges and Park Information

If you want to relax and enjoy an Alaskan vacation, you can spend a weekend or a week at one of the lodges on Lake Clark and have a won-

derful time. (Try late June, July, or early September.) Boating and viewing from the lake can usually be arranged from the lodge you choose, and
if you're at one of the more plush accommodations, you can get airlifted
to one of the various lakes nearby to fish, photograph, or hike. Lodge
owners can give you a good steer for the kind of outdoor recreation
you're interested in. Check with the National Park Service people, either
at *Lake Clark National Park and Preserve Headquarters* (4230 University Drive, Anchorage, AK 99508; phone 271-3751) or at the *Lake Clark
National Park and Preserve Visitor Center* at the field headquarters in
Port Alsworth (1 Park Place, Port Alsworth, AK 99653; phone 781-
2218). Or contact the *Alaska Public Lands Information Center* in Anchorage (605 West Fourth Avenue, Suite 105, Anchorage, AK 99501;
phone 271-2737). All of these can give you further information about the
park.

If you want to explore the backcountry, the hiking and backpacking
are outstanding, and there are opportunities of many kinds. Although
there is no developed trail system, there are many summer and winter
routes that are fine traveling. Game trails (made by moose and bear)
abound, and the alpine tundra is a pleasure to hike on. A 2.5-mile trail
goes from Port Alsworth to beautiful Tanalian Falls, just below Kontrashibuna Lake. Check with the Lake Clark National Park and Preserve
Visitor Center in Port Alsworth (see above) for guides, and to get an idea
about itineraries for backpacking or skiing. Mountaineers and travelers
in general can also get information from this source.

46. Katmai National Park and Preserve

Katmai is a wild, elemental place where great earth forces are obviously,
and gorgeously, at work. You can sense there the overwhelming power of
these forces, which we like to theorize about but do not yet fully understand. From Katmai's pure and primitive landscape you can conjure up
an image of how the world might have looked when land first poured
from the depths of the earth to rise above the sea.

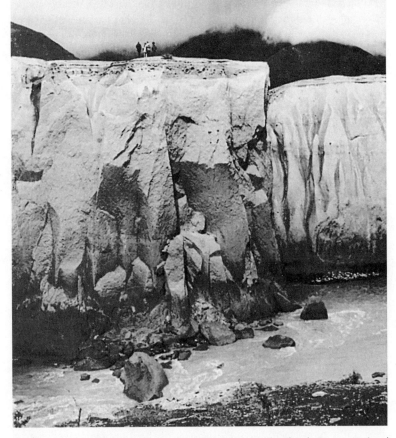

Ash flow strata, Valley of Ten Thousand Smokes, Katmai National Park. Source: National Park Service.

The best-known and one of the most stunning parts of Katmai is the Valley of Ten Thousand Smokes, which was formed as recently as 1912, the result of one of the greatest volcanic eruptions of all time. Fragmentary accounts tell of this sudden, awesome event. Early in June that year, increasingly severe earthquakes shook Mount Katmai and the land around it, and the Native residents of Savonoski on the north and Katmai village on the south had the good sense to leave. On the evening of June 5, when the skies were clear and cool, they could look back and see an ominous black cloud lowering over the three-peaked, nearly 9,000-foot-high summit of the mountain. The earth continued to shudder, and the next afternoon the mountain exploded in a series of thunderous blasts, one so colossal that it was heard in Juneau, 750 miles away. The terrible shaking continued until the night of June 7, when another major convulsion seized the mountain, and a blaze of light over the Katmai area was said to have lit up the peaks "like sunshine." So reported geologist George C. Martin, who was sent to the scene later that summer by the National Geographic Society. This violent illumination apparently marked a prodigious outpouring of incandescent ash that roared at fantastic speed from Novarupta, a vent that opened near Mount Katmai. As the chief of Savonoski village put it with biblical succinctness: ". . . fire come down trail from Katmai." A towering funnel of ash and steam soon rose skyward for several miles and spread an enveloping canopy of darkness. Ash rained from the sky, and fumes heavy with sulfuric acid spewed out with such force that they traveled as far away as Vancouver, British Columbia, where they ate away linens hung out to dry. Across Shelikof Strait, amid thunder, lightning, and storms of ash, the people of Kodiak thought the end of the world had come and, mindful of Pompeii, took to the sea to escape. Ivan Orloff, a Russian on a fishing expedition at nearby Kaflia Bay, wrote his wife, Tania, on June 9: "A mountain has burst near here so that we are covered with ashes, in some places ten feet . . . deep. . . . We cannot see the daylight. In a word, it is terrible, and we are expecting death at any moment, and we have no water. All the rivers are covered with ashes. Here are darkness and hell, thunder and noise. . . . Pray for us." Before it was all over, the skies of virtually the entire North American continent were dimmed by a haze of ash, and the summer of 1912 was notably cool.

When the molten outpour from Novarupta finally did stop, Mount Katmai had collapsed into itself and was 2,000 feet lower than it had been. What had been a high, snowy summit became a broad crater filled with milky blue-green water. At the foot of the mountain, a valley area of 40 square miles was engulfed with searing ash and pumice to a depth of from 300 to 700 feet. The blast of intense heat from the torrent of ash devastated the landscape in every direction; the villages of Katmai and Savonoski had been desolated by what Martin called simply "a breath of hell." In the valley, an eerie scene even more evocative of Hades was in the process of evolving: the streams and waters beneath the fiercely hot ash and pumice had started to shoot out sulfurous steam in thousands of fumaroles. But no one was to see this staggering sight until July 31, 1916.

On that date, Robert Fiske Griggs, a botanist on his second exploratory expedition for the National Geographic Society, labored to the top of Katmai Pass and was about to turn back when he saw a whiff of steam that pulled him a few steps farther, and there he stopped, stunned. Later he reported, "The sight that flashed into view . . . was one of the most amazing visions ever beheld by mortal eye. The whole valley as far as the eye could reach was full of hundreds, no thousands—literally tens of thousands—of smokes curling up from its fissured floor." The air reeked of sulfur. The sound was "as though all the steam engines in the world, assembled together, had opened the safety valve at once." D. B. Church, the photographer on two of Griggs's expeditions stated, "It seemed to me . . . that this was the Devil's own private corner in hell itself." Griggs named the place the Valley of Ten Thousand Smokes. (After further explorations in the area, he said he should have called it the Valley of a Million Smokes.)

By 1917, Griggs had led three expeditions to Katmai. The information he brought back and the photographs taken by Church and others that had been published in the *National Geographic* magazine fired the imagination of the world. Influenced by Griggs's enthusiastic reports and by the prestigious National Geographic Society, President Woodrow Wilson on September 24, 1918, established Katmai National Monument. Seventeen hundred square miles—more than 1 million acres—in size, the monument encompassed only the volcanic area around Mount Katmai, including of course, the by-now-famous Valley of Ten Thousand Smokes. (Griggs, incidentally, returned one more time in 1919 for a last look at the extraordinary scene, and, in 1922, published his book, *The Valley of Ten Thousand Smokes*—highly recommended reading.)

Perhaps it is as well that the place that Church described in 1917 as being so awesome that it "was not for human eyes to see nor human ears to hear" was destined to change both rapidly and completely. Although Griggs was unaware of it, the process of cooling was under way during the years he explored the valley, and today the valley is long since quiet but for wisps of sulfurous smoke at its upper end. The thick blanket of ash that was laid down in three outpourings has compacted into mesas of gray and beige tuff, a type of volcanic rock. Rivers have cut through the tuff like a knife through cake. (One of the valley's major streams is Knife Creek, which seems most fancifully named until you note Knife Peak, from whose glacier it flows, on older maps . . . the name has recently been changed to honor Griggs.) The mists creep quietly over the eerie buff-colored expanses, and the loudest sound is the rush of the rivers and the roar of the winds. But life is slowly and surely beginning to creep back, and one day the valley may once again be green.

While Mount Katmai appears to slumber, not so nearby mountains Mageik, Martin, and Trident, which are smoldering and sending up plumes of smoke and have steam hissing from the rusty yellow throats of fumaroles at or near their summits. (Griggs was struck by the colors of the Katmai landscape and wrote of the "gaudy muds"—gray, yellow, chocolate, red, black, blue—from which "very creditable pictures could be painted.") The Katmai region seems to be just waiting, the cauldron of molten rock deep beneath its surface ready to bubble up again at any time. Geologists have found evidence of at least ten violent eruptions in the vicinity of Katmai during the last 7,000 years, and who knows when another will occur.

Volcanism, however, is only one of the major earth forces displayed in Katmai National Park and Preserve. The land here rises to over 7,600 feet from the deep-blue waters of Shelikof Strait, high enough to hold a small but active glacial system. Snowfields sprawl among the peaks, and glaciers hang down from them: Serpent Tongue Glacier, Knife Creek Glacier, Four-Peaked Glacier, Hallo Glacier, and others. Steam rises from the snowfields draping Mount Mageik. Ice as well as fire has formed, and is still forming, this terrain. Evidence of past, much more extensive and massive glaciation shows in the long lakes that finger the land on the west side of the park; one of these lakes, Naknek, is large enough to be referred to as an inland sea. (It is the fourth largest lake in Alaska and the largest lake in any national park.) To the east, where the mountains rise from the sea, the coast has been sculpted into deep fjords where cascades of water fall over steep slopes above the beaches.

In this awesome primeval place it is somehow reassuring to find that a lovely and varied flora has successfully evolved. Along the coasts glow the deep green of alder and willow. Forests rim the low-lying lakes with tall white spruce, and the balsam poplars—a species of cottonwood—have gained immense girth over the years, sometimes as much as 4 feet in diameter. Birch trees grow with the balsam poplars, coloring the landscape with shimmering soft greens in the summer and warm golds in the crisp air of autumn. The low-rolling hills are tapestries of berries and dwarf birch. Higher, the sturdy, tenacious primitive plants of the alpine tundra take over, pushing to the frigid edge of the ice. It is interesting to see how closely the flora here is related to that of Siberia. I once walked up the gentle slopes of Mount Dumpling from Brooks Camp with a Norwegian botanist who was delighted, but not surprised, to find species after species that confirmed this fact. (Katmai, of course, is only one of many places where the close similarities of the living communities on the two sides of the Bering Strait can be observed.)

Except for the enclaves where people come together in Katmai, notably on the shores of Naknek Lake and at the developed and often crowded visitor accommodations at Brooks Camp, this park is still marvelously wild, and the animals and birds go their ways generally unmolested. The trails you will follow if you hike or backpack off the beaten track here will probably have been made by the bears, a point to keep in mind, for Katmai is one of the last relatively undisturbed homes of the brown bear, and the great animals flourish here. In the wet places and around the lakes and rivers, you may see moose or river otter (a charming sight on the Savonoski River), mink and beaver, or a beautiful brown weasel, with its cream-colored belly, dashing out of sight. Along the little-visited coasts, there are sea lions, hair seals, and the charming sea otters sporting in the deep waters. Throughout, there are the predators—shy foxes (both red fox and the rare Arctic fox are here), wolves, lynx, and wolverines, and, in the skies, hawks and falcons, owls, and bald eagles.

Katmai is a place that is indeed rich in a variety of birds. Dozens of species of songbirds—as many as forty—gather here in the summer to pour out their melodies, mate, and nest. Tundra swans find the lakes here to their liking; if you are lucky, you may see and hear them in flight. (One of Griggs's parties surprised five hundred of them resting on a sandbar.) Arctic terns nest and rear their young on the gravel bars of Katmai's wild rivers and, if you're a river runner, you may choose—as I once did on a Katmai river—to retire from a choice camping spot because a pair of terns had gotten there first and had started a family. It should be noted that leaving such an avian family alone is not only required wilderness manners, but these birds can also hold their own. A furious dive-bombing tern has been known to connect with a human head on occasion, and the hysterical screams of a couple of outraged tern parents can send almost anybody hurrying down a river to get out of earshot.

Among the most prodigious wildlife of Katmai are the fish. Each summer, the Naknek Lake and River system (which empties into Bristol Bay, the world's greatest sockeye fishery) is invaded by nearly a million salmon. The spawning fish jam the waters in dense, rosy crowds; each fish, its life nearly done, is stubbornly bent on finding its place of birth to help start a new generation of its species. If you happen to be in a place like, say, Brooks Camp when the reds are running, you can expect to catch one of these beautiful fish when you toss out your line. At the same time you will be carrying on a tradition that is thousands of years old, for parts of the Katmai area have been inhabited by fishermen and hunters for millennia. There are rainbow and lake trout in most lakes and streams, which are cold and less productive than the river systems; catch-and-release fishing is recommended for these; if you're a devotee of this sport, be sure to bring along your fishing equipment—even if you don't catch anything, you can enjoy being a part of the lovely scene.

The first people to settle here were undoubtedly drawn by the richness of the fishing and hunting resources. Later, they also came in search of a way across the Alaska Peninsula from Bristol Bay to Shelikof Strait, for such a route would save them from a long and dangerous trip by sea

Arctic tern (Sterna paradisaea). *The world traveler that may challenge your presence on many Alaskan rivers. Range: coastal areas and inland rivers and lakes throughout Alaska.*

around the tip of this tumultuous jut of land. From Katmai Bay, they found three such routes—one was the 125-mile drag across Katmai Pass. They must have been a hardy lot; the trails they left demand extraordinary toughness and stamina of anyone who tries to follow them. Their homes, known as *iglu*s or *barabara*s, were built largely underground, and testify to the fact that Katmai's weather was not any more hospitable in the past than it is now. (There are interesting archeological digs at Brooks River, where an eight-hundred-year-old Eskimo building has been reconstructed.)

Katmai's weather, in fact, is modified on the south by the warmer waters of the Pacific Ocean, but it is also in the pathway of storms generated in the Gulf of Alaska. On its northern side, the cold air of the Arctic comes down to pile up against the mountain barrier of the Aleutian chain, of which the Katmai mountains are such a spectacular part. Winters can be cruel and summers cool. Eighty percent of the summer days are overcast, and furious windblown rain can sweep in at any time during the warmer months. Throughout the year there is the wind, forever the wind. Frequently it comes from the south and is funneled through the mountain passes in gales. (Griggs described Katmai Pass as being a two-ended funnel for the winds. He had four different camps blown down in the area.) The wind gusts across the lakes, plowing the waters into high surf. It blows night and day without stopping and can be canoe capsizing as well as tent transporting, so if you visit this area, be prepared. Experienced canoers and kayakers have enormous respect for the wind on the lakes, particularly Naknek Lake; the word is to travel close to shore. Katmai's wind is an earth force of its own. (I once helped rig a tarp as a sail for our rubber raft to take advantage of the wind pouring down the Iliuk Arm and Naknek Lake.)

Records of explorations in the Katmai region are meager, but the Russians obviously found this area long before Alaska became a territory of the United States. They left their religion and their names among the people and place names like Shelikof, Becharof, and Savonoski on the maps. (The name of Savonoski was given not only to a village but to a short, splendid river that gathers the meltwaters of several ice fields in Katmai and carries them into Naknek Lake.) The few Americans to report on the region before the turn of the century nearly all traveled across Katmai Pass to the east from Bristol Bay to Katmai Bay, battling the blizzards or bending into the torrents of wind that so frequently pour through the pass. One of them, Josiah Edward Spurr of the U.S. Geological Survey, crossed Katmai Pass on an expedition in mid-October of 1898 and noted that it was "extremely wild and rugged . . . the most difficult mountain pass we crossed during the journey."

By the turn of the century, the trail—such as it was—over Katmai Pass was feeling the boots of untold numbers of stampeders. They likely had the wind at their backs, however, for they were headed for Nome. They may have been, as Griggs once was, lifted off the ground by the wind and sent flying down the pass, feet barely touching the ground, but they did not bother to record their adventures in this part of the world. It remained for Robert Griggs to put the Valley of Ten Thousand Smokes and the area around it on the map and to help bring about the establishment of Katmai National Monument.

The original monument fortunately proved to be only the beginning for Katmai. The valley was recognized before long to be only one of many extraordinary features here and volcanism only one of the great natural phenomena of the area. Successive presidents—Herbert Hoover in 1931, Franklin Roosevelt in 1942, Lyndon Johnson in 1969, and

Jimmy Carter in 1978—acknowledged the national significance of the region by enlarging the monument (Carter added over a million acres to it); in 1980, Congress gave it national park and preserve status. This wonderful national park system unit totals some 4,137,000 acres, of which 308,000 are in preserve classification.

Some Useful Information About Katmai

Zip code: 99613. Area code: 907.

How to Get There

Times have changed considerably since the Federal Writers' Project volume on Alaska, produced during the 1930s, stated simply that Katmai National Monument was "inaccessible to tourists." But access to Katmai is still limited—as it should be. Road proposals for the area—there have been serious suggestions for a road over Katmai Pass and/or through the Valley of Ten Thousand Smokes (Griggs, himself, having made the first one)—cause the eyebrows of geologists to twitch; the life expectancy of any road in this geologically active area would be dubious. (Taxpayers should note that Alaska's roads have traditionally been funded almost entirely with federal money.) But far more important, roads would destroy the invaluable wilderness values of the Katmai region.

To reach Katmai, you can fly commercial aircraft to King Salmon and from there take an amphibious air taxi (there are several air operators) to Brooks River, where there is a National Park Service ranger station and campground and a privately operated lodge (see below). Or you can travel up Naknek Lake into the park by chartered boat.

If you can afford it, you can of course charter your own float or amphibious plane into Katmai or avail yourself of an air overlook of the region. A flight over Katmai can be one of the finest ways to see many of the wonders in this parkland. I have been lucky enough to see Katmai many times from above and will keep forever memories of evening mists lit by the slanting summer sun smoking over the pale landscape, while the mountains gathered their own golden clouds.

The *National Park Service* has headquarters in King Salmon at the King Salmon Mall, a half block from the airport; write Box 7, King Salmon; phone 246-3305. You can also get up-to-the minute information about conditions in the park and access into it at the *King Salmon Interagency Visitors Center,* located in the King Salmon Airport; write Box 298, King Salmon; phone 246-4250.

Where to Stay

The King Salmon Interagency Visitors Center (see above) can give you the names of overnight accommodations in King Salmon.

The only developed campground in Katmai is at Brooks River. It has tables, fireplaces, water, shelters, and a food cache. Space, however, is limited. Consult the National Park Service (see above) in advance if you plan to use this camp; reservations are required.

An attractive, though expensive, facility that includes cabins with modern plumbing and a lodge serving good food is operated by Katmailand at Brooks River. (See below re bear watching which is readily accessible from this lodge—and from the park service campground.) Another, smaller, more primitive camp at Grosvenor Lake is also run by Katmailand. Package tours to these concessions are available out of Anchorage. Write *Katmailand, Inc.,* 4700 Aircraft Drive, Anchorage, AK 99502; phone 243-5448. Camping equipment, including tents and stoves, fishing equipment, and canoes, can be rented at Brooks River. You can also take your meals in the Brooks River Lodge if you want to camp out. Otherwise, bring your own supplies.

Camping for backpackers, canoers, and river runners is permitted anywhere in the park. A permit can be obtained at the National Park Service headquarters in King Salmon (see above) or at Brooks River. Note to fishermen: A state fishing license is required in the park, and regulations regarding limits, possession, and types of lures must be observed.

Note: Some of the best bear watching in the state is to be had at the Brooks River falls, where, when the salmon are running (July and early August), literally dozens of bears go fishing. The National Park Service has placed a viewing platform at a strategic point, and rangers escort a limited number of people to it from the road. Viewing time is limited, so everyone gets a chance. A remarkable experience!

How to Enjoy Katmai

National Park Service ranger-naturalists present evening programs at Brooks Camp throughout the summer and lead hikes and nature walks during the day. There is no developed trail system in Katmai; consult the National Park Service people in King Salmon (see above) or at Brooks River for specific information about backpacking or backcountry day hiking. Note to hikers and backpackers: Extensive hiking on volcanic material can be very hard on footwear, and it is easy to wear out a pair of boots in a short time in Katmai.

There has been a great deal of pressure from certain quarters to "open up" and "develop" Katmai so that more people can get into it and see it (and local business can thereby profit as well). This would, of course, mean the end of Katmai's special wild qualities, qualities that have survived in so few places on earth and are, even in Alaska, becoming increasingly rare. To date, the cost and logistics of road building in the area have protected Katmai, and the National Park Service, both because of sensitivity and because of lack of funds, has been unable to do much in the way of development. I hope the National Park Service and enlightened people everywhere will continue the protection afforded so far to this remarkable national treasure.

Think twice before undertaking an extensive visit to Katmai—beyond a stay at Brooks River or an outing on one of its lakes or rivers. And before you plan any kind of outing into the backcountry of Katmai, read Dave Bohn's book *Rambles Through an Alaskan Wild: Katmai and the Valley of the Smokes*. (Read the book anyway, if you love the wilderness.) As Bohn puts it:

> There are hundreds of places where you can stay in posh surroundings and watch thousands of other tourists. Don't ask for that here. Katmai is wild country, not a spa. You come to Katmai because it is something else. That something else will be destroyed for *everyone* (that especially includes the bears) if too many of you come. . . . If you are a backpacker with a good pair of legs and can go into Katmai by yourself [author's note: not recommended] or with one or two others, your gain is on behalf of all of us. When you can no longer do it on your own, however, don't ask for a road across the Valley of Ten Thousand Smokes or a chair lift to the top of Mount Katolinat. Instead, pass on the philosophical space to someone else, and in this way the whole of it is not lost.

Katmai is wild country all right, and for the sake of all of us and our children, let it remain so. If you can visit it on its terms, it can give you an unforgettable wilderness experience (that may include some of the most arduous hiking you have ever achieved and some of the worst weather). But consider your priorities—as well as your condition—before you plan a visit to the backcountry of Katmai National Park.

If you do decide to visit Katmai, you might want to consider the possibility of a side trip to the McNeil River Bear Sanctuary to the north of the park. This is one of the best places in Alaska to see and photograph bears. The sanctuary is administered by the Alaska Department of Fish and Game, and visitation is strictly limited, as, again, it should be. A letter to the **Alaska Department of Fish and Game** (Box 25526, Juneau, AK 99802-5526; phone 465-4112) will get you the information you will need. Note: A lottery is used to select (lucky) visitors. If you can afford it, Mike and Diana McBride's Chenik Camp, located near the Chenik River, will almost certainly offer you excellent bear viewing, along with gourmet fare and most comfortable cabins. (Chenik Camp is surrounded by the McNeil River sanctuary.) Write the McBrides at Box 956, Homer, AK 99603.

The waterways on the west side of Katmai National Park make for wonderfully adventuresome kayaking and canoeing. They include Naknek Lake with its lovely Bay of Islands (tree-covered islands stud the north arm of the lake) and the Alagnak River (for rafting). Unfortunately, some of Katmai's shores were oiled in 1989. For information, contact the *National Park Service,* Box 7, King Salmon, AK 99613; phone 246-3305.

47. Aniakchak National Monument and Preserve

One of the strangest, most impressive features of the Alaskan landscape is a remote volcano located about halfway down the Alaska Peninsula. What makes it supremely unique is its caldera, which is one of the largest in the world, with an average diameter of 6 miles. Along with this extraordinary geological phenomenon, Aniakchak also has a rich and varied floral and faunal community. Because it is relatively inaccessible, its ecosystem has survived as one of the least disturbed in Alaska. In recognition of the many exceptional values of this volcanic area, Congress in 1980 established a 138,000-acre national monument there, with a contiguous 376,000-acre national preserve.

There are good reasons why Aniakchak has been left alone. It is a long way off, some 400 miles, from Anchorage, and the nearest community, Meshik–Port Heiden, has only about a hundred people. But more than distance and few people nearby isolate this new parkland; there is also the weather. Rain and fog smother the mountain most of the time. In 1973, an intrepid freelance writer spent six weeks in the crater, and only eight days of his sojourn were sunny. In an average year, the Pacific side of Aniakchak gets soaked with 126 inches of rain, while the Bering Sea side is almost continuously fogged in. Along with this, a microclimate within the caldera brews winds of hurricane force. The visitor just mentioned had his camp blown down twice, watched Niagaras of fog pour over the crater's rim, and, during one storm, had his wind gauge carried off. During this episode, he was forced to take shelter in a depression in the crater wall to save his life. Aniakchak's temperatures, it should be noted, go to 30 degrees below freezing in the winter; in summer, they gyrate between the upper 40s and a possible but unusual 70 degrees.

On top of all this, Aniakchak is still alive, being one of the forty-seven active volcanoes in the 1,600-mile Aleutian Range that have erupted since 1760. Aniakchak went off as recently as 1931, but the great explosion that formed its caldera occurred long before there was any written history. That eruption left a high rim (some 2,000 feet above the caldera floor), which is crenellated into mountains. On early topographic maps, these were shown as a peculiar ring of low peaks. When viewed from the sea (on those rare days when they could be seen), they gave no hint of the extraordinary crater they embraced. For this reason and the weather conditions of the region, the Aniakchak Caldera was not officially discovered until 1922 when an exploratory team of U.S. Geological Survey scientists noted interesting pockets of ash some 30 miles northeast of Aniakchak on the Alaska Peninsula. Following their lead to the southwest, they came upon a whole valley buried in ash at Cinder Creek. With growing excitement, they climbed the slopes above and reached the crater's rim to look down upon the extraordinary sight below them. With the discovery of the immense caldera, the curious circle of mountains on their maps was graphically explained.

To conjure a picture of Aniakchak Caldera, imagine if you can Crater Lake without its lake but with a small turquoise-colored body of water, named Surprise Lake, tucked along one side of it. Imagine the terrain stained mahogany brown and black, deep maroon with darkly smudged yellows, and over it all an openwork pattern of white snow looking like some huge, dazzling piece of lace had been dropped there. Off-center in the bizarre landscape is a small secondary crater, Vent Mountain, which has its own snow-filled caldera. Nearby there is a smaller, perfectly round formation, aptly named Doughnut Cone.

Adding to this whole strange scene is an abrupt gash in the crater's rim called "The Gates," which drains Surprise Lake and lets the white-foaming, boisterous Aniakchak River (floatable, but difficult; see below) race to the flatland below, where it gentles out and flows into Aniakchak Bay. Without this drainage system, the caldera, like that of Crater Lake, would be filled with water, and Vent Mountain would make a creditable second Wizard Island.

Just when Aniakchak erupted is not known, but since there is no evidence of glaciation in the drifts of ash it left, it must have been after the most recent ice age. Geologists estimate the height of the original moun-

The Aniakchak River flowing through "The Gates" in the Aniakchak Caldera wall.
Source: National Park Service.

tain to have been above 6,000 feet; Aniakchak Mountain at 4,400 feet is now the highest point that remains. Before it exploded, Aniakchak was a mass of sedimentary rock of Jurassic age, which rested at a slight angle on its huge base. When the eruption occurred, it threw more than 15 cubic miles of volcanic material over the landscape for 20 miles in every direction. This was three times as much ejecta as Krakatoa spewed out in 1883. Thus Aniakchak's big blowout was truly a monumental geological event.

Aniakchak's more recent activity has been mild in comparison, although in May 1931 it belched flames 7,000 feet into the sky and sent up a plume of ash that reached 30,000 feet and rained down over an area 1,200 miles in diameter. (At the village of Chignik, 60 miles away, ash poured from the air at the rate of a pound per square foot per hour.) A year later, Father Bernard R. Hubbard, the "Glacier Priest," on his third visit to Aniakchak, found a scene that he described as "a prelude to Hell: black floor, black walls, black water, deep black holes, and black vents." Even then, the mountain had not fully quieted, and every morning Father

Hubbard donned his robes and held Mass, using the immense columns of steam that ascended thousands of feet into the sky as altar candles. Living creatures were already returning to the scene of devastation, and Hubbard shared his caldera altar with brown bear and ptarmigan.

The great brown bear continues to be one of the foremost members of the caldera's wildlife population. The bears have been known to seek out the steaming mud ponds, where they wallow as though, in Hubbard's words, in "a Turkish bath." They also leave their immense tracks deeply imprinted in the volcanic ash, and Hubbard noted that they stepped carefully in the same footprints over and over again (as they have probably done for centuries). Caribou use the caldera too. They are members of the 12,000- to 17,000-head Northern Alaska Peninsula herd, and they wander through low passes into the crater to seek snow patches, where they stand in striking silhouette, trying to avoid the torment of mosquitoes. Moose and other mammals large and small use other areas of the new parklands, including the outer slopes of the mountain and its lowlands.

Flower lovers will find a beautiful sampling of Alaska Peninsula plants inside the park's boundaries. When Father Hubbard first visited the caldera before the 1931 eruption (which, incidentally, he predicted), he found a variety of plants growing there, including the ladyslipper orchid and luxuriant ferns that flourished in the moist, warm places.

Some Useful Information About Aniakchak

Zip code: 99613. Area code: 907.

How to Get There

Access to the Aniakchak Caldera is not cheap and is difficult and uncertain. Scheduled airlines serve King Salmon (150 miles distant) and Meshik–Port Heiden (10 miles away), and it is possible to charter a small plane to Aniakchak from either place. People have been known to walk the 10 miles from Port Heiden to the parkland, but it's a rough scramble, with uneven boggy tundra and heavy thickets of brush. You also have to climb at least 2,000 feet to get into the caldera through one of the passes. It is possible to follow the Aniakchak River and enter the crater floor through the Gates. (This hike is even rougher and is not recommended.)

Far easier and more spectacular is an air flight over the caldera, weather permitting. I have lucked out twice in viewing the caldera from the air, and it is an unforgettable sight. If you are very tough and adventurous, you can, of course, be deposited in the crater; it is possible to land a floatplane on Surprise Lake, and wheeled planes can usually find a level stretch on which to set down.

Where to Stay

There are no National Park Service campsites at Meshik–Port Heiden. Camping is allowed anywhere inside the park boundaries.

How to Enjoy Aniakchak

As noted, a flightseeing trip over the Aniakchak Caldera is highly recommended. It is also possible to raft the Aniakchak River, which is designated a wild and scenic river. It is 27 miles in length, and its upper stretch is white water; the final run across Aniakchak Bay is entirely open-ocean travel. You will need a charter pickup from Aniakchak Bay. (This river is recommended only for experts; stretches of the river can be class IV under certain water conditions.) The *National Park Service* in King Salmon can give you further information regarding air charters and the possibility of a commercially run river trip. Write Box 7, King Salmon, AK 99613; phone 246-3305.

Aniakchak is a magnificent, geologically and ecologically important unit of the National Park System. It is a fascinating natural wonder to view from the sky. But, except for the Aniakchak River, this is not recreational country for most people. If you decide to visit it, be prepared for a rough outing, miserable weather, and maybe even another display of volcanism. Aniakchak is still very much alive. Note also: There are no emergency services.

48. Alaska's State Parks

Alaska's state park system, while still relatively young, could well be the envy of almost any state. It contains over 3 million acres of superlative terrain. (This is considerably less than 1 percent of the acreage in Alaska!) Development of the system has largely been devoted to readily accessible areas and especially to waysides along the state's more heavily traveled highways. Of eighty-two units, fifty-seven are designated waysides. These provide welcome places for bikers as well as drivers to stop, stretch, picnic, or perhaps to camp. Some of the waysides are quite large—several hundred acres in size—and can include such amenities as

King salmon (Oncorhynchus tshawytscha), *Alaska's state fish. Range: Southeast Alaskan waters to Chukchi Sea.*

toilets, drinking water, shelters, camping units. Several have boat launchings into lakes or rivers; others serve as trailheads.

The state park people also maintain designated campgrounds and recreation areas. The latter can be several thousand acres in size and have extensive campgrounds, canoe trail systems, snowmobile areas, cross-country ski trails, or other developed recreational facilities. The state historic parks, another unit classification, primarily help preserve some of Alaska's rich history, but in Kodiak (Fort Abercrombie), the historic park also has camping facilities.

The largest units of the state park system are the state parks themselves. Most of these are undeveloped or in the process of development, including Wood-Tikchik State Park, Kachemak Bay State Park, and Denali State Park. Denali was the first major unit in the state park system (1970) and is scheduled to be a focal point of visitor services for Denali National Park. Although facilities here are still limited, there are interesting backpacking opportunities, and you can get to the takeoff point on the Alaska Railroad. (Check with the Alaska Department of Natural Re-

Pacific walrus (Odobenus rosmarus divergens). *Range: Bristol Bay to Point Barrow.*

sources Public Information Center in Anchorage for details; see below.) The most highly developed is Chugach State Park, just outside of Anchorage, which is discussed in some detail in this book.

The Alaska Division of Parks and Outdoor Recreation publishes useful information, including an inventory of its various units, their locations, and the facilities they include. (Pamphlets giving details of some specific areas are also available.) If you're planning an auto or bicycle excursion into Alaska this information can be very valuable to you. To obtain it, write *Alaska Department of Natural Resources Public Information Center,* 3601 C Street, Suite 200, Anchorage, AK 99503; phone 269-8400. A modest fee is charged for use of many state park facilities—and is well worth it.

Wood-Tikchik State Park

The Wood-Tikchik State Park is located about 300 air miles west of Anchorage and is one of the loveliest regions in all of Alaska. There are two sets of lakes adjacent here, each with six gorgeous bodies of water. Each set gathers its waters from a different watershed, and each drains into a different river, although the waters of all end up in Nushagak Bay.

The higher lakes are tucked between soaring peaks where the snow gleams against swathes of emerald green heath tundra. The lower lakes are fringed by dark spruce forests with birches scattered here and there. When the salmon are running, they are so thick in the "river bays" between the lower lakes that it is hard to see the bottom, although the water is as clear as glass.

Under the terms of statehood, Alaska was able to select a large part of this magnificent area, and did so in the early 1960s. Almost immediately, there were strong pressures on the state to subdivide the lakeshores into 5-acre "wilderness estates"—one of its land-disposal classifications. Fortunately, there were even stronger pressures to preserve this region more or less intact, and, in the late 1970s, the state legislature established the Wood-Tikchik State Park, which everyone can enjoy. With its more than 1,500,000 acres, this is the largest unit in the state park system, indeed the largest state park in the United States.

The Wood-Tikchik State Park is still undeveloped, although there are several lodges on private inholdings within the park. It offers superb wilderness experiences, primarily water based, during the summer, although boat and plane traffic are increasing, especially on the lower lake system and lower lakes in the upper system. (The usual caveats about rain, mist, coolness, and wind all apply.) You can fly commercial to Dillingham, where there are tourist facilities. To reach the wilderness part of the park, you fly in a small floatplane. Check with the Alaska Department of Natural Resources Public Information Center in Anchorage (see above); they can help you with further information about the park and with the names of facilities in Dillingham. Dillingham is also the place from which you travel—by boat or by air—to Round and Walrus Islands.

The Alaska Department of Natural Resources Public Information Center can also give you information about guides, air charters, lodges, and more.

49. Pribilof Islands

The only way you can reach the Pribilof Islands is to fly there via Reeve Aleutian Airlines—unless you're lucky enough to somehow find transportation by boat. Once there, the only lodging is the Native-operated hotel on the largest island, Saint Paul. (There is one other sizable island, Saint George, and three little ones—Otter, Walrus, and Sea Lion.) The islands lie in the Bering Sea just about due west of Naknek, and, if the weather is good when you visit them, you will have some fine aerial views of the Alaska Peninsula en route to or from Anchorage.

The great attractions of the Pribilofs are their Russian history (dating back to 1786 and memorialized by, among other things, a wonderful Russian Orthodox church), their colonies of northern fur seals (two-thirds of the total population haul out on Saint Paul Island), their fabulous birdlife (176 species have been recorded on the islands), and their uniquely accessible seabird nesting cliffs.

The Aleuts who inhabit the islands have done an outstanding job of developing tourism as a major source of income. They are protecting their wildlife even as they show it off, which they do with sensitivity, using viewing platforms and blinds for observation stations. (Where else in the world can you see thousands of fur seals without disturbing these engaging animals?) The accommodations on Saint Paul are clean, informal, and more or less of the bedrock type (the bathroom is down the hall). The opportunities to photograph the wildlife are fantastic—if the weather is good. Unfortunately, most of the time it isn't, so be prepared accordingly. Rain, mist, winds, or a combination thereof are usually the order of the day. Nonetheless, a visit to the Pribilofs is highly recommended.

Make your travel arrangements through your travel agent or **Reeve Aleutian Airlines.** Write 4700 West International Airport Road, Anchorage, AK 99502; phone 243-4700.

PART IV

Interior and Arctic

50. Introduction

Once you leave the tumultuous mountains of the Alaska Range and head northward, you encounter the Interior, a country with a very different kind of magic. If Southcentral (and Southeast) Alaska can be described as vertical terrain, the Interior can be described as horizontal. There is a softer feel to this gently tilted landscape, termed the Intermontane Plateau by geologists. Your eyes can reach across vast stretches of space to what seems to be an infinitely distant horizon. True, that horizon may be delineated by high, shining mountains, but more often there is a lower uplift of the land, a bank of hills whose outlines are superimposed and marked by different shades of blue—deep, deeper, deepest—in a curiously two-dimensional effect. The dark, spiky shapes of spruce trees punctuate the grand vistas and fringe the lakes and oxbow sloughs and ponds that gleam like polished black mirrors in the still summer air. Lush green-gold mosses weave themselves together in the muskegs. Gardens of fireweed splash cerise all over the ground as though huge buckets of rich rose-colored paint had spilled here and there.

This is the region in Alaska where on hot summer days thunderstorms move their dark blue-black shadows over the land, trailing sunlit shafts of rain and rainbows. Birches and aspens shake out their soft green leaves that turn silver in the wind. The sun can be so hot and the air so warm that you are tempted to snooze away the afternoon in a proper siesta, but afternoon, evening, night, and morning blend almost imperceptibly into one light-filled day. The light itself has wonderful qualities, flooding golden during the day and often becoming rose or orange as the sun dips lower on the horizon.

Autumn comes to the Interior like a visiting artist for a few brief weeks. The broadleaf trees glow like bright torches; spruce cones turn royal purple; delicate-looking larches pale to a smoky yellow before their needles fall to the ground. The plumes of horsetails float in a soft creamy haze above the forest floor; cranberries turn a brilliant red, and so do the leaves of the bearberries.

Then, as the earth moves more deeply into the dark months of shadow, colors fade to muted browns, tans, and grays. The first chilly rains can freeze and cover the world with a brief shine of ice. The heat of the land—gathered during those sunlit near-twenty-hour summer days— begins to drain inexorably into the infinite depths of space. Day after still, clear day sees the temperature slide lower until the snows come whirling and whispering down to color the land white. Great masses of polar air slide in from the west to be held fast by the high walls of the Brooks and Alaska Ranges, and the cold deepens. During the brief daylight hours of winter, the sun rolls along the horizon like a brass disk and gradually tips out of sight. In this pale slant of sunlight, the soft, dry snow glitters, and floating ice crystals sparkle in the calm air. A small cloud of ice fog forms when you breathe, and when darkness grips the world, auroras come to flame the sky.

Like Alaska itself, the aurora is difficult to describe. Here is one attempt, written about a century ago by Fridtjof Nansen, the Norwegian explorer who spent three years in the Arctic. Two of those years were spent in his ice-bound ship the *Fram*. His classic book is called *In Northern Mists*.

> Nothing more wonderfully beautiful can exist than the Arctic night . . . the aurora borealis shakes over the vault of heaven its veil of glittering silver—changing now to yellow, now to green, now to red. It spreads, it contracts again, in restless change, next it breaks into waving many-folded bands of shining silver, over which shoot billows of glittering rays . . . an endless phantasmagoria of sparkling colour, surpassing anything that one can dream. Sometimes the spectacle reached such a climax that one's breath was taken away; one felt that now something extraordinary must happen—at the very least the sky must fall. But as one stands in breathless expectation, down the whole thing trips, as if in a few quick light scale-runs, into bare nothingness.

It is small wonder that some Eskimos believed the aurora was a heaven where it was always warm and wonderful and life was eternally easy and beautiful.

But the lengthening days of spring dim the northern lights, and, as the skies stay brighter, the fronds of the spruce trees start to drop their loads of fluffy snow until the forests are filled with glittering cascades. Meltwater begins first to ooze and then to stream from the snowbanks, and the first flowers come to star the brown, wet ground. The ice-bound rivers creak and heave until huge blocks of ice break loose and start their

Interior and Arctic Alaska

ponderous journey downstream, sometimes piling up on one another and jamming the rivers until they flood their banks and drown the land. When the ice slabs collide, the air is filled with the deep, primeval sounds of irresistible forces meeting an immovable object.

There is a feeling of timelessness about this elemental land. Although its great rivers have changed their courses, and the land itself—much of it underlain by permafrost—has been patterned and repatterned by the earth-shaping forces of freezing and thawing, and buried and reburied by loess and sediments from the mountains that embrace it, the basic land-scape has remained essentially unaltered for the hundreds of thousands of years it has been above the sea. When the great Pleistocene glaciers

Caribou (Rangifer tarandus). Range: once throughout most of Alaska but for Southeast and Aleutian Islands; now the largest herds are in the northern portions of the state.

covered the Brooks Range to the north and the Alaska Range to the south, they stopped short of this immense plateau. This was the place of refuge for countless living things that could not breach the world of ice and snow surrounding them.

Many of those living things still flourish here, having survived from those times, though, strangely, many great mammals, herbivores and carnivores alike, have disappeared within the ken of prehistoric people. This is the land of muskegs and tundra, tangles of low-growing berries and, in places, of devilish tussocks, sedges, or cotton grass. It is the land of the taiga, the boreal forest community of white spruce, black spruce, alder and willow, larch, birch, and aspen. This is the land of moose, caribou, and wolves, of lynx and snowshoe hares, of the grizzly bear and red fox, the vole and the red squirrel, which is the alarm sounder of the forest. It is also the land of raptors; and on its tundras and in the wetlands of its great rivers, it is the land of migratory birds, hundreds of thousands of winged creatures that follow an undeniable pull to what has been one of earth's stable ecological communities. They come to the Yukon and Tanana wetlands, their wingbeats filling the skies, waterfowl in over-whelming numbers.

Millions more birds—waterfowl and seabirds, many species of shore-birds and songbirds—prolong their migratory flights northward, some finding their way through the passes of the Brooks Range or over these beautiful mountains, others arriving via the Pacific flyway. Their goal is the Arctic Slope with its braided rivers, thousands and thousands of thaw lakes, marshes, and coastal plains—all so rich in insect life during the summer months. As with the Interior, the Arctic Slope escaped glaciation during the Pleistocene ice ages (above ground, that is; below the surface, the ground froze nearly solid and has remained so). As a consequence, the Arctic Slope, too, was a refugium for certain plants and animals and a haven for certain migratory birds, like the eiders, Canada geese, and oldsquaws, which still feel the pull that returns their species to this place summer after summer.

The Arctic Slope is the part of Alaska that may possibly have been formed by the breaking off and rotation of a piece of the Canadian shield around a pivotal point in what is now the Mackenzie River delta. As this huge block of rock swung round through a shallow sea, one theory goes, it helped push up the Brooks Range, which, in turn, contributed an im-mense quantity of outwash and sediments through the millennia to help build up the surface of a new landmass. (In this millions-of-years-long process, geologists explain, oil was trapped between the basement rock and the surface layers; hence Prudhoe Bay.)

Arctic Slope

Although separated from the Interior by the Brooks Range and essen-tially sharing these mountains with it, the Arctic Slope is very different from Alaska's central plateau. This relatively flat and thoroughly frozen slab of land is gripped by continuous permafrost, which may extend as much as 2,000 feet below the surface. Everywhere in the Arctic there is evidence of this phenomenon, but perhaps the best way to get a perspec-tive of what permafrost can do to the land—as well as to enjoy some of its especially picturesque aspects—is to fly over the Arctic Slope in a small plane on a clear summer day. Below you this vast segment of gent-ly tilted earth—snow-free under the summer sun—will be cracked into a network of giant polygons, many of which will be outlined by thin, shin-ing ribbons of water in the troughs that separate them.

You will also see beaded streams wandering across the landscape.

These are small ponds formed at the intersection of ice wedges and connected by short threads of water running between the polygons. You will see literally thousands upon thousands of thaw lakes shimmering in the sunlight, for in the summer, the Arctic Slope is more water than land in places. A few thaw lakes are round, but many are oval or almost rectangular; and while some are tiny, no more than a few feet long, others are 20 miles or so in length. In many areas, their long axis is oriented just west of north, reflecting the general direction of the prevailing winds, which are southeasterly. Contrary to what might be expected, the winds spread the water at right angles to their impact and build up wave-generated shelves on the shores in front of them; hence the long, narrow shapes.

Another Arctic phenomenon that makes interesting viewing from the air is the *aufeis,* which forms in north-flowing rivers. It may look as though there were snowfields on the waterways in midsummer, but, in fact, *aufeis* is something like a riverine glacier. Each season, a layer of ice is formed when overflow water freezes. This can build up into a sizable striated platform of ice, which is as blue as the best of glaciers when seen from the river itself. (Note to river runners: Avoid collisions with *aufeis* and, above all, avoid going under it.)

If you fly far enough north, you will leave behind the patterns of the Arctic land and will see, instead, the extraordinary patterns of the Arctic ice pack. Summer usually breaks the frozen Arctic Ocean up into millions of chunks of ice that, seen from the air, form an incredible silver-white jigsaw puzzle in the dark blue waters. Land and linger, if you can, along the Arctic coast. To stand on the shore of the Arctic Ocean or clamber onto a chunk of beached ice is quite an experience; should you visit this region on a clear midnight when the Arctic sun rolls along the ice-roughed horizon, flooding the world with a cold, golden light, you will enjoy one of Alaska's truly great sights.

From the ground, you may also have a chance to see a pingo, or ice blister. A pingo can result from the draining of a lake. The permafrosted land encroaches into the empty lake basin from all sides until it finally reaches the center, where the icy ground has no place to go but up; hence, a low frozen hill results. A pingo makes a valuable reference point as you travel across what seems to be a flat and featureless landscape.

Although soggy in the summer (not recommended for cross-country hiking), the Arctic Slope can be described accurately as a frozen desert. Precipitation here is the lowest in Alaska and ranges between 5 and 8 inches a year across the sweep of this region. (This includes both rain and snow.) Cold is a fact of life year-round, and spits of snow can sting your face here in July and August. Because the winds sweep constantly over

Aufeis, *Arctic Slope. Source: U.S. Fish and Wildlife Service.*

these vast reaches of open land (Barrow, for example, reports calm conditions only 1 percent of the time), what snow there is seems more often to travel horizontally than vertically, and it piles up only where it meets an obstruction. Windblown snow can cause a whiteout that competes with summer fogs in making ground travel a challenge and flying an uncertainty in this part of the state.

While the climate of the Arctic Slope can be especially bitter, particularly in light of the windchill factor, weather is only one aspect of the unique character of this place. The other is the presence or the absence of sunlight and twilight. Barrow is not completely dark for nearly 119 straight days during the year. (This counts some 67 days when the sun is above the horizon and another nearly 52 days when bright twilight illuminates the world even when the sun is below the horizon. Because of the latitude and the cold, refraction maximizes this twilight period.) On the other end of the scale, Barrow residents go for nearly 67 days without ever seeing the sun, although more or less brief periods of twilight lighten the sky during this long period of darkness. (Interestingly, though, Barrow still receives an overall total of solar energy greater than that received by Palmer, which is just north of Anchorage.)

The flora that live in this world of ice and night has adapted to it in intriguing ways. The tundra plants of the North Slope grow on the polygons there much as they would on small, soggy islands, hanging on for dear life with their shallow roots in the thin "active layer" of soil that covers the forever-frozen ground beneath. Many of the plants mat themselves together thickly to conserve what heat they can, protect themselves from the blasts of wind, and preserve the little snow that falls on them for moisture. They may also form cushions or tussocks so that dead leaves are caught around their roots and protect them. Leathery leaves, which help avoid the desiccation inflicted by the cold, dry winds, are commonplace, just as they are in warmer deserts. And the ability to photosynthesize even in very low temperatures keeps many of these sturdy Arctic dwellers alive.

Few of the tundra plants are annuals, for they would be too hard pressed to mature and seed in the brief weeks that are the growing season of the Arctic summer. The perennials that succeed often reproduce vegetatively, even though they may also be capable of producing seed as a backup means of perpetuating their species. Some of the plants, such as the willows, are able to hybridize readily; this is another mechanism for survival. Others, like the various species of lichens that grow on higher ground, have the advantages of being two plants at once, fungi and algae.

Even as the flowering plants cram a lifetime into the few relatively warm days of summer, some members of this tundra community manage to prepare themselves for what lies ahead. For example, the willows put on their buds for flowers and leaves in early autumn in anticipation of the first sunny day to come the following spring; then they are ready to pop open and take advantage of every moment of sunshine. In such a rigorous regime for growing things, it comes as a beautiful surprise to find crowds of yellow poppies dancing in the Arctic wind, in seeming bright defiance of all the rules.

The Arctic fauna also use interesting mechanisms to succeed in these northerly latitudes. For example, mammals of all sizes and shapes may not only wear a white fur coat at least part of the year, but they will also have good insulating layers of fat. Some of the birds are feathered in white during the winter; other species, of course, time their arrival and departure to the change of the seasons. Your chance of seeing some of the fabled Arctic bears like the polar bear is slim, but not because of their protective coloration: hunting pressures and the impingement of civilization on this once wild habitat have reduced the numbers of these animals and made them very wary. You might, however, hope to repeat the experience of friends of mine who, one sunny summer day, stopped for lunch on a gravel bar in an Arctic river and whiled away a half hour or so with a charming fox, which posed amiably over and over again for photographs.

The Arctic has been inhabited by people for untold ages (at least 27,000 years, according to some anthropologists), and there are many important archeological sites hidden in its frozen ground. Along some of its beaches, the bones of woolly mammoths are embedded in permafrosted cliffs, reminders of animals struck down by the early hunters here who prized these creatures as game. Along other beaches, the artifacts of more recent cultures wash in and out with the storm-driven sea. (In contrast to other parts of Alaska, the tides in the Arctic Ocean can be measured in inches rather than feet.) The present people of the Arctic, the Inupiat, carry on their treasured traditional ways, often practicing the demanding skills that enabled their forefathers to survive in this vast and strangely beautiful frozen world.

Brooks Range

Separating the Interior plateau and the Arctic Slope—and contributing much of the character of both of these vast regions—is the Brooks Range. The range was named for the explorer and onetime head of the Alaskan Branch of the U.S. Geological Survey, Alfred Hulse Brooks. Stretching from the Canadian border to the Chukchi Sea, this Arctic alpine province is a mountain world of extraordinary beauty and variety. The early uplifting of these mountains, which at their highest rise just a little less than 10,000 feet, is pegged at somewhere around 150 million years ago (as compared with the Rockies, which were uplifted starting perhaps 70 million years ago). But the rocks of the Brooks Range also tell of many earlier earth processes. Regions of these mountains lay beneath ancient seas, as long as 360 million years ago, and gathered the grains of long-lost continents that were washed into their waters. Sediments, built up slowly over time, were finally upthrust and metamorphosed so that now they are stained with lovely colors and form fascinating striated patterns. In their stacking, folding, and deformation, there is graphic evidence of the powerful forces that have shaped this part of the earth through many millennia. Evidence of more recent geological activity lies in the heart of the range, where fiercely sharp granitic peaks, young and untempered, have burst through the older formations in an upwelling of the earth's hot magmas.

So large is the sweep of the Brooks Range that it contains several mountain systems within it. The mountains closest to the Canadian border--the Davidson and Romanzof groups—rise higher and higher as they travel westward. Their foothills are clothed with pale-green tundra, which may be powdered with snow off and on during the summer. (It is quite an experience to be caught in an early July storm, as I once was while traveling through these mountains, and watch the perfectly even snow line come lower and lower down the hillside until, only a few hundred feet above you, it gives way to frigid rain.) Through and over these foothills flow the crowds of the Porcupine caribou herd, animals that roam the lands of Canada and Alaska as they follow the instinctive patterns that pull them back and forth across the tundra.

To the west of the Romanzofs are the Franklin, Shublik, Sadlerochit, and Philip Smith Mountains. Among their summits lie scraps of glaciers, reminders of the Pleistocene ice sheets that covered and sculpted this land. Beyond lie the Endicott and Schwatka Ranges, and forming the westernmost end of the range are the pastel-gray and beige De Long Mountains and the Bairds—only 3,000 to 4,000 feet high—which escaped later glaciation and have weathered into beautifully rounded shapes.

To the north, the Brooks Range is bordered by two sets of foothills whose ancient sediments have been tossed up here in tumultuous waves or stacked like shingles. Because it lies beyond the tree line, the bare structure of this fascinating piece of the earth can be clearly seen.

The Brooks Range has an interesting pattern to its drainage; waters flow north, south, and west from its peaks and ridges. North-trending streams—like the Kongakut, Hulahula (there were once more Hawaiians in Alaska than there were the Russians who claimed it, hence place names like this one), Canning, Sagavanirktok (for a while, you were supposed to qualify as an Alaskan if you could pronounce the name of this river, but then, after the pipeline got going, everybody started calling it simply the Sag), and Colville—all rush from the high country to break into braids that intertwine their channels across the gently sloping apron of the northern province. One great river, the Noatak, rises from the granite heart of the range, flows due westward, and then makes a 90-degree angle south to empty into Kotzebue Sound. Most of the south-flowing streams—lovely rivers like the Sheenjek, the Koyukuk, the Dietrich, the John, and the Alatna—contribute to the volume of the Yukon River. But whatever their directions are, the rivers of the Brooks Range, still wild and free, are among Alaska's most beautiful (and sometimes challenging) streams; they can carry you through some of Alaska's most interesting and unique scenery.

The Brooks Range is a redoubt for some of Alaska's finest wildlife. One of my greatest Alaska memories is of floating the Kongakut River on a cold, misty afternoon and looking up to see two Dall sheep lying on the

Lake Norvik, Brooks Range. Source: National Park Service.

dark cliffs above, silently watching our slow progress downstream and somehow embodying the pure spirit of the wilderness. Other wildlife is not so silent, and the thousands of shorebirds that nest along the Arctic rivers of the Brooks Range are not at all shy about announcing their presence—and trying to get rid of yours. Although there are still many grizzlies and wolves (as well as caribou and moose) in the Brooks Range, you may not be as fortunate as wildlife biologist Averill Thayer—who knows and loves this territory so well—who once spent several days on the Sheenjek River in the company of a family of forbearing wolves and a grizzly that was more frightened of him than he was of it.

Gardens of wildflowers brighten the tundra swards of the Brooks Range—marsh marigolds, mertensia, potentilla, anemones—and in the higher terrain, the hiking is good. In wet places, however, you can encounter the ubiquitous tussocks that force even the most nimble hiker into a careful balancing act.

Despite the tussocks, the Brooks Range offers splendid backpacking. It is also a wonderful place to be spot-packed into; you can stay awhile and absorb the beauty and the wildness of this part of Arctic Alaska. As always, of course, warnings about the weather apply, with the added one

that, especially to the north, bone-chilling storms can sweep in any time
of the year, as can bitter winds, and the weather can change with speed
remarkable even for Alaska.

Sometimes people fall in love with a particular part of Alaska, and this
love affair changes their lives. Such was the case for Robert Marshall,
who visited and lost his heart to the Brooks Range during the 1930s. He
climbed and named Mount Doonerak (Spirit Mountain), which broods
above all the other peaks in the Endicotts. He was stunned by the beauty
and grandeur of Boreal Mountain and Frigid Crags, which he christened
and then aptly described as the "Gates of the Arctic." He spent happy
months in the little mining town of Wiseman on the Middle Fork of the
Koyukuk River, where he found the simple and accepting community living a social model he would have liked to see emulated by the rest of the
world. He wrote eloquently and delightfully of his time in this magnificent wilderness, which he was among the first to try to protect. His book
Alaska Wilderness is required reading for anyone who visits the Brooks
Range (see Suggested Reading).

Until recently, many of the extraordinary values of the Arctic—the
cultural, ecological, and scientific among them—were given little attention by our government. The first major federal withdrawal of Arctic
lands was for oil. Incidentally, the Eskimo people had known about the
presence of oil there since time immemorial. The 23-million-acre Naval
Petroleum Reserve Number 4 was established in the 1930s. Subsequent
oil exploration in the reserve yielded no bonanza, but it did inflict major
and perhaps irreparable damage on parts of this fragile tundra. The U.S.
Navy has since turned this acreage over to the Department of the Interior,
and former secretary of the interior James Watt opened up a 6-million-
acre portion of it to renewed exploration. Limited but important scientific research came with the establishment of the Naval Arctic Research
Laboratory in Point Barrow, an effort that has been discontinued. And in
1960 the Arctic National Wildlife Refuge was established in a first official nod to the importance of the Arctic wildlife resource.

Although the state of Alaska, also looking for oil, selected strategic
lands in the Arctic under the statehood act early on, it took bringing in
petroleum at Prudhoe Bay in 1968 to turn the national spotlight onto this
part of Alaska. While the subsequent construction of the Trans-Alaska
Pipeline, with its attendant Haul Road, forever ended the wild integrity
of the region, the 1980 congressional dispositions of Arctic public lands
within and south of the Brooks Range has, at last, acknowledged some
of the major human and conservation values here. Sadly, the Arctic Slope
itself, that vast, fragile, and magnificent area that is unique in the United
States, fared less well. Only a small percentage of it was given adequate
protection by the federal government; oil exploration was authorized in

Junction of the Kokrine River with the Yukon. Kokrine Hills in background. Source: Alaska Environmental Information and Data Center, University of Alaska.

the fragile Arctic National Wildlife Refuge. The rest of this vulnerable and beautiful terrain faces an uncertain future, as does the wildlife it presently supports.

Rivers

Clear and cold, the Colville River offers a relatively easy (class I and II) fifteen-day run from the Kiligwa River to Umiat, with another five days from Umiat to Nuiqsut. You can get in by wheel plane from Bettles or Kotzebue to gravel bars upstream, out by wheel plane from Umiat or Nuiqsut, or you can continue to Deadhorse, where there is commercial air service. Raft or kayak is preferred river craft. The Colville is Alaska's largest river north of the continental divide. It flows through rolling, treeless, Arctic terrain, with good views of wildlife possible but poor fishing likely. For further information, contact the Bureau of Land Management and the Alaska State Division of Forest, Land and Water Management in the Alaska Public Lands Information Center in Fairbanks (see below). Write Nuiqsut (zip code 99789) if you plan to stop in this village.

The Ivishak is a swift, flat-water, clear, class II river. An 80-mile trip on it will take four to five days. Access in is by wheel or float plane from Bettles or Kotzebue. You can fly out by air taxi, or join the Sagavanirktok River and continue on to Deadhorse. Raft or kayak is the preferred craft because of access. Extensive *aufeis* may close the river channels until middle to late June. The Ivishak flows through the Philip Smith Mountains, where there is good hiking, and you may see fine wildflowers and many butterflies in season. For further information, contact the *Arctic National Wildlife Refuge,* Box 20, Fairbanks, AK 99701; phone 456-0250.

The Killik River is a beautiful, clear, swift, Arctic stream. It will take about six days on it to reach its confluence with the Colville, then three more days to Umiat. The river is generally class I and II with possible III rapids. Rafts or kayaks are preferred. Access is by floatplane from Bettles or Kotzebue to lakes upstream. You can be picked up by a wheel plane from a gravel bar at the Colville River, or continue down the Colville to Umiat. There is good hiking in the upper reaches of the river, and you will pass within sight of large sand dunes. For further information, contact the Alaska Public Lands Information Center in Fairbanks or Tok (see below).

The Sagavanirktok River is another clear, swift, north-flowing Arctic stream. You can spend about six days on it from Galbraith Lake to Franklin Bluffs, and add another two days to reach Deadhorse. This is an excellent white-water river for experienced floatboaters; you may encounter class IV rapids in Atigun Canyon; otherwise it is class II and III. The Sag flows through some very lovely country, and parallels the pipeline and Haul Road (or Dalton Highway) for two-thirds of its length. Access in and out may be possible from the road, which will allow the use of canoes. Otherwise, you will need an air taxi and may prefer a folding raft or kayak. For further information, contact the Alaska Public Lands Information Center in Fairbanks or Tok (see below).

The Middle Fork of the Koyukuk River is a relatively easy, clear stream that passes through historic country, has good fishing, and is suitable for a family outing. It can provide a pleasant five-day trip from its headwaters to Bettles, weather cooperating. Access in is by the Haul Road and out by scheduled air service from Bettles. Canoe, raft, or kayak is suitable. The river passes through mining properties in Wiseman, Nolan, Coldfoot, and Tramway Bar: these should be respected. For further information, contact the Alaska Public Lands Information Center in Fairbanks or Tok (see below). There are Native properties along the Koyukuk, and you may want to camp below the high-water line.

The Porcupine River is large and generally slow moving, and poses few challenges to a small-boater. However, it is a historic waterway that flows from Canada into Alaska, and it offers a wonderful eight- to ten-day river experience from Old Crow, Yukon Territory, to Fort Yukon, Alaska, if you don't mind mosquitoes. (There are numerous other places to put in in Canada.) You can take out at Fort Yukon, or continue down the Yukon River. There is commercial air service out of Fort Yukon, or you might want to investigate putting your raft, canoe, or kayak onto a barge at Fort Yukon and returning to Old Crow. The Porcupine passes several Native villages and through a good deal of Native-owned terri-tory: write Tanana Chiefs (zip code 99777) if you wish to stop along the way. And for further information, contact the U.S. Fish and Wildlife Ser-vice (see below). Note: You may have to check in with U.S. Customs in Fort Yukon.

Other interesting river and small-boating opportunities in the Interior and Arctic include: Nigu-Etivluk Rivers (NPS); Black River (USFWS); Kasegaluk Lagoon (BLM and village of Wainwright); Yukon River (USFWS, NPS, BLM); and Alatna River (NPS). Write for information to the agency or village indicated. To reach these agencies, contact the *Alaska Public Lands Information Center* in Fairbanks (250 Cushman Street, Fairbanks, AK 99701; phone 456-0527) or in Tok (Box 359, Tok, AK 99780; phone 882-5667).

51. Fairbanks

In a gentle valley cradled on three sides by subdued rolling hills and within sight of some of the most spectacular peaks of the Alaska Range lies Fairbanks, the city of the Interior. Less than 150 miles south of the Arctic Circle, its location happens to be close to the geographical cen-ter—or what is referred to as the "golden heart"—of Alaska. Like Juneau, this is a town that came into being because there was gold nearby; and like Anchorage, it has strong "ties" to the Alaska Railroad, being its northern terminus. But there the resemblance to Alaska's two other principal cities stops. Fairbanks has a distinctive character all its own. While Juneau has early history, charm, and bearable—if soggy—weather, and Anchorage has size, lots of business activity, and a spectac-ular setting, Fairbanks has the feel of a frontier town, with moose in its gardens, magnificent auroras, the University of Alaska (intellectual center of Alaska) in its backyard, and a climate that demands obeisance of anybody who lives in it. Those who do live here include some of the most independent, colorful, and individualistic people in the state—true Alaskans to the core.

The stories about the uniqueness of Fairbanks folks are legion and apocryphal. For example, some time ago the community hospital became so run down that it clearly would have to be replaced. For three years in a row, the people of Fairbanks voted down a proper bond issue to fund a new medical facility. Conditions worsened and serious medical cases had to be sent to Anchorage for treatment; still the voters said no. Then somebody decided to pass the hat to get the money for a new hospital—and, sure enough, the people of Fairbanks, on their own, came up with more money than was needed. (I asked a friend who told me this story why she enjoyed living in Fairbanks so much and she replied that its faults are its greatest charm.)

An election a few years later provided another example of the independent thinking of the Fairbanks people. To speak for them in the state legislature in Juneau, they elected six representatives in the following order: two Libertarians (the only two in the United States to be elected to any state office that year), one conservative Republican, and three Democrats. Nosed out in this election was a man who was considered a socialist (he was later elected and served several terms).

It might be argued that the environment of Fairbanks accounts for the uniqueness of some of its citizens. To survive in it, one has to be tough and self-sufficient, know what one is doing, and know how to make the right decisions. People who live in lesser climates might find it hard to comprehend what a Fairbanks winter is like. One Fairbanks resident described it to me as not being so bad—there are only three or four weeks when it's below 35 or 40 degrees; he meant 35 or 40 degrees below zero. In that kind of weather, things that most of us take for granted simply won't work. Not only can automobile engines solidify overnight (sometimes even when plugged into a heating system, and many parking meters have plugs), but steering wheels can also lock, frozen stiff, while you're driving down the highway. When it drops down to 60 below zero—and it does—if you throw a glass of water out the window, it will fizz like club soda or freeze before it hits the ground. Soap bubbles become as rigid as glass and roll around on the snow. Ungloved fingers will freeze in a matter of minutes, and so will uncovered noses and cheeks. The smog you breathe (and Fairbanks does have smog) will be frozen. It's almost too cold to cross-country ski in such weather; if you tried it, you

Fairbanks home. Source: Yvonne Mozée.

would find the snow so dry that it has the harsh consistency of sand. Unfortunately, if you plan to keep warm inside, you might find that the
power has gone off and all of your pipes hold nothing but ice. In some
apartment buildings you may be requested not to open your windows
from November 1 to May 1. (Despite all this, some residents bicycle to
work, no matter what!)

People who endure this kind of deep winter climate—which they like
to describe as "dependable cold, none of that messy freezing and thawing"—share experiences that bond them together. Add to this another
shared experience—that of long, almost constant darkness—and the
bond becomes stronger. Perhaps understandably, Fairbanks people tend
to feel a little different, like members of an exclusive club to which you
have to be initiated, a little stronger than people from Outside. You

might encounter this attitude when you visit Fairbanks; you might, for example, hear the contiguous forty-eight states described as "the lesser states."

Along with this, you'll find that most Fairbanks residents are also friendly and hospitable. And when the deep cold of their sub-Arctic winter begins to break, and the dark hours begin to shorten—say, in the latter half of February or the first half of March—interesting things happen in Fairbanks, and the people are happy to share these pleasures of their early spring. Here is how one Fairbanksian describes these happenings:

> Mid-February is the time of the Yukon Quest International Sled Dog Race—the start and the finish alternate between Fairbanks and Whitehorse, Canada. [Fairbanks is the dog-mushing capital of Alaska.] Then, in late February, there is the week-long Festival of Native Arts at the University of Alaska. Mid-March brings the week-long Winter Carnival, featuring international ice-carving competitions, the Limited North American Sled Dog Championship Race, and other events such as just-for-fun stuff like the snowshoe race, businessmen's race, and parka parade (where you can see some incredible handmade traditional caribou/ermine/wolf parkas). The week culminates with the three-day Open North American Sled Dog Championship—a spring race that starts and finishes downtown and features the world's fastest sled dogs.
>
> This is when lots and lots of people come in from the villages and everyone piles up along Second Avenue to watch the races start. You can literally rub elbows with Native elders from Slana or Kotzebue, previous Iditarod and Quest champions, old friends you haven't seen for a year, tourists from Japan and New York—you name it!

And with all these events, there's the added wonder of the winter aurora borealis—or northern lights—and Fairbanks is one of the best places in the world to view this spectacular phenomenon. Late February through early April is also the time to "get out into the mountains" and ski, skijor, or dog-mush; the snow is good and the trails are, too. Cross-country skiers from other countries are taking to the Fairbanks hills in increasing numbers to train. Note: Bureau of Land Management and state park cabins are geared mainly to winter trail use. My friend recommends mid-March as a "wonderful time to visit—lots of sunshine and mild weather," she says.

Fairbanks summers can have lots of sunshine, too, and other warm-weather attractions. (I have been in Fairbanks in July when the temper-

ature was nearly 80 degrees Fahrenheit at 7 P.M., but remember, this is
Alaska, so don't count on finding the same!) There are beautiful rivers
that you can run from right downtown or from an easy bus ride away.
There are pleasant walks to take inside the city limits and fine hiking in
those hills not far away. There's an interesting museum and university
campus to visit, and a public bus system to get you there. There's a lot of
local history to explore from the ground, and a helpful Visitor Information Center to give you a hand in exploring it. And there is the Alaska
Public Lands Information Center to provide you with extensive outdoor
recreation information—videos, naturalist programs, etc. (See Useful
Names and Addresses, below, for both.)

Fairbanks is the hub of a network of roads that lead you to the
Yukon—and beyond, with the opening of the Dalton Highway, also
known as the Haul Road—and to other interesting and historical places.
Along the way, you will find outstanding parks and recreational areas to
visit, as well as some good camping. And, of course, Fairbanks is the
gateway to some of Alaska's most magnificent and remote wilderness,
both in the Interior and in the Arctic. From here, you can fly to takeoff
points for the Brooks Range, the Arctic National Wildlife Refuge, and—
to the west—Nome and Kotzebue and some unique and interesting units
of the National Park Service and the U.S. Fish and Wildlife Service.

Many visitors to Alaska see the state almost entirely from the air, with
twelve- to twenty-four-hour layovers arranged by tour operators in particular places selected for their tourist attractions—whether they be picturesque qualities, good accommodations, or something sensational like
the oil pipeline. Fairbanks is a principal depot for this kind of Alaska
sightseeing, and during the summer you will find it full of tourists. There
isn't a great deal in the way of tourist hot spots here. The usual routine
is to haul busloads of people out to Fox to see the pipeline firsthand, or
to take them to Alaskaland or a gold mining camp, or for a trip on the
riverboat *Discovery III* (see below). Then, the next day, the air tour begins, most likely to Nome, Kotzebue, Point Barrow, Deadhorse (where
the pipeline operation is shown off), and back. If your time is limited,
and you want this kind of overview, you might want to take advantage
of one of the tour packages that will give you such a bird's-eye view
(weather permitting) of the Interior and the Arctic. For this, see your
travel agent.

You might prefer to stay a few summer days on your own in this colorful frontier town. July is a good month to visit, weather-wise (see table
next page) and event-wise. The week-long Golden Days celebration (held
just after the middle of the month) sees many Fairbanksians dressed in
turn-of-the-century costumes to remember the era in which the town was

Average Temperature: Fairbanks

	Daytime High (F°)	Nighttime Low (F°)	Monthly Average (F°)
Jan.	−2.6	−20.7	−11.7
Feb.	7.7	−14.9	−3.6
March	22.2	−5.0	8.6
April	41.0	18.6	29.8
May	58.6	36.3	47.5
June	70.2	47.5	58.9
July	71.6	50.0	60.8
August	65.7	45.2	55.5
Sept.	54.1	34.9	44.5
Oct.	33.3	18.1	25.7
Nov.	11.0	−5.5	2.8
Dec.	−1.0	−17.5	−9.3

founded. Golden Days events include an air show; a "Grande Parade"; concerts in the park; a beard, mustache, and ("only in Fairbanks") hairy-leg contest; as well as a 17-mile foot race that begins with a rededication of the monument to Felix Pedro, the miner who discovered gold in the nearby hills and so initiated the gold rush that launched the town. (More gold was subsequently taken from the Tanana Valley than from the Yukon; see History, below.) Then, around the end of the month, the World Eskimo and Indian Olympics take place. This wonderful event includes a fascinating assortment of traditional Native sports, contests, and dances, and another fashion show of exquisite handmade parkas (Alaskans call them "parkys"). The Olympics not only are great fun but offer interesting insight into Native culture. If you happen to be nearby around this time of year, don't miss it. You can get information as to exact dates each year by contacting the *Fairbanks Visitor Information Center,* 550 First Avenue, Fairbanks, AK 99701; phone 456-5774 or 1-800-327-5774. See What to Do in Fairbanks on a Summer Visit, below, for further summer information.

However or whenever you visit Fairbanks, you can count on a unique experience; this small city can provide you with a dimension of Alaska that you won't find anywhere else.

History

The gently rolling hills that cup the Tanana Valley are clothed in places with aspen, birch, and spruce; in other places, lovely swards of tundra embroidered with tiny shrubs and flowering plants and berries cover the permafrosted ground. Some caribou still travel this country; wolves sing in the night. Bear, beaver, moose, muskrat, lynx, hare, and wolverine also inhabit this subarctic land. The rivers born in the nearby hills run clear, while those that reach from the Alaska Range may be thick with glacial silt; almost all of them carry fish. Along the rivers, shorebirds nest, and in the wetlands millions of wildfowl congregate.

While this land is far from the sea and its bounty—and the climate can be cruel—there is subsistence here for those ingenious and strong enough to take it, people such as the Athabascan Indians. Through many centuries, the Athabascans have hunted game, fished, and gathered the berries here, devising ways to survive in a demanding environment. Long ago they fashioned highly sophisticated traps and snares that enabled them to hunt "in absentia." They invented snowshoes to take them over the winter terrain and double parkas and jackets with separate hoods to protect them from the cold. They kept their history in elaborate songs and dances, and they explained the world about them and its mysteries in parables as well beloved and believed by them as those of the Bible. They exchanged stories (if not insults) with their different neighbors, the Eskimos. In their language, they spoke of themselves as *Dena,* which means "the people" or "us." Where the town of Fairbanks now spreads out was once part of their unboundaried land.

Fairbanks had its beginnings when Elbridge Truman Barnette decided in 1901 to establish a trading post at Tanacross, where the historic trail from Eagle to Valdez crossed the Tanana River. Barnette hoped to supply the sourdoughs who were flooding into the Interior in pursuit of gold. He ran into a series of accidents trying to get to Tanacross and ended up on the Chena River instead of the Tanana. When the river grew too shallow, he landed on what was described as "a high, dry bank with good timber for a cache and cabins." (This "high, dry bank" has since been all but drowned by the flooding Chena.)

Barnette intended to move his goods on to Tanacross until Felix Pedro discovered gold just 12 miles north of his cache in July 1902. Meantime, Barnette had promised his friend "Sunny Jim" Wickersham, the first district court judge of Alaska, that he would name his new trading post for Wickersham's political backer, United States Senator Charles W. Fairbanks (later Theodore Roosevelt's vice president). With gold at its doorsteps, Fairbanks came into being on the banks of the Chena. The next year, two more of Sunny Jim's political allies were immortalized in Fairbanks when two of the town's major streets were named for United States Representatives Lacy and Cushman. In 1904, Wickersham reciprocated in full; he officially moved his court from Eagle to Fairbanks, by then a booming mining town. (Barnette donated the land on which the new courthouse and jail were built; he also got a street named after him, and when a bridge was built from it across the Chena River, the foundation of his original cabin was unearthed.) This added stature and prestige to Fairbanks, recognizing not only that it was the major town in the Tanana Valley but that its founder, E. T. Barnette, had lots of political savvy. (Barnette, however, was forced to skip town only a few years later when the bank he founded went broke and the townspeople discovered he was an ex-convict and turned against him.)

Although Fairbanks was all but burned to the ground on May 22, 1906, rebuilding started the next day, and the local newspaper ran a headline that stated simply: "Fire Cannot Stop Fairbanks." This proved, indeed, to be true over and over again during the following decades; Fairbanks has had between twenty and thirty major fires during its lifetime.

Gold kept the town flourishing until the supply began to run out, and it was getting so low by the late teens that Fairbanks was on the verge of going ghost. (Nonetheless, more gold, over 7 million troy ounces, was taken out of the Fairbanks area than out of the Yukon.) But just in time to save things, the northern terminus of the Alaska Railroad was relocated to Fairbanks (from Nenana), and what would become the University of Alaska was established in College, just outside the town's boundary. The construction of the Alaska Railroad was completed in 1924, and Fairbanks became the major "port" serving the Interior. (Freight brought in by rail was shipped out on a network of rivers to nearby villages—and it still is.) However, by the time of World War II, Fairbanks still had only around two thousand residents, and the community welcomed the input of money and people brought by the location of two military installations nearby, Fort Wainwright and Eielson Air Force Base—formerly Ladd Field.

The building of the Trans-Alaska Pipeline, however, was what brought Fairbanks the biggest infusion of people, money—and problems—that it has had in its history to date. Between 1973 and 1977, Fairbanks became a principal gateway to the North Slope, and a boom city to end all boom cities, as material and pipeline workers flooded in and out, all but bursting the seams of the community. Every room in town (and every tent site) was occupied; there were waiting lines in every supermarket; prices soared; and traffic became gelatinous in a town where traffic jams had once been laughed at. The smog, already a problem, grew worse and worse, especially on cold winter mornings when thousands of cars warmed up their motors and poured their carbon monoxide out into the dense, heavy air. Some of the true Alaskans living in Fairbanks wondered what had become of their cherished way of life.

However, with the pipeline completed and in operation, Fairbanks has returned somewhat to its older ways, and the Yellow Pages of the phone book no longer feature ads for Las Vegas casinos. The city is larger now, older and perhaps wiser, but it is still looking to see another boom take shape in its future.

What to Do in Fairbanks on a Summer Visit

On a warm summer day it is most pleasant to stroll along the streets of Fairbanks. This is a compact, low-rise small city with many of its older buildings still standing to tell of its history. If you start your walk at the Fairbanks Visitor Information Center (Log Cabin) on First Avenue, on the banks of the Chena River, you can pick up a city map, bus schedule, and a copy of the *Fairbanks Walking Tour.* This excellent booklet tells you how to find the most interesting sights and buildings and what their stories are. The Cushman Street bridge across the Chena, by the way, is close to the site of Barnette's first landing.

A walk across this bridge will take you to the *Fairbanks Daily News Miner* building; this newspaper is the oldest institution in Fairbanks, having been published continuously since 1903, when its founder, W. F. Thompson, arrived to "engage in the dissemination of well-known truth." Enjoy the flowers blooming in front of this building and elsewhere, and note the story-high delphiniums that grow around town.

Near the *News Miner* building is the Alaska Railroad station, where you can pick up a schedule if you need one. Directly across from the station is the **Northern Alaska Environmental Center** (218 Driveway Street; phone 452-5021), housed in a small, old-fashioned cottage; it is well worth a visit. (Outdoor travelers please take note, however: there are not facilities here; no place to pitch a tent, no showers, and so on.) Along with getting an upgrade on current environmental endeavors in this part of Alaska, you may also be able to buy birch baskets and T-shirts here (sold as fund raisers), and perhaps authentic Native smoked salmon. You may also want to inquire about wilderness trips being run by the center or about local wilderness guides.

Back across the bridge in downtown Fairbanks, you can visit the **Alaska Public Lands Information Center,** at the corner of Cushman and Third (phone 456-0527). This fills nicely a long-felt need for having the public lands agencies in Fairbanks—National Park Service, Bureau of Land Management (BLM), U.S. Fish and Wildlife Service, and Alaska State Parks—under one roof. (Several other state agencies and the U.S. Geological Survey and USDA Forest Service are also represented.) The Alaska Public Lands Information Center offers daily interpretive programs and films and videos during the summer. Inquire at the Fairbanks Visitor Information Center (see page 324) for the current location of the

Dog Mushing Museum, with its unique and fascinating displays and programs (plus a one-of-a-kind gift shop). It is worth noting that in 1967 all of Fairbanks, including this part of it, was several feet under water when the Chena River flooded.

A short bus trip (better check routes) will take you to what was once Creamer's Dairy and is now a migratory waterfowl refuge administered by the Alaska Department of Fish and Game. There is a nearly 2-mile nature path there that can give you an excellent overview—in miniature—of the typical habitats of the Interior, from floodplain to woodland to bog, seasonal stream and pond to upland forest, thermokarst pond, and tussock meadow. You can even see ice-wedge polygons. The Alaska Fish and Game people have a good descriptive folder that serves as a guide keyed to the signposts along the trail. From late April through early to mid-May, this is one of the best places around to birdwatch. You can expect to see sandhill cranes, trumpeter swans, white-fronted geese, many different ducks, and so on in some quite spectacular migratory shows. There may be many thousands of birds here at a time. Well over a hundred different species have been recorded as visitors to or residents of this particular refuge. The Creamer's Field Nature Path, incidentally, is used by cross-country skiers in winter as well as by joggers in the summer. Directly across the street from Creamer's Field there is a borough park where you may be able to see beavers or muskrats—a good place to take a sandwich for lunch.

Continue out College Road (you can take the same bus) and you'll come to the University of Alaska (more colorful gardens to see). There is another opportunity here to take a short hike or do some more birdwatching at the right time of year. The Experimental Farm lands are heavily used by migratory birds, especially in summer and early fall. There is also a loop trail system that can give you a look at the pleasant countryside surrounding the campus. You can inquire at the University of Alaska Museum for directions (see below), and, while you're there, pick up checklists of Alaska birds and mammals.

The university buildings are also interesting. The Alaska State Constitution—an important step toward statehood—was drafted and signed in 1956 in one of them, Constitution Hall, and the museum has some interesting displays, although you might have to share the space with busloads of tourists trying to see them. Note the huge copper nugget in the lobby, the good array of Alaska's large mammals, and the only confirmed meteorite in Alaska (which resembles a small ham in size and shape, weighs 58 pounds, and was found near Council on the Seward Peninsula). The university, described by one of its faculty as a "fantastic cultural small town," is the site of important wildlife and geophysical research.

If it's a clear day when you're at the university, be sure to look just to the west of south for Mount McKinley; it can be seen from the ridge at the west end of the campus. (McKinley, some 160 miles away, is actually below the horizon; however, because of the angle of refraction occasioned by the latitude, and sometimes intensified by the cold, the light rays can bend in such a manner as to give you a splendid view of this magnificent mountain. Small wonder that the locals who made the first ascent of its north peak in 1910 waved a flag from the top to let their friends back home know where they were!) The mountains closer by to the south are Mounts Hayes, Deborah, and Hess; all are over-12,000-foot giants of the Alaska Range. Mount Hayes is actually 13,700 feet high.

Starting from downtown, you can also travel by bus to Alaskaland, a sort of fairground of the state's centennial celebration (also flooded in 1967). Here you can see the restored riverboat, *Nenana,* one of the largest—if not the largest—of the Interior stern-wheelers; it is on the National Register of Historic Sites. There is also a "Native Village" and a small museum. This is a major tourist attraction these days. (If you're interested, you can also take a boat ride down the Chena River in an operative stern-wheeler, the *Discovery III,* which is berthed off of Davis Road near the airport (see below).

If you'd like to take a local excursion by bike or by canoe or kayak out of downtown Fairbanks, this is perfectly possible; for information, visit the **Alaska Public Lands Information Center** at 250 Cushman, or the **Fairbanks Visitor Information Center** at 550 First Avenue.

Hiking

If the weather's nice when you're in Fairbanks and you like to walk, there are a number of pleasant local strolls to take. Already mentioned are the *Fairbanks Walking Tour,* which will take you around the downtown area; the Creamer's Field Nature Path on College Road; and the loop trail on the university campus. Some of the cross-country ski trails offer good hiking and jogging; ask at the Alaska Public Lands Information Center for directions and other suggestions (see above).

Farther afield, there is some excellent hiking. The Chena River State Recreation Area has many miles of hiking opportunities and offers a good overview of the Interior countryside, from beaver-occupied sloughs to mature spruce forests. A day trip up Granite Tors will give you a nice workout. Ask the Alaska Public Lands Information Center people for details.

The BLM administers some good hiking country in the area. Between Fairbanks and Livengood on the Elliott Highway (which becomes the

Dalton Highway), there is a trail system that leads from the highway into the 1-million-acre White Mountains National Recreation Area. The 20-mile Summit Trail, for instance, starts at Mile 28 and heads eastward over Wickersham Dome. (A hike to the dome itself makes a pleasant four-hour round-trip circuit from the road.) There are a few good scrambles and switchbacks up the steeper slopes. Although water may be available, the BLM advises either carrying your own or boiling (or chemically treating) water from streams or lakes. On this and other hikes, remember to pack out what you pack in and to treat the tundra gently. Note: There is an extensive winter trail system with strategically placed cabins in the White Mountains Recreation Area. Good in late winter and early spring.

The BLM also administers the Pinnell Mountain National Recreation Trail. (It is one of twenty-two trails so designated in the United States.) This is a 27-mile alpine trail that traverses ridge tops around the 3,500-foot level. It is rugged in places and steep, but it offers some fine views of the Alaska Range on the south and the Yukon Flats and Brooks Range to the north, and the hiking through the tundra country is excellent. (This is one of the few places where you might see nesting surfbirds.) From mid-June to mid-July, the wildflowers are gorgeous. This is also a good trail to take around midnight between June 18 and June 25; then the midnight sun is visible from many high points. During this week, you can also see the midnight sun from the Eagle Summit trailhead parking lot. There are trailheads for the Pinnell Mountain Trail at Mile 85.6 and Mile 107.3 (Eagle Summit) on the Steese Highway. You may want to make a short hike from either trailhead, or both, and return to your car, or you could arrange a shuttle or a pickup. Water is scarce along the way, so be sure to carry a full canteen. Refer to the Alaska Public Lands Information Center for further information (see below). (Remember that the protozoan *Giardia lamblia* is present in many Alaskan watersheds; do not drink stream water without boiling it for five minutes or filtering it.)

Small Boating

Fairbanks is the gateway to several accessible rivers that are excellent for river running. You might want to check with the local sporting goods stores for good firsthand information about nearby small-boating opportunities. Or talk to the people in the Alaska Public Lands Information Center (see below); they can give you details about the Tanana, Fortymile, Chena, and Chatanika Rivers, and about Birch Creek and Beaver Creek—all easy-to-reach and locally popular streams. You might also ask about the Delta and Gulkana Rivers.

Driving

Pay attention to any sign that says "DIP." Because Interior roads are frequently constructed on permafrost, there may be massive cave-ins when ice lenses melt because their cover has been removed. (See Permafrost, in Part I.)

If you're traveling to Circle, you'll take the Steese Highway; to Livengood, you'll take the Elliott Highway; to Eagle, you'll pick up the Taylor Highway at Tetlin Junction (off the Alaska Highway). These three historic highways will be more interesting to you if you can get one of the BLM folders, which give good background and describe points of interest along the roads. (They have many points of interest: for example, the Steese Highway has numerous historical sites as well as a National Aeronautics and Space Administration satellite tracking facility alongside it that is open to the public at selected hours—ask when at the Fairbanks Visitor Information Center (see below); the Trans-Alaska Pipeline System (TAPS) parallels the Elliott Highway; the Taylor Highway provides ready access to running the Fortymile River.) Write the Alaska Lands Information Center (see below) to obtain the latest information on these highways. (The BLM puts out some good brochures.)

The Dalton Highway (also known as the Haul Road) cuts between the Gates of the Arctic National Park and the Arctic National Wildlife Refuge, paralleling the Trans-Alaska Pipeline and thus slicing through some of Alaska's most beautiful and vulnerable wilderness. It is possible for commercial vehicles, including tour buses, to drive the 304 miles from the Yukon River crossing (the river is spanned by a 2,290-foot-long bridge with a 6 percent grade—the only bridge across the Yukon) to Prudhoe Bay. Private vehicles can now legally drive to Deadhorse (Mile 414), but not to the Arctic Ocean. If you are determined to see the ocean or want a tour of the Alaskan oil fields, Gray Line of Alaska has a three-day, two-night tour out of Anchorage or Fairbanks (you fly back), called the North Slope Explorer. You spend the first night at Coldfoot, the second in Deadhorse. Sleeping quarters are big trailers recycled from the building of the pipeline. But be warned. The Brooks Range is often socked in with rain or fog in the summer, making for muddy bus windows and chancy scenery and wildlife viewing. For information write: *Gray Line of Alaska,* 300 Elliott Avenue West, Seattle, WA 98119; phone 1-800-628-2449. (There are a couple of tours operated by hotels in Deadhorse. One is *Prudhoe Bay Hotel Tours;* phone 659-2449.)

A road from Fairbanks to the Arctic Ocean may sound enticing, but its 500-plus miles run through unstable and fragile terrain that is subject to extremes of ice and permafrost action; there can be many huge holes and ruts when the ice melts in summer. Maintenance is not only extremely difficult but enormously costly; at present it is minimal. Added to this, the Arctic weather is capricious and can change rapidly; heavy dust can turn to deep and slippery mud with dangerous speed. There are also eighteen-wheel trucks and trailers, pickups, and tour buses barreling along this rough road, spraying windshield-cracking gravel and blinding dust as they go by. And there is only one campground, operated by BLM at Marion Creek (Mile 180), and only one service facility north of the Yukon, at Coldfoot, where the buses stop for the night. Enough tourists come through that there is also a tri-agency (BLM, National Park Service, and U.S. Fish and Wildlife Service) Visitor Center at Coldfoot.

Unfortunately, the state of Alaska not only controls the Dalton Highway but has selected key portions of the Pipeline Corridor (such as the area around Coldfoot) as part of its entitlement. It is the state that is pushing hardest to develop this part of Alaska and "open it up," despite the fragility of the terrain, the relentless weather, and the tremendous pressure this would put on the already beleaguered wildlife. State plans call for some curbs on future development, thankfully. The state wants to limit it to five areas along the Pipeline Corridor; no vehicles will be permitted off the road for 5 miles on either side of the highway, beginning at the Yukon River, and only bow and arrow hunting will be allowed in this area.

Biking

The city of Fairbanks has numerous bicycle trails that you can find on the map you get at the Fairbanks Visitor Information Center (see below). Of particular interest is the trip around Farmer's Loop, which is extensive enough to give you a good overview of the community and its surroundings. You can also take bike trips on the Steese and Elliott Highways, as well as on the Taylor (if you don't mind the traffic you'll encounter on the Alaska Highway getting to Tetlin Junction). Be advised that these roads are mostly gravel. The Tanana Valley State Forest road system (some 150 miles of logging roads) offers mountain bikers some interesting riding. A Fairbanks friend of mine notes: "They [the roads] can give you an intimate feel for the boreal forest system." But watch out for logging trucks! The Alaska Public Lands Information Center (see below) has complete information on the forest roads and other recreational opportunities in the state forest.

Miscellaneous

You can take a 20-mile stern-wheeler trip on the *Discovery III,* one of the last operative stern-wheelers in Alaska. The riverboat carries nine hundred people and travels the Chena River into the Tanana and back at least once a day from June 1 through September. Call 479-6673 for details about sailing.

The University of Alaska Museum is located on the upper campus and is open year-round. You can take a bus to the Wood Center and thence take the shuttle to the museum. Or you can go from the Wood Center to the museum on foot; it's a pleasant campus walk. You may see Denali (Mount McKinley) en route.

Some Useful Information About Fairbanks

Zip codes: as listed. Area code: 907.

Hotels

There are more than two dozen overnight accommodations—hotels and motels, that is—in Fairbanks, plus literally dozens of bed and breakfasts. You can telephone or write ahead to the *Fairbanks Visitor Information Center,* 550 First Avenue, Fairbanks, AK 99701; phone 456-5774 or 1-800-323-5774. Note: Most of Fairbank's larger hotels are on the tourist circuit.

If you're traveling with a family—or another congenial couple or two—you might want to try the *Wedgewood Resort,* 212 Wedgewood Drive, Fairbanks, AK 99701; phone 452-1442. It is not cheap, but not expensive either, and you can get a full-sized apartment with cooking facilities. Two restaurants, and gift shop open in summer. Comfortable and quiet. Bus runs to the door. If you find yourself stuck for a place to stay, try the *Golden North Motel,* 4880 Old Airport Road, Fairbanks, AK 99709; phone 479-6201. Touristy and not too quiet, but they may be able to take you when other places are full.

There are two locally favored out-of-town resorts: *Ester Gold Camp:* Ester, AK 99725; phone 479-2500. Good if you have a car and want an "Alaskan" atmosphere. Close to town and reasonable, but summers only. *Chena Hot Springs Resort:* If you're driving or biking and don't mind traveling about 60 miles out of town, this has a hot swimming pool, a lodge or cabin (and camping) facilities, and, in winter, excellent cross-country skiing. Open year-round. Write Box 73440, Fairbanks, AK 99707; phone 452-7867.

Campgrounds

As of this writing, public campgrounds in Fairbanks are limited; the Chena River State Recreation Site, on University Avenue, is the principal one—inquire at the Alaska Public Lands Information Center (see below). There is a fee. The borough runs a nearby inexpensive campground 2 miles south of North Pole at the *Chena Lakes Recreation Area.* There's lots of campground space (five-day limit), rest rooms, fire enclosures, fishing, swimming, and nonmotorized boating; phone 488-1655. Alaska State Parks also has two campgrounds close to town, both on the Elliott Highway: *Olnes Pond* at Mile 10.5 and *Whitefish Campground* at Mile 11. Phone Alaska State Parks (see below) or the Alaska Public Lands Information Center (see below) for information.

There is also the *Harding Lake Recreation Area* out of North Pole at Mile 42 on the Richardson Highway. This has water and rest rooms (is heavily used locally) and is developed for car and trailer camping. Harding Lake, incidentally, poses a few problems because it has no outlet and therefore limited drainage.

If you have wheels, there are three state park campgrounds within a reasonable distance. One is *Harding Lake* (see above). The *Chena River Recreation Area,* which takes in some 254,000 acres of land, lies between Mile 26 and Mile 52 of the Chena Hot Springs Road. There are several developed campgrounds and many places to camp on river bars and so forth, and there are many picnic tables. Fine hiking and some river running too. You can hike here to a tundra ridge exhibiting dozens of spikelike granite monoliths called "tors." These make for a remarkable sight, especially in moonlight. The *Chatanika River Wayside* at Mile 39 on the Steese Highway has water and rest rooms. Pets are welcome. For all state park campgrounds, phone *Alaska State Parks* at 451-2695.

The BLM has a campground at *Cripple Creek,* Mile 60 on the Steese Highway.

You can pick up a list of private campgrounds at the Visitor Information Center in downtown Fairbanks (see below). Most of these are geared to take care of trailers and RVs as well as tents.

Showers

Norlite Campground, Mile ¼, Peger Road (phone 474-0206). *Monson Motel Campground,* 1321 Karen Way (phone 479-6770), is year-round. *Tanana Valley Campground,* Mile 2, College Road (phone 456-7956), is accessible by bus. These are all privately run campgrounds; consult the Fairbanks Visitor Information Center (see below) for others. Shower, sauna, and swim are available at the *University of Alaska. Mary Siah Recreation Center,* located at Gillam and Fourteenth (next to Ryan Junior High School and Hering Auditorium), has showers. Showers are also available at many laundromats, since many Fairbankians have no running water, another unique aspect of Fairbanks life.

Car Rental

Avis: International Airport; phone 474-0900 or 1-800-331-1212. *Payless:* International Airport; phone 474-0177 or 1-800-237-2804. Free pickup and return. *Hertz* (two locations): International Airport, and Airport Road and Stacia; phone 452-4444 or 1-800-654-8200. *Rent-A-Wreck:* 2105 Cushman; phone 452-1606 or 1-800-478-1606. Free pickup and delivery.

Youth Hostels

Fairbanks International Youth Hostel: This northernmost hostel in the United States is searching for a new facility as of this writing; phone 457-6551 for information. Other hostels in Fairbanks (not official International Youth Hostels) include: *Grandma Shirley's,* 510 Dunbar Street, Fairbanks, AK 99701; phone 451-9816. *Northwoods Lodge,* Box 83615, Fairbanks, AK 99708; phone 479-5300 or (only in Alaska) 1-800-478-5305. *Alaska Heritage Inn* (also a B&B), 1018 Twenty-Second Avenue, Fairbanks, AK 99701; phone 451-6587. *Billy's Backpackers Hostel,* 2895 Mack Boulevard, Fairbanks, AK 99709; phone 457-2034. *Traveler's Hostel,* 1315 Sixth Avenue, Fairbanks, AK 99701; phone 452-5787.

Air Service

Frontier Flying Service, 3820 University Avenue, Fairbanks, AK 99709; phone 474-0014. Serves Bettles, Anaktuvak Pass, Kaktovik, and other points in the Brooks Range. Inquire at Fairbanks Visitor Information Center (see below) for other air carriers and air charters.

Laundromats

There are laundromats at the private campgrounds listed under Showers (see above). Check with the Fairbanks Visitor Information Center (phone 456-5774) for others and for dry cleaners.

Wilderness Guides

There are numerous wilderness guides (for all types of outdoor activities) and outfitters in Fairbanks. Check with the Fairbanks Visitor Information Center, the Alaska Public Lands Information Center, or the Northern Alaska Environmental Center (see below for all).

Useful Names and Addresses

For information regarding all Interior public parklands—*National Park Service, U.S. Fish and Wildlife Service, Bureau of Land Management, State of Alaska*—contact the *Alaska Public Lands Information Center,* 250 Cushman Street, Fairbanks, AK 99701; phone 456-0527. *Alaska State Department of Fish and Game,* 1300 College Road, Fairbanks, AK 99701; phone 459-7200. *Northern Alaska Environmental Center,* 218

Driveway, Fairbanks, AK 99701; phone 452-5021. Open 9 A.M. to 5 P.M. Monday through Friday. *Fairbanks Visitor Information Center,* 550 First Avenue, Fairbanks, AK 99701; phone 456-5774 or 456-INFO (for recorded information on local events); from out of state, phone 1-800-327-5774.

52. Denali National Park and Preserve

In a land of superlatives, it is hard—especially for an observer who loves it all—to single out any one place or any one mountain as being "the very most." But anyone who has seen Mount McKinley in all its snow-shining glory—perhaps rose-colored in early dawn, or stained with blue evening shadows—will probably remember it forever as "The High One." Surely, any viewer will be grateful to see one of the grand sights of the planet, a mountain that rises higher than any other anywhere from the land at its feet to become the summit of a continent. As Charles Sheldon put it so simply after first seeing McKinley in July of 1906, "I can never forget my sensations at the sight. No description could convey any suggestion of it."

A few statistics, however, can help give a small idea of the impressiveness of this snowy mountain massif, which with its "foothills"—those over 10,000 feet, that is—occupies an area approximately 70 miles long and 10 miles wide. Standing 20,320 feet above sea level, the peak of this massif is nearly 4 miles high. Since it rises from a fairly level elevation of a little over 2,000 feet, you see this magnificent mountain occupying some 18,000 feet—well over 3 miles—of sky. In contrast, Mount Everest, the highest peak on earth, has its summit 29,028 feet above sea level, but it rises only 11,000 feet above the Tibetan Plateau.

What makes the McKinley group so high? Geologists explain that the rocks of the area are relatively lightweight (think of them as floating on the earth's mantle) and so are being shoved against one another and piled

Mount McKinley: Denali National Park. Source: Yvonne Mozée.

higher and higher as a result of the Pacific plate being pulled beneath the North American plate in this general region. Geologists add that there could also be another reason for this tremendous uplift: earthquakes and other evidence from local faulting suggest that the boundary of the Pacific plate, delineated by the Denali fault, makes an abrupt turn southward in the region of McKinley. This could serve to concentrate its thrust in a northwest direction. (*A Geologic Guide to Mount McKinley National Park,* by Wyatt G. Gilbert, is recommended reading; see Suggested Reading.)

The height of the mountain, however, is only one of a number of interesting geological features in Denali National Park. The Denali fault system, which is in fact the largest crack in the crust of the North American continent, slices through the park, separating the oldest rocks in Alaska (roughly to the northwest) from the much younger rocks of the Alaska Range. Thus you can see here a great spectrum of Alaska's "recorded" geology.

The range, of course, acts as an enormous barrier between Southcentral and Interior Alaska, and while the Interior was largely ice-free during the last periods of glaciation, a fine glacial system remains on the mountains around McKinley to remind you of how things once were over vast reaches of this countryside.

As though the sheer size and snowy splendor of the McKinley massif were not enough to bedazzle the viewer of this continental phenomenon, many of the older foothills that guard the giant are gorgeously colored. Some vistas look as though a great painter had created a giant mural using every shade of the rainbow—Polychrome Pass is aptly named. A flyover of the park reveals even more striking scenes, for glaciers make fascinating patterns as they actively sculpt this colorful land. Add to this a gentle-looking green cloak of tundra above the tree line, which occurs here at about 2,700 feet. This high, dry tundra makes for delightful hiking, and you can find myriad flowering plants, including dwarf dogwood and tapestries of dryas stitching down the thin layer of soil. (In other parts of the park, the moist tundra has unfortunately clumped itself into the miserable kind of tussocky terrain that is very hard to hike over.)

This is taiga country, and the conifers—the ubiquitous white spruce and black spruce—grow most often in mixed stands with aspen, paper birch, and—in the wetter places—cottonwood. In the light summer breezes, the leaves of these deciduous trees turn and twinkle to catch the soft, slanting light. Along the gravel streambeds cut by the fiercely flowing glacial rivers, the broadleaf trees can grow in pure stands, colonizing the new rough terrain and adding color to the autumn hues. Underfoot, the floors of the sparse forests are often tufted with mosses and lichens.

In this world of extraordinary terrain and frigid subarctic weather, some 37 species of mammals manage to survive, and the count of bird species that use Denali Park totals 157. As the National Park Service notes, cold-blooded reptiles and amphibians can hardly be expected to live happily here (or most other places in Alaska), but one—the wood frog—has succeeding in thriving despite the overwhelming odds against it.

The mountain we call McKinley was viewed in awe by untold generations of Athabascan Indians, who named it Denali, "The High One," but it was first described to the Outside world by a prospector, William A. Dickey, in 1897. Dickey, who was a Princeton graduate, wrote an article for a New York newspaper describing what he correctly identified as the highest peak in North America: ". . . never before," he wrote, "had we seen anything to compare with this mountain." He christened it in honor of William McKinley, who would shortly be elected president of the United States. Five years later, Alfred Hulse Brooks helped survey and map Mount McKinley for the U.S. Geological Survey, and he is credited with being the first white man to venture onto its slopes. He didn't get too far, however, for he wrote that he was ". . . satisfied to have been able to traverse the great lowland to the base and to climb the foothills." It remained for four Fairbanks sourdoughs to make the first successful ascent of the mountain, in 1910; two of their party reached the north (and, at 19,470 feet, the lower) summit, and there they planted the spruce flagpole they had hauled up with them. The flag fluttering from this pole was supposed to alert their friends in Fairbanks—some 160 miles away—that they had made it to the top. Three years later, the south summit was conquered, and, since then, the mountain has been climbed perhaps too often, if the litter left on its slopes is any indication. Early mountaineering parties often used dog teams to get their equipment partway up the giant mountain, until the use of small ski-equipped aircraft became common. Now the parties that get routinely landed on the Kahiltna Glacier might consider what those first climbers went through; how they forded the glacial streams, which, in summer, can rise 4 or 5 feet in a matter of hours, made their way through thickets of brush, across tundra slopes, and onto the snow before they ever really started to climb. Tough folks, those early sourdoughs, who made it to the top in their old clothes, without oxygen, without freeze-dried food, without anything, really, but true grit.

Like many other Alaska places, Denali has had its special advocates, the first one being Charles Sheldon, who discovered this country soon after the turn of the century. An influential member of New York's Boone and Crockett Club, Sheldon spent several years studying the wildlife of the Denali region and led in the effort to gain establishment of Denali as a national park. The establishment of this park is one of the few in history that had the support of the mining community; since there was gold in the Kantishna Hills, to the northwest of the mountain, and a park road would provide ready access to the precious metal, the sourdoughs joined the ranks of park proponents and helped win the park. (In return, mining was permitted inside the park until only recently.) The 90-mile road remains—providing access to a key section of the park. In February 1917, President Woodrow Wilson signed the act establishing the original 1,989,493-acre McKinley National Park. That act left out half the mountain massif as well as important wildlife terrain; in 1980, Congress enlarged the park by 2,426,000 acres, rechristened it Denali National Park, and created an adjacent 1,330,000-acre Denali National Preserve. (The total acreage of the Denali parklands comes to about 6 million.) Thus the name *Denali* (recognizing the aptness of its Athabascan origins) took the place, at long last, of William McKinley, a president from Ohio who never lived to see the mountain. (To date, Congress has not changed the name of the mountain itself.)

Some Useful Information About Denali

Zip code: 99755. Area code: 907.

How to Get There

This is the most accessible unit of the national parks and preserves in Alaska. In summer, you can drive, take the train, or bike to the eastern entrance of the park. From Anchorage (to the south), it is 240 miles and takes about six hours to drive. From Fairbanks, about 120 miles away to the north, it takes closer to three. Buses serve the park from Anchorage and Fairbanks, and there is also air service by small plane. Numerous tours of the park are available; the *Alaska Travel Planner* (see Suggested Reading) gives listings. Note: To protect the wildlife and other wilderness values of the park, private vehicles are not to be driven beyond Savage River (Mile 12) on the Park Road unless they are going—by reservation only—to campsites or "inheld" facilities (see below). Year-round, the *Alaska Railroad* runs to the eastern park entrance from Fairbanks and Anchorage.

Where to Stay

In summer, there are several tourist-serving hotels as well as restaurant facilities, a pizza parlor, a grocery store, a service station, and so on at the entrance to the park. The Denali National Park Hotel is large and well run. Write ahead for reservations, as this facility is heavily used by organized tour groups: *Denali Park Resorts,* 241 West Ship Creek Avenue, Anchorage, AK 99501; phone 276-7234 or 1-800-622-7275. (There are also several restaurants and sleeping accommodations along the highway close to the park.)

There are two inholdings in the park where you can stay. One is at Kantishna, formerly the principal mining area in the region. (Kantishna was the operation that inspired early miners to favor a national park—with a road that would access their digs.) This resort has cabins and a lodge built on old—and patented—mining claims. I stay at the other place if I can—at *Camp Denali* or its sister facility, *Northface Lodge.* Camp Denali was founded after World War II by two women pilots who had ferried bombers to Alaska for transfer to Russia (Women's Auxiliary Air Corp pilots, or WAACs, were not allowed to fly out of the country!). Celia Hunter and Ginny Wood all but built the camp with their own hands outside the then-park, but close to its boundary. It is still much as they designed it, with cabins that have superlative views of Mount McKinley (when it's out, that is). These are worth staying in for their Alaskan mystique if for nothing else: the cabins have no electricity and their "running" water is supplied by a diverted stream, but they are extremely comfortable and cozy. There's a spacious dining room, a lodge for talks and reading, and a laundry and bath facility (with hot-water showers). Most importantly, Wally and Jerri Cole, the second and present owners of Camp Denali, make a wonderful host and hostess: they stress the values of the wilderness and offer excellent interpretive programs to their guests. They also run the nearby Northface Lodge, which does have more conventional baths with all the rooms. Guests at either place share in the programs, the good baked foods that the Coles produce, and grand meals (there are separate kitchens). A stay with the Coles will almost certainly give you an unforgettable Alaskan experience. The Coles meet the train at the park entrance several times a week, so you have your own wildlife tour en route to your accommodations. Be sure to get your reservations well ahead as these are among Alaska's most popular lodges. Address *Wallace Cole,* Box 67, Denali National Park; phone (summer) 683-2290; in winter, write Box 216, Cornish, NH 03746.

There are a half dozen National Park Service campgrounds located along the Park Road as follows: *Riley Creek,* at the eastern entrance to the park (large); *Savage River,* at Mile 12 on the Park Road (large); *Sanctuary River,* at Mile 22 (small); *Teklanika River,* at Mile 28 (large); *Igloo Creek,* at Mile 33 (small); *Wonder Lake,* at Mile 85, tent camping only (backpackers like to spend their first night here).

The National Park Service runs a scheduled shuttle bus service to these campgrounds and to other points of interest along the Park Road. As stated, private vehicles may travel the Park Road beyond Savage River only for campground access to the campsites at Teklanika. Beyond Savage, you must take the shuttle bus. For information about these shuttle buses, campground reservations, and fees, phone *Denali Park Resorts* at 272-7275 or 1-800-622-7275 (address above). If you have extra time, or if you are unable to get shuttle bus tickets, an inexpensive guide to the nature trails around the entrance area is *The Nature of Denali* by Sheri Forbes. You should be able to get it in the Visitor Information Center bookshop.

Backpackers will find many wonderful places to pitch their tents in the wilder regions of this great park. The shuttle bus will drop you at the place of your choice and stop to pick you up along the road when flagged. Discuss with park rangers the kind of itinerary you may want to follow.

How to Enjoy Denali

Denali Park offers some of the finest—and most available—opportunities for wildlife viewing in Alaska. The concessionaire runs a bus tour every day, starting very early, from late spring to early fall (you get a box lunch for the price of the tour; phone *Denali Park Resorts* at 272-7275 or 1-800-622-7275 (address above) for information and reservations. The National Park Service shuttle (which is not so plush) regularly travels the length of the Park Road. (You bring your own lunch for this one.) Seated in either of these vehicles on a routine early morning foray, you can expect to see creatures such as Dall sheep, their delicate creamy silhouettes delineated clearly against the dark foothills of the Alaska Range. You may pass by a grizzly sow with her cub, munching away on berries and unmindful of your presence. Caribou may lift their elegant racks from the green brush or tundra or trot across the uneven ground with their heads held high. (I was once traveling in a shuttle bus along the Park Road when we overtook a caribou jogging down the middle of the road. The animal kept ahead of us for several minutes, and several hundred yards, with everybody aboard madly snapping pictures of its rear end, before he figured out what the monster was behind him. I have also seen a wolf race across the Park Road—dark, sleek, and strong—the epitome of wildness.) And, finally, the little ground squirrels will almost certainly charm you as they sit up perkily in front of their burrows, ready for their instant disappearing act.

If you stop to snack at Polychrome Pass or go on to Eielson Visitor Center (Mile 53 on the Park Road) to lunch, a mew gull may try for a share of your food. It could even be a bird that you've seen before, close to your home—if you live along the Pacific flyway, that is. (Note: Please do not feed these birds—or any other wildlife in the park.) You may also hope to see a long-tailed jaeger, which winters in Japan; an American golden-plover, which winters in the Argentine pampas; an Arctic tern, which may commute from Antarctica; or a northern wheatear or Arctic warbler, which will take to the air for Asia when the weather begins to turn cold.

Keep in mind, however, that—as one longtime lover of and frequent visitor to the park once told a disappointed tourist—"This ain't no zoo." You could be lucky and see just about all the birds and animals mentioned above, and more, in a single morning's outing, but you might only get a glimpse of one or two.

The same, of course, goes for the mountain. If it's "out" the day you set aside to view it, count yourself fortunate indeed; you will see an unforgettable sight. If it's cloud-shrouded, enjoy the rest of the scene (which is gorgeous, no matter what the weather) and try again some other time for your revelation of "The High One."

You can also take day hikes in Denali National Park, utilizing the shuttle bus for your transportation. Or you can backpack in to the park's backcountry. Park rangers can give you a good idea of how to work out the kind of foot travel you have in mind to your best advantage. Note: The shuttle bus travel is (very properly) limited; you may have to wait to use it. Backpacking is likewise, and requires a permit. Inquire at the Visitor Center (crowded) at the entrance to the park.

The rivers in Denali Park are frequently shallow, heavily braided, and very fast-flowing glacial streams—not suitable for pleasant river-running. There is, however, a commercially operated raft trip that you can take down the Nenana River for a short run from the park. Contact Denali National Park (see below).

Comments

For many years, park lovers fought to keep the commercialism of this national park to a minimum: they managed to stop the building of a hotel on the fragile tundra near Wonder Lake (where sewage alone would have posed an unbelievably complex problem), and they managed to gain expansion of the park to preserve some of its principal wildlife and scenic values. As of this writing, however, the park has been managed to accommodate tourism; more than half a million people crowd into it each summer. While access to the Park Road is limited for private cars, buses run up and down the narrow dirt (and dusty) road constantly. People who cannot get on a bus have the option of a flyover in a helicopter. Outside park boundaries, in the preserve, snowmobiling and sports hunting are legal and continue to the border. Not surprisingly, the marvelous wildlife of Denali is being increasingly pressured. Furthermore, the park experience itself is impacted. And there are even more pressures from the state to make the Park Road a loop (tying into the old Stampede Road and its northern boundary) and open it to all traffic. The irreplaceable values of Denali Park should be recognized and honored; this park needs help.

For further information about Denali Park or to register for campsites, write: Superintendent, *Denali National Park,* Box 9, Denali Park, AK 99755; phone 683-2294. Or contact the *Alaska Public Lands Information Center* in Anchorage (605 West Fourth Avenue, Anchorage, AK 99501; phone 271-2737) or Fairbanks (250 Cushman Street, Fairbanks, AK 99701; phone 456-0527).

The late Adolph Murie, another man who gave so much of his life, intellect, and devotion to the Denali wilderness and wildlife, summed up some of the essence of this area and its incalculable value:

> The grizzly has survived in only a few states, more by accident than by our planning for his future. In Alaska we have a great opportunity for giving the grizzly and the rest of the fauna ample room for carrying on their living in a natural, free man-

ner. The grizzly needs extensive wilderness country for his way of life, and wild country is also vital for the highest development of human culture. If we provide for the future of the grizzly, we at the same time provide wilderness for our own needs.

53. Yukon-Charley Rivers National Preserve

The Yukon is one of the great rivers of the North American continent. Gathering its waters all the way from Southeast Alaska to north of the Arctic Circle, it drains approximately 330,000 square miles, an area almost as large as France and Poland combined. It travels 2,300 miles from its headwaters in Canada to its rich delta on the Bering Sea. Only four rivers in the world have a greater capacity—the Amazon, Mississippi, Missouri, and Saint Lawrence. In some places the Yukon is almost 20 miles wide.

Far more than the Arctic Circle, which is, after all, a line on the map, the Yukon physically delineates the northern province of Alaska from the southern. While it has been a barrier in some respects (the only successful bridge to span it is the one built in the mid-1970s for the Trans-Alaska Pipeline, or TAP, Haul Road), the Yukon and its tributaries formed Alaska's earliest transportation network, providing access for people since they first came into this part of the world. From the sea to the Interior and beyond, the river led. In winter, frozen solid, it was easy to travel (and still is, especially by snowmobile); and in the summer, the river was a challenge to the boat builders of their time. (Although motorboats still chug their way up and down the Yukon, it seems a pity that the fine old fabled stern-wheelers no longer do.)

The Yukon is full of history, of course, and archeologists continue to find evidence of people who camped along its course or one of its tributaries many thousands of years ago. The trapping and trading of the late nineteenth century and the great gold rush at the turn of that century, however, probably brought the river its most colorful times. Then the shallow-draft stern-wheelers came more and more to crowd out the

Charley River, Yukon-Charley Rivers National Preserve. Source: National Park Service.

canoes and other small river craft, steaming up and down the silty waters that formed the principal highway system to the gold fields. (Among those who tried to make their way up the length of this broad, brown, powerful stream to its gold-filled tributaries was the mayor of Seattle, who, in 1898, organized a party of fellow citizens for a municipal gold hunt. Alas, they never made it and had to sail back home empty handed.) Before the rush was over, settlements of one kind or another dotted the riverbanks here and there from Whitehorse to Saint Michael. Road-houses, trading posts (the Hudson's Bay Company and Alaska Commercial Company among them), and small towns burgeoned, boomed, and then most of them went ghost. Two in Alaska, Eagle and Circle, managed to survive, relics of those heady bawdy days when all in this northern land that mattered was gold—and the mood of the mighty river.

Between Eagle, the first incorporated city of the Interior, and Circle, once known as the "Paris of the North," roll some 160 miles of the Yukon. Here the river passes between colorful bluffs and palisades while dark-blue cloud shadows move across the more distant mountains. (This is ancient land; in places, the rocks tell the story of the earth since pre-Cambrian times.) Now and then the waters part to embrace a forested island. Raptors ride the thermals above the tundra-clothed hills. In summer, thunderstorms can race up the river, whipping the waters into high waves and sending spindrift into the suddenly cool air. Midway in this particular section of the Yukon, the Charley River pours out its green crystalline waters to be lost in the muddy flow.

The watershed of the Charley drains portions of the Yukon-Tanana uplands that are too far inland to gather enough snow for glaciers to form: hence, the lovely clarity of the Charley's waters, which in early summer dance into white rapids along their 88-mile course. The Charley watershed is a region that largely escaped the hordes of gold seekers, protected in part by those rapids and the mountains that cradle the river but more by the fact that this area had little of the precious metal to offer. (One of its lower tributaries, Bonanza Creek, was obviously better endowed.) Thus this watershed has remained rarely undisturbed and pristine, with only a trapper's cabin here and there within its limits and a primitive and difficult landing strip near its headwaters. Caribou roam its hills, Dall sheep clamber up and down the precipitous cliffs through which the river cuts in places, and this is a place of refuge for the endangered peregrine falcon. The banks along its lower course also contain a fine show of ice lenses in the permafrost—which underlies this entire region.

The 2,527,000-acre Yukon-Charley Rivers National Preserve embraces the watershed of the Charley and takes in about 128 miles of the Yukon River and a portion of the land through which it flows. To the east, it is bounded by the Canadian border and has as its gateway the town of Eagle. Downstream, little Circle City, which once had a library, a hospital, and an opera house, lies a few miles outside the boundary of the preserve, making another point of entry or, if you will, a convenient point of exit.

This unusual unit of the National Park Service offers a variety of experiences to the Alaskan adventurer. Since both Eagle and Circle are accessible by road, it is possible to arrange a trip down (or up) the Yukon to enjoy its scenery, history, wildlife, and wilderness qualities, and to get a feel for its incredible riverine power. Reached by the Taylor Highway (which ties into the Alaska Highway and thence into Fairbanks), Eagle is a fascinating historical town. Around the turn of the century, it was booming as the trading center for the mining area around it, and was as well the port of entry for Canada. It was here that Judge James Wickersham headquartered his first judicial system and had Alaska's first court-house and jail constructed. The U.S. Army established Fort Egbert adjacent to Eagle in 1899 and for the next few years directed a major undertaking to tie it into the rest of the world via the WAMCATS (Washington Alaska Military Cable and Telegraph System). It took Lt. Billy Mitchell (later of Word War I aviation fame) to get the line strung successfully from Valdez, but, by the time WAMCATS was in good working order, the wireless was coming into increasing use, and the need for military maintenance of the old system diminished. (It is worth noting that, in 1905, Roald Amundsen, after completing his two-year navigation of the Northwest Passage, left his ship, the *Gjoa,* ice-bound on Herschel Island and traveled by dogsled to Eagle, the most northern telegraph office. From there, he notified the world of his feat.) Fort Egbert was closed down by the U.S. Army in 1911. Meantime, Wickersham had moved the seat of his judicial operations to Fairbanks. Eagle never recovered its former prestige.

Fortunately, in recent years, Eagle has been given tender care by some of its citizens and the Bureau of Land Management, and, because of their efforts, the town and its environs have been designated a National Registry historical district. Restoration of historical sites and buildings has proceeded, and residents of Eagle conduct walking tours in the summer to show off interesting parts of the town and what remains of Fort Egbert. Nearby Eagle Village belongs to Han Indians, descendants of the earlier settlers on this picturesque bank of the river. There is good camping at Eagle, with pure spring water nearby (a point worth mentioning along the Yukon) and a place to bathe or swim in Mission Creek. And while, as the National Park Service people put it, facilities such as restaurants and lodges "open and close without ceremony," you can always get food at one of the stores.

In Circle, which is accessible by the Steese Highway, you'll find yourself on your own to explore the regional museum and the old buildings and relics of times gone by. There are, however, a restaurant, a lodge (with showers), a bar, and a camping and picnic ground on the banks of the Yukon. The Steese Highway, incidentally, offers a number of good hikes and small-boat trips along its length (see under Fairbanks). And, if you don't mind a few miles on an out-of-your-way gravel road, you can stop off for a good soak in the pool at Circle Hot Springs.

At Eagle, you can charter an air taxi to flightsee, a powerboat, a guide, and camping gear for a trip on the Yukon. Circle has air charter service. Inquire at **Beaver Sports** (3480 College Road; phone 479-2494) in Fairbanks if you want to rent a canoe for a trip from Eagle to Circle, or check with the National Park Service (see below) regarding the possibility of canoe (or raft) rentals in Eagle.

The gentle, tundra-covered domes in the Yukon-Charley Preserve and along the Taylor Highway provide excellent cross-country hiking and, in early summer, fine birding. Around the first of September, the tundra plants begin to turn, and the bearberry, dwarf birch, and blueberry make a kaleidoscope of colors as brilliant as the broadleaf trees of New England.

The Charley River offers a fine wilderness experience. It demands, in return, that you be well equipped, know what you're doing in a canoe or raft, and that you respect its unusual wild values. Keep in mind that this river country is the home territory of an endangered species, the peregrine falcon, and, despite its almost gentle character in the summer, it is fragile terrain. Also note that fishing is undependable. For details about this river and some good advice for creating a minimum impact in your camping, contact the *National Park Service,* Box 167, Eagle, AK 99738; phone 547-2233. The Yukon-Charley Rivers National Preserve people have extensive, very useful information about this beautiful unit of the national park system. Write ahead, or pick it up in Eagle; the park service office also has maps and books for sale.

Air Charters: Tatonduk Flying Service: Box 61680, Fairbanks, AK 99706; phone 474-4697. *Warbelows Air Ventures, Inc.* (3758 University Avenue South, Fairbanks; write Box 60649, Fairbanks, AK 99706; phone 474-0518) runs scheduled air service to about twenty rural villages, including Circle and Eagle, as well as charters. Inquire at the National Park Service (see above) about further air and helicopter service.

54. Arctic National Wildlife Refuge

One of the best interpretive guides to any part of Alaska was the leaflet (no longer in print, alas) put out several years ago by the U.S. Fish and Wildlife Service on the Arctic National Wildlife Refuge. The leaflet (prepared under the aegis of Averill Thayer, a legendary lover and defender of Arctic wilderness) provided the detailed, practical information needed to visit this beautiful, fragile, significant piece of Arctic country. More importantly, it helped the visitor understand, enjoy, and protect some of the wildlife refuge's extraordinary values. Here are a few of the things it said—well worth repeating.

On Wildlife Viewing

On the south side of the Wildlife Refuge the warm summer days bring cumulus clouds, often followed by afternoon rain showers. Many species of wildlife are least active during this time of day when conditions may also be less favorable for pleasant hiking. Hiking conditions and opportunities for wildlife observation are usually best from evening until about noon the next day. The standard calendar day is an artificial designation unsuited to the north. Ignore it, live with the land, enjoy the spontaneity of the wilds.

To aid in seeing wildlife, route your hikes over low hills and other vantage points. Examine the land carefully with binoculars. Look around near you. Don't overlook small creatures such as shrews, voles, lemmings, and insects (other than mosquitoes). When looking for wildlife, wait quietly and move slowly. Animals watching you will be less alarmed. The quiet is important—your experience is more environmental than social, you can talk later.

On Camping

Camping is permitted throughout the Refuge. You will find no artificial trails, trail signs, or campgrounds. With foresight, knowledge, and self-reliance, you'll not need or want them. Camp where you will not disturb wildlife. Camp should be moved every day, at least a few hundred yards, to minimize trampling vegetation and soil. Leave your campsite in a natural condition; leave no trace of your presence. Pack out all containers, film wrappers, etc.—they cannot be disposed of properly in the Wildlife Refuge. Part of your experience is escaping a littered environment.

You may want to think twice, however, about visiting the Arctic National Wildlife Refuge—and not only because this is Arctic country, which can give you a very cold if compelling experience to remember (see below). This is also a very fragile country and a highly sensitive area for the Porcupine caribou herd, which uses the North Slope of the refuge in its migratory travels and for its calving grounds. The Porcupine herd is a beautiful symbol of this last piece of protected Arctic wilderness coast, and it is also essential to the Gwich'in peoples (Native Indians of Alaska and Canada). Not only do the animals provide a staple of the Gwich'in diet, but their migratory passages have become integral and beloved parts of traditional Gwich'in culture. Thus, more than the survival of these great animals depends upon the intactness of the refuge's ecosystem: at stake also is a cherished and irreplaceable way of life. The calving grounds of the Porcupine herd is in the exact area where oil has been deemed most promising, and commercial development of this oil is the most obvious threat to an undisturbed habitat. In the 1980s, the Arctic National Wildlife Refuge made headlines because of this threat, and the number of recreationists visiting the area increased tremendously. Visitation has since leveled off, but certain areas may still be overused. The U.S. Fish and Wildlife Service has not imposed limitations on recreational use of the refuge as of this writing, although this may become necessary. Keep this in mind if you're planning a trip to the refuge.

Also keep in mind that while running a river is a wonderful way to experience a wilderness—and it can be the least damaging to the terrain and its wildlife—north-flowing Arctic rivers can give you a true Arctic experience, in every sense of the word. They can give you an encounter with Arctic weather, which is temperamental, totally unpredictable, and frequently frigid. When I ran the Kongakut River one early July a few years ago, it had been so cold—and it continued to be—that the river was perilously low from lack of runoff. In fact, I have never been so cold in the wilderness as I was on one of those Arctic July days. (We celebrated the Fourth of July in a snowstorm.) The south-flowing refuge rivers travel through country that will likely be warmer, and it is also gentled by trees, if not by its magnificent scenery. In June and July, however, mosquitoes can be out by the millions. (My run of the Sheenjek River is not only memorable for its beauty, but for the fact that I had my own private crowd of mosquitoes that went wherever I did!) "If you're going to enjoy the wilds, don't let mosquitoes or anything else dictate [the] time [of your visit]," advised the Fish and Wildlife leaflet. Necessary advice.

Entering the Arctic National Wildlife Refuge from Barter Island (Kaktovik) may give you an unexpected and memorable Alaskan experience as well—you may have to wait a while to be flown to your destination because of the weather, and there may be a dozen or more people waiting ahead of you. Kaktovik is small; there are minimal tourist facilities; after you have photographed the Arctic Ocean, the whalebones left on the beach by the local hunters, and the polar bear skins stretched to dry on racks here and there around the village, there isn't an awful lot to do. Be sure to bring a couple of good paperbacks along.

Dall sheep (Ovis dalli dalli). *Range: Alaska's high mountains, except in Southeast.*

Despite the fact that the Arctic National Wildlife Refuge is a protected wildlife area, there is no guarantee that you will see the wildlife you set out to view. On our trip down the Kongakut, we encountered members of a film crew who had been waiting for weeks for the caribou to cross the river. When we left, the caribou still had not budged from their place on the North Slope. Neither the caribou nor any wild animal runs on strict schedule.

However, as the Fish and Wildlife leaflet pointed out, a visit to the Arctic National Wildlife Refuge can give you another kind of experience. It may help you to "be aware of self-change, maintain a high level of keenness, promote spontaneity, be self-aware, have patience and make demands on yourself—not on the land." It can also make you even more grateful that we as a people have had the wisdom to set aside, and give at least some protection to, such a priceless national wilderness treasure.

For all refuge information, ask at—or write to—*Arctic National*

Wildlife Refuge, 101 Twelfth Avenue, Box 20, Fairbanks, AK 99701; phone 456-0250.

Note: As of this writing, the fate of the Arctic National Wildlife Refuge is still up to the Congress; immense pressures to open it up are still being applied. Only an aware, supportive, and articulate public can save this superb Arctic wildland and all the life it supports.

55. Gates of the Arctic National Park and Preserve

The 7,052,000-acre Gates of the Arctic National Park and the contiguous 900,000-acre Gates of the Arctic National Preserve embrace the heartland of the Brooks Range, including the Endicott Mountains to the east and the Schwatka Mountains to the southwest. Between these two ranges soar the Arrigetch Peaks, a fantastic array of fiercely steep, slick, and smooth-faced granitic spires. (*Arrigetch* is an Eskimo word meaning "fingers of a hand outstretched," as though the earth here were literally reaching up to touch the skies.) To the north, the parklands also include a small portion of the strangely lovely Arctic foothills with their pale-green tundra and layers of sediments stacked nearly on end. Within the parklands are some magical lakes—Chandler, Walker, and Takahula among them. And among the most outstanding features of this reserve, of course, are Boreal Mountain and Frigid Crags, the two splendid alpine guards that flank the North Fork of the Koyukuk River. These landmark mountains were named the "Gates of the Arctic" by Robert Marshall because they open the way to a more or less unobstructed path to the polar region itself. (Read his book *Alaska Wilderness*—see Suggested Reading—for a vivid description of how he named these peaks.)

The Gates of the Arctic National Park and Preserve encompass terri-

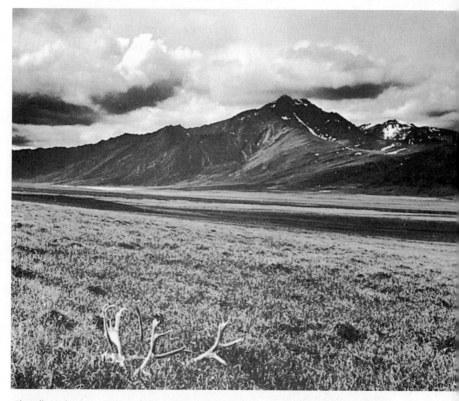

Chandler Lake area, Gates of the Arctic National Park. Source: National Park Service.

tory that was used traditionally by Eskimos, who have roamed the passes here in pursuit of caribou and other wildlife for untold centuries. (Among their legends are tales of their vanquishing another people, the Kutchin Indians, from this same territory, and archeological explorations indicate human occupancy, of one kind or another, in parts of this region that may date back sixteen thousand years.) These national park units were established with a keen awareness of the cultural importance of these lands to the Eskimos and with their participation in many decisions. The Nunamiut village of Anaktuvuk Pass lies within the boundaries of the parkland, as do certain lands selected by the Native corporation of this village and by the Arctic Slope Regional Corporation. (The Eskimo word *anaktuvuk* means "place of caribou droppings.") The park legislation allows for the continuance of traditional hunting practices and other subsistence uses of the land. With an area of this size under park protection, it may be that the animal and plant resources will continue to flourish and that the subsistence way of life may survive, despite increasing pressures on the land and the indigenous culture.

This is no easy environment for people or animals to live in—despite its overwhelming beauty. The climate is demanding, veering from continental zone extremes south of the continental divide, which snakes through the Brooks Range, to the fierce winds and icy temperatures of the Arctic zone to the north. The terrain is, in many places, difficult, and tussock tundra—often composed of big tufts of slippery cottongrass— makes hiking in poorly drained areas a drudgery. ("Tussock walking can be about the most difficult type of arctic hiking," Dr. James Greenough, an ardent Alaskan explorer and outdoorsman wrote. "For every step onto the top of a tussock—a spongy mass of organic matter too wobbly to stand on but too firm to ignore—there is another step down into the narrow, boot-clutching crevasse that surrounds it.") In the more alpine country, it should be added, the tundra is often matlike and makes for fine traveling. Tree line occurs almost precisely along the continental divide and, while on the south of the divide, you may see stands of white spruce fingering the canyons and black spruce leaning tipsily in wet and lichen-tapestried meadows, to the north of the divide, the conifers disappear. Only cottonwoods, among the trees, can make it in any number in this inhospitable region, and then only in a few selected places. (It comes as a great surprise, traveling in the Arctic, to find a forest of cottonwood, or a lone and scraggly spruce prostrate in the tundra struggling to survive.) The alders, however, can attain heights of 20 to 25 feet and diameters of 5 or 6 inches, and low-growing willows are ubiquitous.

Where there are willows in Alaska, there are likely to be moose—a truism that is proved again in the Gates of the Arctic parklands. (Moose, incidentally, comprise the largest percentage of biomass in Alaska.) You may encounter these great beasts along the waterways and marshes and around the lakes. And you may see other familiar Alaskan mammals in this parkland. One of the largest populations of Dall sheep in the state inhabits the high, windy ridges of this region. (The wind, which can chill you to your very core, doesn't bother these hardy creatures, and it performs the important function of keeping the ground swept clean of snow, thus allowing year-round forage.) There are black bears here and grizzlies, although the number of grizzlies is kept in limits naturally by the eating requirement of these huge animals; a single grizzly must have as much as 100 square miles in this spare habitat to support itself. A community of wolves must have an equally large range to keep going here. Of course, a major portion of the wolves' subsistence—and that of the peo-

Mount Igikpak. Source: National Park Service.

ple here as well—is furnished by the crowds of caribou that mill through the mountain passes following in the footsteps of their ancestors.

These Arctic parklands, the Gates of the Arctic Park and Preserve, offer beauty and wildness on, literally, an overwhelming scale. They offer the chance to observe the alpine Arctic wilderness in all its moods. They offer challenging mountaineering, excellent backpacking, and fine river running. But in turn they require good physical condition, a pair of sturdy legs (if you're traveling on foot), good protective equipment, a willingness to put up with insects (the worst mosquitoes I have ever encountered in Alaska were on the Alatna River following a rain), and the ability to get along reasonably happily in poor weather, perhaps while waiting an indeterminate length of time for your air-taxi pickup. They also require a thoughtful approach on the part of the wilderness traveler:

this Arctic wilderness, for all its ruggedness, is extraordinarily delicate. The nest you trample on so carelessly along the shore of Takahula Lake contains a new generation of yellowlegs; the tundra you trample or lay bare for your fire can take years to recover, if it ever does; the wood you scrounge could take decades to be replaced. The Arctic is an area to visit with wonder but also with special respect.

The immediate entryway to the Gates of the Arctic National Park and Preserve is Bettles, a small settlement and a well-developed airstrip just outside the southeast corner of the parkland. Bettles has a general store with the basics (including, for backpackers, freeze-dried food), canoe rentals, outfitters, guides, and air taxis; or check with the National Park Service in Bettles (see below) about available services. Bettles also has a two-story lodge, which, when I first stayed in it, had a slightly drunken appearance and a wavy floor, both of which announced its location directly on the permafrost. A few years ago, however, the building was straightened up and facelifted, and it now appears much more staid and solid. If you don't want to spend the night at the lodge, you can still get a meal there, and, when I last ate there, the portions were generous and the food was good, if simple.

Bettles has a new one-story lodge as well, operated by the same people, which is used primarily during the winter months when the two-story lodge is closed. For both, write *Bettles Lodge,* Box 27, Bettles, AK 99726; phone 692-5111.

There is commercial air service to the village of Anaktuvuk Pass but, as of this writing, there are no accommodations except for a camping area next to the airport. (You should write ahead if you wish to stay in Anaktuvuk Pass; zip code 99721.) Remember that the general stores in villages like Anaktuvuk Pass are hard pressed to supply the local villagers; do not expect to pick up your supplies so far afield. And do not be surprised to find a high school with a good swimming pool at Anaktuvuk Pass: the North Slope Borough is responsible for this educational amenity.

Although there are no developed National Park Service facilities in the Gates of the Arctic parklands, there are many fine places to camp, and the Bureau of Land Management has one developed camping area, the *Marion Creek Campground,* near Coldfoot (write *Bureau of Land Management,* 1150 University Avenue, Fairbanks, AK 99709-3899; phone 474-2300). A good way to make your first visit to these Arctic parklands is to be flown to a lake for a week or two and then picked up, or you may want to run one of the rivers. (The Alatna, John, Noatak, and the North Fork of the Koyukuk all offer wonderful wilderness river experiences. All are accessible by air taxi from Bettles. All are administered by the National Park Service.) As noted, there are also superb rock climbing and mountain climbing challenges. Note: The Arrigetch Peaks are already being crowded with mountaineers; you might want to explore other— "purer"—wilderness peaks; check with the National Park Service.

For further information about Gates of the Arctic National Park and Preserve, contact the *National Park Service* ranger station in Bettles (Box 26030, Bettles, AK 99726; phone 692-5494). In summer, you can also get backcountry information from the *Coldfoot Visitor Center,* operated by the National Park Service, the Bureau of Land Management, and the U.S. Fish and Wildlife Service. It's open from June 1 to September 10; phone 678-5209.

56. Noatak National Preserve

The Noatak River rises in the granite heart of the Brooks Range, its headwaters draining part of Mount Igikpak, which, at over 8,500 feet, towers above its neighboring mountains. (A flyby of Mount Igikpak can be a stunning experience; its upper slopes are breathtakingly perpendicular and sheathed with snow that has been pleated by avalanches into marvelous vertical patterns.) From this high, dramatic mountain world, the Noatak travels more than 425 miles to empty into Kotzebue Sound. Most of its course is due westward, but for the last 100 miles or so it bears abruptly to the south. For much of the way, the Noatak cleaves two beautiful mountain ranges, the Baird Mountains to the south and the De Longs to the north. These ranges swing close to form spectacular canyons above the river and then curve gracefully apart to cradle its huge river basin.

Although born of snowfields and glaciers, the Noatak gathers the clear waters of many rivers along its pathway and it is itself generally clear, dark bottle-green, and smooth flowing, a class II river. In good weather its rapids froth with only medium-sized standing waves, and, when the weather is hot and dry, you may have to avoid rocks and very shallow places. (The river courses through a series of moraines, each of which can be a "rock garden.") Let a summer storm come up, and—as with all Arctic rivers—the character of the river can change radically. The clear waters can rise and become thick with silt in a matter of hours. In the resultant flash flood, the rapids can well up to offer some challenging runs to a canoer or kayaker. In the lower reaches where the current slows down, upriver winds can be—and frequently are—quite literally a drag.

The Noatak is not all that large when compared to, say, the Yukon, but its substantial length makes it one of the most interesting of Alaska's Arctic rivers to run. From its source to its mouth, it travels through a fine spectrum of Arctic scenery, and if you do some exploring in the countryside along the way, you can become familiar with several different Arctic environments. The Noatak will also carry you—without too much effort on your part—through some of the magnificent wilderness regions of the north.

The great basin of the Noatak is particularly rich with wildlife and birds, as well as being almost overwhelming in its sense of size and space. This is the part of the river that has been set aside by Congress in a 6,460,000-acre national preserve. Recognizing its extraordinary natural qualities, the United Nations has also designated this preserve as an International Biosphere Reserve. If you float this part of the river, you may have an unforgettable avian show. Horned grebes, long-tailed and parasitic jaegers, Arctic loons, common loons, Arctic terns, a variety of ducks—these are only a few of the many species that come in from all over the world to breed here. High above you a gyrfalcon or an owl may circle, or you may see a rough-legged hawk or a golden eagle where the river enters its own "Grand Canyon." You will also have a good chance on this run to see the great mammals, like the grizzly and the moose.

If you have time to travel the entire length of the Noatak in a leisurely way, taking, say, a month or more—a fabulous experience—you will have many unique opportunities. You will have a chance to climb a pingo (50 feet high), which will give you a fine view of Mount Igikpak. The forked summit of this mountain prompted its Eskimo name, which means "two great peaks." You can explore Portage Pass, used by prehistoric peoples as well as by early white explorers of this region. You may be piped along your way by lesser yellowlegs, and see Dall sheep, red fox, wolves, and caribou as well as moose and grizzlies. As you drift below the Grand Canyon of the Noatak, you can take a stroll through the Poktovik Mountains or the Igichuk Hills. And should you run this river late in August, you may have a memorable show of autumn colors, made especially intense by the backdrop of the pale Baird Mountains. You can, in fact, spend a summer on this river highway, or you can plan a put-in and take-out for only a week. The National Park Service can give you further details. Consult them in Kotzebue (see below), or at the *Alaska Public Lands Information Center* in Fairbanks (250 Cushman Street, Fairbanks, AK 99701; phone 456-0527).

57. Kotzebue

Since passage of the Alaska Native Claims Settlement Act (ANCSA), Kotzebue has been growing rapidly and is assuming its place as the business and tourist center of northwest Alaska. (Ten years ago, it was more properly a village than a town; now it is the "metropolis"—the largest Eskimo community in the Arctic.) The Northwest Alaska Native Association (NANA), the local Native regional corporation, is interested in tourism and is behind the development of quite elaborate and interesting tourist attractions in Kotzebue. The Nullagvik Hotel, built by NANA, is the most comfortable, and the most expensive, hotel in town.

Kotzebue has no public campgrounds and there is no Youth Hostel as of this writing. It is also not very hospitable terrain when it comes to rolling out a bag; the beach is narrow and slanting, and there is private property to be respected. Plan accordingly—it's kind of all or nothing.

However, Kotzebue is worth spending some time in. It's one of those special Arctic communities where you can watch the sun barely above the ocean, rolling along the horizon at midnight, pouring out a great flood of liquid red-gold light across the water. The evening sea air becomes diffused with a luminescence that is almost tangible. The quality of this light earns a lot of money for film companies; photographers find it difficult to resist. One of Kotzebue's main streets, incidentally, runs right along the beach, and it seems as if everybody in town turns out along it on clear nights—and never goes to bed. You may do likewise.

Kotzebue also has a good natural history museum, in fact, the most sophisticated in the state. This is another NANA enterprise. The museum has interesting dioramas, good specimens of large Arctic mammals, and descriptions of the Native subsistence uses of them. NANA also sponsors a tour that offers insights into the ecology of the tundra and into some of the traditional work ways of the Inupiat Eskimos. There are a number of Native artists in Kotzebue, and you might find prices for some lovely Native artwork lower here than in Anchorage.

Kotzebue is close—minutes by air—to several of the newer units of the national park system. Here is where you make your charter arrangements to visit the Cape Krusenstern National Monument, Kobuk Valley National Park, and the Noatak National Preserve. You can also charter a floatplane here if you wish to run the Selawik River, which is administered by the U.S. Fish and Wildlife Service. The Selawik is a long, low-lying, slow river that winds through country rich in wildlife and birdlife (and mosquitoes). For information, contact the *Alaska Public Lands Information Center in Fairbanks* (250 Cushman Street, Fairbanks, AK 99701; phone 456-0527). Write the village of Selawik (see Alaska Zip Codes appendix), where you can use scheduled air service for your return, regarding your plans. You can also get detailed information from the *National Park Service;* write Box 1029, Kotzebue, AK 99752; phone 442-3890 or 442-3760 (the latter number from mid-May to mid-September only). Or stop by the *Kotzebue Public Lands Information Center* (154 Second Avenue, Kotzebue, AK 99752; phone 442-3760). The center is operated jointly by the National Park Service, the Bureau of Land Management, and the U.S. Fish and Wildlife Service.

58. Kobuk Valley National Park

When you hike the springy tundra of the hills above the Kobuk Valley or watch the pale green waters of the Kobuk River move sinuously westward, you can experience the same sense of timelessness that pervades the Bering Land Bridge Preserve. The Kobuk Valley, too, is an island of unglaciated Pleistocene landscape; and because of its particular soil, climatic, and geographic conditions, it remains remarkably like it was when woolly mammoths lumbered through it many millennia ago. Many of its present plants—grasses, sedges, and a single sagebrush, *Artemisia borealis*—are the same species as those that bent before ice Pleistocene winds. One charming legume, *Oxytropis kobukensis,* has survived from those long-ago times to grow only here in the world.

Although glacial barriers may once have encircled the ancient Kobuk Valley on three sides, the fourth side lay open periodically to the Bering Land Bridge (which, evidence indicates, was carpeted with the same forbs that still thrive in the valley). Thus, this was one of the gateways through which early people wandered, following the bison and mammoths and caribou, stepping unknowingly into what would one day be called the New World. There were many different early people who came this way, leaving the silent evidence of their presence in more than a dozen major archeological sites, including the one at Onion Portage, which has been described as the most important ever found in the Arctic. Along with Cape Krusenstern, Onion Portage (named for the wild chives that grow abundantly here) is used as a kind of archeological yardstick against which all other Arctic sites are now measured; artifacts here have been dated as more than 10,000 years old.

The late J. Louis Giddings, the archeologist who discovered the site at Onion Portage—and uncovered there some thirty layers of artifacts and evidence of at least seven different cultures—was responsible for a magnificent scientific contribution as well as a story that has become popular folklore. Giddings made his first visit to this region in the summer of 1940, rafting his way from the headwaters of the Kobuk toward Kotzebue Sound. As he proceeded downstream, his raft became waterlogged, and, by the time he encountered the first Eskimos along the riverbanks, the raft was barely clearing the surface of the water. As he stood waving his greetings, he appeared to the astonished eyes of the Eskimos to be walking down the river. When he proved, after all, to be only a mortal, he formed a fast friendship with the people of this region.

Along with being highly important in terms of its geological and cultural history, the Kobuk Valley is a region of great interest to botanists, and not only for its relict landbridge flora. Here the boreal forest reaches its most northwestern continental limit, but not in the abruptly drawn tree line that marks its boundary in the Brooks Range. Rather it intertwines delicately with the Arctic tundra; spruce and birch trees stand separately and alone in the lichen-carpeted meadows in a kind of lacy sparseness. This encounter between two major biomes—the tundra and the boreal forest—is one of precarious balance; responding to climatic changes, one or the other pushes forward. Thus in periods of warmth, the forest presses northward; when the climate is cold, the sturdy plants of the tundra invade the open forests and move to the south. This intermingling of forest and tundra is found more commonly in Siberia and Canada, but it is rare in Alaska.

Another interesting and unique feature of this region is the presence here of vast stretches of inland sand dunes. The Great Kobuk Sand Dunes and the Little Kobuk Sand Dunes each lie within hiking distance of the green Kobuk River, the former sprawling over 25 square miles of the land in a true and sizable desert. The temperatures here can crawl above 100 degrees in the summertime, and the air will bedazzle you with its heat. The great yellow dunes, some 100 feet high, look as though they should be in the north of Africa rather than the northwest of Alaska. The result of wind-transported river sand, both sets of dunes have assumed the classical forms of waves and upended U-shapes; they date back at least thirty-three thousand years.

The wildlife in the Kobuk Valley is abundant and varied, and it includes a spectrum of mammals that ranges from the alpine Dall sheep, which skip along the ridges of the Baird Mountains, to migrating herds of caribou and riverine creatures like the beaver, muskrat, and moose, which occupy the watery lowlands. The rivers also carry abundant salmon and sheefish. The Asian flyway and the North American flyway conjoin in this valley so that dozens of birds—waterfowl, shorebirds, and songbirds—from many continents breed here too.

As it has for untold generations, the rich profusion of wildlife in the Kobuk Valley region provides subsistence for people today. The people of the Kobuk have roots that go deep into prehistory, and they have adapted well to the demands of a north-of-the-Arctic climate, which can send the thermometer to 90 degrees in summer or to 60 degrees below zero in winter. As did their ancestors, the Kuuvangmiit hunt the caribou that follow their own ancient migratory patterns as they cross the Kobuk River at Onion Portage. And these people still travel the river to Kotzebue Sound and on to the Chukchi Sea to exchange their inland products—furs and the liver of mud sharks—for seal oil from the coastal dwellers.

Two principal villages of the Kobuk people, Ambler and Kiana, lie outside the boundaries of the Kobuk National Park, and the parklands are open to these Natives and other Alaskans for subsistence use.

The Kobuk Valley National Park is 1,140,000 acres in size. Along with the diverse values outlined above, it contains in its northern section a sensitive region of passes in the Baird Mountains, used historically by caribou. It also contains several intact south-flowing Arctic watersheds as well as a beautiful section of the Kobuk River. One of its loveliest smaller rivers is the Salmon, which is a clear, brilliant aquamarine. Seen from the air, its waters make a stunning pattern as they braid through the pale landscape of the Baird Mountains. The Kobuk itself winds its serene way across the southern section of the park, which is bordered by the Waring Mountains.

The Kobuk Valley National Park, like other National Park Service units in the Arctic, is, and should remain, undeveloped wilderness. This means, of course, that there are no designated campsites, no trails or other facilities or services. The park offers fine spot-camping (you can be flown in from Kiana or Ambler), wonderful backpacking opportunities, and some excellent, if not challenging, river running on the section of the Kobuk inside its borders. The Salmon is a joyous and fast-moving river in places and can be handled by any reasonably experienced kayaker. This is, of course, a place of great interest to archeologically or botanically minded people. June and July are likely to be the clearest months of the summer here; winter use is not advised.

Kotzebue, which lies about 75 miles to the west, is the principal gateway for the Kobuk Valley National Park and the location of the nearest National Park Service facilities. You can reach Kotzebue by daily scheduled air service out of Anchorage or Fairbanks. You can also fly commercially to Kiana and Ambler from Kotzebue, and you can charter from any of these three communities. You may also be able to charter boat service in Kiana or Ambler. There is a lodge at Kiana and guide service available. If you wish to use the facilities of either village or to spend any time in them, you should write ahead and make arrangements (see Visiting Native Villages, in Part I). You can backpack from either Ambler or Kiana into the park.

The subsistence use of the Kobuk Valley region is a vitally important part of the local lifestyle. It is wise to check with the National Park Service to avoid visiting this area when hunting or fishing use is at its height. You should check in with the park service people anyway, if you plan a trip here. Not only can they give you further information, but they would also like a copy of your proposed itinerary. You can write the *National Park Service* at Box 1029, Kotzebue, AK 99752; phone 442-3890 or 442-3760 (the latter number from mid-May to mid-September only). Or inquire at the *Alaska Public Lands Information Center* in either Anchorage (605 West Fourth Avenue, Suite 105, Anchorage, AK 99501; phone 271-2737) or Fairbanks (250 Cushman Street, Fairbanks, AK 99701; phone 456-0527).

Rivers

The Ambler is a small, very clear river that flows through spruce forest. It will take you from six to eight days to make an 80-mile run on it. Its upper section, the most scenic, has many small, class II rapids; the middle reach is braided; the lower is wide, single-channeled, shallow, and slow. The best hiking is in the upstream area. Access in is by wheel plane, and you can take out at Ambler, where there is a scheduled commercial air carrier, or you can continue on down the Kobuk River. For further information, contact the National Park Service (see above). Also write the village of Ambler (see Alaska Zip Codes appendix) regarding your plans.

The Squirrel is a very small, extremely clear stream that tumbles slowly through the low southwest foothills of the Baird Mountains. It makes for an excellent four- or five-day family float trip for relatively inexperienced small-boaters. Fishing, particularly for grayling, is good. Access in is by wheel plane from Kotzebue or Kiana, and out from Kiana, which has scheduled commercial air service. Write the *Bureau of Land Management* (Kotzebue Field Office, Box 1049, Kotzebue, AK 99752; phone 442-3430) for further information. Write Kiana (see below) regarding air charter service and accommodations.

The small, brilliantly clear Salmon can be reached by wheel plane from Kotzebue or Kiana. You can spend from a few days to a week on this beautiful river, which flows through alpine, tundra-covered country in the Baird Mountains. Its lower 25 miles cross the Kobuk lowlands. For further information, contact the National Park Service (see above) and the village of Kiana (zip code 99749) where you may wish to take out.

The Kobuk River can be run 125 miles from Walker Lake to the village of Kobuk. Rapids just below Walker Lake require a portage unless you're an expert small-boater, and there are class II to IV rapids in the lower Kobuk Canyon. Otherwise, this is a class II river. Access in is by floatplane to Walker Lake from Bettles or Kobuk. For further information, write the National Park Service and, if you plan to stop there, the village of Kobuk (zip code 99751). It is possible to continue down the Kobuk to Kiana.

59. Cape Krusenstern National Monument

The 560,000-acre Cape Krustenstern National Monument lies only 10 miles northwest of Kotzebue at its closest point. This is an area that has been set aside for its cultural and archeological values more than for its stark, but very real Arctic beauty. It is a coastal region where storm-shaped beach ridges have been building up the shoreline for at least 5,000 years. Each successive beach has left a ridge—there are 114 of them—and virtually every ridge contains relics of different human occupants. Thus, as you move inland, you travel neatly back in archeological time.

Archeologists digging in these ridges have identified artifacts from every known Eskimo culture in North America. The oldest (most inland) artifacts belonged to the Denbigh Flint people, who lived around 2300 B.C. These first Eskimo hunters of seals and other sea mammals left few traces beyond the beautiful and lethal microblades that they fashioned as arrowheads. Among those who followed the Denbigh hunters were the Old Whaling people (ridge 53), whose culture differed in many ways from their predecessors as well as their successors. Then there were the Choris (ridges 51–44) and Norton (ridges 44–36) cultures and, among the most intriguing of all, the Ipiutak people. The Ipiutaks left their tantalizing artifacts on beaches 35 through 29, and the period of their occupancy appears to have been from the time of Christ to A.D. 600. Skull figures with jet and ivory eyes, curiously fashioned ornaments, and elaborate etched pebbles all have intrigued and puzzled archeologists since their discovery (first, as it happens, at Point Hope not far to the north) in 1939. These artifacts suggest not only superb artisans, but also a culture that included unusual burial practices and perhaps mystic rites of augury, as well as the skillful practice of seal hunting with finely made ivory harpoon points. Interestingly, the Ipiutaks left no shard of pottery; apparently that useful adjunct to living, employed in cultures before and after them, was unknown to them.

The Eskimos who presently use the Cape Krusenstern coast in much the way their ancestors did are descendants of a people who first occupied this region some 1,000 years ago. They followed the Western Thules, who dominated the entire Arctic coast for 800 years, moving across Alaska to settle as far away as Greenland. Today's Eskimos may see, in their own lifetimes, the beach they know and use overridden by wind-driven ice floes and the beginning of a new beach take shape.

The land of the Cape Krustenstern Monument includes low, rolling, and stark grayish-white hills that are fringed with yellow-green tundra. The slanting, changing light works magic on these hills, and you may find a rough-legged hawk perched on the crest of one, or a family of red foxes patrolling the slopes. In autumn, the skies here fill up with geese, and, if you're hiking inland, you may come upon muskox. There is also the flat coastal area in the monument, where there are the many ponds and lagoons whose black waters may rest on some of the earlier beach ridges. All of this earth has been profoundly shaped by ice as well as by the sea, and the powerful winds that cut across it scythe it clean of most vegetation. (Any tent pitched here, by the way, is subject to a battering by those winds.) Still, the tundra plants—dwarf birch and willow, wild sour dock, and many berries used by Eskimos today in their subsistence lifestyle—manage to cling to the soil and bind down the sea-transported sands and gravels.

If you have a grand scenic experience in mind, this is not an area to seek out, especially if your time in Alaska is limited. True, you can hike or backpack across the tundra-covered ridges, whale-watch for the white belugas that shimmer by, or look at the myriad and interesting birds that summer here (the ponds and lagoons are among the most northern nesting sites of the Aleutian tern, and there are yellow wagtails that drop in from Siberia, and jaegers here from Japan). If you're seriously interested in geology, you can also find in this new monument the only Illinoisian esker known to have survived in Alaska; it is an oblong mound some 225,000 years old.

This is country with other and profound values. It is still used by the Eskimo people for subsistence much as it was used by their ancestors. In summer, the big white canvas tents go up along the shore. Children run and laugh along the beaches. The spring hunt for seals on the frozen seas may be over, but the men have whales and fish to bring in. Later, the gathering of berries and herbs will get under way.

This is homeland to people who do not always welcome the small plane roaring over them and intruding on their beaches—with good reason. Local guides may be able to take you on a visit where you will not intrude. Air taxis serve this area, and you may be able to rent a boat in Kotzebue (recommended). If you decide you want to visit the Cape Krustenstern area, be sure to go over your plans at length with the National Park Service people. You can write ahead or spend some time with the park service people in Kotzebue before you venture into this very special place. Address: *Kotzebue Public Lands Information Center,* 154 Second Avenue, Kotzebue, AK 99752; phone 442-3760.

60. Bering Land Bridge National Preserve

Fire and ice together have helped to preserve some of the remarkable history of the 2,770,000 acres of the Bering Land Bridge National Preserve. This region was once a part of the wide pathway where the first hunters wandered to find, unknowingly, the North American continent. The pathway has been submerged by melting glaciers, but the permafrosted land holds intact the leaves and twigs of plants that grew those thousands of years ago; a beaver's dam constructed industriously in Pleistocene times, tiny insects, small mammals, and the remnants of larger mammals such as the woolly mammoth are here as well, preserved in near-perfect condition. Sealed beneath the outpourings of volcanic ash that have buried parts of this area, there are also samplings of whole vegetative systems that flourished millennia ago.

Those early people who came this way left few marks of themselves or clues to their cultures, although there are exciting traces of their presence sealed here into the ground, and there are well-based hopes that more will be found. Later peoples, however, left strange cairns, now thickly covered with moss and lichens, which stand against the pale northern sky. Why did they stack these flat slabs of volcanic rocks on the crests of low craters? Perhaps they were building beacons to give points of orientation in this relatively flat and seemingly featureless landscape; perhaps they were trying to funnel the many caribou that once filled this region (but do so no more) into traps where the animals could be easily taken; or perhaps these cairns had a deeper, religious significance. No one knows the answer, but these monuments are interesting reminders of people who knew this land long before we came to it.

There are also significant volcanic features in several parts of the

Bering Land Bridge National Preserve. The land bridge was still intact when volcanoes here last spewed out their lavas and ash to freeze in the near-Arctic cold. (The Arctic Circle just tips the northern boundary of the preserve.) It must have been terrifying to the wanderers passing through to witness the massive flows of lava, one of which, the Imuruk, is the most northern flow of major scale in the United States. Even more frightening would have been the vast explosions that formed the beautiful clear maars—unusual volcanic lakes—which occur in pairs here, a great geological rarity.

There are many other lakes and lagoons and clear-water streams as well as low, wet tundras, all prime avian habitat, which makes for spectacular birdlife in the preserve. During the lengthening days of springtime, the skies fill up with birds coming in from all over the world—sandhill cranes, ducks, geese, swans, and shorebirds by the thousands. In the brackish marshes, the air vibrates with the cries and movements of loons. Songbirds arrive as well, seeking the dry upper tundra for their homes. Of the 112 species of migratory birds that crowd the preserve each year, many come from Asia, Europe, and even Africa; thus it is possible to see here, routinely, numerous Old World birds. (A note of caution: Parts of the shores of many of the preserve's loveliest lakes are thick with the green droppings of geese.)

There are many mammals here as well, and you can hope to see grizzly, reindeer, muskox, moose, and, at certain times of the year, seals, walruses, and whales along the coast. You will also find a remarkably rich flora thriving in what might seem at first glance to be a barren land. There are almost 250 species of flowering plants that burst into bloom during the long summer days, splashing colors on the ground or hiding shyly for you to find them. In late August and early September they paint the landscape in brilliant hues, just as they did when the first people came this way.

While this is obviously not a place to come for spectacular alpine or riverine scenery, there are several very special values here. In this gently rolling treeless land of lava and tundra, you can gain a true sense of timelessness. This terrain looks much as it did, it is believed, at the time those earliest people moved across it, perhaps in pursuit of one of the woolly mammoths whose ivory tusks lie frozen in the permafrost. If you are interested in birds or archeology and paleontology, this may be a part of Alaska that you will especially want to see.

A unique place, the Serpentine Hot Springs, lies on the southeast side of the preserve and is accessible by air charter from either Nome or Kotzebue (it is about midway between the two towns). A friend of mine writes: "In addition to its body-soothing attractions, the hot spring has

Muskox (Ovibus moschatus). Range: once found throughout Arctic but later greatly re-duced in number; now being reintroduced in selected places (the parent herd is on Nunivak Island). Source: U.S. Fish and Wildlife Service.

an unusually varied flora around it, and the area attracts distinctive birds. The surrounding hills look like castle battlements; gentle domes bristle with tall, thin granite spires, or tors. At twilight, you may feel that you are in a haunted netherworld."

There are no accommodations in the Bering Land Bridge Preserve. Primitive campgrounds may be developed along some of the lakeshores in the future, but for now, if you come here, you will be on your own. You will need to be a good and well-equipped backpacker to enjoy this area, and there should be two or more in your party in what is a vast, remote part of the world. There is not much driftwood along the preserve's beaches and virtually none inland, so carry a stove. While Nome and Kotzebue (the gateways to the preserve) both have reasonably well-stocked stores, supplying backpackers is not a major priority, and you should bring your own freeze-dried food and any other special items you'll need.

The climate of the preserve is generally maritime in summer, averaging in the mid-40s along the coast and the mid-60s inland between mid-June and mid-September. When the Chukchi Sea is ice-free—from mid-June to late October—there is apt to be cloud cover and fog in the area since the humidity is relatively high. When freeze-up occurs, the climate becomes continental, and winters can be bitterly cold.

Some Useful Information About Bering Land Bridge Natural Preserve

Zip code: 99762. Area code: 907.

How to Get There

The Bering Land Bridge National Preserve can be reached by air from Kotzebue or Nome, and the bush pilots in both of these towns may be able to offer you good information about the area as well as expert air service. For a current list of air charter services, check with the National Park Service people in Nome, or contact the Nome Convention and Visitors Bureau (see below for both).

If you choose Nome as your point of entry (and the National Park Service would like to use Nome as the official gateway), you can also go by road to within hiking distance of the preserve. There are two Native villages very close to the preserve, Shishmaref and Deering, and if you would like to visit these villages, be sure to write ahead to make arrangements (see Alaska Zip Codes appendix). The people living there, understandably, do not care to be just dropped in on. (There are some very fine carvers in Shishmaref, and you may be able to find their work in Nome or Kotzebue.)

Nome is a fascinating relic of gold-rush times and is worth a visit on its own merits. It is a town joke that the churches outnumber the bars one year and vice versa the next. (There are, in fact, about a dozen of each in this community of only a few thousand souls.) Nome is strung out along the coast of the Bering Sea and is periodically slammed into and flooded by intense storms that sweep in from the west. In 1974, there was a real holocaust, and Nome was declared a disaster area. The story goes that, during this particular storm, one bartender nearly drowned while trying to sweep the flooding ocean waters out of his saloon. If you're interested in Native artwork, Nome is a good place to look for it; the prices are usually reasonable.

Note: Nome is the finish point for the annual Iditarod dogsled race, held in late winter. It is also the takeoff point for some excellent birding.

The main street of Nome. Source: Yvonne Mozée.

It is, hopefully, slated to be the American anchor for the proposed Bering International Park.

Where to Stay

Nome has a few heavily used tourist hotels, which are bare boned and expensive. If you plan to use one, consult your travel agent and make reservations. There are also bed and breakfasts as well as furnished apartments. And you can check with the Methodist Church if you're ever stranded here.

Useful Names and Addresses

For more details about the Bering Land Bridge National Preserve, write the *National Park Service,* Box 220, Nome; phone 443-2522. Plan to go over your itinerary with them and also let them know when you leave the preserve. Or contact the very helpful people at the *Nome Convention and Visitors Bureau,* Box 240, Nome; phone 443-5535; fax 443-5832.

Appendix A

How to Order Alaska Topographic Maps

The U.S. Geological Survey (USGS) has mapped Alaska on several scales. Most detailed are topographic maps (also know as topos or quad-rangles) on a scale of 1:24,000. Only a few of these exist, covering such areas as Anchorage and environs, Fairbanks and environs, and the Kenai Peninsula. The most generally useful maps have a scale of 1:64,000; this series blankets the state. The third major series consists of regional maps at a scale of 1:250,000, excellent for orientation but lacking detail for hiking. There are also USGS maps for national parks and other conservation units, on varying scales.

You can select maps from USGS's *Alaska Catalog of Topographic and Other Published Maps* and the *Alaska Index to Topographic and Other Map Coverage*. These publications are available free with a call to 1-800-USA-MAPS (1-800-872-6277). To order maps, write USGS Map Distribution, Box 25286, Denver, CO 80225; phone 1-800-HELP MAP (1-800-435-7627); fax 303-202-4693.

Appendix B

Checklist of Alaska Birds

by Dan Gibson, University of Alaska—Fairbanks. Viewing index and breeding status by Brad Andres, U.S. Fish and Wildlife Service.

Alaska's bird checklist includes 445 documented species and an additional 35 unsubstantiated species. Below are presented the common name, a viewing index, and the breeding status for all 480 species. The viewing index is defined as the chance of encountering the species while birding in Alaska (in the right habitats during the proper season) and decreases, from highest to lowest, in the following way: almost certainly, possibly, with work, with much luck, not likely, minute chance. The ratings incorporate regional abundance of the species and the accessibility to them. Spring and early summer are the most productive times for birding in Alaska. Consult Robert H. Armstrong's *Guide to the Birds of Alaska* for information on seasonal and regional abundances and Nick Lethaby's *A Bird Finding Guide to Alaska* for information on birding sites.

	Chance of Viewing	*Breeds?*
Loons		
Red-throated loon	Almost certainly	Yes
Arctic loon	With work	Yes
Pacific loon	Almost certainly	Yes
Common loon	Almost certainly	Yes
Yellow-billed loon	Possibly	Yes
Grebes		
Pied-billed grebe	With work	No
Horned grebe	Almost certainly	Yes
Red-necked grebe	Almost certainly	Yes
Western grebe	With work	No
Clark's grebe	Minute chance	No
Tubenoses		
Short-tailed albatross	With work	No

	Chance of Viewing	*Breeds?*
Black-footed albatross	Almost certainly	No
Laysan albatross	Possibly	No
Northern fulmar	Almost certainly	Yes
Mottled petrel	Possibly	No
Cook's petrel	Not likely	No
Pink-footed shearwater	Minute chance	No
Flesh-footed shearwater	Minute chance	No
Buller's shearwater	Minute chance	No
Sooty shearwater	Almost certainly	No
Short-tailed shearwater	Almost certainly	No
Manx shearwater	Minute chance	No
Fork-tailed storm-petrel	Almost certainly	Yes
Leach's storm-petrel	Almost certainly	Yes
Pelicans, Cormorants		
American white pelican	Not likely	No
Double-crested cormorant	Almost certainly	Yes
Brandt's cormorant	With work	Yes
Pelagic cormorant	Almost certainly	Yes
Red-faced cormorant	Possibly	Yes
Frigatebirds		
Magnificent frigatebird	Not likely	No
Bitterns, Herons, Egrets		
American bittern	With work	Yes
Yellow bittern	Not likely	No
Great blue heron	Possibly	Yes
Great egret	With much luck	No
Chinese egret	Not likely	No
Snowy egret	Minute chance	No
Cattle egret	With work	No
Green heron	Not likely	No
Black-crowned night-heron	With much luck	No
Waterfowl		
Tundra swan	Almost certainly	Yes
Whooper swan	With work	No
Trumpeter swan	Almost certainly	Yes
Bean goose	With work	No
Greater white-fronted goose	Almost certainly	Yes
Lesser white-fronted goose	Not likely	No
Snow goose	Almost certainly	Yes
Ross' goose	With much luck	Yes
Emperor goose	Possibly	Yes
Brant	Almost certainly	Yes

	Chance of Viewing	*Breeds?*
Barnacle goose	Minute chance	No
Canada goose	Almost certainly	Yes
Wood duck	With much luck	No
Green-winged teal	Almost certainly	Yes
Baikal teal	Not likely	No
Falcated teal	With much luck	No
American black duck	Not likely	No
Mallard	Almost certainly	Yes
Spot-billed duck	Not likely	No
Northern pintail	Almost certainly	Yes
Garganey	With work	No
Blue-winged teal	With work	Yes
Cinnamon teal	With work	No
Northern shoveler	Almost certainly	Yes
Gadwall	Almost certainly	Yes
Eurasian wigeon	Possibly	No
American wigeon	Almost certainly	Yes
Common pochard	With work	No
Canvasback	Possibly	Yes
Redhead	Possibly	Yes
Ring-necked duck	Possibly	Yes
Tufted duck	With work	No
Greater scaup	Almost certainly	Yes
Lesser scaup	Almost certainly	Yes
Common eider	Almost certainly	Yes
King eider	Possibly	Yes
Spectacled eider	Possibly	Yes
Steller's eider	Possibly	Yes
Harlequin duck	Almost certainly	Yes
Oldsquaw	Almost certainly	Yes
Black scoter	Almost certainly	Yes
Surf scoter	Almost certainly	Yes
White-winged scoter	Almost certainly	Yes
Common goldeneye	Almost certainly	Yes
Barrow's goldeneye	Almost certainly	Yes
Bufflehead	Almost certainly	Yes
Smew	With work	No
Hooded merganser	Possibly	Yes
Common merganser	Almost certainly	Yes
Red-breasted merganser	Almost certainly	Yes
Ruddy duck	With work	Yes
Vultures, Hawks, Falcons		
Turkey vulture	Not likely	No

	Chance of Viewing	*Breeds?*
Osprey	Possibly	Yes
Bald eagle	Almost certainly	Yes
White-tailed eagle	With much luck	Yes
Steller's sea-eagle	With much luck	No
Northern harrier	Possibly	Yes
Sharp-shinned hawk	Possibly	Yes
Cooper's hawk	Minute chance	No
Northern goshawk	Possibly	Yes
Swainson's hawk	With work	Yes
Red-tailed hawk	Possibly	Yes
Common buzzard	Minute chance	No
Rough-legged hawk	Possibly	Yes
Golden eagle	Possibly	Yes
Eurasian kestrel	With much luck	No
American kestrel	Possibly	Yes
Merlin	Possibly	Yes
Northern hobby	With much luck	No
Peregrine falcon	Possibly	Yes
Gyrfalcon	Possibly	Yes

Gallinaceous Birds

Spruce grouse	Possibly	Yes
Blue grouse	Almost certainly	Yes
Willow ptarmigan	Almost certainly	Yes
Rock ptarmigan	Almost certainly	Yes
White-tailed ptarmigan	Possibly	Yes
Ruffed grouse	Possibly	Yes
Sharp-tailed grouse	Possibly	Yes

Rails, Coots, Cranes

Yellow rail	Minute chance	No
Virginia rail	Not likely	No
Sora	With much luck	Yes
Eurasian coot	Not likely	No
American coot	With much luck	Yes
Sandhill crane	Almost certainly	Yes
Common crane	Not likely	No

Plovers

Northern lapwing	Minute chance	No
Black-bellied plover	Almost certainly	Yes
Greater golden-plover	Minute chance	No
American golden-plover	Almost certainly	Yes
Pacific golden-plover	Possibly	Yes
Mongolian plover	With much luck	Yes

	Chance of Viewing	*Breeds?*
Snowy plover	Not likely	No
Common ringed plover	With work	Yes
Semipalmated plover	Almost certainly	Yes
Little ringed plover	With much luck	No
Killdeer	Possibly	Yes
Eurasian dotterel	With work	Yes
Oystercatchers, Stilts, Avocets		
Black oystercatcher	Almost certainly	Yes
Black-winged stilt	Not likely	No
American avocet	Not likely	No
Oriental pratincole	Not likely	No
Sandpipers		
Common greenshank	With work	No
Greater yellowlegs	Almost certainly	Yes
Lesser yellowlegs	Almost certainly	Yes
Marsh sandpiper	Not likely	No
Spotted redshank	With much luck	No
Wood sandpiper	With work	Yes
Green sandpiper	With much luck	No
Solitary sandpiper	Possibly	Yes
Willet	Minute chance	No
Wandering tattler	Almost certainly	Yes
Gray-tailed tattler	With work	No
Common sandpiper	With work	Yes
Spotted sandpiper	Almost certainly	Yes
Terek sandpiper	With much luck	No
Upland sandpiper	Possibly	Yes
Little curlew	Not likely	No
Eskimo curlew	Not likely	No
Whimbrel	Almost certainly	Yes
Bristle-thighed curlew	Possibly	Yes
Far Eastern curlew	With much luck	No
Long-billed curlew	Minute chance	No
Black-tailed godwit	With much luck	No
Hudsonian godwit	Almost certainly	Yes
Bar-tailed godwit	Possibly	Yes
Marbled godwit	With work	Yes
Ruddy turnstone	Almost certainly	Yes
Black turnstone	Almost certainly	Yes
Surfbird	Possibly	Yes
Great knot	With much luck	No
Red knot	Possibly	Yes
Sanderling	Possibly	Yes

	Chance of Viewing	Breeds?
Semipalmated sandpiper	Almost certainly	Yes
Western sandpiper	Almost certainly	Yes
Rufous-necked stint	With work	Yes
Little stint	With much luck	No
Temminck's stint	With much luck	No
Long-toed stint	With work	No
Least sandpiper	Almost certainly	Yes
White-rumped sandpiper	With work	Yes
Baird's sandpiper	Possibly	Yes
Pectoral sandpiper	Almost certainly	Yes
Sharp-tailed sandpiper	Possibly	No
Purple sandpiper	Not likely	No
Rock sandpiper	Almost certainly	Yes
Dunlin	Almost certainly	Yes
Curlew sandpiper	With much luck	No
Stilt sandpiper	Possibly	Yes
Spoonbill sandpiper	Not likely	No
Broad-billed sandpiper	With much luck	No
Buff-breasted sandpiper	With much luck	Yes
Ruff	With work	Yes
Short-billed dowitcher	Almost certainly	Yes
Long-billed dowitcher	Almost certainly	Yes
Jack snipe	Not likely	No
Common snipe	Almost certainly	Yes
Pin-tailed snipe	Not likely	No
Wilson's phalarope	With much luck	No
Red-necked phalarope	Almost certainly	Yes
Red phalarope	Possibly	Yes

Jaegers, Gulls, Terns

Pomarine jaeger	Possibly	Yes
Parasitic jaeger	Almost certainly	Yes
Long-tailed jaeger	Almost certainly	Yes
South Polar skua	With much luck	No
Laughing gull	Minute chance	No
Franklin's gull	With much luck	No
Little gull	Minute chance	No
Common black-headed gull	With work	No
Bonaparte's gull	Almost certainly	Yes
Heerman's gull	Not likely	No
Black-tailed gull	With much luck	No
Mew gull	Almost certainly	Yes
Ring-billed gull	With work	No
California gull	With work	No

	Chance of Viewing	*Breeds?*
Herring gull	Almost certainly	Yes
Thayer's gull	Possibly	No
Lesser black-backed gull	With much luck	No
Slaty-backed gull	Possibly	No
Western gull	With much luck	No
Glaucous-winged gull	Almost certainly	Yes
Glaucous gull	Possibly	Yes
Great black-backed gull	Not likely	No
Black-legged kittiwake	Almost certainly	Yes
Red-legged kittiwake	With work	Yes
Ross' gull	With work	No
Sabine's gull	Possibly	Yes
Ivory gull	With work	No
Caspian tern	With work	Yes
Common tern	With much luck	No
Arctic tern	Almost certainly	Yes
Forster's tern	Minute chance	No
Aleutian tern	Possibly	Yes
White-winged tern	Not likely	No
Black tern	With much luck	No

Auks, Puffins

Dovekie	With work	Yes
Common murre	Almost certainly	Yes
Thick-billed murre	Possibly	Yes
Black guillemot	With work	Yes
Pigeon guillemot	Almost certainly	Yes
Marbled murrelet	Almost certainly	Yes
Kittlitz's murrelet	Possibly	Yes
Ancient murrelet	Possibly	Yes
Cassin's auklet	Possibly	Yes
Parakeet auklet	Possibly	Yes
Least auklet	Possibly	Yes
Whiskered auklet	Possibly	Yes
Crested auklet	Possibly	Yes
Rhinocerous auklet	With work	Yes
Tufted puffin	Almost certainly	Yes
Horned puffin	Almost certainly	Yes

Doves, Cuckoos

Rock dove	Almost certainly	Yes
Band-tailed pigeon	With work	Yes
Oriental turtle-dove	With much luck	No
White-winged dove	Not likely	No
Mourning dove	With much luck	No

	Chance of Viewing	Breeds?
Common cuckoo	With much luck	No
Oriental cuckoo	With much luck	No
Yellow-billed cuckoo	Not likely	No

Owls

Oriental scops-owl	Not likely	No
Western screech-owl	With work	Yes
Great horned owl	Possibly	Yes
Snowy owl	Possibly	Yes
Northern hawk-owl	Possibly	Yes
Northern pygmy-owl	With work	Yes
Barred owl	With work	Yes
Great gray owl	Possibly	Yes
Long-eared owl	With much luck	No
Short-eared owl	Almost certainly	Yes
Boreal owl	Possibly	Yes
Northern saw-whet owl	Possibly	Yes

Nightjars

Lesser nighthawk	Not likely	No
Common nighthawk	With much luck	No
Whip-poor-will	Not likely	No
Jungle nightjar	Not likely	No

Swifts, Hummingbirds

Black swift	With work	Yes
Chimney swift	Not likely	No
Vaux's swift	Possibly	Yes
White-throated needletail	With much luck	No
Common swift	Not likely	No
Fork-tailed swift	With much luck	No
Ruby-throated hummingbird	Not likely	No
Anna's hummingbird	With work	No
Costa's hummingbird	Not likely	No
Calliope hummingbird	Minute chance	No
Rufous hummingbird	Almost certainly	Yes

Hoopoes, Kingfishers

Hoopoe	Not likely	No
Belted kingfisher	Almost certainly	Yes

Woodpeckers

Eurasian wryneck	Not likely	No
Yellow-bellied sapsucker	With much luck	Yes
Red-breasted sapsucker	Possibly	Yes
Great spotted woodpecker	Not likely	No

	Chance of Viewing	*Breeds?*
Downy woodpecker	Almost certainly	Yes
Hairy woodpecker	Almost certainly	Yes
Three-toed woodpecker	Possibly	Yes
Black-backed woodpecker	With work	Yes
Northern flicker	Possibly	Yes
Pileated woodpecker	Minute chance	No
Flycatchers		
Olive-sided flycatcher	Possibly	Yes
Western wood-pewee	Possibly	Yes
Yellow-bellied flycatcher	With much luck	Yes
Alder flycatcher	Almost certainly	Yes
Willow flycatcher	With much luck	No
Least flycatcher	With work	Yes
Hammond's flycatcher	Almost certainly	Yes
Dusky flycatcher	Not likely	No
Pacific-slope flycatcher	Almost certainly	Yes
Eastern phoebe	Not likely	No
Say's phoebe	Possibly	Yes
Great crested flycatcher	Not likely	No
Tropical kingbird	Not likely	No
Western kingbird	With much luck	No
Eastern kingbird	With much luck	No
Scissor-tailed flycatcher	Minute chance	No
Larks		
Eurasian skylark	With work	Yes
Horned lark	Possibly	Yes
Swallows		
Purple martin	With much luck	No
Tree swallow	Almost certainly	Yes
Violet-green swallow	Almost certainly	Yes
Northern rough-winged swallow	With work	Yes
Bank swallow	Almost certainly	Yes
Cliff swallow	Almost certainly	Yes
Barn swallow	Almost certainly	Yes
Common house-martin	Not likely	No
Jays, Crows		
Gray jay	Almost certainly	Yes
Steller's jay	Almost certainly	Yes
Clark's nutcracker	With much luck	No
Black-billed magpie	Almost certainly	Yes
American crow	With work	Yes
Northwestern crow	Almost certainly	Yes

	Chance of Viewing	*Breeds?*
Common raven	Almost certainly	Yes
Titmice		
Black-capped chickadee	Almost certainly	Yes
Mountain chickadee	With much luck	No
Siberian tit	With work	yes
Boreal chickadee	Almost certainly	Yes
Chestnut-backed chickadee	Almost certainly	Yes
Great tit	Minute chance	No
Nuthatches, Creepers, Wrens		
Red-breasted nuthatch	Possibly	Yes
Brown creeper	Possibly	Yes
Winter wren	Almost certainly	Yes
American dipper	Almost certainly	Yes
Muscicapids		
Middendorff's grasshopper-warbler	Not likely	No
Lanceolated warbler	Not likely	No
Wood warbler	Not likely	No
Dusky warbler	With much luck	No
Arctic warbler	Almost certainly	Yes
Golden-crowned kinglet	Almost certainly	Yes
Ruby-crowned kinglet	Almost certainly	Yes
Narcissus flycatcher	Not likely	No
Red-breasted flycatcher	With much luck	No
Mugimaki flycatcher	Minute chance	No
Siberian flycatcher	Not likely	No
Gray-spotted flycatcher	With much luck	No
Gray-breasted flycatcher	Not likely	No
Siberian rubythroat	With work	No
Bluethroat	Possibly	Yes
Siberian blue robin	Not likely	No
Red-flanked bluetail	With much luck	No
Northern wheatear	Possibly	Yes
Stonechat	With much luck	No
Mountain bluebird	With work	Yes
Townsend's solitaire	Possibly	Yes
Veery	With much luck	No
Gray-cheeked thrush	Almost certainly	Yes
Swainson's thrush	Almost certainly	Yes
Hermit thrush	Almost certainly	Yes
Eye-browed thrush	With much luck	No
Dusky thrush	With much luck	No

	Chance of Viewing	*Breeds?*
Fieldfare	With much luck	No
American robin	Almost certainly	Yes
Varied thrush	Almost certainly	Yes
Northern mockingbird	With much luck	No
Brown thrasher	Not likely	No
Accentors, Wagtails, Pipits		
Siberian accentor	With much luck	No
Yellow wagtail	Almost certainly	Yes
Gray wagtail	With much luck	No
White wagtail	With work	Yes
Black-backed wagtail	With work	Yes
Brown tree-pipit	Not likely	No
Olive tree-pipit	With much luck	No
Pechora pipit	With much luck	No
Red-throated pipit	With work	Yes
American pipit	Almost certainly	Yes
Waxwings, Shrikes, Starlings		
Bohemian waxwing	Almost certainly	Yes
Cedar waxwing	With work	Yes
Brown shrike	Not likely	No
Northern shrike	Possibly	Yes
European starling	Possibly	Yes
Vireos		
Solitary vireo	Not likely	No
Warbling vireo	Possibly	Yes
Philadelphia vireo	Not likely	No
Red-eyed vireo	With work	Yes
Wood Warblers		
Tennessee warbler	With work	Yes
Orange-crowned warbler	Almost certainly	Yes
Nashville warbler	Minute chance	No
Northern parula	Minute chance	No
Yellow warbler	Almost certainly	Yes
Chestnut-sided warbler	Minute chance	No
Magnolia warbler	With work	Yes
Cape May warbler	Not likely	No
Yellow-rumped warbler	Almost certainly	Yes
Black-throated gray warbler	Minute chance	No
Townsend's warbler	Almost certainly	Yes
Hermit warbler	Minute chance	No
Black-throated green warbler	Not likely	No
Prairie warbler	Not likely	No

	Chance of Viewing	Breeds?
Bay-breasted warbler	Minute chance	No
Palm warbler	With much luck	No
Blackpoll warbler	Possibly	Yes
Black-and-white warbler	Not likely	No
American redstart	Possibly	Yes
Ovenbird	Not likely	No
Northern waterthrush	Almost certainly	Yes
Kentucky warbler	Minute chance	No
Mourning warbler	Not likely	No
MacGillivray's warbler	Possibly	Yes
Common yellowthroat	Possibly	Yes
Wilson's warbler	Almost certainly	Yes
Canada warbler	Not likely	No

Tanagers, Grosbeaks, Buntings

Scarlet tanager	Not likely	No
Western tanager	Possibly	Yes
Rose-breasted grosbeak	Minute chance	No
Black-headed grosbeak	Minute chance	No
Blue grosbeak	Not likely	No
Lazuli bunting	Minute chance	No
Indigo bunting	Not likely	No

Sparrows

Rufous-sided towhee	Not likely	No
American tree sparrow	Almost certainly	Yes
Chipping sparrow	Possibly	Yes
Clay-colored sparrow	Not likely	No
Brewer's sparrow	With much luck	Yes
Lark sparrow	Not likely	No
Savannah sparrow	Almost certainly	Yes
Fox sparrow	Almost certainly	Yes
Song sparrow	Almost certainly	Yes
Lincoln's sparrow	Almost certainly	Yes
Swamp sparrow	With much luck	No
White-throated sparrow	With much luck	No
Golden-crowned sparrow	Almost certainly	Yes
White-crowned sparrow	Almost certainly	Yes
Harris's sparrow	With much luck	No
Dark-eyed junco	Almost certainly	Yes
Lapland longspur	Almost certainly	Yes
Smith's longspur	Possibly	Yes
Chestnut-collared longspur	Minute chance	No
Pine bunting	Not likely	No
Little bunting	Not likely	No

	Chance of Viewing	*Breeds?*
Rustic bunting	With work	No
Yellow-breasted bunting	Not likely	No
Gray bunting	Not likely	No
Pallas's reed-bunting	Not likely	No
Common reed-bunting	With much luck	No
Snow bunting	Possibly	Yes
McKay's bunting	With work	Yes

Blackbirds

Bobolink	Not likely	No
Red-winged blackbird	Possibly	Yes
Western meadowlark	With much luck	No
Yellow-headed blackbird	Not likely	No
Rusty blackbird	Almost certainly	Yes
Brewer's blackbird	With much luck	No
Common grackle	Not likely	No
Brown-headed cowbird	With work	Yes
Northern oriole	Minute chance	No
Brambling	With much luck	No

Finches

Gray-crowned rosy-finch	Almost certainly	Yes
Pine grosbeak	Almost certainly	Yes
Common rosefinch	With much luck	No
Purple finch	With much luck	No
Cassin's finch	Not likely	No
House finch	Minute chance	No
Red crossbill	Possibly	Yes
White-winged crossbill	Possibly	Yes
Common redpoll	Almost certainly	Yes
Hoary redpoll	Almost certainly	Yes
Eurasian siskin	Not likely	No
Pine siskin	Almost certainly	Yes
American goldfinch	Not likely	No
Oriental greenfinch	With much luck	No
Eurasian bullfinch	With much luck	No
Evening grosbeak	With much luck	No
Hawfinch	With much luck	No

Old World Sparrows

House sparrow	Not likely	No

Appendix C

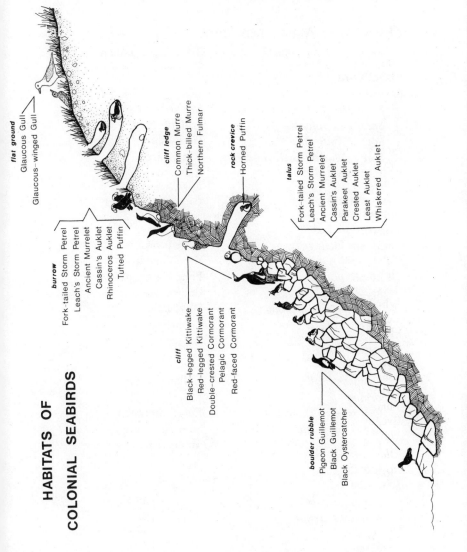

HABITATS OF COLONIAL SEABIRDS

flat ground
Glaucous Gull
Glaucous-winged Gull

burrow
Fork-tailed Storm Petrel
Leach's Storm Petrel
Ancient Murrelet
Cassin's Auklet
Rhinoceros Auklet
Tufted Puffin

cliff ledge
Common Murre
Thick-billed Murre
Northern Fulmar

cliff
Black-legged Kittiwake
Red-legged Kittiwake
Double-crested Cormorant
Pelagic Cormorant
Red-faced Cormorant

rock crevice
Horned Puffin

talus
Fork-tailed Storm Petrel
Leach's Storm Petrel
Ancient Murrelet
Cassin's Auklet
Parakeet Auklet
Crested Auklet
Least Auklet
Whiskered Auklet

boulder rubble
Pigeon Guillemot
Black Guillemot
Black Oystercatcher

Appendix D

Checklist of Alaska Mammals
by Stephen O. MacDonald, University of Alaska Museum

Insectivora
Soricidae

Sorex cinerus (incl. *jacksoni*)	Masked shrew
Sorex pribilofensis	Pribilof shrew
Sorex monticolus	Dusky shrew
Sorex palustris (incl. *alaskanus*)	Water shrew
Sorex arcticus	Arctic shrew
Sorex hoyi	Pygmy shrew

Chiroptera
Vespertilionidae

Myotis lucifugus	Little brown bat
Myotis keenii	Keen's myotis
Myotis volans	Long-legged myotis
Myotis californicus	California myotis
Lasionycteris noctivagans	Silver-haired bat
Eptesicus fuscus	Big brown bat

Lagomorpha
Ochotonidae

Ochotona collaris	Collared pika

Leporidae

*Oryctolagus cuniculus**	European rabbit
Lepus americanus	Snowshoe hare
Lepus othus	Tundra hare

Rodentia
Sciuridae

[*Eutamias minimus*	Least chipmunk]
Marmota monax	Woodchuck

Marmota broweri	Alaska marmot
Marmota caligata	Hoary marmot
Spermophilus parryii	Arctic ground squirrel
Tamiasciurus hudsonicus	Red squirrel
Glaucomys sabrinus	Northern flying squirrel

Castoridae
Castor canadensis	Beaver

Cricetidae
Peromyscus maniculatus	Deer mouse
Peromyscus sitkensis	Sitka mouse
Neotoma cinerea	Bushy-tailed woodrat
Clethrionomys rutilus	Northern red-backed vole
Clethrionomys gapperi	Gapper's red-backed vole
Microtus pennsylvanicus	Meadow vole
Microtus oeconomus	Tundra vole
Microtus longicaudus	Long-tailed vole
Microtus coronarius	Coronation Island vole
Microtus xanthognathus	Yellow-cheeked vole
Microtus miurus	Singing vole
Microtus abbreviatus	Insular vole
Ondatra zibethicus	Muskrat
Lemmus sibiricus (incl. *nigripes*)	Brown lemming
Synaptomys borealis	Northern bog lemming
Dicrostonyx torquatus	Collared lemming (prob. multispecies complex)

Muridae
*Rattus norvegicus**	Norway rat
*Mus musculus**	House mouse

Zapodidae
Zapus hudsonius	Meadow jumping mouse
Zapus princeps	Western jumping mouse

Erethizontidae
Erethizon dorsatum	Porcupine

Cetacea

Balaenidae
Balaena mysticetus	Bowhead whale
Eubalaena glacialis	Northern right whale

Eschrichtiidae
Eschrichtius robustus	Gray whale

Balaenopteridae
Balaenoptera musculus	Blue whale

Balaenoptera physalus	Fin whale
Balaenoptera borealis	Sei whale
Balaenoptera acutorostrata	Minke whale
Megaptera novaeangliae	Humpback whale

Physeteridae

Physeter catodon	Sperm whale

Monodontidae

Monodon monoceros	Narwhal
Delphinapterus leucas	White whale, beluga

Ziphiidae

Berardius bairdii	Baird's beaked whale
Mesoplodon stejnegeri	Stejneger's beaked whale
Ziphius cavirostris	Cuvier's beaked whale

Delphinidae

Orcinus orca	Killer whale
Globicephala melaena	Long-finned pilot whale
Lagenorhynchus obliquidens	Pacific white-sided dolphin
Grampus griseus	Risso's dolphin
Stenella coeruleoalba	Striped dolphin
Lissodelphis borealis	Northern right whale dolphin

Phocoenidae

Phocoena phocoena	Harbor porpoise
Phocoenoides dalli	Dall's porpoise

Carnivora

Canidae

Canis latrans	Coyote
Canis lupus	Wolf
Alopex lagopus	Arctic fox
Vulpes vulpes	Red fox

Ursidae

Urus americanus	Black bear
Ursus arctos	Brown bear
Ursus maritimus	Polar bear

Procyonidae

*Procyon lotor**	Racoon

Mustelidae

Martes americana	Marten
[*Martes pennanti*	Fisher]
Mustela erminea	Ermine
Mustela nivalis	Least weasel
Mustela vison	Mink

Gulo gulo	Wolverine
Lutra canadensis	River otter
Enhydra lutris	Sea otter
Felidae	
[*Felis concolor*	Mountain lion]
Felis lynx	Lynx
Otariidae	
Eumetopias jubatus	Steller's sea lion
Zalophus californianus	California sea lion
Callorhinus ursinus	Northern fur seal
Odobenidae	
Odobenus rosmarus	Walrus
Odobenus rosmarus divergens	Pacific walrus
Phocidae	
Phoca vitulina	Harbor seal
Phoca largha	Larga seal, spotted seal
Phoca hispida	Ringed seal
[*Phoca groenlandica*	Harp seal]
Phoca fasciata	Ribbon seal
Erignathus barbatus	Bearded seal
Cystophora cristata	Hooded seal
Mirounga angustirostris	Northern elephant seal

Artiodactyla
Cervidae

Cervus elaphus *	Wapiti
Odocoileus hemionus	Mule deer
Odocoileus hemionus sitkensis	Sitka black-tailed deer
Alces alces	Moose
Rangifer tarandus	Caribou
Bovidae	
Bison bison *	Bison
Oreamnos americanus	Mountain goat
Ovibos moschatus *	Muskox
Ovis dalli	Dall's sheep

*introduced   [ ] not substantiated

Appendix E

International Youth Hostels in Alaska

Staying at an American or an International Youth Hostel anywhere almost always guarantees an interesting experience—despite the name, age doesn't matter, and your fellow hostelers may have come from the farthest corners of the earth—and the cost is always very reasonable. There are more than a dozen hostels located in various parts of Alaska, and as of this writing, their rates range from $10 to $18 a night (don't be surprised if prices increase). The Alaskan hostels vary as much as their rates and offer everything from sleeping-bag accommodations on church property, to a hike-in (6 miles) into an "extreme wilderness location," to a comfortable dormitory with many amenities in downtown Anchorage. Some hostels have saunas, some are heated by wood that you cut, some have a laundry, some are open year-round and some only seasonally, and many have kitchens where you can prepare your meals. Some are open all year, others only in summer. All have certain requirements: no smoking or drinking is allowed on the premises; length of stay and hours are limited; and you're expected to help out with daily chores. A letter of inquiry or a telephone call in advance is wise; it is frequently possible to make paid reservations ahead of time, and you can find out all details.

Here are the names, addresses, and telephone numbers of several hostels in Alaska:

Anchorage International Youth
  Hostel
700 H Street
Anchorage, AK 99501
907-276-3635

Fairbanks International Youth
  Hostel
Box 72196
Fairbanks, AK 99707
907-456-4159

Girdwood: Alyeska Home Hostel
Box 10-4099
Anchorage, AK 99510
907-783-2099

Haines: Bear Creek Camp and
 Hostel
Box 908
Haines, AK 99827
907-766-2259

Juneau International Youth
 Hostel
614 Harris Street
Juneau, AK 99801
907-586-9559

Ketchikan Youth Hostel
First United Methodist Church
Grant & Main Streets
Box 8515
Ketchikan, AK 99901
907-225-3319

Ninilchik: Eagle Watch Hostel
Mile 3, Oil Well Road, Box
 39083
Ninilchik, AK 99635
907-567-3905

Palmer: Sheep Mountain Lodge
HCO 3 Box 8490
Palmer, AK 99645
907-745-5121

Seward: Snow River International
 Hostel
HCR 64, Box 425
Seward, AK 99664
907-440-4287

Sitka Youth Hostel
303 Kimsham Street
Box 2645
Sitka, AK 99835
907-747-8661

Tok International Youth Hostel
Box 532
Tok, AK 99780
907-883-3745

For further information, write **American Youth Hostels,** Alaska Council,
700 H Street, Anchorage, AK 99501; phone 907-562-7772.

Appendix F

Alaska Native Regional Corporations (Profit and Nonprofit)

Ahtna, Incorporated
Copper River Native Assoc. Inc.
Copper Center, Alaska

Aleut Corporation
Aleutian/Pribilof Island Assoc.
  Inc.
Anchorage, Alaska

Arctic Slope Regional Corp.
Arctic Slope Native Corp.
Barrow, Alaska

Bering Straits Native Corp.
Kawarak, Inc.
Nome, Alaska

Bristol Bay Native Corp.
Bristol Bay Native Assoc.
Dillingham, Alaska

Calista Corp.
AVCP
Anchorage and Bethel, Alaska

Chugach Natives, Inc.
Chugachmuit
Anchorage, Alaska

Cook Inlet Region, Inc.
Cook Inlet Native Assoc.
Anchorage, Alaska

Doyon Limited
Tanana Chiefs Conference
Fairbanks, Alaska

Konaig, Inc.
Kodiak Area Native Assoc.
Kodiak, Alaska

NANA Corp.
Mauneluk, Inc.
Kotzebue, Alaska

Sealaska Corp.
Tlingit/Haida Central Council
Juneau, Alaska

Thirteenth Regional Corp., Inc.
(For Alaska Natives living out-of-
  state)
Seattle, Washington

Appendix G

Alaska Zip Codes

Community	Zip Code	Community	Zip Code
Akhiok	99615-9998	Boundary	99780-8998
Akiachak	99551-9998	Brentwood	99687-6000
Akiak	99552-9998	Brevig Mission	99785-9998
Akutan	99553-9998	Buckland	99727-9998
Alakanuk	99554-9998	Butte	99645-9707
Aleknagik	99555-9998	Candle	99752-8999
Alexander Creek	99695-0020	Cantwell	99729-9998
Alitak	99697-0210	Cape Lisburne	99752-9999
Allakaket	99720-9998	Cape Newenham	99576-8995
Ambler	99786-9998	Cape Pole	99950-0010
Amook	99697-0220	Cape Romanzof	99658-8999
Anaktuvuk	99721-9998	Cape Yakatagu	99574-8998
Anchor Point	99556-9998	Central	99730-9998
Anderson	99744-9998	Chalkyitsik	99788-9998
Angoon	99820-9998	Chefornak	99561-9998
Aniak	99557-9998	Chenega Bay	99574-8098
Anvik	99558-9998	Chevak	99563-9998
Arctic Village	99722-9998	Chickaloon	99674-1100
Atka	99547-9998	Chicken	99732-9998
Atmautluak	99559-8999	Chignik	99564-9998
Atqasuk	99791-9998	Chignik Lagoon	99565-9998
Attu	99619-0090	Chignik Lake	99548-9998
Auke Bay	99821-9998	Chiniak	99615-5500
Badger	99711-9998	Chisana	99780-8999
Baranof	99835-8997	Chitina	99566-9998
Barrow	99723-9998	Chuathbaluk	99557-8999
Beaver	99724-9998	Chugiak	99567-9998
Bell Island	99950-0001	Circle	99733-9998
Beluga	99695-0100	Clam Gulch	99568-9998
Bethel	99559-9998	Clarks Point	99569-9998
Bettles Field	99726-9998	Clear	99704-9998
Big Lake	99652-9998	Coffman Cove	99918-9998
Birch Creek	99740-8999	Cold Bay	99571-9998
Border	99780-9700	Coldfoot	99701-0900
Boswell Bay	99574-8999	College	99708-9998

Community	Zip Code	Community	Zip Code
Cook Inlet	99501-2898	Girdwood	99587-9998
Copper Center	99573-8998	Glennallen	99588-9998
Cooper Landing	99572-9998	Gold Creek	99676-8999
Cordova	99574-9998	Golovin	99762-6998
Council	99762-8999	Goodnews Bay	99589-9998
Craig	99921-9998	Grayling	99590-9998
Crooked Creek	99575-9998	Gulkana	99586-8999
Cube Cove	99850-0360	Gustavus	99826-9998
Deep Bay	99950-0030	Haines	99827-9998
Deering	99736-9998	Halibut Cove	99603-6400
Delta Junction	99737-9998	Happy Harbor	99950-0330
Denali National Park	99755-9998	Healy	99743-9998
		Healy Lake	99706-0300
Dillingham	99576-9998	Hobart Bay	99850-0190
Dot Lake	99737-2299	Hollis	99950-0070
Douglas	99824-9998	Holy Cross	99602-9998
Dutch Harbor	99692-9998	Homer	99603-9998
Eagle	99738-9998	Hoonah	99829-9998
Eagle River	99577-9998	Hooper Bay	99604-9998
Edna Bay	99950-0040	Hope	99605-9998
Eek	99578-9998	Houston	99694-9998
Egegik	99579-9998	Hughes	99745-9998
Eielson Air Force Base	99702-9998	Huslia	99746-9998
		Hydaburg	99922-9998
Ekuk	99576-8999	Hyder	99923-9998
Ekwok	99580-9998	Icy Bay	99574-8996
Elfin Cove	99825-9998	Igiugig	99613-4198
Elim	99739-9998	Iliamna	99606-9998
Ellamar	99574-8997	Indian Mountain	99706-0267
Elmendorf Air Force Base	99506-9998	Ivanof Bay	99695-0050
		Kake	99830-9998
Emmonak	99581-9998	Kaktovik	99747-9998
Ester	99725-9998	Kalskag	99607-9998
Excursion Inlet	99850-0090	Kaltag	99748-9998
Falls Bay	99574-8994	Karluk	99608-9998
False Pass	99583-9998	Kasaan	99950-0340
Fire Cove	99950-0290	Kasigluk	99609-9998
Flat	99584-9998	Kasilof	99610-9998
Fort Richardson	99505-9998	Kenai	99611-9998
Fort Wainwright	99703-9998	Ketchikan	99901-9998
Fort Yukon	99740-9998	Kiana	99749-9998
Freshwater Bay	99850-0350	King Cove	99612-9998
Fritz Creek	99603-6000	King Salmon	99613-9998
Funter Bay	99850-0140	Kipnuk	99614-9998
Gakona	99586-9998	Kitoi Bay	99697-0020
Galena	99741-9998	Kivalina	99750-9998
Gambell	99742-9998	Klawock	99925-9998

Community	Zip Code	Community	Zip Code
Knik	99687-7999	Nightmute	99690-9999
Kobuk	99751-9998	Nikiski	99635-9998
Kodiak	99615-9998	Nikolaevsk	99556-5000
Kokhanok	99606-0998	Nikolai	99691-9998
Koliganek	99576-5098	Nikolski	99638-9998
Kongiganak	99559-5198	Ninilchik	99639-9998
Kotlik	99620-9998	Noatak	99761-9998
Kotzebue	99752-9998	Nome	99762-9998
Koyuk	99753-9998	Nondalton	99640-9998
Koyukuk	99754-9998	Noorvik	99763-9998
Kwethluk	99621-9998	North Pole	99705-9998
Kwigillingok	99622-9998	Northway	99764-9998
Lab Bay	99950-0310	Nuiqsut	99789-9998
Lake Minchumina	99757-9998	Nulato	99765-9998
Larsen Bay	99624-9998	Nunapitchuk	99641-9998
Levelock	99625-9998	Nyal	99642-9999
Lime Village	99627-8999	Old Harbor	99643-9998
Little Diomede	99762-7098	Olga Bay	99697-0050
Long Island	99950-0350	Ouzinkie	99644-9998
Loring	99950-0090	Palmer	99645-9998
Lower Kalskag	99626-9998	Paxson	99737-9299
Manley Hot	99756-9990	Pedro Bay	99647-9998
Springs		Pelican	99832-9998
Manokotak	99628-9998	Perryville	99648-9998
Marshall	99585-9998	Petersburg	99833-9998
May Creek	99588-8999	Pilot Point	99649-9998
McCarthy	99588-8998	Pilot Station	99650-9998
McGrath	99627-9998	Platinum	99651-9998
Meadow Lake	99687-7700	Point Baker	99927-9998
Mekoryuk	99630-9998	Point Hope	99766-9998
Mentasta Lake	99780-6999	Point Lay	99759-9998
Metlakatla	99926-9998	Polk Inlet	99950-0370
Meyers Chuck	99903-9999	Pope Vannoy	99606-8999
Minto	99758-9998	Landing	
Moose Pass	99631-9998	Portage Creek	99576-8998
Moser Bay	99697-0040	Port Alexander	99836-9998
Mountain Village	99632-9998	Port Alice	99950-0170
Naknek	99633-9998	Port Alsworth	99653-9998
Nanwalek	99603-6600	Port Clarence	99762-8998
Napakiak	99634-9998	Port Graham	99603-8998
Napaskiak	99559-6198	Port Heiden	99549-9998
Naukati Bay	99950-0550	Port Lions	99550-9998
Neets Bay	99950-0160	Port Moller	99571-8999
Nelson Lagoon	99571-8998	Port Protection	99950-0180
Nenana	99760-9998	Port San Juan	99574-8995
New Stuyahok	99636-9998	Port Walter	99835-8999
Newtok	99559-8996	Port Williams	99697-0090

Community	Zip Code	Community	Zip Code
Prudhoe Bay	99734-9998	Tatitlek	99677-9998
Quinhagak	99655-9998	Telida	99627-8998
Rampart	99767-9998	Teller	99778-9998
Red Devil	99656-9998	Tenakee Springs	99841-9998
Red Mountain	99603-8999	Terror Bay	99697-0130
Rowan Bay	99835-8998	Tetlin	99779-9999
Ruby	99768-9998	Thorne Bay	99919-9998
Russian Mission	99657-9998	Tin City	99762-9999
Saint George Island	99591-9998	Togiak	99678-9998
		Tok	99780-9998
Saint Marys	99658-9998	Tokeen	99950-0230
Saint Michael	99659-9998	Toksook Bay	99637-9998
Saint Paul Island	99660-9998	Trapper Creek	99683-9998
Salcha	99714-9998	Tuluksak	99679-9998
Sand Point	99661-9998	Tuntutuliak	99680-9998
Savoonga	99769-9998	Tununak	99681-9998
Scammon Bay	99662-9998	Twin Hills	99576-8996
Seal Bay	99697-0230	Two Rivers	99716-9998
Selawik	99770-9998	Tyonek	99682-9998
Seldovia	99663-9998	Uganik Bay	99697-0140
Seward	99664-9998	Ugashik	99613-8998
Shageluk	99665-9998	Unalakleet	99684-9998
Shaktoolik	99771-9998	Unalaska	99685-9998
Sheldon Point	99666-9999	University of Alaska	99775-0001
Shishmaref	99772-9998		
Shungnak	99773-9998	Uyak	99697-0150
Sitka	99835-9998	Valdez	99686-9998
Skagway	99840-9998	Venetie	99781-9998
Skwentna	99667-9998	View Cove	99950-0250
Slana	99586-0770	Wainwright	99782-9998
Sleetmute	99668-9998	Wales	99783-9998
Soldotna	99669-9998	Ward Cove	99928-9998
Solomoy	99762-8997	Wasilla	99687-9998
South Naknek	99670-9998	Water Fall	99950-0270
Sparrevohn	99519-6950	West Point	99697-0170
Sterling	99672-9998	Whale Pass	99950-0280
Stevens Village	99774-9998	White Mountain	99784-9998
Stony River	99557-8998	Whittier	99693-9998
Sutton	99674-9998	Willow	99688-9998
Takotna	99675-9999	Wiseman	99790-9801
Talkeetna	99676-9998	Wrangell	99929-9998
Tanacross	99776-9998	Yakutat	99689-9998
Tanana	99777-9998	Yes Bay	99950-0320
Tatalina	99627-9999	Zachar Bay	99697-0200

Appendix H

Suggested Reading

There is a wealth of fascinating literature on Alaska. The following list—mostly of background and historical books—only cracks the door. Readers are urged to explore further. Although many of these classic works are out of print, you can find them in your library or, if you're lucky, in a used-book store.

Alaska. Published ten times a year, *Alaska* magazine presents a typical Alaskan point of view. For subscriptions, write Alaska Magazine, Box 2016, Augusta, GA 30903; phone 706-722-6060.

The Alaska Almanac. Annual. Anchorage: Alaska Northwest Books. Up-to-date facts on Alaska's past and present.

Alaska Geographic. A quarterly publication of the Alaska Geographic Society, this full-color series on Alaska's lands and people is available in bookstores or by subscription. The Alaska Geographic Society also has over sixty books in print on specific regions of Alaska or resource-related topics, such as Native cultures, glaciers, forests, and so on. To subscribe to *Alaska Geographic* or to receive a book catalog, write Alaska Geographic Society, Box 93370, Anchorage, AK 99509; phone 907-562-0164.

Alaska Regional Profiles. Sponsored by the state of Alaska in cooperation with the Joint Federal–State Land Use Planning Commission for Alaska. Published in the late 1970s, this six-volume series—covering the Arctic, Yukon, Southcentral, Southwest, and Southeast areas of Alaska—is still considered a valuable reference, especially for environmental and geographic information about the state. It is available at state libraries in Alaska.

Alaska State Vacation Planner. A free travel guide published annually by the Alaska State Division of Tourism. Write Box 11801, Juneau, AK 99811-0801; phone 907-465-2010. Recommended as a good source for tourist facilities.

The Alaska Wilderness Guide. 7th ed. Bellevue, Wash.: Vernon Publications, 1993. By the editors of *The Milepost* (see below), this paperback contains facts, maps, backpacking advice, accommodations, fishing data, and so on; it is particularly helpful in providing information about Alaska's rural villages. Look for the latest edition or, to order, phone 1-800-726-4707.

Armstrong, Robert H. *A Guide to the Birds of Alaska*. 4th ed. Anchorage: Alaska Northwest Books, 1995. The easiest reference book for Alaska birdwatchers.

Berton, Pierre. *The Klondike Fever: The Life and Death of the Last Great Stampede*. New York: Knopf, 1958. Written long before the Prudhoe Bay "stampede," as the title shows, this is a classic history of gold rush days and gives a marvelous sense of the country.

Bohn, Dave. *Glacier Bay: The Land and the Silence*. San Francisco: Sierra Club Books, 1967. Another sensitive study of a very special place.

————. *Rambles Through an Alaskan Wild: Katmai and the Valley of the Smokes*. Santa Barbara, Calif.: Capra Press, 1979. A book of perceptive photographs and provocative text for all lovers of wilderness.

Brooks, Alfred H. *Blazing Alaska's Trails*. 2d ed. Fairbanks: University of Alaska Press, 1973. This and other writings of this early explorer are recommended.

Brown, William E. *Alaska's National Parklands: This Last Treasure*. Anchorage: Alaska Natural History Association, 1982. A naturalist's look at the Great Land.

Burroughs, John, et al. *The Harriman Expedition, 1899*. Magnolia, Mass.: Peter Smith, 1990. A series of essays by some of the best minds of the time who accompanied Harriman on a fairy-tale voyage up the Inside Passage and on to Kodiak—and the sun shone on them almost every day that summer of 1899.

Case, David S. *Alaska Natives and American Laws*. Rev. ed. Fairbanks: University of Alaska Press, 1984. The best background book on the congressional acts that have so profoundly changed the Alaskan Native way of life.

Colby, Merle. *A Guide to Alaska, Last American Frontier*. St. Claire Shores, Mich.: Scholarly Press, 1981. This Federal Writers' Project is full of anecdotes and historical tidbits that you won't find elsewhere. This treasury of background facts also conveys vividly how Alaska was only a few decades ago.

Crisler, Lois. *Arctic Wild*. New York: HarperCollins, 1991. A lovely look at the way the wilderness was.

De Armond, R. N. *The Founding of Juneau*. Juneau: Gastineau Channel Centennial Association, 1990. A well-researched and charming account of how Juneau came to be. De Armond is "the" dean of Alaska's historians: if you find his name on anything else, be sure to read it.

Diel, William. *Rocks, Ridges, and Glaciers: A Geologic Tour of the Denali Highway*. Anchorage: Alaska Natural History Association, 1995. A nontechnical guide to some unique—and accessible—geological features, such as kames, eskers, and palsas.

Dufresne, Frank. *No Room for Bears: A Wilderness Writer's Experiences with a Threatened Breed*. Anchorage: Alaska Northwest Books, 1991.

Embick, Andrew. *Fast and Cold: A Guide to Alaska Whitewater*. Helena, Mont.: Falcon Press, 1994. There are few Alaska rivers that the author, a

Valdez physician and expert kayaker, has not run. Some invaluable advice for river rats (and would-be's).

Fejes, Claire. *The Villagers: Athabascan Indian Life Along the Yukon River.* New York: Random House, 1981. Adds insights and understanding to Native ways of life.

Fischer, Victor. *Alaska's Constitutional Convention.* Fairbanks: University of Alaska Press, 1975. History by one who has helped make it.

Forbes, Sheri. *The Nature of Denali.* Anchorage: Alaska Natural History Association, 1995. An inexpensive and helpful nature guide to the most accessible trails—around the park entrance—in Denali National Park.

Ford, Corey. *Where the Sea Breaks Its Back.* 2d ed. Anchorage: Alaska Northwest Books, 1992. The story of Bering and Steller and the way the Russians discovered Alaska.

Giddings, J. Louis. *Ancient Men of the Arctic.* Seattle: University of Washington Press, 1985. Archeological facts by one of the legendary figures in the field.

Gilbert, Wyatt G. *A Geologic Guide to Mount McKinley National Park.* Anchorage: Alaska Natural History Association, 1979. Adds greatly to an understanding of some of Alaska's complex geology.

Goetzmann, William H., and Sloan, Kay. *Looking Far North: The Harriman Expedition to Alaska, 1899.* Princeton, N.J.: Princeton University Press, 1983. An account of the fabled voyage of the Harriman expedition, when Burroughs and John Muir (and other great men) went exploring sunny Alaska.

Griggs, Robert F. *The Valley of Ten Thousand Smokes.* Washington, D.C.: National Geographic Society, 1922. A wonderful story of discovery and subsequent travels in the Katmai region.

Gruening, Ernest. *The State of Alaska.* New York: Random House, 1968. Interesting history by one of the first movers and shakers in modern Alaska's politics. Gruening emerges as a great political figure in the state.

Hammond, Jay. *Tales of Alaska's Bush Rat Governor.* Kenmore, Wash.: Epicenter Press, 1994. Adventure-filled and hilarious autobiography of Alaska governor and bush pilot Jay Hammond.

Hopkins, David M., ed. *The Bering Land Bridge.* Stanford, Calif.: Stanford University Press, 1967. Two dozen provocative, often fascinating, essays by Russian and American scientists inform the reader of the remarkable role the Bering Land Bridge has played in the life of the northern regions.

Hulten, Eric. *Flora of Alaska and Neighboring Countries.* Stanford, Calif.: Stanford University Press, 1968. The Alaskan botanists' bible.

Kauffmann, John. *Alaska's Brooks Range: The Ultimate Mountains.* Seattle: The Mountaineers Books, 1992. As a Park Service planner in the 1970s, Kauffmann helped design the great Brooks Range parks of today. Now he tells of the past of these mountains and worries about their future as visitor numbers grow.

Leopold, A. Starker, and Darling, Frank Fraser. *Wildlife in Alaska: An Ecological Reconnaissance.* Reprint. Westport, Conn.: Greenwood Press,

1973. A good place to start to get a perspective on Alaska's wildlife and the basis for its survival.

Lethaby, Nick. *A Bird Finding Guide to Alaska*. McMinnville, Ore.: Cinclus, 1994. Covers mostly coastal sites, but there are also descriptions for the interior between Anchorage and Fairbanks. Emphasis is on species uncommon in the Lower Forty-Eight.

Lethcoe, Jim, and Lethcoe, Nancy. *Cruising Guide to Prince William Sound*. 2 vols. Valdez: Prince William Sound Books, 1986. Indispensable guides for sailors and/or kayakers in beautiful Prince William Sound. Vol. 1 covers the western area of the sound; vol. 2, the eastern.

London, Jack. *The Call of the Wild*. Reprint ed. New York: Bantam, 1991. People are still telling stories like this one about Alaska's dogs.

Lopez, Barry. *Arctic Dreams*. New York: Bantam, 1996. A lovely book, beautifully evocative of the special magic of the far north.

Marshall, Robert. *Alaska Wilderness: Exploring the Central Brooks Range*. 2d ed. Berkeley: University of California Press, 1970. This is one of the Alaska classics and should be read by anyone going into the Brooks Range or the Arctic.

McGinnis, Joe. *Going to Extremes*. New York: Dutton, 1989. Although this Cheechako's look at Alaska has raised some northern eyebrows, it gives an Outsider's viewpoint, which may be useful to a first-time visitor.

McPhee, John. *Coming into the Country*. New York: Farrar, Straus and Giroux, 1991. Beautifully written, this catches much of the spirit of the place.

Mergler, Wayne, ed. *The Last New Land: Stories of Alaska, Past and Present*. Anchorage: Alaska Northwest Books, 1996. A remarkably comprehensive anthology of Alaska literature, from Native myths and legends to contemporary Alaskan writers.

The Milepost. Published annually on March 1. Bellevue, Wash.: Vernon Publications. A complete travel planner and guide to Alaska and western Canada. A must for automobile travelers. To order, phone 1-800-726-4707.

Miller, John, and Miller, Kristen, eds. *Alaska Stories: Tales from the Wild Frontier*. San Francisco: Chronicle Books, 1995. Includes modern and historic writings.

Miller, Mike, and Wayburn, Peggy. *Alaska: The Great Land*. San Francisco: Sierra Club Books, 1974. Background information on Alaska, its history, and conservationists' efforts to preserve its wilderness. Beautiful photographs.

Milton, John P. *Nameless Valleys, Shining Mountains: The Record of an Expedition into the Vanishing Wilderness of Alaska's Brooks Range*. New York: Walker, 1970. A haunting, lovely literary exploration of the Arctic.

Mitchell, Donald C. *Sold American*. Hanover, Mass.: University Press of New England, 1997. A first-rate history of what has happened to Alaska Natives and their land in the years 1867–1959. The author promises a follow-up of the story from 1960 to the present.

Moore, Terris. *Mt. McKinley: The Pioneer Climbs.* Seattle: The Mountaineers Books, 1981. Some fascinating reading for mountaineers—active
or armchair types—by a man who climbed Mount McKinley himself.

Mosby, Jack, and Dapkus, David. *Alaska Paddling Guide.* 3d ed. Anchorage: J and R Enterprises, 1992. Expert advice from two experienced and
expert paddlers.

Muir, John. *Letters from Alaska.* Edited by Robert Engberg and Bruce Mer-
rell. Madison: University of Wisconsin Press, 1993. Classic comments by
one of Alaska's greatest lovers.

———. *Travels in Alaska.* San Francisco: Sierra Club Books, 1988. Muir
and Alaska at their best.

Murie, Adolph. *The Grizzlies of Mount McKinley.* Seattle: University of
Washington Press, 1985. More classic Alaskan writing. A must for people interested in Alaska's wildlife.

———. *The Wolves of Mount McKinley.* Seattle: University of Washington
Press, 1985. A companion volume to Murie's *Grizzlies of Mount McKinley.*

Murie, Margaret E. *Two in the Far North.* Anchorage: Alaska Northwest
Books, 1997. A delightful recollection of Alaska as viewed by two sensitive people, the other being Olaus, her husband.

Murie, Olaus J. *Journeys to the Far North.* Palo Alto, Calif.: American West
Publishing, 1973. With his wife, Margaret, and his brother, Adolph,
Olaus Murie should be sought out for accounts of the natural world of
Alaska, as well as for beautiful drawings.

Murphy, Claire Rudolf, and Haigh, Jane. *Gold Rush Women.* Anchorage:
Alaska Northwest Books, 1997. Profiles and photographs of two dozen
of Alaska's pioneering women.

Naske, Claus-M., and Slotnick, Herman E. *Alaska: A History of the 49th
State.* 2d. ed. Norman: University of Oklahoma Press, 1994. A good,
standard overview.

———, and Rowinski, L. J. *Anchorage: A Pictorial History.* Virginia Beach,
Va.: Donning, 1981. Good for graphics rather than text.

Nelson, Richard K. *Hunters of the Northern Forest: Designs for Survival
Among the Alaskan Kutchin.* 2d. ed. Chicago: University of Chicago
Press, 1973. A thought-provoking study of the people of the Kutchin vil-
lage, Chalkyitsik, Alaska.

———. *Hunters of the Northern Ice.* Chicago: University of Chicago Press,
1986. Another perceptive study of Alaska's Native people.

———. *Make Prayers to the Raven: A Koyukon View of the Northern Forest.* Chicago: University of Chicago Press, 1996. Nelson at his best,
which is very good, indeed.

Nienhueser, Helen, and Simmerman, Nancy. *Fifty-Five Ways to the Wilderness in Southcentral Alaska.* 4th ed. Seattle: The Mountaineers Books,
1994. Look for latest revised text. An invaluable guide to hiking out of
the Anchorage area. Good for families. Some canoeing information, too.

Orth, Donald J. *Dictionary of Alaska Place Names.* Washington, D.C.: U.S.

Government Printing Office, 1967. Geological Survey Professional Paper #567. Tells not only how, but often why, place names got onto the map of Alaska. Fascinating reading.

Pewe, Troy L. *Permafrost and Its Effect on Life in the North.* Corvallis: Oregon State University Press, 1966. Reprint available from Books on Demand, Ann Arbor, Mich.: phone 1-800-521-0600. A good start to understanding the phenomenon of permafrost. (See also *Alaska Regional Profiles,* above).

Piggott, Margaret. *Discovering Southeast Alaska with Pack and Paddle,* 2d. ed. Seattle: The Mountaineers Books, 1990. An excellent guide for people wanting to get around in the Southeastern out-of-doors.

Pruitt, William O., Jr. *Animals of the North.* New York: Harper & Row, 1967. Written in simple, poetic language, this book informs and enchants. Although a "children's book," it is really for all ages.

Schwatka, Frederick. *A Summer in Alaska.* St. Louis: J.W. Henry, 1893. A sometimes hilarious account of some early intrepid adventuring in Alaska.

Searby, Ellen. *Alaska's Inside Passage Traveler.* Juneau: Windham Bay Press. Annual. An invaluable aid to ferry travelers in Southeast.

Service, Robert. *The Spell of the Yukon and Other Verses.* New York: Putnam Berkley, 1989. Some say it's doggerel, but others say this poetry truly captures the spirit of the gold rush—perhaps despite itself.

Sheldon, Charles. *The Wilderness of Denali.* New York: Charles Scribner's Sons, 1960. For visitors to Denali National Park, this gives some of the background of how the park came to be, related by the man most responsible for its establishment.

Sherwonit, Bill. *To the Top of Denali.* Anchorage: Alaska Northwest Books, 1990. Climbing adventures on North America's highest peak.

Sherwood, Morgan B. *Alaska and Its History.* Seattle: University of Washington Press, 1967. An interesting and somewhat eclectic presentation that's well worth reading.

————. *Exploration of Alaska, 1865–1900.* Fairbanks: University of Alaska Press, 1992. A readable and informative history of thirty-five years in Alaska's history.

Simmerman, Nancy. *Alaska's Parklands: The Complete Guide.* Seattle: The Mountaineers Books, 1991. (Look for latest edition.) Recommended reading for all national park visitors.

Specht, Robert. *Tisha.* New York: Bantam, 1984. The story of a young white teacher in a Native village in days gone by.

Sydeman, Michelle, and Lund, Annabel. *Alaska Wildlife Viewing Guide.* Helena, Mont.: Falcon Press, 1996. Well-illustrated and concise information. Part of the National Watchable Wildlife Program, sponsored by land management agencies and conservation organizations.

Vierick, Leslie, and Little, Elbert L., Jr. *Trees and Shrubs of Alaska.* Washington, D.C.: Department of Agriculture Handbook #410, 1986. Paperback. Required reading for anyone interested in the flora of the Great Land.

Waterman, Jonathan. *In the Shadow of Denali: Life and Death on Alaska's Mount McKinley.* New York: Dell, 1994. Maybe the most personal book yet about Denali.

——. *Surviving Denali.* 2d. ed. New York: American Alpine Club, 1991. Some of the pitfalls (and pleasures) of climbing North America's highest mountain.

Wexell, Sven. *The Russian Expedition to America.* New York: Collier Books, 1962. Some insights into a few of the Russians' adventures.

White, Helen A., ed. *Alaska-Yukon Wild Flowers Guide.* Anchorage: Alaska Northwest Books, 1974 (12th printing, 1996). Although limited, this is the handiest Alaska flower guide around. This and other Alaska Northwest books are widely available in Alaska, or your bookstore can order them. For a catalog of Alaska Northwest publications, phone 1-800-452-3032.

Wickersham, Hon. James. *Old Yukon: Tales, Trails, and Trials.* Washington, D.C.: Washington Law Book Co., 1938. The good judge not only helped make Alaskan history but wrote about it in an entertaining way.

Mysteries

Three Alaskan mystery writers—Sue Henry, Dana Stabenow, and John Straley—are currently in print, with new books coming out frequently. For mystery lovers, they offer an insight into Alaskan customs, climates, and present lifestyles. Recommended. Three starters are:

Henry, Sue. *Termination Dust.* New York: Avon, 1996.
Stabenow, Dana. *Blood Will Tell.* New York: Berkley, 1997.
Straley, John. *Death and the Language of Happiness.* New York: Bantam, 1997.

Pertinent Legislation

Public Law 72-339, July 7, 1958. Alaska Statehood Act.
Public Law 92-203, December 18, 1971. Alaska Native Claims Settlement Act (ANCSA).
Public Law 96-487, December 2, 1980. The Alaska National Interest Lands Conservation Act (ANILCA).
Public Law 101-626, November 28, 1990. Tongass Timber Reform Act.

Index

*Page numbers in italic refer to illustrations. In some entries, page numbers are grouped regionally into **Interior/Arctic, SC/SW** (Southcentral/Southwest), and **SE** (Southeast).*